# Global Business Leadership

The second edition of this bestselling textbook has been fully updated with a synopsis of the latest changes in the fields of intercultural communication and leadership development. This includes new benchmark interviews from some of the world's foremost companies; a wealth of proven guidelines, tools, and models, including Wibbeke's own Geoleadership Model and two new chapters focusing on the influence of gender and technology on culture and leadership.

This new edition also emphasizes practical examples of individuals and organizations that have utilized the core concept of "Geoleadership"—including updated research from those at the forefront of various industries, including finance, healthcare, and manufacturing.

With contributions and endorsements from some of the most important thought leaders in leadership development and intercultural communication, this edition offers a resource for designing, delivering, and evaluating successful leadership theories and practices to both students and practitioners.

**E.S. Wibbeke** is the most noted intercultural leadership guru in the world. Dr. Wibbeke spent 20 years in business leadership and management roles for Fortune 500 firms, including a decade in the Silicon Valley, and is an international consultant and professor of leadership and management. Dr. Wibbeke has taught at many international institutions, including American Intercontinental University, the Thunderbird School of Global Management, University of California at Santa Cruz and the University of Liverpool, UK.

**Sarah McArthur** is founder of *sdedit, a writing and editing firm based in San Diego, California. With nearly two decades of experience in the publishing field, Sarah has worked with such influential clients as Marshall Goldsmith and Anthony Robbins, and is co-editor of *Coaching for Leadership: Writings on Leadership from the World's Greatest Coaches* and *The AMA Handbook of Leadership*.

# Global Business Leadership

## Second Edition

**E.S. Wibbeke and Sarah McArthur**

Routledge
Taylor & Francis Group

LONDON AND NEW YORK

First published 2008
By Butterworth Heinemann/Elsevier

Second edition published 2014
by Routledge
2 Park Square, Milton Park, Abingdon, Oxon OX14 4RN

and by Routledge
711 Third Avenue, New York, NY 10017

*Routledge is an imprint of the Taylor & Francis Group, an informa business*

*British Library Cataloguing in Publication Data*
A catalogue record for this book is available from the British Library

*Library of Congress Cataloging in Publication Data*
Wibbeke, E. S.
  Global business leadership / E.S. Wibbeke and Sarah
  McArthur. – 2 Edition.
    pages cm
  Includes bibliographical references and index.
  1. International business enterprises–Social aspects.
  2. Leadership–Social aspects. 3. Intercultural communication.
  4. Business communication–Social aspects. 5. Sex role in the
  work environment. 6. Corporate culture–Cross-cultural studies.
  I. McArthur, Sarah. II. Title.
  HD62.4.W583 2013
  658.4'092–dc23

                                                        2012050055

ISBN: 978-0-415-62981-2 (hbk)
ISBN: 978-0-415-62982-9 (pbk)
ISBN: 978-0-203-76871-6 (ebk)

Typeset in Times New Roman
by Cenveo Publisher Services

Printed and bound in the United States of America by
Edwards Brothers Malloy

### E.S. Wibbeke

This book is dedicated to the first and best example of leadership I have ever seen—my mother, Rose. *Cronáim thú*. To my husband, Michael, whose patience and understanding made this second edition possible. *Ich liebe dich*.

### Sarah McArthur

Dedicated to Homer, from whom I learned and with whom I've found that anything is possible!

# Contents

viii   *Contents*

# List of Exhibits

# List of Figures and Tables

**Figures**

## Tables

# Acknowledgments

## E.S. Wibbeke

This second edition was made possible through the efforts and generosity of many amazing individuals, primarily my co-author, Sarah McArthur. This has been a true collaboration. Jane Dodge proved to be a most effective research librarian and editorial assistant, and Maureen Guarcello is poised to be an emerging leadership scholar in her own right. The continued support of my colleagues and mentors were invaluable during this second edition: Jack Aschkenazi, Geert Hofstede, Robert Moran, Alan Richter, Edgar Schein, and George Simons. I am also most grateful to all of the thought leaders interviewed for this new edition. Their experience and expertise made this a unique book to write. I am also honored to have worked with a wonderful editing team at Routledge/Taylor and Francis, including Rosemary Baron and David Varley.

## Sarah McArthur

First and foremost, very special warmth and gratitude goes to my friend and co-author, Eileen Wibbeke. Her focus, dedication, and knowledge are an inspiration! This book would not have been possible without the outstanding work of Jane Dodge and Maureen Guarcello. Jane's knack for research and her calm, can-do demeanor were a great help and comfort during the writing process. Maureen's focus and positive attitude, in addition to her extraordinary research, editing, and writing capabilities were indispensable. Very special thanks go to each of the thought leaders who took the time to be interviewed. Their insights into global business leadership are invaluable to this second edition. Also, many thanks to my family Sarah Beynon, John Falchi, Amanda, Declan, and Halle McBride, and Scott, Eddie, and Hugh McArthur; to my friends Foxy Mc and Doug Baker, and to my mentors Marshall Goldsmith, Laurence S. Lyons, and Frances Hesselbein. Finally, a note of sincere gratitude to the outstanding editorial team at Routledge/ Taylor and Francis, who, through their diligence and care, made bringing *Global Business Leadership* to publication a joy.

# Foreword by Warren Bennis

The art of leadership is not based on quick formulas for success. It flows from becoming an integrated person, one who is able to discover and define—and redefine—oneself in the face of surprises and challenges in today's changing world. Dr. E.S. Wibbeke and Sarah McArthur's second edition of *Global Business Leadership* delves into just what it takes to become a leader who is prepared to face the challenges of global leadership. The Geoleadership Model they detail is a comprehensive approach derived from validated research. Its key dimensions are critical in preparing leaders for intercultural competence.

The model's seven foundational dimensions serve as a guide to leaders for both initial preparation and for re-tooling. The first dimension of the model presents the greatest challenge and opportunity for any leader: simply to care. Caring is a vital concept; it means tempering one's ego, while taking calculated risks. It means learning to engender trust that transcends difference. Care means balancing profit with meaningful concern for stakeholders. Any business leader can lead by dependence, fear, or guilt, but this can create obligation and resentment rather than loyalty and trust.

Global leaders are now able to communicate with their followers by sending an email, text, or tweet. Digital technology and international competition have altered how business is conducted. In this new business landscape, leaders must communicate the organization's vision clearly, attending to the importance of both timing and tone. How a message is received will differ per cultural differences in perception.

Consciousness is not a word found in American business jargon, typically. The truth is that self-awareness is vital. An authentic leader interacts with followers with awareness of any self-bias. This requires global business leaders to be more mindful about their energetic presence based on who they are, and not just, what they do. The business leader needs to see the difference between doing and being.

I often talk about the differences between leaders and managers. Dr. E.S. Wibbeke and Sarah McArthur discuss these contrasting roles as well, but do so with the unique idea that these contrasts exemplify how leaders deal with ambiguity. Global business leaders must develop a tolerance for working with contrasting methods, perspectives, and value systems when constituents can be located anywhere in the world. Whether in New York or Hong Kong, leading across ten different time zones and ten different countries means paying attention to the uniqueness of all individuals and their perspectives. Interest in other perspectives requires being curious about another individual holistically. Within a globally interdependent economy, business leaders must possess a learning aptitude and attitude towards growing contrasts.

Contrasts and contexts are closely related. A business leader must be continually able to evaluate a situation and how to act within it, even as the context changes. The business leader's consciousness may be challenged to be outside the leader's cultural comfort zone. By adding a global layer to this discussion of context, the authors demonstrate that the synthesis of full self-expression is what defines leadership. Everything the business leader does reflects who he or she is, despite the cultural context from both established and emerging markets.

*Global Business Leadership* is a thoughtful tome on the subject. Leaders need to have the capacity to imagine and articulate exciting future possibilities. They need a long-term perspective (i.e. a succession plan), which is the essence of successful change. Change is not a natural human condition, but an opportunity to learn. With the current state of a multi-generational workforce, a global economic crisis, and a technological revolution, leaders must not only manage change but also be comfortable with it in their own lives.

Learning assumes that a business leader is capable to be open to new ideas and retain a sense of curiosity. Dr. E.S. Wibbeke and Sarah McArthur term this as capability and discuss where and when a leader is deficient in a certain capability or competency, and then adjustments can be made. Most important is the ability of the business leader to facilitate an effective organizational culture, despite geography, and be capable of intercultural learning agility.

I am impressed with this work. The authors have built a sustainable global business leadership model that is unique in its layering of cultural complexity. Since the first edition of *Global Business Leadership* was published in 2008, others have written on the topic, and even universities have developed global business leadership courses. Dr. E.S. Wibbeke and Sarah McArthur have set the standard for how national culture affects business leadership decision-making through the Geoleadership Model. I applaud the efforts of these two authors and recommend this second edition to my colleagues and students as a valuable source of how business, culture, and leadership intersect. Culture at times may be invisible, but it plays an increasingly important role in influencing the mindset of constituents around the world!

*Dr. Warren Bennis*
Professor, University of Southern California, and
author of over 30 books on leadership and change.
His most recent book is *Still Surprised:*
*A Memoir of a Life in Leadership.*

# Preface

The greatest challenge facing leaders in this era of globalization is working effectively through cultural barriers to achieve business goals and objectives. Although U.S. corporations have been expanding across international boundaries for decades, the rapid global advance of technology, especially the Internet, as well as changes in investment *processes* and trade relationships, has eliminated previous barriers, thus opening markets and necessitating an even greater level of competence. The risk of not possessing the appropriate organizational capability, specifically in leadership, is great. This book seeks to provide U.S. business leaders with a cultural road map to navigate these vast oceans of cultural differences in leadership styles. We hope its content and strategies will prove useful to leaders in all business professions as well as students of international commerce. Finally, may this revised volume further the leadership competencies of leaders in business-related fields who seek to understand how cultural understanding is key to uncovering new global opportunities.

*Global Business Leadership* examines the dynamic role of leadership from an intercultural perspective. Learning how other cultures define and exert leadership is crucial in gaining and maintaining market share. Intercultural knowledge in this sense denotes how other cultures approach concepts such as ambiguity and change—the means to the unspoken side of business. Today's leaders are confronted with a plethora of published data about both their colleagues and competitors; however such information does not begin to cover the ways others form opinions or make decisions. Such intangible concepts can only be grasped through stepping back and examining the cultural underpinnings of another's background and development. The latter is done by making the connections between what a culture values and how it views leadership. Only through the committed exchange of ideas with diverse constituencies will U.S. leaders begin to cross the cultural divide growing in the global business arena.

In addition, past research pointed to specific competency variables without detailed explanations and input from intercultural participating experts. Dr. Wibbeke's doctoral dissertation presented such intercultural feedback. Pedersen and Connerley[2] determined that most leadership literature focused on data obtained from study participants and researchers from the United States, whereas this dissertation encompassed feedback from intercultural researchers from Africa, the Americas, Asia, Europe, and the Middle East. Further, in this book, there is a unique perspective on the new global workforce. This book is aimed at undergraduate and graduate business students, as well as career professionals, and current and future leaders of commerce.

Knowledge leaders of today are operating in a flat world. Physical borders have been dropped across trading zones, such as the European Union and Mercosur, and leaders deal daily with multiple groups in numerous countries, both online and offline. The Internet has become the great equalizer where small firms can appear large and where the attainment of knowledge becomes currency. Competent global leaders become great assets to their organizations when they can improve their global shrewdness consistently through interaction with their diverse business counterparts around the world.

Since the first edition of *Global Business Leadership*, we have worked with some consultants who effectively connect culture to leadership in the U.S. definitively, and we will include some of their expertise in this second edition. However, we find that most consultants still fail in this area, as they have not sufficiently linked leadership development to cross-cultural understanding, especially as it relates to globalization. We will address these issues and inadequacies within the present framework of a globally competent leader. This matter will be discussed in this volume because it helps to improve communications, increase effectiveness, and enable leaders to be both more understanding and more understood across boundaries.

*Global Business Leadership* is organized into twelve chapters. The first chapter discusses the challenges facing both leaders and organizations and the paradigm of a changing global landscape. The seven key principles of this new leadership paradigm lead to an explanation of the Geoleadership Model. The second chapter provides in-depth definitions of both culture and leadership and how competency in both realms is inextricably linked. The third chapter focuses on care, the first concept of the Geoleadership Model, and introduces the first case study of the book. The fourth chapter highlights the principle of communication and looks at how an organization delivers its message globally. The fifth chapter discusses the variable of consciousness and how self-reflection by a leader can lead to greater cultural adaptability. The sixth chapter investigates the idea of contrasting worldviews and how such meaning is interpreted differently in other cultures. The seventh chapter hones in on leading within context of a given situation. The eighth chapter describes how leaders must retain an adaptive global mindset and remain flexible when confronted with the increasing speed of organizational change. The ninth chapter concentrates on the importance of a leader's learning agility in remaining capable of thriving in a global space. The tenth chapter focuses on the influence of gender on leadership, while the eleventh chapter highlights how technology both helps and hinders how a leader relates to followers.

The final chapter summarizes and updates the book's principal messages. It underscores our belief that culturally competent leaders are essentially globalists and change agents in the global marketplace. In the conclusion, we propose that leaders in the era of globalization combine the seven principles of the Geoleadership Model to increase their competence: care, communication, consciousness, contrasts, context, change, and capability. The rationale of this work is that the globally competent leader embodies all seven of these principles and practices them consistently while leading an organization with global reach. Gender and technology are also taken into consideration as influencing factors on the act of leadership.

The following definitions serve to delineate the intended meanings of certain concepts presented in this book:

- *American and North American*: For the purposes of this book, the term *American* refers strictly to the United States.
- *Competence/Competency/Competencies*: The term *competence* reflects a specific range of skill, knowledge, or ability.
- *Cross-cultural*: The terms *cross-cultural, global, intercultural*, and *international* appear interchangeably to describe variables relevant to many cultures around the world.
- *Culture*: Reflects the learned and shared knowledge, beliefs, and rules of social groups that influence behavior.
- *Global Leadership*: Reflects the act and art of creating shared meaning and action that leads to achieving desired results across global boundaries.
- *Intercultural*: Please see *cross-cultural* above.
- *Leadership*: How an individual influences others to act for certain goals that represent the values and motivations of both leaders and followers.
- *Situational Leadership*: Reflects how the external environment and situation exerted influence on a leader's behavior.

When global leaders or would-be leaders appreciate the concepts and interdependence of the seven Geoleadership principles, then the transformation of mindsets and organizations can occur. Essentially this book on Geoleadership is a further discussion on the topic of organizational leadership, which stemmed from Dr. E.S. Wibbeke's doctoral dissertation, entitled *Intercultural Leadership Competencies for U.S. Business Leaders in the New Millennium*. A select panel of intercultural experts provided consensus on what exact intercultural leadership competencies were necessary for U.S. business leaders in the globalized marketplace. This dissertation appeared to be the first Delphi research study on intercultural leadership competencies solely conducted on the World Wide Web. This showed that this research does not require participating experts to interact in face-to-face communications, which made the method useful in conducting surveys with qualified participants in a global arena.

In conclusion, the doctoral research and subsequent work for this second edition of *Global Business Leadership* stems from our professional experience and research in the fusion of business, culture, and leadership. In today's dynamic, multicultural marketplace, we have always been keenly aware of "living between cultures" and trying to take one mindset and adapt it to be effective with others of different mindsets. As confirmed globalists, we are optimistic that this book will demonstrate the incredible value of seeing the cultural foundation of decision-making and how leaders committed to learning this will only thrive in this time of global change. As academic and business professionals, we are convinced that our message is relevant across borders.

*Dr. E.S. Wibbeke*
San Diego, California, 2013

*Sarah McArthur*
San Diego, California, 2013

# 1   Geoleadership challenges

## Failure to survive

It may be a small world but are we worlds apart? Today's organizational leaders are faced with a fast-paced marketplace operating within a context of multicultural, paradoxical complexity to achieve results.[2] More accurately, globalization has created an awareness of this complexity that was always there but not recognized. Now, there is no choice. Leaders at all levels of organizations, and especially those at higher levels, must work across national and cultural boundaries to achieve goals and objectives. While corporations have been expanding across international boundaries for some time, the rapid global advance of technology, as well as changes in investment processes and trade relationships, has eliminated previous barriers, thereby opening markets and necessitating an even greater level of competence. The risk of not possessing the appropriate global mindset, specifically in leadership, is enormous. How big is the problem?

> *Corporations have been building leadership models that dismiss multicultural competencies. Fewer than 10 percent of the models examined over the past several years contained any language alluding to global work.[3]*

There must be an integration of both multicultural and performance dimensions in constructing global leadership competency models.[4] In order to remain competitive, global business leaders need to be able to adapt to diverse national, organizational, and professional cultures.[5] What is more, leaders must be aware of the pitfalls of working in global contexts and the potential risk of lost opportunities.

## New challenges for leaders

Leaders of today are faced with global opportunities and challenges. In recent years, global business has grown beyond economic exchanges between nations to include cultural engagements, thus weaving a complex social component into global business practices.[6] The challenge is how to manage our multiple simultaneous cultural identities. A leader who can accommodate and master these challenges practices what we refer to as Geoleadership™.

Interpersonal communication and interaction pose several leadership challenges for intercultural leaders and managers. Differences in language, in cultural preferences for pace, social penetration, intonation, spatial distance, implicit versus explicit styles and more, play a role in the success or failure of any intercultural communication.

Communication technology presents challenges for leaders working in intercultural contexts. Instant communication technology connects the globe providing businesspersons with unprecedented opportunities. Consultants can log on and instantly connect with clients in London, Paris, or Istanbul. Managers can videoconference on the spot with counterparts in South Africa and can transfer documents around the world in seconds. Workers know when they send a PowerPoint presentation to Saudi Arabia their counterparts will be able to open it with a simple keystroke. The seemingly worldwide acceptance and use of "common" technologies, both hardware and software, create an illusion of familiarity.

However, it does not follow that, because a significant proportion of people worldwide run on Windows software, they think the same, have the same values, or face the same issues. In reality, our computer operating systems may be one of the few things that humanity has in common. There is a risk in our over-reliance on technology to solve all of our problems. After all, more plumbing does not increase the quality of our water.

Reflect for a minute about the variety of cultures there are just within the United States, sometimes within the same city. Los Angeles has a different feel about it from New York. In San Francisco, North Beach (the Italian quarter) is quite different from Chinatown. For example, is it not noticeable that the suburbs are different from urban centers? These settings are different because they make up what are referred to as subcultures: cultures within cultures. Some of these subcultures are ethnic-based; others are professional or economy-based differences. Ethnographic, demographic (age, gender, residence), status (educational, social, economic), and affiliation (formal and informal) all are combined in our cultural identity.

Yet, the issue is much broader than just the diversity encountered in today's domestic workforce. In organizations today, workforce diversity means working across national and geographic boundaries, with employees from various countries reporting to a manager in yet another country. The business leader of today is dealing with the world. The tendency of American business leaders to emphasize getting to "back-end" results quickly while most of the world's cultures emphasize "front-end" loading has proved costly.

Someone once quipped that the "only good *change*, is the change rattling in your pocket."[7] Amusing as that statement is, the implicit message is that change is okay when it belongs to you as an individual, when it is your idea; however, when change happens to you, it is not as easy a proposition. The cliché of the early 1990s that "change is constant" is now passé.

In this global business marketplace, gone is the illusion of certainty. Organizational life for leaders and managers is fraught with *ambiguity*. There are no cradle-to-tomb employment agreements. Technologies become obsolete and replace each other minute by minute rather than year by year, or decade by decade. Industries long considered stable are no longer so. The entire life cycle of a single economy can elapse before your child reaches preschool. Leaders do not have the luxury of taking for granted anything once thought of as material. Please see Exhibit 1.1 as an example of the dynamic workplaces in the new millennium.

---

### *Exhibit 1.1* **Dynamic workplaces in the new millennium**

**The perception from outside the cubicle**

You understand that our concept of time has changed if you manage a global team of workers with reports in Tokyo, Rome, Munich, Paris, Dublin, Manila, Mumbai, Beijing, and Abu Dhabi, who interact with a business partner in Bangkok. You have a weekly teleconference on Monday morning; but, when is Monday morning?

You are past "change as a constant" when you have been hired by one megacorporation, survived a company split, a merger (that was really an acquisition), led a divisional downsizing, were spun-off, then became an allied business, were promoted four times, reported to twelve different executives, had your office relocated five times, lived on two continents simultaneously, all within 30 months. You are also past the old "change management" models.

One only needs to look at the recent history of Yahoo!. There have been five different CEOs in as many years. One of the founders of the Internet pioneering firm, Jerry Yang, steps down as CEO, with a refusal to be bought by Microsoft, and the stock falling to record lows. In 2009, Carol Bartz, former CEO of Autodesk, replaces Yang, and within three years and many job and cost cuts throughout the company, Bartz is fired. Scott Thompson, president of eBay's PayPal division, becomes Yahoo!'s new CEO, its fourth within five years. After laying off 14 percent of the workforce in April 2012, Thompson then is fired due to misrepresentation of his educational background, and former Google executive, Marissa Mayer, becomes the new Yahoo! CEO.

(Information accessed at the following link, http://www.globalnews.ca/timeline+key+events+involving+yahoo+and+its+performance/6442680644/story.html)

Source: Global News. (2012) Timeline: Key events in Yahoo and its performance. http://www.globalnews.ca/timeline+key+events+involving+yahoo+and+its+performance/6442680644/story.html

Learning how to interact with other cultures takes effort beyond superciliously learning another culture's language. For the American business leader operating in another culture, business interaction requires a deeper cultural understanding about how things are done. Additionally, there are certain leader roles that, by themselves, require a high level of skill. One such skill is *negotiating*. The fact is cultures vary in perceptions about negotiating; some frown upon it, especially in certain situations, while other cultures rely on it as an integral aspect of any business exchange. Mismatches commonly occur between culturally different individuals due to misunderstandings about discretionary power, about what is and is not negotiable.

Another issue frequently blocking negotiations between culturally different individuals is approach. For example, cultures that adopt "positive face" will display sociability and solidarity in their interaction style, often using informality, friendliness, and use of first names to show "inclusiveness" or lack of distance. This approach may create a sense of uneasiness for members of a culture whose approach is to adopt a position of "negative face," showing deference and distance to other parties for fear of offending them or threatening their face. The concept of "face" refers to a person's public self-image, that which they desire to present to others. Positive face comes from a desire for appreciation and approval from others. Negative face is the desire to not be imposed on or to impose upon others.[8] The concept of "face" as a projected public image can be found across most cultures.

When people do not have a common frame of reference—as is found within a culture—misunderstandings, *conflict*, and productivity problems tend to arise. A manager described a situation within his team: individual members tend to support members from their own culture and consistently clash with team members from other cultures. An atmosphere of tension and hostility pervaded the team and without intervention resulted in business loss. Conflict resolution is yet another aspect of intercultural business relationships, as with negotiating, that requires a high level of knowledge. The majority of intercultural conflicts are caused by misunderstandings about different norms, styles, communication rhythms, values, and approaches.

*Motivation* presents a dual challenge for intercultural business leaders. On one level, *motive*, which is directly linked with values, presents a test of a leader's ability to understand what causes someone to do what they do. On a related level, providing a motivational work environment for employees who are different in their needs and expectations requires that a leader accurately interpret situations and respond in a culturally acceptable manner. The leader who assumes that what worked wonderfully to provide a motivational work environment in their native culture will also work to motivate a division of employees in Taiwan will experience a serious problem.

The strategy of sending U.S. corporate leaders and managers abroad for *foreign assignments* is not new. However, increasingly, corporations recruit leaders and managers to take foreign assignments to solve dicey business problems in their overseas locations. An entire consulting industry has sprung up in the U.S. to serve organizations that need to maximize the success of these personnel decisions because the success rate in the recent past has been poor. The chief reason for the lack of success is culture clash—rigid American managers sent to foreign cultures with a mandate to "fix the problem" encountering a culture with a different mindset.[9] If you can experience culture shock, as an American, traveling two states over, or from one telephone interaction to another, imagine what you would feel, as a unilingual American manager with no previous travel outside the U.S., when your corporation transfers you to an overseas assignment in Taiwan. For example, when different student exchange programs select high school students to go abroad, it selects students who have (1) the ability to fail, (2) a sense of humor, (3) a low goal–task orientation. Task-oriented people tend to have more difficulty adjusting in an unfamiliar culture.

## New challenges for organizations

In an increasingly competitive global marketplace, organizational leaders must believe that they can make a positive impact on others. This self-confidence leads to credibility being the foundation of leadership, so that followers will be apt to comply. The values of the leader drive the commitment to the organization from both followers and leaders. In the dynamic marketplace of today, leaders who focus on the future set themselves apart, while still realizing that leaders are not alone—leadership is indeed a team effort. In regards to teamwork, trust is crucial. Leaders must lead by example and face change head on by viewing challenges as opportunities, and not as obstacles. Modern leaders also need to be strong learners and provide an atmosphere of learning agility. Most companies realize that the ability to create or acquire human capital or talent assets can provide a singular competitive advantage. Leadership talent may be *the critical driver* of corporate performance and a company's ability to maintain competitive advantage far into the future.[10]

Read any respected business magazine, business journal, or website sponsored by a respected business school producing MBA graduates, and what you will find is a phenomenal level of agreement on two things related to global business: (competent) leaders, in general, are in short supply, and intercultural leaders require an entirely new and broader set of skills.

Competent leaders are in short supply chiefly because of demographic trends and because the job demands and requirements have expanded.[11] Currently, the United States is producing too few leaders with comprehensive international perspectives and experiences to meet the demands.[12] With current demographic trends, including the upcoming retirements of many "baby boomers" (i.e., people born between 1946 and 1964), the U.S. leadership talent shortage is projected to continue into the next several decades. Susan Lund, James Manyika, and Sree Ramaswamy have written an insightful article "Preparing for a new era of work" on how the global talent shortage is becoming more of a worry for business leaders than economic or political downturns.[13]

It is no longer enough to possess leadership skills learned from a domestic education or experience. Corporate boards and stockholders increasingly rely on their executives and managers to navigate the tangled jungle of global business. American employees outfitted with only their professionally oriented degrees and experience rely on their leaders and managers to guide them through the complexity of intercultural contexts. Companies must not only equip their leaders with additional skills; they must prepare leaders to navigate varied ethnic, religious, national, and cultural contexts to meet worldwide business demands. Companies should embrace this crisis as an amazing opportunity. Crises make leaders. Anybody can succeed when things are easy. But, real leadership is required when things get tough.[14]

## Paradigm shift

There is a shift currently that will in the end define all leaders as global leaders. This shift is masking the difference between leadership and global leadership due to the global complexity of the business and cultural context where leaders operate. Over the past several decades, leadership assessment frameworks have emerged to highlight not just managerial skills models with no mention of intercultural skills, but also more extensive leadership competency models that include a global layer.[15]

### *How interdependent are we as a global village?*

If you think that you are untouched by globalization, think again. Today, roughly two-thirds of all companies worldwide compete globally. As is clear from the global expansion maps included in Figure 1.1, an extraordinary amount of

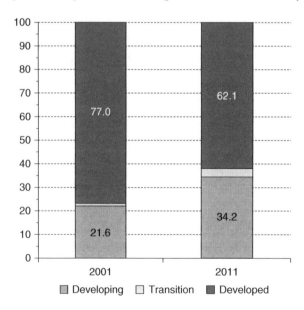

*Figure 1.1* Global corporate expansion, 2001 and 2011 (source: United Nations Conference on Trade and Development. Manyika, J., and Ramaswamy, S. (2012). *Statistics at a glance*. http://unctad.org/en/Pages/Statistics.aspx).

expansion has occurred during the last ten years. Global leadership is no longer the arena for just expatriates working overseas or top executives responsible for operations across geographies.

Not only are North American companies expanding abroad, but foreign interests have reciprocally bought into North American companies, and foreign companies are expanding operations in the U.S. and Canada.[16] What are the current statistics on foreign direct investment in the U.S. alone? Let us take a look at Figure 1.2.

*Global organizations*, then, are those that produce and sell goods or services in more than one country, have operations in foreign markets, and have established interdependencies, such as suppliers, who are foreign-based.[17]

The problem is that American companies needing to solve costly business problems abroad find themselves in a quandary, namely, how to entice U.S. managers (men and women) to leave their home country, uproot their families, to relocate half a world away to some culture they previously had only read about in magazines or seen glamorized in a Hollywood movie. Enticements generally consist of bonuses, additional hardship premiums for those who move to developing nations, and the promise of promotion. Multiple factors inform how these individuals ultimately perform, but research shows a positive relationship between geographic relocation and career advancement, about 2.6 advancements over a 20-year period.[18] It should be noted that studying international relocation is unwieldy because each individual situation is unique; however, laying a strong foundation is critical for all managers and organizations. What we are just beginning to deal with is determining the right preparation.

In addition to extraordinary business leadership skills, a leader now needs cultural intelligence. Cultural intelligence requires transcending one's own cultural background to interact with diverse and unknown intelligences.[19] People with high cultural intelligence are able to discern what true behaviors represent

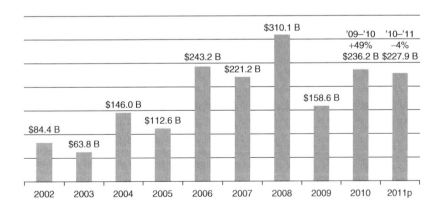

*Figure 1.2* Foreign direct investment in the United States, 2001–11 (source: Organization for International Investment (2012). *Foreign direct investment in the United States*. http://www.ofii.org/docs/FDIUS_3_14_12.pdf).

for individuals and groups compared to which behaviors are not universal or aberrational.[20] The gap between the universal and the aberrational is what we call culture.[21] Having this level of competence requires a comprehensive understanding of intercultural distinctions. Moreover, intercultural competence requires a highly developed sense of awareness to discern the global as well as the local similarities and distinctions within each context and within truly intercultural contexts.

The illustration of cultural intelligence exemplifies the many, complex layers involved in Israeli culture.

> In small countries, producing only for self-consumption does not pay. Israel gradually came to understand that it must produce for export, and the natural next step was to open subsidiaries abroad. As is true for most countries, Israeli executives, as home country nationals (HCNs), usually manage subsidiaries. Israel is located in the Middle East, but it is influenced by Middle Eastern, European, and Anglo-Saxon cultures. In general, Israeli executives have at least college degrees and are more or less fluent in English. Many have completed graduate school in the United States, England, or France. Those who acquire Ph.D. degrees often work in academia or as consultants.[22]

### Why is culture such a big deal?

When we operate from our own ethnocentric worldview, we develop perspectives and beliefs that we hold to be true. This is only natural. However, it can quickly feel unnatural when we encounter the customs, values, and laws of people from other cultures, who also hold their perspectives and beliefs to be true. Therein lays the dilemma. Nobody is right; nobody is wrong, just different! The simple truth is: culture is important because culture controls our life with or without our permission.

Leading across national boundaries is no small task. We know from Geert Hofstede's landmark cultural research[23] and E.T. Hall's germinal research on language,[24] that people differ across cultures along certain dimensions, such as individualism versus collectivism, power distance, short versus long-term orientation, time orientation and patterns, and pace of speech, to name a few. Moreover, research has demonstrated that differences occur within cultures, too. Even within a national culture, there are regional variations between individuals relative to the culture as a whole. This can be due to many things including immigration, and regional ethnic and political differences.

The world is a very different place outside our own country's borders. In 2012, there were 195 countries and an additional 72 dependent areas in the world. Each of these entities has a unique composition including cultural, religious, and geographic differences among its population. Some nations like New Zealand have as few as four major ethnic groups, while others like Nigeria are comprised of more than 250 ethnic groups.[25] The key to being successful in international business is recognizing how different things are and doing the homework necessary to understand with whom you are doing business.[26] Exhibit 1.2 presents a recent situation that serves as a good example.

---

### *Exhibit 1.2* **Israel and its place in the global marketplace**

Relative to its size, Israel is very involved in international business. The Israeli high-tech industry is well positioned among the top five world leaders in the field (Israel Ministry of Foreign Affairs, 2004) and has research centers and offices abroad. Israel while a small nation is experiencing a constant growth in expatriate managers.

Furthermore the growth of Israeli firms has been documented. About 215 Israeli small or medium enterprises (SME) have offices in New York City, according to the American–Israel chamber of commerce and industry in New York (AICCI, 2002); of these SMEs, 21 are listed on the NASDAQ. In December 2002, there were 125 Israeli companies listed on the NASDAQ and 18 Israeli companies traded on various European stock exchanges, including London, Zurich, and Brussels (Israeli Stocks Traded on European Exchanges, 2003). The American–Israel chamber of commerce in Atlanta (AICCSE, 2004) lists 47 Israeli companies based in Atlanta in various fields, from high-tech to biopharmaceuticals and shipping. In the second quarter of 2005, American firms invested in Israeli firms an amount of over one billion dollars, the latest transaction being the purchase of the Israeli firm shopping.com by e-Bay for an amount of $620 million.

*Source*: Aschkenazi, J. (2008). *Israeli expatriate managers, knowledge transfer and retention*. Saarbrücken, Germany: VDM Verlag Dr. Müller.

---

## Leadership evolving

### *New roles for leaders*

For centuries domestic and global economies have continually grown and transformed. Each emergent economy builds upon the former iteration. For example, the emergence of the "knowledge economy" in the 1990s was compared in strength and scope with the emergence of the manufacturing economy of the 1890s along with the mass-production economy of the 1940s and 1950s. Using historical events to help frame current and burgeoning economies is not the only tool we have at the analytical workbench these days. Just as it is important to take the global perspective into account, we can pull information from neighboring disciplines to help describe changes in our global economic trends.

Philosophy, sociology, modern political theory, and international relations all support illustrations and considerations of our current economies.[27] Despite the United States having been touted as the de facto leader of the knowledge economy because of our widely perceived educational and technological advantages, we witnessed the wholesale offshoring of jobs empty the corporate parking lots of economic centers in areas including Silicon Valley, California. This sea change, toward the knowledge economy, brought about widespread changes to how people in organizations work, and to the value of the positions of those working in the United States and abroad. Research is beginning to show differences in foreign labor tasks, some resulting in lower employment in the United States indeed, but some positions are complementary, creating a stronger output or overall product.[28]

With all the talk about new economies, though, it is important to understand what is meant by "new economy" before we discuss the implications of the various new economies themselves. What people mean when they talk about new economies is the creation of a new basis *for* an economy. For example, moving from a manufacturing economy to a knowledge economy indicates that the wellspring here is the flow of information and the creation of "knowledge" rather than material goods. Economists and management writers have been talking for some years now about the differences between older economies that are/were valuated on physical assets, such as facilities and equipment, and the new economy that is measured on the less tangible assets such as intellectual capital and patents. Thus, in the new economy, growth occurs through innovation rather than mass production. However, while there is widespread agreement that a defining aspect of the new economy is the increased importance of knowledge, defining what we mean by *knowledge* as it pertains to the concept of *economy* may be the most important issue. *Knowledge* is an intellectual product. *Intellectual capital* has been defined as valuable considerations and innovation, and as having three parts. One facet of intellectual capital is that of human capital, followed by relational, and organizational capital. At the heart of the knowledge economy are the discovery and management of intellectual capital.[29]

The knowledge economy includes the high-technology sector, service functions, and cultural industries among others. The Fordist modes of leadership and organization have long since been automated, lending time and resources to this new economy.[30] This is where industries such as software, biotechnology, and information technology hardware reside. These industries employ occupations such as engineers, scientists, programmers, and designers, whose major output is research and development that translates into new products and services. These industries are driven not by machinery, skilled shop workers, or even capital, although these continue to play a role, individuals engaged in research, design, and development drive these industries. At this point it is easy to imagine that the leadership styles from the mass-production economy and the knowledge economy differ today. Additional industries support the organization and distribution of human capital, since intellectual capital has three parts and multiple subdivisions therein.[31]

We now see the emergence of yet another economy, referred to as the "creative economy." This emerging trend is based upon the same principles of intellectual capital as the knowledge economy, but focuses upon social factors rather than the economics. Theorists believe that the human capital behind the creative economy is more interested in music, arts, and outdoor recreation, than the drivers of most of our former economies.[32]

With the globalization of the world's business, we are increasing the diversity of our business partners. And through mergers and acquisitions, and less formal cooperations like joint ventures (JVs) and partnerships, we have also added diversity to the gene pool. In business practice, we see two trends occurring together: on the one hand, an increasing standardization of the world; and on the other hand, an ever-growing diversity. When we connect the two, we have the essence of what the new innovation is all about. The joining of things we share, as well as the things that differ, is the essential task of leadership. It is, perhaps, this mode of leadership that we are currently missing. Theory has not caught up with the changing world and it has little to offer, nor has it provided a general framework to advise practitioners. The theory base has suffered from (scientific) reductionism and is not surprisingly highly segmented into the separate and unconnected domains of creativity, invention, and business development. There is no generalizable theory that informs professional practice (nothing to help leaders, HR professionals, or team leaders) for today's world.

Our research seeks to build an integrative theory. Whilst there is "nothing as practical as good theory," according to Kurt Lewin,[33] I would add that there is nothing like contemporary professional practice to build good theory. Next to the societal level creative thinking can be stimulated on three levels: individual, team, and organizational. The creation of a culture of innovation often starts with the individual, the entrepreneur, the whiz kid. There are few innovative organizations that don't have some unusually creative individuals. They are constantly challenging the organization's routines, irritating their more conservative colleagues, and making many mistakes along the way. On the individual level we need to go beyond existing models like Kolb's learning styles, neuro-linguistic programming (NLP), Kirton Adaptation Innovation Inventory, and Hermann's Brain Dominance (left vs. right brain, limbic vs. cerebral). Most models suffer from the fundamental flaw that they are based only on linear scales, where one orientation excludes the other. There might indeed be relationships between certain dominant orientations and the creative competence of an individual, but an important point has been missed.

"Stop!" some would say. Many have done solid research that shows a correlation between certain of the above preferences and creativity. The creative process is essentially a process where different logics are united and as such create a new reality. If we look at the Japanese garden, we see it is an invitation to accumulate different viewpoints so that every tour is a creative act. If we walk together, it connects your point-of-view with my point-of-view.

If we review almost 50 years of social science research on diversity in teams, the reality appears much less clear-cut. Elizabeth Mannix and Margaret Lean[34]

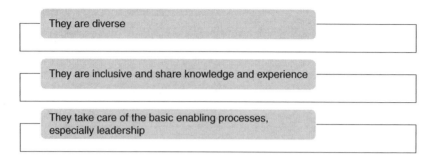

*Figure 1.3* Components of innovative teams.

have attempted to disentangle what researchers have learned over the last 50 years and they have concluded that visible differences—such as those of race/ethnicity, gender or age—are more likely to have negative effects on a group's ability to function effectively. By contrast, underlying differences—such as differences in functional background, education, or personality—tend to lead to performance improvement. In particular, underlying differences can facilitate creativity or group problem solving—but again, only when the group process is carefully supported. Teams are successfully innovative when they combine three main factors as shown in Figure 1.3.

When we look critically at what type of diversity leads to creativity in teams, we find that the invisible characteristics dominate. In particular, functional differences in skills, information, and expertise have been shown to improve performance because they give rise to a stimulating debate, and this leads to creativity and improved problem solving. These findings support the view that diversity in teams creates a positive environment of constructive conflict—an environment in which ideas synergistically evolve into higher-level outcomes than would be achievable in more homogeneous teams. We describe this phenomenon as the reconciliation of dilemmas created by different points of view. The tensions deriving from these dilemmas are the main source of creativity; the reconciliation of these dilemmas is the essential challenge and is thus the competence required of a team leader.

Creative individuals and inventive teams are both necessary, but this is not sufficient to generate conditions for an organization to be innovative. Organizations need to take a specific path to turn creative individuals and inventive teams into sustainable innovations by creating an integrated corporate culture. It is a bumpy path with many crossroads and many crises to be overcome. And the path never ends, because the culture of creativity needs to continuously integrate all the fundamental logics of an organization into a culture of sustainable innovation. The dynamics and processes are quite different from those we've discussed for the individual and at the team level. But what they have in common is that many key (and frequently recurring) dilemmas have to be reconciled. And the methodologies that enable us to diagnose and provide routes to improvement for corporate culture need to evolve from a rather static snapshot picture to a dynamic process of reconciling competing values.

A prerequisite for an innovative organization is the reconciliation of the variety of organizational cultures, in order to face the challenging dynamic world in which it operates. In this way, it can overcome the limitations of the dominant culture into which it will otherwise tend to drift, looming from crisis to crisis. There is synergy among all our pairs of extreme cultures. It is this that distinguishes creative and productive cultures from stagnant and ineffective cultures taken to extremes.

Interestingly, what we have found is that there are more similarities between the knowledge and creativity economies than between the older industrial economies. Unlike older economies that are and were based on scarcity, or the depletion of resources, the knowledge economy's fundamental unit of measure is information (knowledge, intelligence, etc.), which can be used, reused, and can actually grow through its utilization. The creativity economy's units of measure are concepts. Because of mediating technologies, such as the Internet and mobile computing, the effect of location is reduced significantly. Virtual marketplaces and virtual organizations are created offering speed and agility. Both of these new economies require that organizations recognize "intellectual capital" (the brainpower of employees) as their chief asset. However, the organizational shifts and challenges accompanying the knowledge economy and technology are highly dependent upon the situation and organization.[35]

In 2012, the A.T. Kearney Global Cities Index[36] was released for the third time. The index measures cities' global engagement across five dimensions. These include business activity, human capital, information exchange, cultural experience, and political engagement, as shown in Figure 1.4.

### *What are the implications of all this change for global business leaders?*

Sweeping changes, not seen since the Industrial Revolution, impact the organizational makeup and outputs of global and knowledge-based businesses. With change in the organization comes an implied requisite for changes in leadership; whose rewards and measures of success in a global world have also changed in form and function.[37] Immediate rewards like bonuses and promotions may still result, but scholars and business leaders posit that the traditional incentives take a backseat to long-term vision and relationship building.[38]

Economies based on knowledge and creativity require organizations to possess a level of management sophistication different than anything previously seen. Supervision and training, though important for some industries, becomes outdated when it is employed in the new economies. Former management functions are replaced with critical thinking and "cultivation of creative problem-solving skills."[39]

When leaders exercise the thinking skills and principles associated with creative problem solving, not only do they benefit from the outcome, but the lessons

| New York |
| --- |
| London |
| Paris |
| Tokyo |
| Hong Kong |
| Los Angeles |
| Chicago |
| Seoul |
| Brussels |
| Washington, D.C. |
| Singapore |
| Sydney |
| Vienna |
| Beijing |
| Boston |
| Toronto |
| San Francisco |
| Madrid |
| Moscow |
| Berlin |

*Figure 1.4* 2012 A.T. Kearney Global Cities Index (source: Adapted from 2012 Global Cities Index and Emerging Cities Outlook study by A.T. Kearney and The Chicago Council on Global Affairs).

and training are also imparted on the trainee cultivating future leadership skills.[40] Although "creativity" sounds like a loose term, it is possible to maintain the structure of a specific job description, while incorporating creative elements into the role, creating an opportunity to develop both the employee and the leader.[41]

Perhaps the greatest change in leadership perspective is that leaders must understand that the very concept of leadership, and therefore its practice, varies between cultures. This understanding is an essential factor in possessing intercultural leadership competence.[42] Exhibit 1.3 expands upon leadership comprehension and the value of reflection and the learning edge among global business leaders.

In order to acquire or develop new competencies all leaders, including business leaders, must first know what specific competencies to develop and how to acquire them. A recent Aboriginal classroom study shows the value of "both ways" education, with staff acting as both intercultural teachers and leaders.[43]

Technology and communication indicate that the trend toward globalization is likely irreversible, that truly intercultural leaders are in short supply, and that the "new intercultural leader" is and will be operating at a much higher level of capability than ever before. The question is what those capabilities are and how leaders can acquire them.

---

### *Exhibit 1.3* **Paths to creating global business leaders**

Is necessity truly the "father of invention"? Perhaps not, but necessity often provides the opportunities for individuals to gain valuable experience. This can be seen through such variables as trial-and-error, hardships, making mistakes, or learning on the fly. Global business leaders can also receive experience training through such pathways as intercultural communication training, targeted skills training, negotiation and conflict resolution training, and language training. Such leaders can make part of their personal development plans the act of networking wherein they participate in multicultural associations, attending regular global leadership conferences, and even connecting through technology such as Skype and WebEx. On the same wavelength as experience and training, budding global business leaders can themselves become part of global virtual teams, task forces, and action learning groups. Such teams and groups would be necessary for targeted assignments to be completed, whether they be multicultural team assignments, international assignments, exchange programs, or early career programs. When such assignments are in progress, or even completed, global business leaders can greatly benefit from assessment tools such as 360 degree feedback, cross-cultural assessments, cultural simulations, and role plays. Finally, throughout the career of a global business leader, coaching is paramount for success. From mentoring, feedback, cultural guides, role models, and executive coaching, continuous feedback allows for the effective growth of a truly successful global business leader. It is important to remember that all leaders were once followers themselves.

---

## Seven key principles of a new leadership paradigm

### *Framing context*

It is quite challenging, even with the best of intentions, to think about anything without your thoughts being steeped deeply in cultural meaning—that includes the well-intended and well-researched book you are reading now. We simply do not exist outside of a cultural and social context. The following colloquial story will illustrate this point. Say you were born on the beach of an uninhabited island in the middle of some ocean, and orphaned immediately at birth because your poor mother and father were washed out to sea before you laid eyes on them, and you were "raised" by native orangutans. You would still be a creature of your culture. In this case, your culture would be those native primates.

   The problem with even the best-intentioned recommendations for leadership competence in intercultural contexts is that they still have a cultural bias. In other words, the very concept of leadership is culturally bound. Leadership is not what *you* think of as leadership everywhere else on this planet.

*Here are some examples to illustrate the point*

In French, leadership, "conduite," means to guide one's own behavior, to guide others, or command action.[44] In France, although the French are famous for protesting, authority holds deference and respect.

In German, leadership, "Führung," means guidance, and in organizations, it is construed to consist of uncertainty reduction. The leader guides action. Further, leaders guide by the rules in such a way as to motivate.[45]

In Chinese, leadership, "领导," means the leader and the led. The leader is one who "walks in front" and guides the group through teaching "the way." Here, the implication is that leadership can only be a relational activity.[46]

In Arabic, there is a word "Sheikh" that has different meanings according to the regional culture within the Middle East. Literally, "Sheikh" means a man over 40. However, in the Gulf and Saudi Arabia, "Sheikh" means a person from the Royal Family. In Egypt, "Sheikh" means a scholar of religion. In Lebanon, "Sheikh" means a religious leader even among Christians. The socioeconomic and political culture of the Middle East plays a role in influencing the definition of leadership. In general, it is agreeable among people from the Middle East that leadership is tied to seniority before any other qualification.

During the period when Egypt was a monarchy, it was improper to present King Farouk as the leader of Egypt. However, they used the term leadership to describe heads of the opposition parties. During the 1950s, many Arab countries were ruled by military officers. Since then "leadership" has become a descriptive term of presidency. There have been great business innovators who were recognized as leaders for their role in starting new industries. However, that was before the 1952 revolution. Now, in the Middle East the term leadership is a political term, nothing else, with the exception that in Iran, leadership is a religious term more than a political one. As far as organizational or business leaders, they cannot share the term no matter how great their contribution.[47]

### Is there one best way to lead, or is leadership, at best, contextually dependent?

In the first-ever web-based Delphi study on intercultural leadership competence, leading intercultural experts from around the world participated in a consensus-building effort to determine the critical competencies for intercultural leadership and in how leaders can acquire them.[48] While the study's inquiry questions directed to the panelists focused on U.S. business leaders to delimit the research properly, panelists concluded that their recommendations held for all leaders engaged in global enterprise. The researcher's investigation yielded both surprising and anticipated results.

From the analysis, the researcher and independent analyst identified seven critical factors considered necessary for intercultural leadership competence. These seven critical factors were integrated and form the foundation for Geoleadership, a new intercultural leadership model.[49] In the section following, we present and briefly describe the seven factors considered necessary for intercultural leadership competence. Figure 1.5 provides a graphic representation of the Geoleadership Competency Model.

**Care** Global business leaders should hold and maintain equal concern for the bottom line and for stakeholder groups. One of the clearest and starkest criticisms of American leaders and businesses is perceived to be that their

*Figure 1.5* The Geoleadership Competency Model (source: Sheridan, E.S. (2005). *Intercultural leadership competencies for U.S. business leaders in the new millennium.* Unpublished doctoral dissertation. University of Phoenix, AZ).

focus is on profit, seemingly above all other considerations. While we can agree that one objective of business is profit creation, we also believe that a longer (term) and broader (social systems) view serves business, ultimately.[50]

**Communication** In order for business leaders to lead effectively in intercultural situations, such leaders necessarily must engage and interact with those cultures in whose countries they work, if not with many cultures. Closely related to context is that leaders must reach out to people in other cultures with a desire to understand and appreciate that culture and its people.[51] Leaders must learn communication skills that promote listening and open, respectful dialogue.

**Consciousness** Nowadays, a person filling the role of leader and manager needs to develop self-awareness. A leader's awareness must be expandable as contexts shift around them, such that the leader becomes clear of a personal cultural background and bias relative to that of other people. Building consciousness means being able to expand your awareness.[52]

**Context** Global business leaders must develop the ability to perceive, discern, and adapt to the situations within which they work, and to suspend judgment. As trite as it may seem the old expression "when in Rome, do as the Romans do" seems to apply. We want to be careful here, not to suggest that leaders patronize the people they interact with in intercultural contexts. In truth, we submit that American business leaders have some work to do in authentically interacting with other cultures. What all of this means is that all global business leaders must attend to the situation in which they find themselves. Leaders need to understand each culturally learned behavior in the context of where that behavior originates and appears.[53]

**Contrasts** Leaders must be able to work comfortably and effectively with ambiguity. Developing a tolerance for working with contrasting perspectives, methods, and with differing value systems is critical. Working in ambiguous contexts requires patience and it requires consciousness. Working at such a high level of consciousness means that leaders must be able to perceive multiple levels of meaning simultaneously.[54]

**Change** Postmodern organizations require adaptive leaders who demonstrate flexibility in adapting to dynamic cultural environments. Intercultural leaders must shift from the old mechanistic mindsets of the industrial era to the flexible adaptive perspective of organizational life as what it is, a complex sociocultural system.

**Capability** In order for a leader to be effective in intercultural situations, there must be development of sufficient personal and organizational capability. Intercultural competence requires that leaders are able to assess their own and others' capability and build it where there is deficit.[55] Most important is the leader's influence in facilitating an organizational culture capable of intercultural learning agility.

In this second edition of *Global Business Leadership*, we have included interviews with individuals who exemplify the competencies highlighted in the

Geoleadership Model. Each leader, in his or her own words, discusses what makes a great global business leader and what mistakes such leaders continually make. The first interview in Exhibit 1.4 is with John Ryan, the president and CEO, for the Center of Creative Leadership.

---

### *Exhibit 1.4* Interview with John Ryan, president for the Center of Creative Leadership

"Creative Leadership" according to the Center for Creative Leadership (CCL), is "the capacity to think and act beyond the boundaries that limit our effectiveness." Astute and far-sighted, this definition lends itself to the focus of CCL, which is to help leaders face obstacles, whether they be in the global marketplace, locally, or in non-profit groups and government agencies. Initiated in 1970, CCL has a long legacy of creating new knowledge to expand the field of leadership. At the helm of this organization today is John Ryan, current president and CEO, whose insights on global leadership you'll find in the interview that follows.

*What are the most important decisions you make as a leader of an organization of which you have been a part?*

Leaders need to make the right decisions in three key areas. No. 1 is setting direction, which means developing a realistic and competitive strategy. No. 2 is creating alignment. This is not about merely organizing people, which is instead the role of management. It's more about establishing effective communication up, down and across the organization to foster empowerment. No. 3 is prioritizing talent decisions. It is crucial to hire well, ensure everyone is in the right position and give individuals and teams the resources to execute strategy. This might sound trite, but so few leaders give talent the focus it deserves.

*How do you encourage creative thinking within your organization (i.e., given the type of industry in which you operate)?*

To encourage creative thinking and create a culture of innovation, leaders need an innovation strategy that is developed from the bottom-up and recognizes people as the key source of competitive advantage. As my CCL colleague Dan Buchner notes, most leaders are educated in traditional "business" thinking, which attacks problems in linear, logical and established ways. To take organizations to the next level, we must also develop our ability to use "innovative" thinking—to intuit new ideas, ask "what if?" consider multiple options, and embrace ambiguity. A creative leadership culture recognizes and skillfully manages the tensions between business thinking and innovative thinking. Productive new products and services will result.

*What is one characteristic that you believe every global business leader should possess?*

Every global leader needs to develop learning agility, which is the ability to make meaning from their experience. When you are an agile learner, you can challenge the status quo, take on tough situations and remain calm in the face of them. To become that kind of leader, we first need to expose ourselves to new challenges, ideas and subjects. Then, we need to be disciplined about creating time to reflect on what we've learned and how we can put it into action. There's little point, after all, in having the experience but missing the meaning. Jack Welch has said that an organization's ability to learn and translate that learning into action very quickly is the ultimate competitive advantage.

*What is the biggest challenge facing a global business leader today?*

The biggest challenge facing global leaders today is quite clear: There's not enough leadership talent in organizations, and the talent that does exist needs to work more interdependently. Great leaders are needed to make organizations thrive in a world characterized by Volatility, Uncertainty, Complexity, and Ambiguity, (VUCA), described by futurist Bob Johansen in his newly updated book *Leaders Make the Future*. The pace of change in the world keeps accelerating, so global executives need to make building their leadership pipelines a top priority. They also need to recognize and reward leaders who take responsibility for developing a new generation of leaders, even as they also pay attention to strategy and the bottom line.

*What effect do you think national culture has on business leadership decision-making? (This can also include how your own native national culture affects your decision-making.)*

The danger of being too heavily influenced by a particular national culture is that it narrows your view of the world. We all live in certain cultures and can buy into their assumptions, both good and bad, too easily if we're not careful. The antidote to being overly influenced by a particular culture is to value cognitive diversity and take steps to create it on your teams. In other words, we need to put together teams and organizations with many people who think differently, have different backgrounds and see the world in different ways. Is it good for me to have a half-dozen people on my executive team who look, think and act just like I do? Absolutely not. We're going to miss opportunities and falter on important decisions. We need to have a sense of humility and recognize the limits of our own knowledge and experience. Then we bring in people who can help expand it. To make sure we're on the right path, it's also important to review periodically our strategies and key decisions, and re-do them when necessary.

*What are your thoughts on globalization and how important is it leaders embrace the importance of change management in order to remain competitive and promote innovation? Can you give an example of a leader or organization that did not change (or did change) and what were the results of the change both for the individual leader as well as for the organization as a whole?*

Kodak, which recently sought bankruptcy protection, is a great example of how difficult it is to remain innovative and competitive in a world of accelerated change. This was a great company for 100 years, and it did many things right. It developed innovative technology; it was recognized for its strong ability to align its people around key strategies. But success also requires looking into the future and anticipating and preparing for changes in the marketplace, even if we can't know what's coming with certainty. Kodak, which developed many digital photo technologies in the market today, was never able to capitalize on its own innovation—but its competitors were. One lesson here: an ability to innovate and align talent does not matter much if you're aligning around the wrong strategies. A second lesson: we can never rest on our laurels. It is critical to practice continuous dissatisfaction, which means taking time to celebrate accomplishments but never getting complacent about them. Some competitor is always coming for your business.

*What is one mistake you witness business leaders making more frequently than others? Can you provide an example of where you have seen this mistake being made and the resolution (if any) of the situation?*

Probably the biggest mistake that business leaders make—and I've been guilty of this as well—is not spending enough time on talent acquisition, onboarding, development, and retention. When your daily schedule is hectic, and you're trying to hit your numbers, develop new business and put out all the fires that keep coming up, it's easy to treat the hiring of people on your team as just one more thing you need to check off your list. But, unlike many of the daily fires we face, the hiring of key people has long-term, serious implications for your organization. If you hire the wrong people, you have greatly compromised your ability to execute your strategy now—and compromised the future of the organization. So take the extra time needed to find the right women and men for your key roles and get them on board—and then work hard to develop and keep them. The extra work needed to do that might cause inconvenience in the short term, but it will define your success over the long term.

*Can you name a person who has had a tremendous impact on you as a leader? Maybe someone who has been a mentor to you? Why and how did this person impact your life?*

Andy Wilkinson, my first boss when I was a young pilot in the U.S. Navy, had a powerful and lasting influence on me as a leader. In ways both large and small, he embodied effective leadership. He took a strong interest in my personal development, provided honest feedback (which was sometimes a little painful to hear but always delivered professionally), thought of how to keep us connected with our families, and helped me get my next job. I was always learning from him. What more could you ask from a leader? In many ways, I have spent my career trying to live up to the potential he saw in me.

*Within the global economy, how important is it that a global business leader understands the key features of the Geoleadership Model? (http:// www.geoleadership.com/model.asp)*

The Geoleadership Model reflects many of the most important skills CCL has identified through research projects globally for leading effectively across boundaries and cultures. In our experience, effective leadership always starts with self-awareness and a thorough understanding of the context in which you are leading. With that foundation in place, adaptability and communication become crucial qualities for leading across boundaries, particularly geographic ones. And it is always important to keep in mind a longer-range goal of building capability, in this case intercultural expertise at every level of the organization. The Geoleadership Model superbly articulates those skills and how they must work together—making it a model that global business leaders should be sure to study.

*What do you like to ask other business leaders when you get the chance?*

I'm privileged, through working at CCL and serving on various boards, to talk with first-rate leaders very frequently. It is always tempting to ask "What keeps you up at night?" But, instead, I ask "What makes you excited to get up in the morning?" Their answers are inspiring and many times similar: the chance to learn something new, to make a difference, and to work with great colleagues. I'm grateful to have all three of those opportunities every day at CCL.

***

Not surprisingly, John Ryan purports that the Geoleadership Model reflects similarly the skills and characteristics that CCL has found significant to effective global leadership in its many research projects over the last 40 years. The fact that we are finding the same things to be true is a great support and inspiration as we continue our research and as we show leaders how to use the Geoleadership Model to build long-range capability and intercultural expertise throughout their organizations.

**John R. Ryan** is president and CEO of the Center for Creative Leadership (CCL), a top-ranked, global provider of executive education that unlocks the leadership potential of individuals and organizations. A retired U.S. Navy Vice Admiral, Ryan joined CCL's Board of Governors in 2002 and became President in 2007. From 2005 to 2007, he served as Chancellor of the State University of New York (SUNY). Previously, Ryan served as President of the State University of New York Maritime College and as Interim President of the University at Albany. From 1998 to 2002, Ryan was Superintendent (President) of the U.S. Naval Academy, winning widespread praise for his focus on academics, strategic planning, and fundraising. A former Navy pilot, Ryan commanded squadrons, wings, and forces in Asia, Europe and the Middle East during a 35-year career in the military. Ryan serves on the Board of Directors for Cablevision (Bethpage, NY) and CIT Group Inc. He is also a member of the U.S. Naval Academy Foundation Board. Ryan received a B.S. from the U.S. Naval Academy and an M.S. in Administration from George Washington University.

Our first interview was with a thought leader on leadership; now the content shall shift to a thought leader in the field of intercultural communications. We feel it highly appropriate that these interviews open our book, as their content reiterates the fact that we simply do not exist outside of a cultural and social context. When we look at leadership, it is through the lens of a cultural bias. All of our interviews will illustrate this fact, and many of our interviewees will mention it. How we communicate cross-culturally, then becomes of huge import as our next interview with Fons Trompenaars will reveal in Exhibit 1.5.

**Exhibit 1.5** **Interview with Fons Trompenaars, founder and director of Trompenaars Hampden-Turner (THT)**

Fons Trompenaars is a world-recognized expert on how culture influences international management. With Charles Hampden-Turner, he developed a seven-dimensional model of culture, which defines five orientations human beings have to deal with each other. Fons directs a consultancy, which works with companies to provide training in the areas of sustainability and globalization. Dutch-born Trompenaars was recently recognized as one of the 50 Most Influential Management Gurus by Thinkers50 (sponsored by Harvard Business Review).[56] His work in the field of cross-cultural communication illustrates how leaders can be successful in a cross-cultural, global world.

*What are the most important decisions you make as a leader of an organization of which you have been a part?*

Let me start with a quote by my wonderful colleague Charles Hampden-Turner: "*Outstanding leaders sense dilemmas facing their industries and their organizations before their competitors and tend to find solutions more quickly. The more formidable the dilemma, the greater the gain from resolving it first!*"[57]

This is what it is all about: leaders reconcile dilemmas and managers want to make choices. Leaders frequently suffer from insomnia, because they are not able to resolve a dilemma they face. It is difficult "not to have made it," but even more difficult not knowing "what to make." Then, even worse—the successful integration of conflicting values frequently leads to the creation of one or more new dilemmas. It is a continuous process.

*How do you encourage creative thinking within your organization (i.e., given the type of industry in which you operate)?*

There are many counterproductive forces related to the process of innovation. First, we find that the commodification of education—a prime killer of creativity—has not helped to make people more innovative. In fact, the opposite is true. Second, current practices in organizations, from the Sarbanes-Oxley Act to the Hay System of Job Evaluation, have not been an effective framework for the creative person that supports or enables breakthrough services. In contrast, there seems to be an increasing drive for us to control our processes as much as we can and to avoid mistakes at all costs. Despite the fact that we seem to have tried to numb our creative processes, the countervailing powers are at least as big.

*What is one characteristic that you believe every global business leader should possess?*

It is the competence to recognize, respect, reconcile, and realize the integration of opposing orientations. A good global leader knows to distinguish between a dilemma and a problem. With problems you just need to have the competence to make the right choices. But choices are killing when you deal with a dilemma. With a dilemma you need to try to bridge the opposites.

*What is the biggest challenge facing global business leaders today?*

What are these dilemmas that international leaders face? Of course you have to inspire as a leader and you have also to listen. You need to follow the orders of HQ to fulfill the global strategy and you have to have local success by adapting to regional circumstances. You have to decide when to act yourself but also when and where to delegate. As a professional you need to input your own day-to-day contribution and at the same time to be passionate about the mission of the whole. And you need to simultaneously use your brilliant analytical power while enabling the contribution of others.

You need to develop an excellent strategy while simultaneously having answers to why the strategy misses its goal.

The view of leadership taken here is that leaders find themselves *between* conflicting demands and are subject to an endless series of paradoxes and dilemmas. There are non-stop culture clashes and by culture we mean not simply the cultures of different nations, but those of different disciplines, functions, genders, classes, and so on. Some well-known leadership dilemmas are listed in Figure 1.6. Their exact descriptions are less important than the capacity for trans-cultural competence or paradoxical problem solving which underlies them all.

Figure 1.6 describes an army of current challenges. Are leaders the "authors" of strategy and policy or do they orchestrate the necessary participation? Do leaders deal in high-level abstractions or in concrete details? Can a leader be a servant also? Such questions culminate in what is, perhaps, the biggest crisis of the day. Are leaders people hired by shareholders to channel the lion's share of profits in their direction, or do they lead a learning, developing community?

*What effect do you think national culture has on business leadership decision-making? (This can also include how your own native national culture affects your decision-making.)*

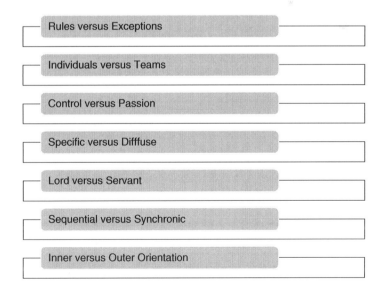

Rules versus Exceptions

Individuals versus Teams

Control versus Passion

Specific versus Difffuse

Lord versus Servant

Sequential versus Synchronic

Inner versus Outer Orientation

*Figure 1.6* Leadership paradoxes and dilemmas.

The two main cultural differences that affect decision-making in an international environment are the degree to which one allows people to participate and whether it is done top-down or bottom-up. International leaders are frequently facing the integration of team spirit (in which cooperation dominates) versus individual creativity and empowerment. The effective leader knows how to mold an effective team out of creative individuals. In turn, the team is made accountable to support the creative genius of individuals as they strive to contribute the best for the team. This has been described as *co-opetition*.[58] At Lego,[59] maker of popular children's toys, there is no problem in finding enough individuals to generate enough ideas. The challenge lies with the "business system" or community, which has to translate those ideas into the reality of viable products and services. It was not unusual for the community or system to impede the realization of good ideas, especially where ideas came from senior people, while juniors were expected to be concerned solely with implementation.

There is top-down versus bottom-up. Getting things done is important for manager performance. But doesn't the doing of vulgar and mundane things need to be in balance with our private life? As a leader you need also to be able to be yourself. However, from our research findings we conclude that our leaders are not different from what they do. They seem to be one with what they do. One of the most important sources of stress is when being and doing are not integrated. An overdeveloped achievement orientation that does not harmonize with what the person suits in their lifestyle and themselves leads to ineffective behaviors.

We have seen in another recent book, *Building Cross-Culture Competence*,[60] that successful leaders do things in harmony with who they feel they are and vice versa. They have been able to reconcile Private and Work Life. This is not an easy way, but "the Servant Leader" does not only use his ascribed status top-down to have his people achieve better bottom-up. It is also used to have family life and business support each other.

*What are your thoughts on globalization and how important is it for leaders to understand the context(s) under which they operate in a given situation and/or organization?*

Globalization has taken a new direction lately. There have been many stages from multi-local, through international and global. Now we have to go for transcultural. A second ethnocentric phase is the one of *defensiveness*. In this phase, people do experience cultural diversity; however the world is immediately divided into "us" and "them," whereby "us" is—of course—superior to "them." This is typified by an internationalizing manager who is convinced that his organization (and the technology it represents) is the very best. Local differences are not really appreciated. If the threat of the defensive phase is being reduced by the assumption that, at the core, all persons are equal, one then enters the phase of *minimization*. This final level of ethnocentrism is approached in the so-called *global organization*, if we use the terminology used by Goshal and Bartlett.[61] One sees that cultural differences exist, and are tolerated, but a strong corporate culture, such as IBM in the past, or GE, creates a strong pressure towards conformity. In the global organization, there is a strong drive towards standardization. Management teams consist purely of nationals that have grown the business from home.

Bennett[62] has characterized the first phase in *Ethnorelativity* as the phase of *acceptance*. The managers of the organization have, through longstanding international contacts, understood that they have their own cultural context determining their behavior, and that other cultures give meaning to their lives in other ways. These organizations will pay serious attention to attracting staff from different and diverse cultures, and will fully understand the value of cultural diversity, far beyond the formal rule-based interpretation of diversity that we see so often. The top management of such an organization will, however, still typically consist of nationals from the country where headquarters are based, but there will be one or two exceptions. A good example of this *International Organization* (Ghoshal and Bartlett) is Walt Disney, which relates slightly to the countries (France and Japan) where they also have their theme parks. The last but one phase is referred to as *adaptation*. Managers are able to look through different lenses onto the world. They adapt easily to changing local circumstances. The Anglo-Dutch companies Royal Dutch Shell and Unilever (not by coincidence both bi-national organizations) are good examples of this group. And work gets done in the *Multi-National Organization*. Their managers are used to doing in Rome as the Romans do. Their organizations are easy to recognize, because they put a lot of effort into language training, and have many traditional cross-cultural training programs such as "doing business with the Japanese". *Trans-national Organizations*, of which probably ABB and Applied Materials would be the best examples I know, have actually entered a sixth phase: that of complete *integration*. When visiting Applied Materials, I learned that their top management of seven included seven different nationalities (even omitting the double nationalities), and that the organization was directed from different centers, of which several were outside the United States. Because all international activities are performed in multi-cultural teams, all managers are familiar with swapping from one cultural context to another. They view themselves as moving from one culture to the other, and do not perceive themselves as being at the center of the world. They very often use the interface between cultures as a platform from which to develop a hyper-culture that transcends and makes use of the differences.

*What is one mistake you witness business leaders making more frequently than others? Do you think that some leaders are not self-aware enough to successfully understand the changing contexts around them while doing business globally?*

One of the mistakes is that global leaders think that cultural differences can be pushed aside by standardization of processes: one brand, one HR policy, one IT system worldwide. And if it does not work, push harder. This type of globalization has failed dramatically. Then there are the more sensitive leaders who say that you need to adapt to local circumstances. They are finding out that if you increasingly deal with a multi-cultural environment it is impossible to find out to whom to adapt to.

Indeed there is not enough (self-) awareness about this topic in particular the need to go trans-cultural and combine your own values and standards with the local ones.

*Can you name a person who has had a tremendous impact on you as a leader? Maybe someone who has been a mentor to you? Why and how did this person impact your life?*

In academia it was my tutors at Wharton: professors Hasan Ozbekhan and Russ Ackoff. And obviously my business partner and co-author, Charles Hampden-Turner. In business I have been very impressed and inspired by Bob Galvin of Motorola and Ginny Rometti from IBM. They both combine intelligence with a great human touch.

***

As we experience the paradigm shift that is transforming leaders into global leaders (or is finding them moving to extinction), we must navigate in a new direction. Perhaps, having moved through the stages of multi-local, through international and global leadership, we will move towards transcultural leadership as Trompenaars envisions, wherein leaders will understand that the essential factor of leadership as well as its practice varies between cultures and leaders with this understanding will be the link to a transcultural, global world.

**Fons Trompenaars** is recognized around the world for his work as a consultant, trainer, motivational speaker, and author of various books on all subjects of culture and business. As founder and director of Trompenaars Hampden-Turner (THT), an intercultural management firm, he has spent over 25 years helping Fortune 500 leaders manage and solve their business and cultural dilemmas to increase global effectiveness and performance, particularly in the areas of globalization, mergers and acquisition, HR, and leadership development. Trompenaars has translated his approach into innovative, practical, and profitable results in all areas of international business for BP, Philips, IBM, Heineken, AMD, Mars, Motorola, General Motors, Merrill Lynch, Johnson & Johnson, Pfizer, Citibank, ING, PepsiCo, and Honeywell.

He has written 13 books including the best seller and "Book of the Year" *Riding the Waves of Culture* and was voted one of the top 20 HR Most Influential International Thinkers 2011 by *HR Magazine*. He is also ranked in the Thinkers50 to be one of the most influential management thinkers alive in November 2011 and shortlisted as making substantial strides in the contribution to the understanding of globalization and the new frontiers established by emerging markets.

## The bottom line

Globally, societies are changing and so are organizations. Globalization and other changes create a new business climate, which requires different competencies from leaders. The risk of not becoming competent at leading global organizations and businesses is a costly failure. It has always been important for leaders to be competent at interpersonal relations, communicating, decision-making, visioning, problem solving, negotiating, influencing, and inspiring. However, in a constantly evolving global environment, where there are multiple and varying environments, leaders need new skills that enable them to traverse new territory. The role of leader has shifted at the same time that the expectations of leaders are less clear because of cultural differences, economic changes, generational shifts, political and social upheaval.

One of the primary reasons why so many global businesses have failed is due to unresolved cultural differences. Cultures vary widely in how they view business including how to lead and how to follow. Even with the minimal understanding of cultural differences that can be learned through distant study, the going can be tough and frustrating.

The combination of globalization, complex societal changes, demographic changes, and the lack of skilled business leaders being graduated from business schools has created a global talent crisis. Juxtaposed to this phenomenon is a postmodern perspective of leadership as being something that can emerge anywhere in an organization when it is needed.

## The journey to new leadership frontiers

In Chapter 1, we portrayed the complexities facing global business leaders today, and offered concrete examples of effective global leadership. Chapter 2 provides an overview of culture theory, leadership theory, and a discussion about the interaction of culture and leadership. In Chapters 3–9, we detail each of the leadership model competencies and then we present case interviews of business leaders who are trying to expand their markets and reach their company's potential. Chapter 10 explores leadership and gender and Chapter 11 shows the juxtaposition of technology and leadership. Chapter 12 summarizes how Geoleadership can be integrated into the business community as a whole. Through the case interviews, we demonstrate the use of the Geoleadership Model[63] so that you can see how to employ it in your own situations. Appendix A contains the original data, which validate the Geoleadership Model.

A competent intercultural leader has vision, yet is not rigid; is intentioned, yet not self-serving; is engaging, yet not political; is decisive, yet consensual; above all, s/he is cosmopolitan.

To be a true Geoleader, one must recognize that cultures are always evolving and that an individual's intercultural education will never end.

# 2　Culture and leadership

> "Good means not merely not to do wrong, but rather not to desire to do wrong."
>
> —Democritus[1]

Globalization presents unprecedented complexity for leaders.[2] Leading any social milieu requires that you possess, and act from, a set of values and principles (standards of behavior), and it is especially helpful when your values support rather than thwart your endeavors. Challenges include the distance involved with global partnerships, conducting business and customs differently across cultures, and the problems generated through cultural barriers; including an inability to see culture from a perspective other than that afforded to us by our own culture.[3] What is culture and how does it affect leadership and organizations?

## Defining the indefinable

Culture remains an often misunderstood concept within organizations.[4] Culture may appear specifically related to ethnicity, nationality, demography, or status; as the classic definition states, culture is "the collective programming of the mind that distinguishes the members of one human group from another."[5] The term itself is derived from a Latin root *colere*, which means to prepare and develop.[6] Thus, in this definition we can see the other form of the original word, which is (to) cultivate, meaning to grow. We accept the definition of culture proposed by Moran, Harris, and Moran: "Culture is a distinctly human means of adapting to circumstances and transmitting this coping skill and knowledge to subsequent generations."[7]

A general theory that explains culture has only been in the Western lexicon since the mid-twentieth century and essentially holds that culture is an interpretive and adaptive mechanism used by humans to understand and deal with their own nature and the environment around them. Human interest in culture surely is not new. One can speculate that being able to understand people beyond one's own tribe has been at least a secondary pursuit for as long as humankind has wandered from home terrain. The systematic examination of culture as social phenomenon began in earnest with early folklorists and anthropologists.

A number of early groundbreaking studies and writings about culture began appearing in the 1880s with such classics as Frazer's *The Golden Bough*, Radcliffe-Brown's *The Andaman Islanders*, van Gennep's *Rites of Passage*, Benedict's *Patterns of Culture*, and other notable scholars such as Margaret Mead. The majority of these works, however, concerned cultures not of the so-called modern world. It was not until the late 1950s that studies of culture began to concern themselves with contemporary culture. In 1959, Hall published his now famous, *The Silent Language*, in which he postulated the idea that cultures can be typed according to certain characteristic dimensions of behavior. Although Hall did not conduct empirical investigation, working in the U.S. Foreign Service provided suitable opportunity for participant-observation.

Hall posited that all cultures could be categorized along two dimensions: as being either high or low context and as being either polychronic or monochronic in their time orientation. The central premise undergirding high versus low context is that communication constitutes a transaction of information. In high-context cultures, information is passed with most of the information in the physical location or internalized by the person, and very little is coded within the explicit transmission. In contrast, a low-context communication contains as part of the explicit message the bulk of the information. Distilled, this means low-context cultures are more explicit and high-context cultures are more implicit in their communication style.

In high-context societies, people have close connections and long history, and many aspects of culturally sanctioned behavior are implicit because most members know what to do and what to think from years of interaction with each other. Societies such as China, Japan, India, and France are considered high context. Conversely, in low-context societies, such as the United States and the United Kingdom, people tend to have many connections but of shorter duration or for some specific reason. In these societies, cultural behavior and beliefs tend to be explicit so that those coming into the cultural environment know how to behave.

In Chinese culture, communication tends to be very efficient. In business, people tend to discuss issues during the time they work, sometimes over a meal. When it comes to meetings, Chinese have a tendency discuss things in advance and consider meetings ceremonial where the already commonly agreed decision will be announced. This is important in the way of "giving and keeping face." Conversely, the American and German way of conducting business meetings is to inform the attendees of a meeting about the hard and necessary facts during the actual meeting. In Chinese culture, issues, circumstances, and relationships are as important as work so they would comment only during a more private or appropriate occasion.

People from India or China, when hired by a North American company, tend to ask many questions, and can be perceived by their Western counterparts to be overly inquisitive before they commit to something. Americans might sometimes

| Factor | Monochronic Culture | Polychronic Culture |
|---|---|---|
| Actions | One task at a time | Multiple tasks handled at once |
| Focus | Concentration is on one job | Distractions and interruptions occur often |
| Time management | Time commitments are important | Time is present but not imperative |
| Respect for property | Seldom borrow or lend property | Regularly borrow and lend property |
| Planning | Adhere to plans | Plans remain fluid and change |

*Figure 2.1* Monochronic and polychronic cultures (source: Adapted from Hall, E.T., and Hall, M.R. (1990). *Understanding cultural differences: Germans, French, and Americans*. Yarmouth, ME: Intercultural Press).

find such behavior intrusive and unnecessary. The non-Americans may place great importance on ambience, decorum, the relative status of the participants in a communication and the manner of the message's delivery. Conversely, American employees keep work and friendship away from each other as much as possible. Discussions at work in a professional environment would be to the point and concise. High-context cultures are often misunderstood as being too relationship-oriented. The fact is that these cultures tend to value relationships more than the task. These differences in cultural ways of life create misunderstandings and miscommunication.

Hall's second postulate concerns cultures' orientation to time—that is, how each culture perceives and structures time. Figure 2.1 illustrates Hall's monochronic and polychronic cultures.[8]

Culture has been described as a mental exercise in its systematic sending, sorting, and processing of information.[9] Although it is not visible, artifacts and behaviors serve as reminders that culture is present.[10] Group experiences surrounding particular symbols present visible representations of the seemingly invisible construct.[11] As members of a culture share experiences, scholars and practitioners work to unpack the construct and analyze the independent pieces and patterns.[12] These properties include assumptions, beliefs, and values.

When shared collectively, such properties become acculturated norms and accepted behaviors. Within organizations, for example, these properties can be observed as artifacts, behaviors, underlying assumptions, and espoused values through vision and mission statements, organizational logos and other company propaganda, as seen through the germinal work of Edgar Schein.[13] Understanding culture, as Schein contends, becomes as much about learning how the process came to be, as it is about tracking similarities and differences across different cultures.[14]

## Dimensions and patterns of culture

Many models exist to help sort out the differences among national cultural values.[15] The germinal work of Hofstede provides one of the more convenient models highlighting the differences among cultures, through the study of one company, IBM.[16] Hofstede determined that five universal categories of culture describe the basic problems of humanity with which every society must cope. Hofstede determined the five dimensions by studying workers in 75 different countries and regions.[17] The benefit of studying one company across countries was that it allowed for the control of many variables in the workplace, where nationality stands out as the major difference across samples. The five dimensions that emerged are displayed in Figure 2.2.

*Power distance* (PDI) refers to "the extent to which the less powerful members of institutions and organizations within a country expect and accept that power is distributed unequally."[18] Hofstede defined *institutions* as the basic elements of society. Such institutions include the family or school. People work within organizations. Power distance appears relative to other variables such as social class, education level, and occupation. The United States ranks low on power distance, which signals greater equality between social levels.

The second dimension, *individualism versus collectivism* (IDV), refers to the extent to which ties between individuals are loose or integrated. More individualistic societies, such as the United States, stress the importance of the individual in work and society, whereas collectivist societies stress the importance of the group over an individual's needs. In the IBM study, individualism was associated with a work orientation concerned with personal time, freedom,

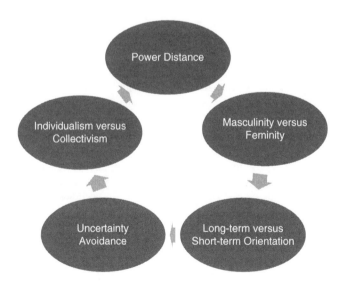

*Figure 2.2* Hofstede's five dimensions.

and challenge.[19] The collectivistic group focused more upon the interdependence between the employee and the organization. Confrontation is more likely in individualistic countries such as the United States.[20]

The third dimension is *masculinity versus femininity* (MAS).[21] A masculine culture values people and organizations that are aggressive and competitive, such as the United States. Masculinity stands for a preference for heroism, assertiveness, and material success; femininity stands for a preference for relationships and modesty. Masculine societies focus more on achievement in the workplace, as opposed to the more feminine countries that might focus on quality of life.[22] Overall, masculine countries strive for a performance society, while feminine countries strive for a well-being society.

The fourth dimension is *uncertainty avoidance* (UAI): how far members of a culture can go before they reach a boundary when they feel threatened by the unknown.[23] Uncertainty avoidance measures the amount of ambiguity a society will tolerate. The countries high in uncertainty avoidance prefer rules, regulations, and structure. In contrast, countries with low uncertainty avoidance prefer few laws or rules. The United States reflects a lower uncertainty avoidance score and focuses on a greater level of tolerance for a variety of ideas, thoughts, and beliefs.

The fifth dimension describes a culture's *long-term versus short-term orientation* (LTO). Short-term orientation focuses on personal steadiness and stability. The short-term orientation tends to be more past and present oriented. Long-term orientations are associated with persistence and preserving status and order. The United States reflects a more short-term orientation in its business environment.[24]

Hofstede's five universal categories of culture provide an overview of some differences in national culture that must be resolved in the global environment. It is important to gain a more complete understanding of the intercultural leadership criterion for its communication and maximization by leaders for business success. American business organizations and leaders must transcend their traditional ethnocentric framework and learn to adapt in a world of cultural differences. The first step for business leaders is to learn to understand how cultural differences affect leadership and life within and across organizations.[25] See Exhibit 2.1 for an interview with Geert Hofstede.

Questions surrounding the validity and resilience of Hofstede's work for more than 30 years are answered through consistent replications and confirmations of his findings. In his 2001 book, Hofstede shares over 200 additional studies, employing the five dimensions and further supporting his work.[26]

The fluidity of culture and society prompts regular study of Hofstede's dimensions. These analyses fostered the introduction of a sixth dimension called *indulgence versus restraint* (IVR). The dimension, supported by scores from 93 countries, and coined by Hofstede collaborator, Michael Minkov, addresses societal allowances or prohibitions upon gratification. "Indulgence stands for a society that allows relatively free gratification of basic and natural human desires related to enjoying life and having fun. Restraint stands for a society that controls gratification of needs and regulates it by means of strict social norms."[27] (More statistical information on Hofstede's dimensions can be found on the Dimension Data Matrix website http://www.geerthofstede.com/dimension-data-matrix.[28])

---

**Exhibit 2.1 Interview with Geert Hofstede, professor emeritus University of Maastricht, The Netherlands**

Influential Dutch researcher in the fields of organizational studies, organizational culture, cultural economics, and management, Geert Hofstede has provided all of us in the field with one of the most comprehensive studies of how values in the workplace are influenced by culture. In his interview, he succinctly and wisely answers our questions about global business leadership.

*What are the most important decisions you make now or have made as a leader of an organization of which you have been a part?*

I have been a scholar, not a leader.

*What is one characteristic that you believe a global business leader should possess within an organization today?*

They should have international experience as a subordinate.

*What is the biggest challenge facing global business leaders today in corporations?*

The biggest challenge is becoming a victim of greed.

*What effect do you think national culture has on business leadership decision-making at Fortune Global 500 organizations? (This can also include how your own native national culture affects your decision-making.)*

This depends on the place where they spent the first ten years of their life.

*How do you think leaders from both governmental and non-governmental organizations view leadership differently? Are such organizations more affected by the national culture in which they are headquartered (i.e., the United Nations is situated in the U.S.), versus the culture of the organization itself, despite its geographic location?*

Again, this depends on the place where they spent the first ten years of their life.

*What is one mistake you witness business leaders making more frequently than other Fortune Global 500 organizations? Can you provide an example of such a mistake, particularly one in which the leader did not understand the importance of appropriate intercultural cues?*

Hans Wijers of AKZO, the Netherlands, selling Organon Pharmaceuticals, one of the most prominent and innovative research labs of the country, to Merck Sharp & Dohme from USA who closed it almost immediately for short-term shareholder gain.

*What are your thoughts on globalization and how important is it for leaders to hold and maintain equal concern for the bottom line and the stakeholder groups. Would a broader, longer-term social systems approach to leadership be feasible within the global business arena?*

This is a question about which I have written. Please ask your readers to see my article "Business goals for a new world order: beyond growth, greed and quarterly results". *Asia Pacific Business Review*, 15(4), 2009, 481–8.

*What do you like to ask other business leaders when you get the chance?*

I ask them to tell me about a day in their life when they were about 16.

*** 

Regarded as one of the leading representatives of intercultural research and studies, the findings of Hofstede's research and his theoretical ideas are used worldwide in both psychology and management studies. It's very interesting to note that Hofstede believes that global leaders are most affected by the national culture in which they spent the first ten years of their lives, and not as much as those in which they resided after these first years.

**Geert Hofstede** *is an influential Dutch researcher in the fields of organizational studies and more concretely organizational culture, also cultural economics and management. He was born in Haarlem, the Netherlands, on October 2, 1928. Raised in The Hague and Apeldoorn during the German occupation of World War II, he has an M.Sc. in Mechanical Engineering from Delft Technical University, 1953, and a Ph.D. in Social Psychology, from the University of Groningen, 1967. He currently lives in Velp, the Netherlands. He has been married since 1955 to Maaike van den Hoek. They have four sons who live in the Netherlands, Belgium, Germany, and France; they have ten grandchildren aged 25 to 5.*

## The effect of culture on leadership and organizations

For people interacting within organizations, culture assumes a multi-focal role that combines personal, national, ethnic, professional, religious, and corporate characteristics.[29] Since cultural influences derive from individual cultural values, people often experience difficulty locating the source and impact of these phenomena.[30] Understanding culture helps lower the anxieties and frustrations associated with "unfamiliar" and seemingly "irrational" behavior within organizations.[31]

There are several ways to identify how culture influences leadership. Primarily, culture shapes the image of the ideal of a particular nation or organization.[32] These ideals vary between cultures.[33] Culture influences the personality traits and work values of leaders and followers in a country or organization, and these different assumptions which we each abide by succeed or fail based upon the participants and their respective cultural backgrounds.[34]

To a significant extent, culture determines the actual pattern of leadership behaviors in a country or organization. Cultural values and norms likely influence the attitudes and behaviors of leaders in ways unconscious to them.[35] In addition, cultural values reflect societal norms in the relationships between individuals. These norms specify acceptable forms of leadership behaviors. For example, the norms appear as societal laws limiting the use of power to influence the decisions and actions of others.[36]

Intercultural leaders must balance multiple factors and concerns.[37] Commercial imperatives focus on the salient leadership capabilities that corporations must possess to respond successfully to customer needs and competitive threats. Globalization increases the need to understand the impact of diverse backgrounds and philosophies. Leaders in the early twenty-first century need to look at the world with a local–global perspective and develop products and strategies that work within as well as across borders. The current reality is that the forces of globalization are drawing all cultures into a virtual and time-independent global business zone.[38]

Corporate executives in the early twenty-first century need to develop business and leadership characteristics that are effective outside of their own national boundaries. In the multinational, indeed global, environment, American traditions are not the only force. National differences in mental programming have become increasingly important because an increasing number of activities in the world demand the cooperation of people from different nations. As previously mentioned, cultural difference is one of the most significant and troublesome variables for multinational businesses to solve.[39]

As the business world becomes more global, it is necessary to understand that each culture views the world differently and that managerial practices that are effective in one culture may be ineffective in another. Leadership theories previously focused on firms, perspectives, and objectives most relevant to American managers and leaders. Typically, ethnocentrism has been the dominant tendency for U.S. business leaders operating abroad, as if language, values, and behaviors were standardized and homogenized throughout the world.[40]

## A briefing on leadership theory

Interest in leadership as a concept and a practice is not new. All of the world's major religions discuss the topic of leadership from Confucianism, to Islam, to Hinduism, to Judeo-Christian texts going back thousands of years. While addressing leadership from these vantage points now is not the point, it is important, nevertheless, to understand that for as long as human beings have been recording their histories, leadership has been a topic of interest across all cultures. Examining definitions across cultural perspective reveals that there is both consensus and dissonance among the meanings attributed to leadership.

Defining the term "leadership" is challenging, but the following are agreed-upon constructs involved with leadership: process, influence, group involvement, and common goals.[41] From the essentialist perspective, leadership consists of a core set of traits, behaviors, skills, or characteristics that cuts across situations, cultures, philosophies, and moral systems.[42]

From the contextualistic viewpoint, leadership can be understood only as a complex irreducible system that is highly influenced by social, cultural, psychological, processual, circumstantial, and historical factors. Table 2.1 depicts the various leadership theories and in which category they fall.

The leadership literature generally deals with the essentialist and contextualist perspectives as though they are incompatible theories. In the following section, we discuss these two perspectives from the view that they are not necessarily contrary, but rather complementary. We briefly introduce their origins and describe the major tenets and assumptions of each perspective. However, we avoid the tendency to try to define leadership because, in our experience as interculturalists and social and management scientists, while leadership is learnable, knowable, and practicable, it is also emergent and evolving; what it is not is definable without consideration of propinquity. In other words, while leadership is definable in this moment, in this place, and while some of its components may endure the next human evolution, in the next decade today's definition may not be entirely suitable. Moreover, while we may accurately define leadership presently for the American business culture, our definition, derived from our own culturally-biased understanding of leadership, may not at all be representative of leadership conceptualized in other cultures. Viewed from an intercultural lens, leadership may be understood as consisting of elemental characteristics that may exhibit continuity and/or mutability. One organization though that continually presents recommended research on leadership study is the Center for Creative Leadership (www.ccl.org).

### The essentialist perspective

The majority of essentialist leadership theories originated in the United States or other Western-perspective countries. Arguably, many essentialist leadership theories are characteristically ethnocentric. To the North American reader, an example of how ethnocentric perspectives color our world is the annual event in sports of the World Series of Baseball.

While the sport of baseball is now, in 2013, played in a few countries more than just in the U.S., at the time of its inception, baseball was strictly an American sport. Imagine the surprise of foreign visitors to the U.S., in the fall of 1952, at the notion that the New York Yankees were the "World Champions of Baseball" given that no team outside the U.S. played in the World Series. To some Americans, "World Series" literally meant that "the world" consisted of the

Table 2.1 Overview of leadership theories

| Essentialist | | | | | Contextualist |
|---|---|---|---|---|---|
| Trait 1500–1990s | Behavior 1940–2001 | Situational and Contingency 1960–current | Power 1500–present | Charisma Transformational/ Transactional 1800–present | Cognitive 1980–present |
| Machiavelli 1513 Great Man<br>Stogdill 1948 Desired Traits<br>Flanagan 1951 Critical Incidents<br>Katz 1955 Skill Taxonomy<br>McGregor 1960 Theory X, Y<br>McClelland 1965 Stories<br>Boyatzis 1982 Traits and Competencies<br>Yukl 1989 Trait Correlates<br>*Universal Principles*<br>Greenleaf 1970 Servant<br>Covey 1990 Principle-Centered<br>Spiritual 1992 Bullis & Glaser<br>Mayer, Davis, & Shoorman 1995 Trust | Lewin et al. 1943 Autocratic Democratic, and Laissez-faire<br>Katz et al. 1950 Michigan<br>Flanagan 1951 Behavior<br>Fleishman et al. 1953 Ohio State<br>Merton 1957 Role Theory<br>Yukl 1971 Participative Leadership<br>Mintzberg 1973 Managerial Roles<br>*Process*<br>Yukl 1989 Behavioral Determinant<br>Howell & Costley 2001 Adaptive Behavior | Sartre 1956 Temporality Theory<br>Fiedler 1964 Contingency Model<br>Hersey & Blanchard 1969 Situation Model<br>Evans et al. 1970 Path Goal<br>Vroom & Yetton 1973 Normative Decision Model<br>Graen et al. 1975 Leader, Member Exchange<br>Kerr & Jermier 1978 Group Maintenance<br>Boje 1980; 2001 Problem, Solve, Learn Model | Machiavelli Will to Power 1513<br>Weber 1947 Feudal Bureaucratic French & Raven 1959 Sources Social Exchange<br>Graen et al. 1975 Vertical Dyad | *Charisma*<br>Weber 1947 Charisma<br>House 1977 Impression Management<br>Bass 1985<br>Conger & Kanungo 1987<br><br>*Transformational Transactional*<br>Weber 1947 Transformational<br>Burns 1978 Transformation and Transactional<br>Bass 1985 Transformational<br>Bennis & Nanus 1985 Transformational<br>Schein 1985 Culture Change | *Emergent*<br>Gronn, 2002 Distributed<br>Pearce and Conger 2003 Shared<br>Linsky and Heifetz 2002 Adaptive<br>Hazy 2004 Coexistent<br>Uhl-Bien 2006 Relational<br>Lichtenstein et al. 2007 Complexity<br><br>*Context*<br>Birnbaum 1992 |

*Cognitive*
Bensimon, Neumann, & Birnbaum, 1989
Bolman & Deal 1991
Martinko 1995
Attribution
McCormick 2002
Self-efficacy
*Cultural*
Ferguson 1984
Anti-bureaucratic Feminist Leadership
Rosener 1990
Genderization of Leadership
Helgesen 1990
Gender Barriers
Calais & Smircich 1991
Feminist Leadership
Astin & Leland 1991
Social Change
Cantor & Bernay 1993
Metaphors
Tierney 1993
Pluralistic Leadership
*Cross-Cultural*
House, Wright, & Aditya 1997
*Globe*
Dickson, Den Hartog, & Mitchelson 2003
Ethical Leadership

*Source:* Adapted from Boje, D. (2005). *Teaching Sites:* http://business.nmsu.edu/~dboje

United States. To other Americans, it meant that baseball was exclusive to the U.S. and therefore could be viewed as "the world" of baseball. Even now, with baseball flourishing in other countries, American baseball teams still play in the "World Series of Baseball" each year. Of course, people from the U.S. are not the only people who operate with an ethnocentric perspective of the world. The point is that cultural bias influences our perspective of life; therefore, cultural bias influences our theories about everything.

In reviewing the leadership literature, it is striking how American theory particularly dominates. Arguably, one reason why essentialist leadership theories dominate the body of literature on leadership globally is that North American and some European countries, as centers of capitalism, led the spread of globalization. It is important to understand, however, that even within the essentialist school of thought, there are cultural variations.

The worldview of essentialism is deeply rooted in the philosophies of Plato and Aristotle who posited that there are two realities of the universe: one that is the essence and the second that is perceived. The essential universe is that which is perfect and ideal, and the perceived universe is that which is in a constant state of flux. In this view, the goal of scientific observations is to identify that which is ideal. From this, it is easy to see the leap to conceptualizing leadership as consisting of essential attributes that must be common across all of creation, since these ideals are in fact at the essence of leadership.

Essentialists believe that realities exist outside of our independent perceptions and experiences, rather than considering our perceptions to be the drivers of how we experience reality.[43] To the essentialist, natural objects operate the way they do because to operate otherwise would be contrary to their natures. Therefore, natural laws are metaphysically necessary, and consequently, there are necessary connections between events and material effects.

### How do essentialists view leadership?

The answer is that, to essentialists, because leadership is a natural effect, it is subject to the laws of nature and has a fundamental character that governs its operation. What this means to leadership theorists of this philosophical bent, is that social scientists must search for leadership's ideal character. An essentialist, then, seeks to establish a general theory of leadership that permeates all human experience. Simply stated, essentialists seek to identify and prove pure leadership irrespective of human variability.

Within the essentialist leadership perspective, the major theories include trait, behavioral, power, exchange, and situational. These five groupings of leadership theory are probably the most recognizable theories to North American business leaders and managers. To say that essentialist leadership theory has shaped the American business culture is a gross understatement. Countless American MBA graduates have been minted from the essentialists' mold. Dozens of "how-to" books, innumerable management development programs, and a myriad of corporate leadership cultures have been cast from the "ideal leader" paradigm.

Early *trait* theorists sought to determine what makes some leaders great, and what characteristics distinguish leaders from followers. The trait approach assumes that certain physical, social, and personal characteristics are inherent in leaders. The objective of this exercise was to identify the right sets of traits and characteristics in order to select the right people to become leaders. The problem is that trait research has not been able to identify a set of traits that can consistently distinguish leaders from followers. In an important review of the leadership literature published in 1948, Ralph Stogdill concluded that the existing research had not demonstrated the utility of the trait approach. It turns out that in some studies many followers exhibited the same traits, and more so, than some so-identified good leaders. Because of the lack of consistent findings linking individual traits to leadership effectiveness, researchers abandoned empirical studies of leader traits in the 1950s.

*Behavioral leadership theories* approach leadership from the perspective that leadership is a learned skill rather than inborn in particular people as trait theory postulated. However, behavioral theories approach the concept of leadership again from the viewpoint there is a specific set of behaviors demonstrated by leaders that distinguishes them from other people.

The most well-known behavioral leadership studies took place at Ohio State University[44] and the University of Michigan in the late 1940s and 1950s. Interest in the Ohio and Michigan studies provoked countless other leadership studies and both studies continue to be widely cited. The Michigan study[45] undertook to determine the principles and methods of leadership that led to productivity and job satisfaction.

The Michigan study identified two factors that consistently appeared in the observation of leaders. Initiating structure, sometimes called task-oriented behavior, involves planning, organizing, and coordinating the work of subordinates. Consideration involves showing concern for subordinates, being supportive, recognizing subordinates' accomplishments, and providing for subordinates' welfare. From the study, two general leadership orientations were identified: an employee orientation and a production orientation. Leaders with an employee orientation showed genuine concern for interpersonal relations. Those with a production orientation focused on the task or technical aspects of the job.

The conclusion of the Michigan study was that an employee orientation and general supervision rather than close supervision yielded better results. The study's author, Rensis Likert eventually developed "four systems" of management based on these studies; he advocated System 4 (the participative-group system, which was the most participatory set of leader behaviors) as resulting in the most positive outcomes.

One concept based largely on the behavioral approach to leadership effectiveness was the Managerial (or Leadership) Grid, developed by Blake and Mouton, shown in Figure 2.3.[46]

The grid combines "concern for production" with "concern for people" and presents five alternative behavioral styles of leadership. A leader who emphasized neither was practicing "impoverished management" according to the grid.

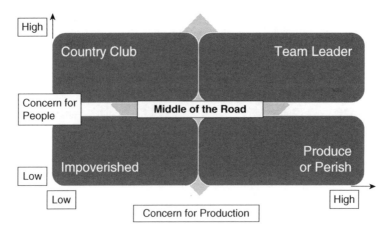

*Figure 2.3* The Blake Mouton Managerial Grid.

When a leader emphasized concern for people and placed little emphasis on production, he was considered a "country-club" manager. The leader emphasizing a concern for production, but who paid little attention to the concerns of subordinates, was deemed a "task" manager. A leader who tried to balance concern for production and concern for people was termed a "middle-of-the-road" manager. In the last quadrant, leaders who were able to exhibit simultaneous high concern for production and high concern for people were practicing what Likert referred to as, "team management." According to the prescriptions of the grid, team management was the "ideal" leadership approach. The Managerial Grid became a major consulting tool and the basis for countless American corporate leadership development programs.

The assumption of the leader behavior approach is that there are certain behaviors that are universally effective for leaders. Unfortunately, empirical research has not demonstrated consistent relationships between task-oriented or person-oriented leader behaviors and leader effectiveness.

*The situational* approach to leadership presumes that the best way to manage is to tailor leadership direction to the particular circumstances faced within an employee group. The situational approach to management assumes that the right thing to do depends on a complex variety of critical internal environment contingencies. However, it is important to understand that situational theory does have essentialist roots.

Essentialists document idealized and universal personality traits and situations and match the leader's orientation with certain organizational situations. Fiedler is one of the early writers on situational theory, examining how a leader's personality or behavior affects leadership performance focusing on aspects of the organization.[47] The "essential" leader's personality traits are task-oriented versus relationship-oriented. The "essential" leadership environment feature is situational control marked by: (1) the leader being or feeling accepted and supported by group members; (2) the task is clear-cut and structured; and (3) the leader has the ability to reward and punish, and thus obtain compliance. The task-motivated leader performs best in both high and low situational controls. Relationship-motivated leaders perform best in situations in which control is moderate. Fiedler's conclusion is that leaders perform best in situations that match their leadership style. All leaders can be understood as having an enduring style that can be matched to a static environment that can be identified at some point in time. Experience, training, and organizational turbulence are also conditions that can be "fixed" and examined in relation to leader effectiveness.

From *power theory*, leadership is understood as the leader's use of power and influence with a group of people. The power approach, postulated by French and Raven, views leadership as the exertion of power to influence followers' behaviors.[48] Accordingly, leaders derive power from five identified sources, or bases, of power. Again, the essentialist notion of the "ideal" shines through as essential power sources and standardized use of those power sources regardless of context.

*Social exchange theory* proposes that leaders and followers exchange one thing for another. According to the theory, transactional leaders and their followers exchange transactions between task execution and rewards.[49] Transformational leaders cultivate followers' higher needs.[50] In this view, the transformational leadership process is mutual and elevates the follower and leader. The "essence" of leadership according to this theory is social change measured by intent and by the fulfillment of human needs and expectations toward ideal goals. Transformational and transactional leadership are idealized types, characterized by essential, timeless, unchanging features that purportedly can be identified across culture, situation, and context. Finally, this theory posits that it is possible for leaders to identify the "true" and essential needs of followers—exact universal psychological, economic, spiritual, aesthetic, and safety needs.[51]

### The contextualist perspective

In the 1980s, some researchers began to challenge assumptions of universality by examining human phenomena through cultural, cognitive, contextual, and processual lenses.[52] To contextualists, essentialism seemed to be a way of controlling nature and oppressing people. Contextualists believe that a complex system of cultural, social, psychological, and historical differences constitute human experience.[53] They do not deny that phenomena such as leadership exist; however, they posit that such phenomena are more complex, multifaceted, and varying than previously envisioned.

In the leadership arena, researchers examined cultural differences in an effort to understand whether different countries value different traits or influence strategies. They also examined social differences to understand whether race and gender affected leadership.[54] Researchers in the field of psychology investigated different psychological orientations, for example, different types of cognitive orientations among leaders. This research continues as it was only initiated in the past decade.[55] Organizational theorists began studying whether different organizational contexts require different leadership—including processual change that occurs in response to distinctive organizational histories and cultures.[56] Historians have begun to examine whether different (historical) periods require different approaches to leadership.[57]

One concept underlying much of contextualist theory is that reality is socially constructed. Social constructivism is the belief that reality is developed through people's interpretation of the world and a denial of essences.[58] Accordingly, reality is a social and cultural construction, not an idealized form beyond our immediate perception. By examining multiple interpretations, a shared sense of reality can be detected; nevertheless, our understanding of reality is always partial and imperfect. Each of us generates our own "rules" and "mental models," which we use to make sense of our experiences.

More recently, contextualist scholars have challenged previously held universal truths and essences because, in this view, there is no objective vantage point (or reality) and our perceptions are the only thing we can come to know.[59] Contextualists also question whether universal essences or truths even exist beyond our perceptions. Instead, knowledge is seen as contingent to local conditions and contexts.

### *How do contextualists view leadership?*

Contextualists believe that leadership is shaped by individual, (local) conditions, circumstances, time, and variations of human experience. To contextualists, there are no universal, essential, and transcendent aspects of leadership. Within the contextualist leadership area, the foremost theoretical schools include cognitive, cultural, and processual.

*Cognitive theories of leadership* describe how leaders have different perspectives or lenses.[60] For example, Bolman and Deal's research[61] demonstrated that leaders tend to examine situations through one or more lens or cognitive orientations (e.g., political, symbolic, structural, or human resource). Building a contingency theory, the researchers demonstrated that different situations might require different cognitive approaches to leadership; a political orientation might serve a leader in one situation while a bureaucratic orientation is important within another. They break from the related, yet essentialist-oriented "situationalist" efforts of matching situation and leader type. Instead, they describe how leaders often try to lead organizations by finding the one best way and then are stunned by the turmoil and resistance that they invariably generate. Bolman and Deal argue that leaders must be passionately committed to their principles, but flexible in understanding and responding to the events, situation, and contexts around them that are constantly shifting and changing. Accordingly, leaders must assume a posture of learning knowing that leadership is organic and emergent, not static and precise. Research demonstrating that leaders have vastly different cognitive orientations led to more social/cultural studies about other types of differences among leaders' approaches and beliefs.[62]

*The social/cultural leadership* literature examines gender and race[63] as well as cross-cultural issues.[64] Studies of women leaders have demonstrated that they tend to understand, define, and enact leadership in distinctive ways from men.[65] Women's leadership styles emphasize reciprocity, mutuality, and responsibility toward others; is collective and participatory; focuses on relationships and empowerment; and highlights outcomes as a central goal of leadership.[66] In contrast to men's leadership styles, women de-emphasize hierarchical relationships, individualism, and one-way power relationships.[67]

Although fewer American cultural diversity studies exist, research on racial or ethnic differences in the U.S. have found that leadership styles vary from the earlier research conducted on all white, male samples. For example, Native Americans emphasize community, wisdom, and spirituality as important for leadership and African Americans describe a non-hierarchical, community-based definition of leadership.[68] *Cross-cultural* studies in the last decade provide superb examples of the contextualist perspectives.[69] One study provides a historical perspective that chronicles a decline in the quest for universal leadership principles and a rise in awareness of differences over the past decade.[70] The research examines issues from differences related to individual countries, to an examination of country groupings based on similar contexts or histories.

In general, cross-cultural studies reveal unique ways that leadership is defined among Eastern (collective, holistic, spirituality based) and Western cultures (hierarchical, authority-based, and individualistic).[71] Some cross-cultural studies examined difference based on general societal differences such as the tendency to be either individualistic (focus on individual achievement and rights) versus collective societies (focus on collective achievement and rights) and found remarkable differences.[72]

Along with the differing mental models, cross-cultural studies have also examined how the context affects leadership.[73] Some researchers argue that the leadership literature has overemphasized micro perspectives.[74] Conversely, they argue, macro perspectives that take context and complexity into account have received limited attention. Many contextual and processual theories of leadership emerge from anthropological approaches applied to the study of organizational phenomena.[75]

Ethnographic and folkloristic studies illustrate that organizations and societies have particular histories and cultures that affect organizational phenomena, including leadership.[76] It turns out that contexts are so distinctive that comparison across them is often not meaningful. For example, Tierney's analysis of leadership showed that it is like a spider's web—each web being unique to the spot in which it is created.[77] Comparably, leadership is unique within each context and is dynamic, emergent, and evolving over time. Since leadership is a process, it is volatile and sensitive to changes. The conclusion of these cultural studies, to contextualists, is that universal essences have little value in this emergent understanding and context of leadership.[78]

Postmodern leadership theories have moved 180 degrees from the perspective that "leadership" per se indwells positional leaders, to the notion that "leadership" occurs as an event interactively within social milieus.[79] The latest of the postmodern theories, *complexity leadership theory*, provides an integrative theoretical framework for explaining interactive dynamics acknowledged by several emerging leadership theories. Viewed this way, leadership is an interactive event in which knowledge, action preferences, and behaviors evolve, thereby provoking an organization to adapt. Leadership is understood as a product of interactive dynamics and leaders as people who influence the interaction between social actors and their environments. Accordingly, adaptive leadership means that leadership occurs (anywhere in a social context) when interacting agents generate adaptive outcomes. Individuals act as leaders in this dynamic when they mobilize people to seize new opportunities and tackle tough problems. As the situation changes, different people may act as leaders by leveraging their differing skills and experience.

### How can understanding both essentialist and contextualist perspectives enrich one's view of leadership?

The appeal of essentialist theory is that it provides a convenient platform on which we can construct ideal leadership models. Being able to create a leadership style that is constructed from such a platform can afford a leader with confidence and provides a handle for meaning-making. Arguably, deriving meaning is an endeavor closely linked with vision, and vision is perhaps the only universal characteristic of effective leadership that appears across all cultures.

The attraction of contextualism is that it has illuminated our understanding of leadership, by showing the diverse contexts in which leaders operate. It has given voice to multiple points of view and shined a light on the obvious—that our globe is full of diverse peoples. Moreover, it provides the answer to why one-size-fits-all does not.

Accepting the coexistence of the notions that constructing an ideal leadership model is practical and, that leadership models must allow for emergent variance, provides leaders with an expansive toolkit. Explicitly stated this means accepting the premise that, underlying fluidity there is regularity, underlying similarity there is diversity.

## The culture–leadership link and intercultural leadership competency

Using different lenses to view culture and leadership allows scholars and practitioners the opportunity to view these phenomena in different ways. For example, a culture-specific perspective reflects the notion that the occurrence and the effectiveness of certain leadership behaviors are unique to a given culture. The culture-universal position, in contrast, argues that certain leadership behaviors are comparable across cultures and that many universal leadership behaviors exist.[80]

As we expand our analysis of culture, we find there are different ways of conveying the information.[81] Two options include "dimensions" and "descriptions." Dimensions of culture are developed from quantities of empirical data, often generated through a large-scale survey. There are multiple dimensions, but a common way of viewing societies is through the dimension of economic modernity.[82] The interview in Exhibit 2.2 with Irwin Jacobs, Chairman Emeritus of Qualcomm, will demonstrate this idea of varied dimensions.

---

### *Exhibit 2.2* Interview with Irwin Jacobs, founding chairman and CEO emeritus for Qualcomm

Irwin Jacobs, a graduate of the Massachusetts Institute of Technology (MIT), is the founder of Qualcomm, a U.S. semiconductor company that manufactures and markets digital wireless telecommunication products and services. He also serves on the Board of Trustees for the Salk Institute. In his interview, he imparts his thoughts on how to manage the dynamic changes in the global business environment.

*What are the most important decisions you make as a leader of an organization of which you have been a part? (This can also be answered from the perspective of what is the most important decision a leader/client makes in his or her organization.)*

I co-founded two companies, the first Linkabit and the second Qualcomm. Although in neither case did I have a business plan nor product in mind when starting, an early decision was to focus on innovating in digital communications and wireless, on not considering incremental improvements to existing products but rather to take large development risks which, if successful, would yield products with a significant market advantage. A second decision was to hire only the brightest people, to invest in a great working environment, and to encourage individual initiative.

As the business grows, many of the key decisions involve allocation of limited resources, of people and dollars and one's personal time, to various projects, judging status, probability of success, and impact if successful, and to new market and customer development. Occasionally, a key strategic decision must be made, such as, in the case of Qualcomm, whether to bet the company on CDMA development, and later, when successful, whether to focus on the two businesses of technology innovation and licensing and integrated circuit development and sales and to sell the handset and infrastructure manufacturing businesses.

*What is one characteristic that you believe every global business leader should possess?*

A great leader must lead by example, not by fiat. He or she must set an example of integrity, of openness to new ideas, of understanding details as well as the larger picture, of communicating well, and of not shooting the messenger when a problem arises but helping find a solution. As a company gets larger, and Qualcomm is now over 23,000 people, communication gets harder and harder. When you start up, you can wander the corridors and have people come to your office. Then as the company gets larger, this doesn't quite work anymore. We provide a lot via email, so we can discuss ideas. We avoid a hierarchical structure, so if people have ideas they can communicate them among the groups who would be interested and not just up the organizational line. Because of its size, Qualcomm cannot be a completely flat organization, but we have tried to keep it relatively flat. We've done this particularly so that groups can communicate broadly among themselves in order to find ways of spurring innovation. We bring people together with the idea of trying to come up with new ideas, pass them around, and massage them a bit.

*What are the biggest challenge facing global business leaders today?*

The world is changing very rapidly. Change brings opportunities but also global competition. The challenge is to not fight change, but to recognize and welcome the new opportunities provided by change. A company must be organized with the resources and the will to react quickly. You must be prepared to run a little faster than everybody else to keep your lead, and to do so in good times as well as bad.

*What effect do you think national culture has on business leadership decision-making? (This can also include how your own native national culture affects your decision-making.)*

Establishing a strong corporate culture is important when you start, but even more important as you grow, with a workforce and customers in many countries. I believe that a corporate culture that has integrity, that values innovation, that is adaptive to change, that is very competitive, and that above all values employees and customers is one that works across borders. Depending on national background and education, it may take new employees more or less time to recognize and accept the culture. We occasionally have problems with employees we hire from another large company who have a different work experience. They may have much more trouble adapting to a culture that expects them to be self-reliant and innovative, often expecting to be directed hour by hour. On the other hand, we usually find hires just out of college quickly adapt to our corporate culture, even with different personal and national backgrounds.

*Do you think the corporate culture, whether it is a small or large organization such as Qualcomm, is set at the top by the CEO? Or is it an amalgamation of a groundswell from the followers up through the ranks?*

The culture is set from the top. People generally take their cues from the leadership. If it is a culture they feel comfortable with, then they will value it and pass it along to coworkers. I came from a university background, so in my two companies I modeled the business climate on the openness of a university. As a professor, one is continually stimulating others intellectually, encouraging questions, and looking for elegant solutions. This works well in business and does pass down through the organization.

*What are your thoughts on globalization and how important is it for leaders to develop their own self-awareness so as to adjust to the changing context(s) under which they operate in a given situation and/or organization? (This consciousness could include the leader's own cultural self-bias while operating with diverse constituents.)*

Within your own company, you have reasonable control over shaping the climate you desire and leading employees in a common direction. Customers, however, are generally different in different parts of the world. If you have product you wish to sell worldwide, you must have local presence, not only in marketing and sales, but also R&D. It is important to recognize and to adapt to local tastes. Local suppliers may also behave differently in different locations, and you must adapt to local situations and not become impatient or frustrated. Finally, governments are sensitive to the size of your local workforce and to the contributions you are making to their country and are not simply extracting profits.

*What is one mistake you witness business leaders making more frequently than others? Do you think that some leaders make such errors due to their inability to be self-aware of their own national cultural bias, as mentioned above?*

It can be fatal to fail to recognize the suddenness of change and to allow your company to adapt too slowly, to avoid taking risks. Markets can change very quickly, and you cannot be lulled by today's success and assume that you have more time to adapt to the change and to possible new competition. A successful leader must be open to inputs from around the organization, delegating reasonable levels of authority to those close to the action and who can play the role of first responders. Many once-great companies have foundered by adapting to change too slowly because they held decision-making too tightly at a central point, frustrating change.

*Can you name a person who has had a tremendous impact on you as a leader? Maybe someone who has been a mentor to you? Why and how did this person impact your life?*

While a graduate student, I met Professor Claude Shannon and became excited about the broad potential of his innovative work in information theory. The subject was rather theoretic at the time, but provided insight into many applications. His clear thinking and clever approach to problems helped me develop my intuition and to appreciate the importance of pursuing elegant solutions. After graduating and joining the faculty at MIT, I had the opportunity to work with Professor Jack Wozencraft to develop a new course in communications based on the application of Shannon theory, culminating in the textbook *Principles of Communication Engineering*. The many requests for consulting that resulted from the book when I moved to California led directly to the formation of Linkabit.

*Within the global economy, how important is it for leaders to hold and maintain equal concern for the bottom line and for the stakeholder groups? Do you think a broader, longer term social systems approach to leadership is feasible in the global business arena?*

It is most important to take a long, not short, term view of the bottom line in balancing the needs of different stakeholders. In a public company, shareholders and analysts often focus on quarterly profits and it is necessary to explain carefully why certain costs have important long term benefits. One is R&D for future products which should be maintained consistently even during a down economy to support revenue growth when the economy improves. Another is costs to ensure employee morale. One of the greatest costs to a business is the loss of an employee. Employees identify with and contribute greatly to a company when they participate in exciting work and are compensated well, of course, but also when they identify with and feel proud of their company. Thus, community involvement and social cause support do contribute to the bottom line and can be justified as a long term benefit. Such involvement is also noticed by government and customers, particularly in foreign countries, and results in benefits enjoyed as a good corporate citizen.

*What do you like to ask other business leaders when you get the chance?*

What excites you? What is it that you see coming over the horizon that will impact business and that will make a difference to customers? And, especially these days, where is the local and global economy going and how do you see politics in different regions impacting business, both positive and negative?

***

Providing an environment in which innovation is fostered and recognized has made Qualcomm one of the leading technology companies in the world, and Irwin Jacobs is an example of a true Geoleader. It is also important to remember that all leaders were once followers who were mentored and taught by others who paved the way, both locally and globally.

**Dr. Irwin Mark Jacobs** is founding chairman and CEO emeritus for Qualcomm. As CEO through 2005 and Chairman through 2009, he led the growth from startup to Fortune 500 Company. As CEO, Dr. Jacobs oversaw Qualcomm's revolutionary innovations in Code Division Multiple Access (CDMA), a technology fundamental to today's 3G mobile wireless standards. He established a business model and a climate of innovation that continues to drive the company.

Dr. Jacobs previously served as co-founder, CEO and chairman of Linkabit Corporation, leading the development of Very Small Aperture Earth Terminals (VSATs) and the VideoCipher® satellite-to-home TV system. Linkabit merged with M/A-COM in August 1980, and Dr. Jacobs served as executive vice president and a member of the Board of Directors until his resignation in April 1985. Over 100 San Diego communications companies trace their roots to Linkabit. From 1959 to 1966, Dr. Jacobs was an assistant, then associate professor of Electrical Engineering at Massachusetts Institute of Technology (MIT). From 1966 to 1972 he served as Professor of Computer Science and Engineering at the University of California, San Diego (UCSD). While at MIT, Dr. Jacobs co-authored with Jack Wozencraft a textbook in digital communications *Principles of Communication Engineering*. First published in 1965, the book remains in use today. Dr. Jacobs holds 14 CDMA patents and received a Bachelor's degree in Electrical Engineering in 1956 from Cornell University and Master of Science and Doctor of Science degrees in Electrical Engineering from MIT in 1957 and 1959, respectively. He and his wife Joan have been cited by *Business Week* and *Chronicle of Philanthropy* among the 50 Most-Generous Philanthropists in the United States.

### Can research pinpoint which cultural dimensions are most important for leadership behavior?

Some researchers suggest that individualism versus collectivism could be one of the most important dimensions of cultural variation.[83] Collectivist cultures expect successful leaders to be supportive and paternalistic, whereas individualist cultures more likely value an achievement orientation and participative leadership. Other researchers suggest that power distance is particularly important for leaders.[84] In low-power distance cultures, subordinates expect consultation, whereas in high-power distance cultures subordinates expect leaders to act more direct and autocratic. Understanding the results of cross-cultural leadership research could be very helpful to leaders in intercultural interactions. For example, researchers interpreting their results indicate that it would be inappropriate to train leaders in very high-power distance cultures to use participative decision-making since the leaders in these countries are supposed to have all the answers. By inviting subordinates to become involved, followers would see the leader as weak and incompetent. In addition, subordinates in long-term orientation cultures would be more likely than those in short-term cultures to accept development plans that had a longer period.

### Prior research on intercultural leadership competency

At the cognitive level, a leader arrives in a new cultural situation as ignorant, but then moves into the novice level of awareness.[85] The importance of cultural exchange reveals itself to the leader in this novice round.[86] In the next round, the leader transitions to having an understanding and appreciation of the cultural situation. This round also exists as the attitudinal and values level. Moving toward acceptance and internalization, the leader reaches the behavioral level, or mastery round, and arrives at transformation. This was where intercultural competency becomes a leadership practice.[87]

In another view, intercultural leadership competence is the ability to manage uncertainty, create learning systems, and manage cross-cultural ethical issues.[88] A culturally competent individual possesses personal, social, business, and cultural literacy.[89] Such literacy provides the leader with the tools to understand, value, and leverage cultural differences and situations.[90] Moreover, cultural empathy and contextual analysis provide for intercultural competence.[91]

Intercultural competence also occurs when a leader remains aware and deals with complexity.[92] Exemplary intercultural leaders retain the ability to model the way, inspire a shared vision, and enable others to act in any situation.[93] This implies that interculturally competent leaders are able to communicate and motivate others. These leadership competencies occur with the leader retaining an open mind and respect for others.[94]

The first level to build in constructing interculturally skilled leaders is an awareness of the culturally learned starting points in the leader's thinking.[95] This foundation of intercultural awareness is important because it controls the leader's interpretation of all knowledge and utilization of all skills. The need for intercultural awareness seldom appears in the generic training of leaders.[96] The intercultural skilled leader does not take awareness for granted. Sue, *et al.* suggested a cross-cultural competency model.

Such proposed cross-cultural competencies and objectives encompass leader' awareness of their own cultural values and biases, including attitudes and beliefs.[97] Culturally skilled leaders move from being culturally unaware to being aware and sensitive to their own cultural heritage and to valuing and respecting differences.[98] These leaders are aware of how their own cultural backgrounds and experiences and attitudes, values, and biases influence interactions with others. Such leaders are able to recognize the limits of their competencies and expertise. Culturally skilled leaders are comfortable with differences that exist between themselves and others in terms of race, ethnicity, culture, and beliefs.[99]

Interculturally competent leaders possess specific knowledge about their own racial and cultural heritage and see how such backgrounds affect their definitions of normalcy.[100] Culturally skilled leaders possess knowledge about their social impact on others. They are knowledgeable about communication style differences. This includes how the leader's style may clash with minority groups, with effective leaders knowing how to anticipate the impact it may have on others.[101]

In some nations, leadership means establishing direction and influencing others to follow that direction.[102] Moreover, we know that one of the few universal attributes ascribed to leadership competence is the ability to develop and communicate a vision. An effective intercultural business leader needs to possess clarity of vision to find compatibility with every new intercultural situation.[103] Many competencies are related to being able to understand national cultural differences. Without developing these competencies, an intercultural leader will not be successful in working abroad.

There is a need for leadership theories that both transcend and accommodate culture. The study from which the Geoleadership (Intercultural Leadership) Model was derived sought to determine how business leaders could develop the knowledge, skills, behaviors, and models necessary to interact with dissimilar others in a way that led to mutual appreciation.

In the following chapters, we present the principles of Geoleadership. We define each principle and describe its attributes as seen through the lens provided by the global interculturalists who participated in the study. Each chapter will also include a brief section related to attitudes and behaviors that support the principle and through presentation of interviews with thought leaders in the areas of business, culture, and leadership. Another such interview is with leadership guru Sally Helgesen, who outlines her thoughts in Exhibit 2.3.

---

**Exhibit 2.3** Interview with Sally Helgesen, author of *The Female Advantage* and *The Web of Inclusion*

Ranked by Leadership Gurus as number 15 in its survey of the world's most influential leadership experts, Sally Helgesen is the author of six books. Most recently she published *The Female Vision: Women's Real Power at Work*. Her best-selling *The Female Advantage: Women's Ways of Leadership* is hailed as "the classic work" on women's leadership styles. Sally approaches global leadership from a unique angle and as such she provides great insights that many business people might not even think to consider.

*What are the most important decisions that a leader of an organization must make?*

The most important issue to me now is how global leaders can address present problems and/or crises that arise on a daily, monthly, or yearly basis, and reconcile these with long-term strategies. In today's environment, things change rapidly and unpredictably, and this is having a huge impact on organizations of every kind. Making decisions to be flexible in changing times and also to stay committed to a long-term strategy or vision is very important. It's important for global leaders not to be pulled away from their mission and also to recognize that they must have some flexibility. This is a very tough balance. It is particularly difficult for the for-profit sector because of the extreme volatility of the marketplace and the demand that it puts on many organizations for short-term responses to dominate the market. This is a huge challenge for global leaders, and I see it continuing to be so.

*How have global leaders you have worked with encouraged creative thinking within their organizations?*

One of the most useful ways to think creatively within an organization is to encourage people and leaders alike to learn from completely different types of organizations. If a global leader is in a for-profit, he or she can learn a lot from non-profits, military, religious, and social service organizations. How challenges are faced across industries and sectors is very important. There is a lot of information out there and things move so rapidly, that leaders often say their organization is different and that they have distinctive challenges or a different type of culture. That may be true, but there is a lot that leaders can learn from outside their sectors, if they are open and willing to learn.

*What is one characteristic that you believe every global business leader should possess?*

Every global leader should possess humility. Today, the tasks are huge, the terrain is uncertain, and global leaders face significant challenges of an unpredictable future. Global leaders with a degree of humility are more open to different solutions from different places. They have more freedom to act because of this openness, and they have the capacity to see emerging solutions and patterns that are difficult to see if one is a captive of his or her arrogance. A lot of organizations encourage and reward arrogance as a global leader works his or her way up the corporate ladder; yet, in top leadership humility is demanded.

*What is the biggest challenge facing global business leaders today?*

From my perspective, which has to do with people rather than strategy or logistics, I would say the biggest challenge in dealing with people, both internally and with customers and clients and the broad range of people who now consider themselves stakeholders in any given organization's business, is being able to meet people's need to feel as if they are part of something that is important, that matters, and that has real consequences in the world. People want to feel that they are part of a joint effort that makes a difference. How do you make people feel as if they're part of something that's important, while maintaining awareness of the provisional nature of what the organization has to offer right now?

*What effect do you think national culture has on business leadership decision-making? (This can also include how your own native national culture affects your decision-making.)*

National culture has a significant effect on business leadership decision-making. From a U.S. perspective, and having done a lot of work in other parts of the world as well, I see that we exalt decisiveness and the ability of our leaders to make quick decisions. In doing so, our leaders may make decisions without all the information. In the U.S. we have a can-do bias, a heroic leadership bias, where we require our leaders to think big and bold, and to act and execute. This can lead to overreach. It behooves global leaders to be intensely aware of what the dominant leadership model is in their own culture, so that they can be, make sure that they're kind of not getting caught up in that game.

*What are your thoughts on globalization and how important is it for leaders to develop their own self-awareness so as to adjust to the changing context(s) under which they operate in a given situation and/or organization? (This consciousness could include the leader's own cultural self-bias while operating with diverse constituents.)*

"Self-awareness" is so important when we're talking about the cultural diversity that every organization has to deal with now. Global leaders must be self-aware if they are to be sensitive to the culture-boundedness of themselves, their organizations, and the people around them. This operates in two ways. It operates in the cultural diversity space. Often leaders will make analogies or references or use metaphors assuming they will make sense to people, but culturally they do not translate. These can be about anything from work ethic to vision to common purpose. These things are very different in different cultures around the world, and they are also different within our own culture.

   Being aware of this takes a high degree of self-awareness. Global leaders should also recognize the factors that made them excel. How transferrable are these to different situations? Chances are that they are not applicable. Leaders often run into trouble trying to repeat successes when the scope of the global arena is completely different. Self-awareness is crucial to avoid projecting oneself as what a culture or organizational culture should produce—it is critical to flexibility and adaptability, which are key to success in the global arena.

*What is one mistake you witness business leaders making more frequently than others? Do you think that some leaders make such errors due to their inability to be self-aware of their own national cultural bias, as mentioned above?*

As alluded to in the previous question, business leaders get caught in "should." "People who work here should…" "If someone is a good worker they should…" This idea of what people "should" do is often leaders wanting people around them who are just like them. It's a very narrow view of what an organizational culture could be. It was appropriate in the Industrial Era. I remember working at IBM in the '70s and '80s. You could always tell whose employee someone was, because his briefcase would be identical to his boss's and he would dress in the same way. If his boss wore a rumpled suit, he'd wear a rumpled suit. If his boss wore a sharp suit, he'd wear a sharp suit. Organizations were adept at turning out people who were in the image of the leader.

This isn't a useful concept anymore. It doesn't mean that organizations shouldn't have strong, cohesive cultures, but there is a difference between a culture and a cult. When teams are created in the image of a leader or culture, then you have a cult, which will lack sustainability. And, it will limit creative thinking. People become primed to replicate responses that have already been developed, which is the essence of not being creative.

*Can you name a person who has had a tremendous impact on you as a leader? Maybe someone who has been a mentor to you? Why and how did this person impact your life?*

Jane Jacobs, the writer, and urban theorist who wrote *The Death and Life of Great American Cities,* had a great impact on my life. Jane changed how we think about urban development. If you walk around an urban area tomorrow, you will see her ideas in action. She was very active in a number of political movements, including helping to stop a master plan to build three ten-lane highways across Manhattan. She moved to Toronto and became wide-ranging in her interests, including writing a response to Adam Smith's *The Wealth of Nations* with her book called *The Wealth of Cities.* I was fortunate to speak at a celebration of her work in 1997, and more recently I was invited to participate in a symposium of her work. After reviewing her work, I realized what an influence she'd had on me. She was a highly creative and independent thinker who had a big impact on cities. I've tried to do something similar in organizations, and I feel more confident with my work knowing that she had so much success from a very independent point of view. She has been a role model to me and given me courage to continue when I've wondered why I do what I do.

*Within the global economy, how important is it that a global business leader understands the key features of the Geoleadership Model?*

Having a geopolitical understanding of how the world works and the changes that are taking place today is essential for leaders in organizations today. But, this is highly specific. The Geoleadership Model is important, and gives leaders a way to think about leadership development in their organizations, but this is not my area of expertise.

*What do you like to ask other business leaders when you get the chance?*

I don't ask them what keeps them up at night. This is one of the most over-asked questions in the world of organizations. I like to ask them: How are you preparing your organization to draw from the widest, most creative, and most robust talent base in the years ahead? Where do you see that talent base as located? How are you going to address it? How are you going to present your organization as a place that's desirable for extremely talented people to build a career? What are you going to do to make sure that they have the opportunity to act on their best talents, so that they can feel the sense of satisfaction and contribution that talented people want to feel?

***

With her focus on "self-awareness" and adaptability as the keys to global leadership, Sally Helgesen reaffirms our statement that different people might lead in different situations depending on their skills and experience. Leaders who understand this dynamic are far more likely to be successful in a wide range of situations, as they delegate leadership responsibilities to others.

**Sally Helgesen**, an internationally acclaimed author, speaker, and consultant, is ranked by Leadership Gurus as number 15 in its survey of the world's most influential leadership experts and cited as one of the top 35 authorities in the field by *Leadership Excellence* magazine. Sally develops and delivers leadership programs to corporations, partnership firms, universities, and associations around the world.

Sally is the author of six books, most recently *The Female Vision: Women's Real Power at Work*, which breaks new ground by exploring how women's strategic insights can strengthen their careers and benefit their organizations. Her best-selling *The Female Advantage: Women's Ways of Leadership*, hailed as "the classic work" on women's leadership styles, was translated into 12 languages and has been continuously in print for 22 years. *The Web of Inclusion: A New Architecture for Building Great Organizations* was cited in the *Wall Street Journal* as one of the best books on leadership of all time. Sally is a contributing editor to *strategy+business magazine* and a member of the New York and International Women's Forums. Articles about her work have been featured in *Fortune, The New York Times, Fast Company*, and *Business Week*. She lives in Chatham, NY.

### The bottom line

Humans are quite similar as beings in some ways; however, as cultures we vary widely in our worldview. Everything we do is influenced by cultural norms and this includes how we conduct and lead business organizations.

There are important similarities and differences in how cultures perceive leadership. Intercultural leaders must have a solid understanding of how leadership is perceived and practiced in their own cultures and should undertake learning about how leadership is perceived and practiced in other cultures.

While leadership theorists largely agree that there is no one-size-fits-all leadership model that can fully prepare a leader for the journey, some do argue that there can be more standardization of leadership practice. Other leadership theorists argue that leadership is bound by the context and no universal principles exist that can properly prepare a leader for all situations. Some argue, and we agree, that there can be a degree of standardization of essential leader practice, but that it is also important for leaders to be adaptive to their dynamic contexts.

# 3 The principle of "Care"

"Men would live exceedingly quiet if these two words, mine and thine, were taken away."

—Anaxagoras[1]

Western cultures are often thought to have a lower consideration for other cultures. Part of this observation includes dynamics of the culture itself; as Western communication puts the message sender in a "principal position." Traditional Western models of communication, and their accompanying cultural connotations, are changing, but are not without challenges.[2] Less successful and altogether unsuccessful leaders facing intercultural situations tend to operate from their own cultural background without regarding the cultural context. Successful leaders, on the other hand, operate quite differently.

One theme for discussion in this chapter concerns successful intercultural leaders and the commonalities found among their experiences. Successful intercultural leaders seem to take the time to learn about the cultures with which they come in contact prior to beginning their foreign assignments. In each case we reviewed, the leader read about the culture, took time to visit the foreign country, began learning the language of the host culture, and made a point of getting to know people in the host culture. The majority of the successful intercultural leaders reviewed purposely demonstrated concern for the host culture by asking questions focused on seeking to understand the interests, values, and goals of the people they made contact with from the host culture. We will discuss more about cultural awareness and appreciation in the chapter on consciousness.

Another issue is the tendency to focus only on short-term profit, which can mean long-term disaster. Relatedly, in too many situations, U.S. business leaders appear to be hyper-focused on corporate profit and pleasing shareholders irrespective of any other stakeholder group.[3] In the observation of many intercultural experts, people of other cultures perceive the tendency for U.S. business leaders to emphasize profit as disrespectful and uncaring. Whether this is true is almost irrelevant because perception often precludes further evaluation.

In the American business culture, the tendency toward performance orientation and an emphasis on profit has not gone unchallenged. As early as 1984, when Freeman first introduced the idea of the "stakeholder," awareness of multiple interests in business emerged.[4] The term stakeholder is defined as "any group or individual who can affect or is affected by the achievement of the organization's objectives."[5] Other theorists define stakeholders in relation to the organization. In general, stakeholders can be seen as drivers of corporate responsibility. In addition, internal and external stakeholders can be seen as a reflection of the organization.[6] Accordingly, groups like consumers and employees are stakeholders; moreover, society as a whole is also included since whole communities can be affected by the actions of an organization.

---

# "CARE"
## DEFINED

Balanced interest and value for profit and stakeholders.

---

Stakeholder theorists claim that all stakeholders have their own intrinsic value, and believe that leaders/managers must account for the interests of all stakeholders. In this view, the ultimate goal of the firm is to balance profit maximization with the long-term ability of the corporation to remain viable as a socially responsible entity.[7] One of the criticisms of stakeholder theory has been the obvious ethical dilemma faced by leaders when trying to balance the various interests of stakeholder groups.

Theorists have developed a stakeholder-agency perspective to aid leaders in dealing with the stakeholder-balancing act. In this view, the firm is a nexus of contracts between resource holders (stakeholders).[8] A similar approach proposes structural configurations on the stakeholder/organization relation to explain why different stakeholders influence organizations in different ways. The structural nature of the organization/stakeholder relation, the contractual forms, and the available institutional support influence the extent of stakeholder impact on an organization.[9] The first step is the process of diagramming the intricate, complex web of relations by the compatibility of ideas and material interests. The second step is to identify necessary relations that are internal to a social structure and contingent ones that are external or not integrally connected. In a third step, leaders build decision rules and in the fourth step build outcome scenarios based on the findings from the first three steps.

Implicit in stakeholder theory is that leaders must engage and consult with their various stakeholder groups in all major decisions. This principle is consistent with interculturalists' recommendations related to how U.S. business leaders can better operate in other cultures. The prevailing opinion is that U.S. business leaders must demonstrate authentically that they "care" beyond economic indicators, meeting objectives, and *spreading the American way.*

Related to the practice of considering stakeholder perspectives and profitability is another point repeatedly emphasized by interculturalists, namely, the idea of taking the long view or sustainability view of business. We want to be clear, that we are not suggesting that businesses should not concern themselves with profitability. However, what interculturalists advocate, and we concur, is that global business leaders would benefit from thinking of *both* short- and long-term perspectives. The long view and the sustainability view of business means that businesses should meet today's global economic, environmental, and social needs without compromising the same opportunity for future generations. The movement toward sustainable business is growing and now includes the perspectives of several streams of societal interests including financial investment, responsible business ethics, and of course environmental preservation. We see the boundaries between for-profit and nonprofit blurring. We see entrepreneurial spirit moving business organizations closer to taking on corporate social responsibilities.

Taking the long view requires that business leaders envision scenarios that serve both immediate and long-term goals. It requires that leaders not bury their heads in the sand in denial of the uncertainties that the future always holds; but, rather, choosing to imagine the possibilities and planning for how those could be met. The ultimate goal of taking a long view of business is to enable leaders to tolerate ambiguity, accept, and act with the knowledge that the future holds risk and to be prepared even for failure. The degree to which leaders should focus on longer view business strategies abroad should depend on the comparability between the home and host culture. From our experience and from the cultural research that shows all cultures place importance on time—monochromic, polychronic, and including what is referred to as future orientation[10]—leaders should investigate how a potential host culture perceives time and the future beforehand.[11]

Also related to the concept of sustainability is the practice of holding a local–global mindset. Although we discuss the principle of context in a later chapter, operating with a local–global mindset does involve attention to context. Operating with a local–global mindset simply means thinking and acting in a local context with an awareness of the consequences to places and people beyond. It follows the simple concept of systems thinking that what is done to one part of the system affects all other parts of the system.

Context awareness, local–global mindset, stakeholder awareness, and sustainability all require a leadership practice that facilitates comprehensive decision-making processes. Without advocating any particular decision process, based on our research, we do recommend that leaders base any business process, including making decisions, on the styles of both the host culture and the home culture.

A final element of the Care Principle concerns leaders acting from purposeful rather than habitual approach. Often in our pursuits, we have observed leaders and managers who appear to operate on, what could be described as, autopilot. The mistaken assumption underlying autopilot leadership is that learning stops at graduation or after the first successful job assignment. Our conviction is that leadership, like most professions and life itself, requires continuing education. We recommend that leaders who aspire to or find themselves faced with global, intercultural business assignments devote 20–30 percent of their time engaged in some type of meaningful learning experience. We discuss more about how leaders can prepare themselves for global assignments in another chapter.

While our principal audience is leaders and managers of commercial organizations, we recognize, too, that there is a growing number of hybrid organizations, nonprofit organizations, and even government and municipal organizations for whom intercultural leadership competency is important. To be quite clear, everything that a leader says and does has far-reaching effects, some more than others. A recent example in the news that played out on the world stage provides an important lesson related to the principle of Care.

During the closing ceremony for an international shooting competition held in Kuwait in March, 2012, Maria Dmitrienko took the stage with her fellow athletes from Kazakhstan to receive her gold medal. As is custom, the event planners played her country's national anthem, "My Kazakhstan." They had, however, downloaded an unauthorized version of the anthem that was part of the film parody, *Borat*. This version contained insults to Kazakhstan and had been banned in that country. Ms. Dmitrienko remained standing politely for the ceremony, but Kazakhstan officials demanded an apology.

Business leaders can help themselves, their organizations, and the other cultures with which they interact by demonstrating concern about the individuals in other cultures and by seeking to understand the other culture's values and interests. American business leaders, in particular, but all leaders must be aware that they are a member of a culture that is just one culture among many without assuming dominance. An interview with Dr. George Simons in Exhibit 3.1 will provide an expert interculturalist's opinion on this topic.

---

### *Exhibit 3.1* Interview with George Simons, owner, George Simons International

Interestingly and appropriately to this chapter, George Simons is the creator of the award-winning Diversophy games for developing diversity and intercultural competence in the training room and online learning. Developing diversity and learning intercultural competence through games helps to reinforce leaders' commitment to understanding culture and building a peaceful and economically and socially sound world, which is the epitome of the Care Principle.

*What are the most important decisions you make as a leader of an organization of which you have been a part? (This can also be answered from the perspective of what is the most important decision a leader/client makes in his or her organization.)*

As a consultant, there is always the important decision to be made about the larger direction of the organizations in which we work. This raises important ethical and moral issues such as oneness. Within the framework of the organization is the consistency of its values and behaviors, as well as understanding its role in the larger society, its impact on social welfare, and the ecology both positive and negative. It is essential that these issues not remain unaddressed in the everyday conduct of business. This makes the decision of how and when and where and with whom one raises these substantial issues a very important, even critical one.

*What is one characteristic that you believe every global business leader should possess?*

Certainly we encourage endless curiosity that leads to the ferreting out of reliable and relevant resources through the asking of intelligent questions and listening to what one hears. The leader should know where and how the organization is headed and how that can be directed both for the general good and for the welfare and success of the organization itself.

*What is the biggest challenge facing global business leaders today?*

The biggest challenge facing global business leaders today is awareness of the corrupting nature of capitalism and its destructiveness and dehumanization of people who are now conceived of almost solely as "human resources" and "consumers." Global leaders must realize that there is more than one bottom line and that the one they are fixated on has responsibility to the others.

*What effect do you think national culture has on business leadership decision-making? (This can also include how your own native national culture affects your decision-making.)*

In the U.S.A., we have become a "survival of the strongest and richest" society. We propagate that version of Darwinism under the guise of "democracy" around the world with unending commercial and military warfare. The powerful, whether in Syria or the U.S.A., will turn to violence if thwarted. This is a human tendency, not simply a national one, which needs constant monitoring. This is blatantly obvious in our language by the use of bellicose terminology as we create "war" on everything we want to change.

*What are your thoughts on globalization and how important is it for leaders to develop their own self-awareness so as to adjust to the changing context(s) under which they operate in a given situation and/or organization? (This consciousness could include the leader's own cultural self-bias while operating with diverse constituents.)*

Globalization is largely colonialism. It is a wolf in sheep's clothing. People in less powerful societies are not dumb, but they are often needy and they give into the temptation to become economic "rice Christians" in response to corporate power and policy. A McDonald's "sweet and sour burger" is not Cantonese cuisine! The force of wealth is constantly on the attack, and real guns will be brought forth if dollars are not doing their job.

*How do you think leaders from both governmental and non-governmental organizations view leadership differently? Are such organizations more affected by the national culture in which they are headquartered (i.e., the United Nations is situated in the U.S.), versus the culture of the organization itself, despite its geographic location?*

While the United Nations Headquarters is in New York, its agencies are quartered all over the world and its representatives reside globally. However, it needs restructuring, as the Security Council is currently a lobby for the great powers and does not provide a real leadership function because of this. The question is more relevant for the European Union, where there is always the tension between leadership, position-taking, and bureaucracy, now of course aggravated by the current financial crisis.

*What is one mistake you witness business leaders making more frequently than others? Do you think that some leaders make such errors due to their inability to be self-aware of their own national cultural bias, as mentioned above?*

One mistake I witness business leaders making more frequently than others is assuming that a day or two of cultural indoctrination (kiss, bow, and shake hands, etc.) will suffice to work with other cultures (until they come around to our way of thinking and behaving). This has led to massive failures in mergers acquisitions and joint ventures, to say nothing of negotiating lasting and productive relationships in both private and public realms. There is the ridiculous assumption that, because an organization is international, or has an international mission or market, that it therefore contains within itself the knowledge that it needs to succeed in a multicultural environment. In some cases that knowledge may be there, but it is latent and not brought forth or used to the degree required. In a number of outstanding cases of failure, intercultural and diversity measures were taken at the outset in lending organizations; however, the efforts were not continued, nor was progress monitored until it was too late. The most outstanding example of this is DaimlerChrysler, where primitive cultural values continued to operate beneath the surface and then surfaced with disastrous consequences.

*Can you name a person who has had a tremendous impact on you as a leader? Maybe someone who has been a mentor to you? Why and how did this person impact your life?*

Benjamin Spock taught me that you are never too old to learn and lead. The people I revere hardly ever come from the business world, but are individuals who think outside the box in ways that make life fuller and more meaningful. Mentors at work have not just been people who help you learn how to do the job and do it right, but those who know how the work fits into both the productivity of the organization and the social network of those who are stakeholders in the productivity. I have been lucky to have a couple of these mentors, beginning with a mentor from a job I had in high school. These mentors have helped me understand the workplace and the people within it. They have helped me to perform and made me feel at home even in difficult situations.

*What are your thoughts on globalization and how important is it for leaders to hold and maintain equal concern for the bottom line and the stakeholder groups. Would a broader, longer-term social systems approach to leadership be feasible within the global business arena?*

They may have missed their chance already. The Arab Spring, the Occupy Movement and growing unrest worldwide with unjust exploitation and environmental destruction point toward what will ultimately be more violent attempts at suppression of resistance. For example, it is clear to the rest of the world, if not to the U.S.A., that little of the help or support sent abroad actually goes to much of anyone but U.S. contractors supplying U.S. interests. Most of us try our best to exercise morality and appropriate ethics on an everyday basis. Sometimes it is insightful to realize, that if the socially constructed realities that we live in, organizational, political, etc. are invisible, the backdrop of our efforts, which can often turn our best energies into something similar to "rearranging the deck chairs on the Titanic."

*What do you like to ask other business leaders when you get the chance?*

The questions I would ask run something like this: "Why do you do what you do?" "What would you do if suddenly you had to stop the role you are in?" Sometimes it is insightful to ask the same question in another way, "What will you be doing when you are done with what you are doing now?" This is essentially a question of what life is about and goes beyond the business and busyness of the moment to where our hearts should be taking us. It can generate not only better directions for ourselves, but also a great deal more compassion and empathy for others. Perhaps the question is simply answered with an "I don't know," however, the question stimulates people to at least momentarily raise their consciousness beyond the level of accepted everyday norms and structures so that they can both evaluate and express preferences for others if needed.

***

In his interview, Dr. Simons makes the important point that just because an organization is international does not mean that it has within itself (or that its people have) the knowledge to succeed in a multicultural environment. This is very true and it is for this reason that we and many others continue our research and study of what makes a great global leader.

**Dr. George Simons**, born in the small Western reserve town of Bedford, Ohio, of immigrant families from Poland and Austria, attended Catholic grade school there and went on to high school in Baltimore, Maryland, for two years and then returned to Ohio. Dr. Simons did collegiate studies at Borromeo, John Carroll University, Notre Dame University (Master's degree in the History of Ritual) and Claremont (doctoral degree in Psychology). Dr. Simons is currently an independent consultant residing on the Côte d'Azur in France. From there, he travels worldwide doing training and consulting for both private and public organizations as well as developing a line of intercultural learning tools called diversophy®. Dr. Simons writes for the Cultural Detective® series of intercultural learning instruments and is an author and reviewer of both books and articles.

## Taking the high ground

One tendency in discussions of ethics is that people have ethical perspectives that they generally—unless they have taken courses in ethics or religion—do not understand. Moreover, many people cannot identify the ethical perspectives of other people, and may misinterpret another person's perspective as being unethical when in fact the other person is arguing from a different ethics tradition. Before discussing the various ethics traditions, we will first define the term *ethics*.

Ethics has two meanings. The first definition is the moral principles that guide and influence behavior (and decisions). The second definition of ethics is the branch of knowledge concerned with moral principles. It is the first definition with which we concern ourselves. Many people think these two terms, *ethic* and *moral* are interchangeable. The simple answer is, not exactly. Ethic (a set of moral principles) is a *noun*. We use moral, an *adjective*, to describe the set of principles we use to judge *right* and *wrong* behavior and, *good* versus *bad* human character, or *just* and *unjust* behavior. Therefore, the question remains, where do our ethical perspectives come from, and what are those perspectives?

Ostensibly, we begin early in our lives learning ethics from our caretakers. In the following sections, we provide the answers to these questions without spending much time on the history of these perspectives since this is not a book about ethics. We will first discuss Western ethics traditions, and then examine some other ethics traditions of other world cultures.

In Western cultures, the three traditions of ethics are the ethics of *purpose* (teleology, with its roots in the work of Aristotle), the ethics of *principle* (deontology, with its roots in the work of German philosopher, Immanuel Kant), and ethics of *consequence*, sometimes known as utilitarianism (its roots in the work of Jeremy Bentham and John Stuart Mill).

### Ethics of purpose (teleology)

A teleological perspective is concerned with the "end"—or purpose—of the person. In this view, the person decides what "should be done," and this *end state* is the "good" to which s/he strives. Conduct, which supports that "good" is judged *right*, and conduct hindering that "good" is judged *wrong*. There is a two-step approach in the ethics of purpose. The first is to decide what should be done, and the second is to find the appropriate means to achieve that end.

In the Western vernacular, there is a common expression, "the ends justify the means" which describes this process. Some people have criticized this philosophy, perhaps rightfully so. For believers of this perspective, goodness is judged from having a properly "good" purpose, or *intention*, in mind. For critics of this perspective, intention is not the only criterion with which behavior should be judged.

Let us take the example of Jerrod, a doctor, who, responding to an emergency call, gets in his car and drives faster than the speed limit in an effort to arrive at a hospital in time to save the life of a patient. On one hand, the doctor's intentions would be judged as good from an ethics of purpose perspective, regardless of his breaking the prevailing speed law. On the other hand, ethics of purpose cannot justify the law breaking and, in the judgment of teleology's critics, especially if on the way to the hospital, the doctor caused an accident.

Purists of the teleological perspective would challenge this last judgment by saying that in the true spirit of Aristotelian analysis, there is a close relationship between the means and the end. In other words, a purely "good" intention, in this case the doctor wanting to save a patient, cannot be separated from the means. Therefore, if the doctor's intention is to save life, there must be integrity in how he conducts himself in achieving that end. This means that the doctor must act in such a way as to keep the integrity of his conduct in relation to his intention. In this case breaking speed laws and crashing his car compromises the integrity between his purpose and his actions.

### Ethics of principle (deontology)

Now while the idea that an ethical perspective based on the notion of principles sounds straightforward, this perspective is a bit complex. Immanuel Kant was an academician whose writings posed considerable challenges. His perspective was that all actions must be judged by the premise used to decide the action. If, whatever premise is used, it can be judged as universally applicable, then the action, necessarily, must be judged as ethically "right." Consider the following example of how this universal law works.

All persons have dignity.
Connie is a person.
Therefore, Connie has dignity.

This rationale implies a universal law, what Kant called the "categorical imperative," that can be applied to all persons. These categorical imperatives command us to obey, because we "will" the law, we create the categories to which the rules apply.

Now, let us return to the earlier example of Jerrod the doctor. We have, already, a categorical imperative, which states that it is the duty of all doctors to preserve human life. We know that Jerrod is a doctor. Therefore, it is Jerrod's duty to save life. If, in the course of his actions, Jerrod speeding in his car hits a pedestrian in a crosswalk, how would we judge him according to our categorical imperative? We would say that his conduct violated a universal law, and therefore was an unethical act. In other words, we must always act in such a way that we treat humanity, never simply as a means, but always as an end as well. Implicit in this statement is consistency, the groundwork for universal law, created through "free will."

### Ethics of consequence (utilitarianism)

In the ethics of consequence, the focus is on positive and negative effects of a decision or action on the affected people. To judge an act or decision, we need to know what are "the probable consequences" and what those consequences mean for the affected people (or stakeholders). We also need to know how the *positive consequences* compare with the *negative consequences*. With this information, we can choose right action that does the most good for the most people and does the least harm. It is from the utilitarian perspective that we get the expression "the greater good," meaning the greatest utility. Utilitarianism began as a social movement. Ethics of consequences, then, is a public or social ethic. Utilitarians developed an ethic with which they could simply judge whether an action or policy caused pleasure and happiness or caused pain and unhappiness.

One of the classic debates that arose out of the utilitarian movement pits the interests of the individual against the interests of the public. However, John Stuart Mill, who greatly expanded on Bentham's work, believed that neither side, a majority of thousands, nor an individual, could reasonably expect that their perspective be any more or less justified.

Now, for one final review of Jerrod's conduct. According to an ethic of consequences, Jerrod's choice to ignore prevailing traffic laws created a potential to harm any number of people. In addition, by choosing to speed, he took a risk that his conduct could delay his safe arrival at the hospital. In reality, Jerrod hit a pedestrian, and although the pedestrian escaped major injury, he did sustain injury. Moreover, Jerrod was delayed from his objective because he was compelled to treat the injured pedestrian. However, suppose that there were two pedestrians, a little boy, who was hit, and his mother, and the mother who was quite disturbed by the driving behavior of Jerrod, hesitated to allow Jerrod to treat her son. Now, we have two pedestrians harmed, a patient waiting at the hospital, a surgical unit frantic because their doctor is late and has not called, and a doctor who has lost sight of his oath. From an ethic of consequence, we must view Jerrod's decision as a wrong one because it caused harm to several people and resulted in no perceivable positive consequences.

## Beyond Western ethics traditions

During a period just under 3000 years ago, a series of religious, philosophical, and ethical changes took place, which have greatly influenced human morality. Several highly influential teachers appeared, each of whom advocated for a moral, ethical, and spiritual wisdom grander in scope and beyond any one society. In China there was Confucius and Lao Tzu; in India Siddhartha Gautama (Buddha); in ancient Persia the Prophet Zoroaster, and in ancient Israel the great Hebrew prophets Jeremiah, the Second Isaiah, and Ezekiel. Thereafter, the first philosophical ethics of the Western tradition in the work of people like Socrates, Plato, and Aristotle appeared. These teachers were followed, some centuries later, by the two most influential figures on ethical perspectives, Jesus of Nazareth and the Prophet Muhammad. Quite rapidly, the messages of these highly influential figures led to the growth of major new movements, which are for the most part both ethical and religious with the exception of the ancient Greek moral philosophers.

In the sections following, we overview the major of the non-Western ethical traditions. It is important that the reader keep in mind that in many societies and cultures around the world ethical frameworks and practices are based not on secular philosophy, but rather on spiritual and religious doctrine and sacred writings. Therefore, to understand how people of African, Arab, many Asian and Middle Eastern cultures make decisions, one must first understand their religions.

### *Islamic ethics*

To appreciate Islamic ethics it is vital first to understand Islam, a religion that has its origins in seventh century Arabia. The word Islam itself means "peace" or surrender to God (Allah). The central tenet of Islam involves the acceptance of Oneness, or unity with God, and the recognition of Muhammad as the one true prophet. Accordingly, Muhammad, the messenger sent from Allah, is the recipient of the sacred scripture of Islam, which is called the *Quran*. Islamic Law derives from the *Quran*.

From the *Quran*, comes the Islamic ethical tradition. Islam does not separate religion from other human pursuits including government and business, ethics, in principle and practice, originate from Islamic religious doctrine. The doctrine of Oneness is central in Islamic belief, ethics tradition tends to be God-centered, also. In other words, it is God's will, which forms the basis for evaluating human conduct and ethical behavior. Human actions in such a Divine-centered worldview become purposeful, and are driven by the goal to serve, submit, and surrender to God's will.

The *Quran*, then, is the primary source in the Islamic ethics, giving guidelines and is the central source for deducing Islamic ethical and moral behavior. These moral guidelines emanate mostly from passages that describe the attributes of the Muslim God. For instance, the *Quran* presents God as a possessor of divinely beautiful attributes. Therefore, the faithful are those people who are perceived to have internalized these attributes in their interaction with others. As the embodiment of human perfection, Muhammad's conduct and behavior becomes the norm and standard through which the ethical ideals of the Muslim community are determined. This means that it is incumbent on people following Islamic Law to try to behave by the standards "known" by the faithful to be Divine attributes. For example, if kindness is one Divine attribute, then the expectation is that people should behave kindly toward one another.

Islamic ethical attitudes towards the environment derive mostly from Muhammad's teachings and personal conduct. If, among other definitions, ethics is the codification of the rules for behavior, the way we make decisions about right and wrong, and the values that underlie such decision-making then, represents a vital resource of reference for a systematic regulation of Muslim life and activity. In other words, all rules concerning prohibitions and what is permissible, stretching from rules governing ritual observances, social transactions (like commercial and family laws), are supposed to be sanctioned by Islamic Law. Islamic Law has classified human actions into five basic categories as shown in Figure 3.1.

The implications of the Islamic codification of human actions are that there is some ambiguity and that there is a close relationship between ethics and law. Ambiguity is evident in the actions that are categorized as recommended, reprehensible, or indifferent/morally neutral. In the case of the ambiguous categories of human actions, the law becomes neutral. In other words, Muslim conduct that may be classified under these categories, although in some instances it may be judged undesirable or harmful, is nevertheless exempted from civil penalties.

Islam is often described as an "action-based" religion meaning that beliefs must be accompanied by necessary actions. The ethical implications of this, is that human intention alone to "do good" is insufficient. From the Islamic perspective, good intentions must translate into good actions. For example, and continuing with our story of Jerrod, it is not enough for Jerrod to say that he intended to remove broken bottles on the road; he should actually remove them. Otherwise, if any individual were endangered, Jerrod would be morally responsible. The point is that good intention must be acted out and not confined to an individual's thoughts.

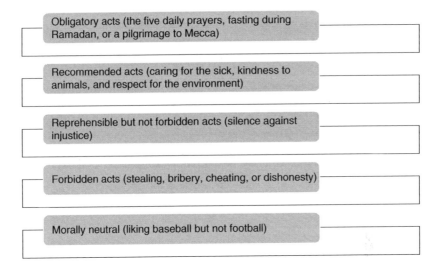

*Figure 3.1* Five basic categories of human actions per Islamic law.

Like most traditions, Islam is not free from diverse points of view. For example, the extent to which the imperative to apply and enforce God's will through application of Islamic Law is entrenched as forced morality. For example, Muslim countries such as Saudi Arabia and Sudan have made Islamic Law, civil law. Similarly, even in countries where Muslims live within secular democracies, Muslims have not shied away from demanding that Islamic Law should govern them. In other words, as the symbol of human excellence, Prophet Muhammad represents the ethical ideal. Based on this centrality of Muhammad within Islam, parallel to legal or Islamic Law based ethics, a less legalistic ethics has emerged that stresses the compassionate side of God rather than the punitive dimension of God.

In summary, morality in Islam is based on the following basic beliefs and principles. Allah is the source and creator of all goodness, truth, and beauty. Human beings are representatives or agents of God on earth. All things in creation are created for the service of humans. Allah as a just God does not place unnecessary burdens on humans. All that humans do must be done in moderation. Except for the explicitly forbidden, all things are permissible. The ultimate goal is to attain the pleasure of Allah. Accordingly, Islam has lain down in the form of religious and social duties regulations that have moral and ethical implications for organizing human life. These are meant to assist Muslims in their quest towards moral progress and improvement of inter-human relations. A critical reflection on Islamic ethics indicates that Islamic morals are goal driven. The ultimate goal and concern is the desire to attain the pleasure of Allah. Such a view has led some Muslims to assert that morality cannot be imposed by human authority but must emerge from the world of the individual.

### *Hindu ethics*

The ethical tradition of Hinduism is a cultural and historical tradition so rich and complex that some see it as a federation or plurality of religions rather than a single religious stream. An amazing variety of religious beliefs, practices, customs, and trends can be found within the wider Hindu community. There are a number of ways or paths in Hinduism that will enable the seeker to achieve final spiritual liberation from the problems of suffering, bondage, and ignorance. A Hindu may choose whichever path fits his/her circumstances. The three main paths are shown in Figure 3.2.

Following one or more of these three paths will eventually bring the seeker to a genuine realization of, and encounter with, the one Divine Reality, which has numerous manifestations: Shiva, Vishnu, Krishna, Durga, and Ganesh.

There are many Hindu Scriptures, and a Hindu may choose to focus on any number of these Scriptures as his or her preferred holy book; this might be the popular *Bhagavad Gita*, the time-honored collection known as the *Four Vedas*, or the *Ramayana*.

Ahimsa (practicing non-harmfulness toward all living creatures, a theme stressed by Mahatma Gandhi) is universal in Hinduism.

Hinduism is a constellation of traditions, and the diversity continues into modern times. Hinduism has been described as a tolerant and flexible spiritual tradition. Religious and social practice in Hinduism is crucially important; Hinduism is a tradition in which "doing and acting" are more fundamental than "believing." This doing can take many forms: popular worship, various ritual performances, yoga, prayer, chanting, good deeds, participation in festivals, pilgrimages, and many other things. One important context in which Hindu religion has been learned and lived out over the centuries is within families.

Many Hindu philosophers today perceive an act as truly amoral only if it is taken out of *informed* choices that are *freely* made. Hinduism is, perhaps, the most spiritual of the world's religions. Yet the tradition contains a full range of worldly and otherworldly values. For example, the *Bhagavad Gita* describes the four goals of life: Moral and ritual action; Economic and political activity; Desire and pleasure; Ultimate spiritual liberation. One significant teaching of the *Gita* is

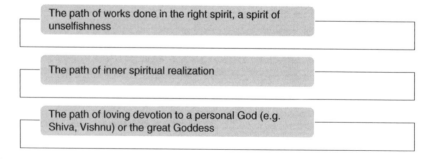

*Figure 3.2* Three paths of Hinduism.

Karma *actions* (i.e. any actions, whether right or wrong) coupled with the consequences of actions)

Dharma *right/appropriate actions* (including moral actions, and appropriate ritual actions)

*Figure 3.3* Hindu terminology.

that you do not need to leave the world and society behind in order to find God; you can continue to act fully in the world in all manner of ways, but you should do so in a spirit of action without attachment. This means action without desire, without ambition, without selfishness, without vested interest. An explanation of Hindu terminology is explained in Figure 3.3.

Karma effectively means, as you sow, so shall you reap. Act morally, and this will affect your future lives for the good; act selfishly and negatively, and in your future lives you will experience negative and miserable circumstances. Consequently, moral considerations are based on whether or not the person's desire to do something either provides insurance for a good next life, or provides a strong enough motivation to outweigh the thought of future life repercussions.

By contrast, Buddhists believe that karma is generated only by intentional human actions. Karma in Hinduism does not involve some fatalistic belief that there is no human freedom, that everything is always predetermined. Although what a Hindu is now is a result of past (and unchangeable) forces and influences, from this moment on the Hindu is relatively free to shape his or her own future destiny.

Dharma is a very important principle in Hindu traditions and has two contextual meanings: applied to the universe, dharma implies orderliness and coherence of the universe and of nature; and, applied to the human and social realms, dharma implies proper action, right action, and moral action. The link between these two meanings is simply that dharmic action is right action that conforms to the order that lives in all things.

Some dharmic virtues are universal and obligatory for everyone (e.g., honesty, temperance, patience, hospitality, and kindness), while other applications of dharma are contextual, depending on the caste to which you belong (Brahmins, Rulers/warriors, Farmers/traders, Servant workers), or the stage of life you are passing through (Spiritual student, Married householder, Contemplative forest-dweller, Holy wanderer).

There are a number of traditional social practices in Hinduism that are based simply on a principle of: do not do things because you feel that you must do them; do them when you understand and sincerely accept the call of genuine moral obligation.

### African ethics

It is important to understand that it is not possible to generalize across African cultures, given the large number and variety. Nonetheless, for our purposes here, we provide as much universality as possible without compromising accuracy. There is agreement among scholars that there are a number of patterns in most African cultures. For example, all African cultures share the concept of ancestor veneration.

The importance given to ancestors is demonstrated by the fact that ancestors are the perceived guardians of ethics and morality. Arguably, such a view stems from the understanding that since ancestors are those who have lived exemplary lives in the world of the living, they continue to be preoccupied with regulating the affairs of their communities even in their temporary absence. In a sense, they are still concerned about the moral integrity of their communities. For disregard of what constitutes moral virtues renders the community vulnerable to harmful spirits, misfortune, and subsequent destruction. Relatedly, a universal concept across African societies is that the notion of what is wrong and right, desirable and undesirable, acceptable and disliked is evaluated based on whether it has the approval or non-approval of the ancestors. In other words, in deciding on a course of action, the question becomes how conduct will invite the pleasure or earn the wrath of the ancestors.

Given that African ethics and morality are based on the veneration of ancestors, the general character of African ethics, the central concern, is the management of life and maintenance of well-being within society. Individual ethical choices are made within the context of the community, that is, community in the inclusive sense. In such a context, individual actions are evaluated and judged based on the effect that they have on the life of the community. In particular, within the South African context, this view finds expression in the concept of *Ubuntu* and a similar notion is expressed in the Shona concept of *Ukama*, implying the relatedness between humans, environment, god, and ancestors. Simplified, the concept underpins the very communal nature of African society and by extension its ethics. The well-being of the individual and his or her interests are possible through the community where the community becomes a web of relationships. This is well expressed in the Zulu saying, *Umuntu ngumuntu ngabantu* (You are a person through others). In other words, the well-being of the individual and his or her interests is possible through the community. As an ethical principle, *Ubuntu* then places a high value in sound human relations. Therefore, in traditional societies no one was a stranger, hospitality to strangers and the spirit of sharing were respected values of a community. Likewise, cruelty, murder, cheating, or stealing was sufficient to warrant ostracizing the individual through public censure (i.e., for the shameful or immoral act). Therefore, in a sense the act of ostracizing the individual served as some kind of a form of deterrent punishment.

In ethical terms, it is the collective wisdom of the ancestors and elders that becomes the basis or point of reference for moral decisions or choices that the individual or community makes. Morality is the creation of the community and emerges from its social institutions. It is lived within the community so what an individual does directly or indirectly affects the whole society. Therefore, tradition demands that those who have done shameful or immoral acts must be cleansed before they can be accepted back into the community. In summary, the community's history and life experience are the source of African ethics. This source may vary and evolves from social customs, religious beliefs, regulations, social taboos, proverbs, and certain symbols.

### Confucianism

Confucianism is a philosophy concerned with humans, their achievements and interests, rather than with the abstract beings and problems of theology. In Confucianism, man is the center of the universe: man cannot live alone, but with other human beings. For human beings, the ultimate goal is individual happiness. The necessary condition to achieve happiness is through peace. To obtain peace, Confucius discovered human relations consisting of the five relationships that are based on love and duties. Great Unity of the world should be developed. All humans are good and always striving to be better, be loyal, and live morally. The focus is on comprehensive truths rather than logic; the more comprehensive, the closer the truth. Confucianism emphasizes sympathizing for others when they are suffering; always searching for a higher sense of sympathy for people. This belief system also entails the belief that the ultimate personal harmony in life are the relationships one has during human existence.

### Taoism

Taoism is a constellation of related Chinese philosophical and religious traditions and concepts. These traditions influenced East Asia for over 2,000 years and some have spread internationally. Taoist propriety and ethics emphasize the Three Jewels of the Tao; namely, compassion, moderation, and humility. Taoist thought focuses on *wu wei* ("non-action"), spontaneity, humanism, and emptiness. An emphasis is placed on the link between people and nature. Taoism teaches that this link lessens the need for rules and order, and leads one to a better understanding of the world.

The word *Tao* means the "path" or "way," but in Chinese religion and philosophy it has taken on more abstract meanings. Tao is rarely an object of worship, being treated more like the Central Asian concepts of dharma. Most traditional Chinese Taoists are polytheistic. Nature and ancestor spirits are also common in popular Taoism. Organized Taoism distinguishes its ritual activity from that of the folk religion, which some professional Taoists (*Daoshi*) view as debased. This sort of shamanism is eschewed for an emphasis on internal alchemy among the "elite" Taoists. A discussion of adapting to other cultures and their ethics follows in section 3.2.

## *Exhibit 3.2* Interview with Alan Richter, founder and president of QED Consulting

As the founder and president of QED Consulting, Alan Richter's company's clients have included not only Fortune Global 500 companies, but also leading nonprofit and public sector organizations, such as the United Nations (and a number of UN agencies and organizations, including UNICEF, WHO, and FAO), NASA, and Wharton School of Business. The organization specializes in the areas of Leadership, Values, Culture, and Change, and in the alignment of Strategy, People and Processes. We find his expertise to be of immense value in our discussion of the Care Principle, especially the section on ethics, wherein we discuss that people from different ethical perspectives can easily misinterpret others' perspectives as being unethical even though it may be in fact that they are just acting in a situation from a different ethics tradition. As you'll read in his interview, Alan believes that people are grounded in their own culture which, while providing a foundation for leadership, can be limiting without adaptive strategies.

*What are the most important decisions you make as a leader of an organization of which you have been a part? (This can also be answered from the perspective of what is the most important decision a leader/client makes in his or her organization.)*

The most important decisions I make are about who to partner with, which resources to use, and on which new products we as an organization should focus.

*What is one characteristic that you believe every global business leader should possess?*

I believe every global business leader should possess a global mindset. To me, this is the willingness and ability to see the world from multiple perspectives.

*What is the biggest challenge facing global business leaders today?*

The biggest challenge facing global leaders today, I believe is dealing with very fast change and technological innovations—and keeping up with the complexity of data.

*What effect do you think national culture has on business leadership decision-making? (This can also include how your own native national culture affects your decision-making.)*

We are grounded in our culture and way of seeing the world, so it provides a foundation but also a limitation if one does not develop flexible/adaptable strategies.

*What are your thoughts on globalization and how important is it for leaders to develop their own self-awareness so as to adjust to the changing context(s) under which they operate in a given situation and/or organization?(This consciousness could include the leader's own cultural self-bias while operating with diverse constituents.)*

A significant key is being able to connect national culture to universal values. No country should be outside of the UN's Declaration of Human Rights framework.

Global leadership means balance. Global leaders should focus on results and people, values and ideas, and on keeping a long-term focus. This is key for businesses as well as government and nonprofits.

*How do you think leaders from both governmental and non-governmental organizations view leadership differently? Are such organizations more affected by the national culture in which they are headquartered (i.e., the United Nations is situated in the U.S.), versus the culture of the organization itself, despite its geographic location?*

I believe there is more similarity than difference between public and private organizations. We all need to deal with values, strategy execution, innovation, and managing talent.

*What is one mistake you witness business leaders making more frequently than other Fortune Global 500 organizations? Can you provide an example of such a mistake, particularly one in which the leader did not understand the importance of appropriate intercultural cues?*

I don't have one simple answer to this one. There are so many mistakes made, but I'm not sure of frequencies of common misunderstandings across culture. Perhaps the biggest common mistakes are breaches of ethics—conflicts of interest, abuse of authority, corruption—and no industry or country is immune from these. And there are frequent misunderstandings across cultures that can lead to awful outcomes. So understanding different communication styles is imperative.

*Can you name a person who has had a tremendous impact on you as a leader? Maybe someone who has been a mentor to you? Why and how did this person impact your life? Was this person from the same native and/or organizational culture than you?*

A role model for me, not mentor, is Nelson Mandela. He was such an exemplary leader! A man of integrity, compassion, brilliantly creatives, and able to unite people toward goals.

*What do you like to ask other business leaders when you get the chance?*

I like to ask them: What's new? What's exciting? What's working? What innovative best practice can you share?

***

Every organization is founded on a set of values and a belief system that drive its function within the global marketplace. Alan's succinct answer that it is breaches of ethics that are the most common mistakes leaders make supports the notion that an organization will suffer greatly if its leaders do not uphold the values of the organization. Living the organization's values, learning right from wrong, and communicating and following through on what's "right" for the greater good is of the greatest importance as we knit our organizations together to form a global business tapestry.

**Alan Richter** is the president of QED Consulting, a 25-year-old company based in New York. He has consulted to corporations, organizations, and universities for many years in multiple capacities, primarily in the areas of leadership, values, culture, and change. Dr. Richter is the creator of many successful training tools such as the award-winning Global Diversity Game©, the Global Diversity Survey©—a self-assessment tool which measures how we deal with difference, and the Global Leadership Survey©—a global leadership style self-assessment tool. As a pioneer in the global diversity and inclusion field he has worked closely with many organizations including: American Express, Avon, Chubb, Deloitte, Delphi, Ernst & Young, Gartner, GE, Home Depot, the ILO, Investec, NASA, Nokia, PricewaterhouseCoopers, Prudential, RBS, Sasol, Sony, Sumitomo, UBS, UNICEF, the United Nations, Wharton, WIPO, Wipro, the WMO, and the WTO. He has worked in Africa, Asia, and Europe, in addition to the Americas. Dr. Richter has also been a presenter at many conferences and is on the Board of the South African American Chamber of Commerce. He holds an M.A. and a B.A. B.Sc. from the University of Cape Town, and a Ph.D. in Philosophy from Birkbeck College, London University.

## The moral you

Supporting all ethical traditions, there is a system of morality. Morals are the principles we use to judge right and wrong, just and unjust behavior, and good versus bad human character. It is our moral principles that guide our behavior and with which we form our opinions about our behavior and that of other people. No matter what culture you are from, you possess a set of morals.

Previously, we discussed ethical frameworks and the bases for the various ethical perspectives to which people subscribe. Further, we also noted that our ethical perspectives develop in us from an early age through our interactions with caretakers, religious institutions, schools, and general societal influences (television, media, role models, etc.). If our moral principles guide us and we learn them through interaction with our caretakers and early influences, the question remains of how we develop moral principles.

In this section, we discuss the prevalent Western theory of moral development to date as refined and researched by Lawrence Kohlberg, a professor of Education at Harvard University. Kohlberg based his theory on the earlier work of Piaget done in the 1930s. Kohlberg posited his refinement of Piaget's theory in the early 1960s and the work of both theorists continues to be utilized in research today.

### *The formation of moral principles*

An important aspect of any developmental process is that it occurs over time. In other words, development means something transforms. Moral development is no exception to this rule. People progress forward—never backward—through stages of moral development. What transforms is the person's cognitive structure. Simply put, the way that people intellectually construct their thoughts evolves over time due to the influences of their environment and their own personality formation.

The research on moral development demonstrates three important characteristics. First, people exhibit consistent moral judgment through each stage. This means that during any stage, a person will behave similarly in character with that stage. They do not move backwards, and they do not suddenly behave as though they were in an advanced stage and then retreat to a far earlier stage. Second, people pass through the stages sequentially; they do not go forward, then slip back, then move forward again, unless they experience extreme trauma. Third, as people progress through the stages, they incorporate the essential aspects of earlier stages. However, they tend to use the highest stage understood.

The result of this developmental process is that people progress from a simplistic moral perspective of right and wrong to an increasingly complex and differentiated model of moral reasoning. What causes some individuals to progress and others to remain in earlier stages has to do with many factors such as the ability to empathize with other people, and their capacity for remorse. Generally, when an individual is stuck at a psychological level they will be stuck at a moral development level as well. Next, we describe each of Kohlberg's three stages of moral development. The three stages in human development are Preconventional, Conventional, and Postconventional, as shown in Figure 3.4. Within each of these stages are subsets, which we describe as well.

Preconventional

Conventional

Postconventional

*Figure 3.4* Kolberg's three stages of moral development.

**Level One: Preconventional** In this stage, children respond to cultural rules of right and wrong by perceiving the connection between behavior and, physical pain or pleasure.

*Stage One: Punishment and Obedience Orientation.* People (children) in this stage of moral reasoning equate right and wrong with the dictates of authority and the punishment associated with a given action. In other words, the consequences of the child's action determine how s/he interprets the goodness or badness of those actions. The child seeks to avoid punishment and respects authority based on the avoidance of punishment, not based on a value for elders.

*Stage Two: Instrumental Relativist Orientation.* Children in this stage of reasoning begin to factor their own wants and needs in their choices. If something satisfies the child's own needs, then it is worth the risk of punishment. Simply put, the child in this stage begins to understand that s/he can satisfy his/her needs through behaving in an approved manner. S/he will behave in such a way because s/he is convinced that there is reward—a *quid pro quo relationship.* Occasionally in this stage, the child even considers the needs of other people.

**Level Two: Conventional** Once children reach the conventional stage, they begin to associate their own behavior with maintaining the expectations of their social groups. In this stage, they learn conformity and loyalty to the rules of their families and other important social groups.

*Stage Three: Interpersonal Concordance Orientation.* Children in this stage of reasoning are often entering adolescence, and become concerned with what is good for others. There is a preoccupation with being a "good" girl or boy. They have a larger perspective, and see themselves as part of a society with its rules and regulations.

*Stage Four: Law and Order Orientation.* Individuals in this stage of reasoning have an increased sense of social order. They tend more to rely on "the rules" as laid out by the society to make their moral choices. Maintaining social order and doing one's duty are important.

**Level Three: Postconventional** Once individuals enter this stage, they begin to evaluate moral values and principles in terms of the merit of the rule or value apart from the particular authority or group.

*Stage Five: Social Contract–Legalistic Orientation.* Individuals in this stage maintain their emphasis on social order, but they see it less as a black-and-white set of rules and more as mutually agreed-upon standards. They also factor in the individual's rights when making moral choices. They do not see the social system as perfect, but believe that it is still necessary to avoid chaos.

*Stage Six: Universal Ethical-Principle Orientation.* Kohlberg's final (and most controversial) stage represents the epitome of human moral reasoning. Individuals in this stage realize that sometimes what they choose democratically is not necessarily in the best interest of the society. They make their moral choices based on their internal ethical standards, which take into account the universal good.

### Kohlberg's classic dilemma

In the next section, we provide an example of how to understand and use Kohlberg's model of moral development. Kohlberg used this particular example in his research. Kohlberg's description starts with children who receive their orientation to values and ethics. However, as a person matures, the individual should expand upon this original psychological construct. As one grows, so should this moral sense of responsibility.

### Heinz steals the drug

In Europe, a woman was near death from cancer. One drug might save her, a form of radium that a druggist in the same town had recently discovered. The druggist was charging $2,000, ten times the drug's actual cost to make. The sick woman's husband, Heinz, went to everyone he knew to borrow the money, but he could get together only about half of what the drug cost. He told the druggist that his wife was dying and asked him to sell the drug cheaper or let him pay later. The druggist said "No." The husband got desperate and broke into the man's store to steal the drug for his wife. Should the husband have done that? Why or why not?

*Level One: Preconventional* In this stage, personal needs determine right or wrong. Favors are returned along the lines of "You scratch my back; I'll scratch yours." In the Heinz case, the person wants to avoid apprehension—either for stealing the drug or for not doing enough to save his wife. Wanting to avoid punishment will be his main motivator.

*Level Two: Conventional* Someone operating from this level will value both following the law and doing what is best for a person. They would see the situation as either "it is against the law to steal" or "it is okay to steal the drug because he is trying to help his wife."

*Level Three: Postconventional* Someone operating from Level Three has altruistic ideals in mind. They value human life over a potentially arbitrary law and they would believe that you have to consider the situation.

Kohlberg's theory is value-free. Heinz could have stolen or not stolen the drug with moral reasoning from *each* level.

### Moral responsibility

Does understanding the stages of moral development help us understand better the behavior of organizations? Does it help us understand our own behavior? Can we better grapple with the issues facing our business world today?

From our perspective the answer to all these questions is, yes. As members of organizations, we carry the expectations that we, as adults, are fully prepared to make appropriate decisions. By understanding our own moral reasoning and understanding that we have in our grasp the cognitive tools to make appropriate decisions, we necessarily assume responsibility for our actions. Along with other cultural biases, intercultural leaders must be aware of their own ethical and moral principles. As we have indicated with other organizational considerations, intercultural leaders must be aware that ethics and moral standards differ across cultures and this area of knowledge and understanding must be learned at a local level along with language and other cultural norms, laws, and customs.

### Integrative ethics model

In any situation, there are nine elements to consider, the person or "agent" (who), the act (what, including all potential consequences), alternative acts (all options considered—which does the greatest good for the most people, causing the least harm to the fewest number of people), the "agency" (how it will be carried out), the scene (where), occasion (when), the purpose (why), the actors (all stakeholders to whom something is or may be done), and consent and/or notification.

When all nine of these elements are considered, and all the ethics traditions are linked together, the strengths of those traditions enable us to build an integrated ethical framework. Such a framework gives us a comprehensive basis with which to make decisions. For organizations, it can provide a methodology and practice that can allow members to avoid disagreements and help decision-makers prevent harmful conduct. Making ethical decisions must start at the top of the organization and be practiced throughout the organization.

U.S. business leaders will need to be in constant and clear contact with all stakeholders to show a firm commitment as well as understanding from the perspective of each stakeholder group. Whether business decisions are made online or offline, a set of rules needs to be developed to analyze how each decision

A Geoleader can demonstrate the principle of Care through the following practices and behaviors:

- Clarify and understand the membership of each stakeholder group.
- Meet with representatives of each stakeholder group to understand their interests, values, and goals.
- Communicate commitment and concern for stakeholder perspectives and interests.
- Analyze all business decisions from the perspective of each stakeholder group.
- Develop decision rules to be used in making business decisions that consider stakeholder interests.
- Develop outcome scenarios as a step in strategic planning.

*Figure 3.5* The principle of "Care" in practice.

will affect each stakeholder interest. In doing so, leaders can attempt to plan more strategically in order to achieved desired outcomes. Profit seems to remain the guiding principle in most business dealings, but it is changing the way leaders view the conduit for profit (i.e., global employees) that is vital. There needs to be a thought shift from currency to care in order to sustain long-term relationships in markets that have not yet been fully developed and promise untapped opportunities.

The mental revolution to which Taylor referred was that the antagonism and conflict between management and worker had to stop. Management, and ownership, had to stop focusing on increasing their profit at the expense of worker and consumer. Workers had to stop focusing on increasing their wages at the expense of the company ownership and management and the consumer. Taylor said it best, "The great revolution that takes place in the mental attitude of the two parties under scientific management is that both sides take their eyes off of the division of the 'surplus' (profit) as the all-important matter, and together turn their attention toward increasing the … surplus," through mutual effort, cooperation, and honorable intention. Newer perspectives toward profit and corporate responsibility indicate that by "doing good" companies will reap reputational gains, thus supporting successful business development.[12]

## The bottom line

Sensitivity, concern, and appreciation for other cultures are primary requirements for the new intercultural leader—we call this the principle of Care. Leaders can improve both profit and intercultural relations by adopting a "long view" or sustainability view of business strategy. Adopting a local–global dialectic ability can help leaders to demonstrate their commitment to both corporate and regional needs. By dialectic ability, we mean that leaders should engage in the perspective taking dialogue necessary to consider all stakeholders.

Leaders must adopt a purposeful rather than habitual behavior pattern. The lesson learned from most global business failures is that what works on home turf will not necessarily work in another culture. Moreover, what works in one foreign culture will not necessarily work in yet another culture. Leaders must consider the differences as well as the similarities across cultures in order to be successful in all cultures.

# 4 The principle of "Communication"

"We have two ears and one tongue so that we would listen more and talk less."
—Diogenes[1]

The prevailing theme of this chapter is that business leaders need to engage with individuals from other cultures in order to understand their own cultural background and biases. Past research indicates that culturally skilled leaders move from being culturally unaware to being aware and sensitive to their own cultural heritage and to valuing and respecting differences.[2] These leaders were aware of how their own cultural backgrounds, experiences, and attitudes, values, and biases influenced interactions with others. Theorists suggest that leadership is central to the human condition, and further that the follower is a social animal.[3] Intercultural experts concur that through engaging with diverse cultures, a leader becomes more aware of a personal cultural framework.[4]

Intercultural competency experts agree that building intercultural understanding is the top priority for American business leaders to lead and motivate others.[5] The more leaders understand the behaviors of both their own employees and others outside the organization, the better able they are to direct the organization.[6] Theorists[7] suggest that effective intercultural leaders are able to communicate and motivate others. These competencies occur when the leader retains an open mind and respects others. Leadership also results when an individual can influence, motivate, and enable others to contribute toward the effectiveness of an organization.[8]

Theorists and practitioners alike, agree that effective communications remains the top competency for global business leaders.[9] Research informs us that the ability to communicate clearly is paramount for a globally competent leader.[10] Additionally, exemplary intercultural leaders are able to communicate and motivate others and are knowledgeable about communication style differences.[11] Effective communication remains crucial as the forces of globalization are pulling all cultures into a virtual and time-independent business zone.[12]

The problem for American business is that too many organizations have operated with an ethnocentric approach to their ventures abroad. Operating with an ethnocentric mindset means that U.S. business leaders tend to consider language, values, and behaviors as standardized and homogenized throughout the world.[13] Dealing with language involves an interaction between the text on the one hand, and the culturally based world knowledge and experientially based learning of the receiver on the other.

## Intercultural communication

All communication is cultural. People communicate by drawing on learned patterns, rules, and norms. When people interact, two factors influence the nature and quality of the relations, namely, *situation* and *disposition*. We discuss situational factors in chapters devoted to context, contrasts, and immersion. In this section, we discuss the dispositional (psychological and sociological) factors that influence interpersonal contact, specifically related to *intercultural communication*. Intercultural communication is the management and transmission of messages for creating meaning across cultures.

Intercultural communication difficulties are the cause of many problems in global business contexts. The way people communicate varies widely between, and even within, cultures, let alone between and among regions, professions, socioeconomic classes, genders, and organizational cultures. At a basic level, communication between humans involves desire (intention plus motivation) and prediction (calculation plus expectation). In other words, people make communication decisions based on their desire and the expected response from the receiver, whether or not they are conscious of this intricate process.

At a psychological level, people base communication strategies on their assessment of the receiver, whether s/he is different, or similar to others with whom the sender has previous experience. At a sociological level, people base communication strategies on assessment of the receiver's similarity to the sender, that is within group, or aspirational group affiliation. In addition to these psycho-cognitive and sociocultural processes, culture affects several aspects of communication interactions. Language, even between same-language speaking groups (e.g., France and Quebec; U.K., U.S., and Australia), is the most obvious difference; however, there are a number of other equally important cultural distinctions.

The areas of cultural variability, related to intercultural communication, include non-verbal communication (facial expression, gestures, and posture) tone and volume, pace, social distance (how far apart are the speaker and receiver), time orientation, uncertainty-avoidance, locus of control, conflict orientation, and worldview.

Intercultural communication involves situations where there is communication between persons with different cultural beliefs, values, or ways of living. Cultural differences may be minimal, for example between a German and an Austrian, or may be great, as between a Scot and a Malaysian. At best, intercultural

# "COMMUNICATION"
## DEFINED

In order for business leaders to lead effectively in intercultural situations, they must engage and interact with those cultures in whose countries they work with a desire to understand and appreciate that culture and its people.

communication can be difficult if the communicator and the receiver share few mutual languages and practices.

The culture of a receiver of communication acts as a filter through which he/she interprets the message. This filter may color the message to the point that the message received may not match the message sent. The source of the communication will most often be within the context of the sender. Ostensibly, culture influences every facet of the communication experience. The message that is received is actually more important than the message that the communicator sent. In other words, effective communication depends on the accuracy of the message received.

Non-verbal communication, particularly in relation to verbal channels, is highly culture-dependent and relies on cultural heritage. Every person is influenced how to move and communicate from a very early age. Hence, it plays a significant role with regard to intercultural communication and in fully understanding what is being communicated.

Hall differentiated between low-context and high-context communication. Low-context communication focuses on verbal elements and is characteristic of cultural groups from North America, the U.K., and Germany. High-context communication blends verbal messages with a lot of bodily behavior, motions, and signs; this typifies Central/Eastern Europe, the Mediterranean region, South America, among others.

Although language plays a significant role in meaning-making, non-verbal elements of communication accentuate language to emphasize meaning, even affecting the need for verbal elaboration. Much like verbal communication, non-verbal communication, including posture and bodily expression, carries a meaningful message that other people receive and process as shown in Figure 4.1. Similarly, words have multiple meanings to people and so too do behavioral messages sent through other non-verbal channels. Messages sent through non-verbal channels tend to mean different things by various cultural groups, often crossing the borders imposed by verbal language restrictions, but also generating new challenges in societies with multiple cultures.

Daniel Goleman[14] identified four main domains of emotional intelligence (EI or EQ), namely: self-awareness; social awareness; self-management; relationship

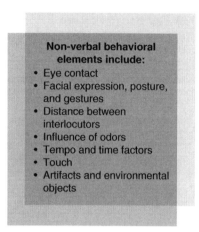

**Non-verbal behavioral elements include:**
- Eye contact
- Facial expression, posture, and gestures
- Distance between interlocutors
- Influence of odors
- Tempo and time factors
- Touch
- Artifacts and environmental objects

*Figure 4.1* Non-verbal behavioral elements.

management and positive impact on others. The estimate is that 90 percent of emotional communication is a non-verbal component. This includes body posture, movements and gestures, facial expressions, eye contact, touching, interpersonal distance. and greetings.

General knowledge about cultures and emotional intelligence facilitate the following important aspects of intercultural communications, all of which are necessary for intercultural leaders.

- Developing an understanding of bases of cultural differences (categorization, differentiation, in-group/out-group distinction, learning styles and attribution)
- Understanding the influences that culture has on communication and associated behaviors
- Acquiring a level of intellectual curiosity, openness, tolerance, and empathy towards foreign cultures and their inhabitants.

EQ, through its emphasis on intercultural awareness, empathy, self-awareness, and social skills, can strongly aid intercultural communication competences. This begs the question of what constitutes intercultural communication competence and how all this relates to the concept of connection within the Geoleadership framework.

Competent intercultural communication requires behaviors that are effective and appropriate. Effective intercultural communication means that people are able to achieve desired personal outcomes. To do so, competent intercultural leaders should be able to interact within a social environment to obtain mutually accepted goals. This presumes that competent leaders, as communicators, are able to identify their goals, assess the resources necessary to obtain those goals,

accurately predict the other communicator's responses, choose mutually workable communication strategies, enact those communication strategies, and, finally,
accurately and mutually assess the results of the interaction.

Appropriate communication necessitates the use of messages that are expected
in a given intercultural context, and actions that meet the expectations and
demands of the situation. This criterion for communication competence requires
the leader to demonstrate an understanding of the expectations for acceptable
behavior in a given situation. A competent intercultural leader must recognize
appropriate communication means recognizing the constraints imposed on their
behavior by different, culturally defined, sets of rules, avoiding violation of those
rules with inappropriate (perceived as impolite or offensive) responses, and enact
communication behaviors in an appropriate (e.g., clear, truthful, considerate,
responsive) manner.

The two criteria of effectiveness and appropriateness combine to influence the
quality of the interaction. Spitzberg[15] suggests four communication styles based
on the criterion in Figure 4.2.

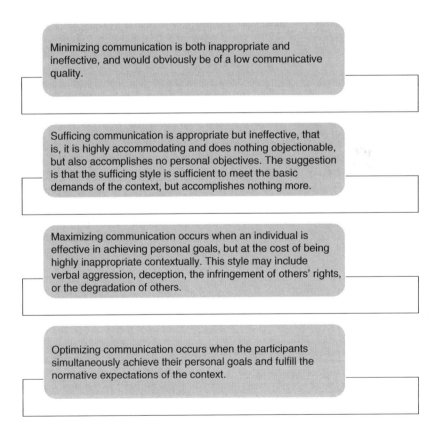

*Figure 4.2* Spitzberg's four communication styles.

While seemingly simplistic, this framework provides understanding of the dialectics of the competence criteria in intercultural social contexts. When communicators interact effectively and appropriately, they are co-orienting and coordinating their behaviors (verbal and non-verbal) to accomplish social functions, obtain personal goals, and conform to the normative expectations of the situation.

Interestingly though, some researchers examining "interculturality" suggest that intercultural communication is an interactive process whereby cultural differences are established not through external forces, but rather from the interactants themselves.[16] In other words, cultural identity is constituted by, through, and during intercultural exchanges. The implication is that in our intercultural conversations cultural identity is situationally emergent rather than normatively fixed. Despite there being sometimes obvious physical differences between two conversants (i.e., a person of Asian race and a person of Caucasian race), we do not enter intercultural communication interactions with dossiers printed on our foreheads that provide each other with cultural identification. In short, intercultural relationships require effortful, meaningful, and (dialectical) exchanges. Exhibit 4.1, an interview with Todd Fortner of the CAIP Group, provides a good example of the mindset and practice of an intercultural leader who epitomizes the concept of Communication.

---

### *Exhibit 4.1* Interview with Todd Fortner, president and board member of CAIP Group

Todd Fortner is president and board member of CAIP Group (Changshu Automotive Trim Company). The company was founded by Mr. Luo Xiaochun in 1992, and is headquartered in Changshu City. With facilities throughout China, it is the fastest growing privately run systems manufacturer of automotive interiors components. Todd, an American born and raised in Detroit Michigan, is a true testament to successful intercultural communication. Learn how he communicates across borders in the following interview.

*What are the most important decisions you make as a leader of an organization of which you have been a part? (This can also be answered from the perspective of what is the most important decision a leader/client makes in his or her organization.)*

To me, there are three important decisions global leaders need to make. The first is about setting the strategy and vision for the organization. How they inform people where the company is currently and where it's headed. How do they create a vision of the future that people will want to engage with and give their talents and energy to because they believe it will benefit them as much as it does the company? Second, how do they execute the vision? Where do they allocate resources (people, money, budgets)? Third, what sort of measurement system will help us track how well we are doing and will let us quickly know if we get off track?

*How do you encourage creative thinking within your organization (i.e., given the type of industry in which you operate)?*

Initially, many of our vehicles at CAIP Group were developed, designed, and innovated elsewhere. Because China is now moving up the value chain in terms of developing, engineering, innovating, and creating products for domestic Chinese consumers, our corporate culture is moving towards creation, craftsmanship, and customization. We have to be more at the forefront of understanding what people want today, tomorrow, and years from now, so we are day dreaming much more. (Love the word daydreaming! I like to use the word *day dreaming*. It sounds freer than brainstorming to me, which sounds like something is under pressure to get the right answer before the world crashes!)

*What is one characteristic that you believe every global business leader should possess?*

For global business leaders, it's not enough to be smart. We have to have stamina and endurance for the long haul. With our culture of fast food, quick results, instant information, and rapid response, we forget that it takes time to build solid relationships. CAIP Group was not an overnight success. It's been a long, hard trench warfare-type process. It hasn't been easy. I work in China, which has 5000 years of history. I recognize that change doesn't happen overnight. I stay focused on what's important, on making good products, and on making the customer happy. If our customers are happy, they will pay more for the product. It takes time to build customer loyalty. And, it takes time to build teams who can create that customer loyalty.

*What is the biggest challenge facing global business leaders today?*

The biggest challenge facing global business leaders today is overcoming difference in values. Differences in values can create significant misunderstandings. Work ethics differ, focus differs (for instance faith versus profit). In many places though, values are becoming more similar. There are niches where people from around the world are becoming more similar to each other. But, there are a lot of people who are not benefiting from globalization and it is creating tension in the world, and more quickly with the advent of technology, the Internet, the Smart Phone, etc.

For example, in China, the system is based on strong personalities, on people and relationships, versus in the West we have a "fair" system based on rules and laws. In business this is an issue when operating in another country, because the global leader is concerned with who's in charge and what's going to be successful. I believe people are happier with a leader who is leading them someplace, and who is concerned about their personal well-being along the way.

*What are your thoughts on globalization and how important is it for leaders to understand and embrace the rapid pace of technology? How has it changed the global landscape for business as a whole?*

To me, globalization is the awareness that there is a better standard of life in other places. For most people, whether they are in Africa, Asia, or North America, free and available information is setting a standard for their life and lifestyle that they try to reach. How this translates into the commercial aspect or consumer behavior, whether it's a socialist or capitalist system or how the businesses organize themselves is becoming less important. Global leaders now realize that they have to make a product or provide a service that reaches a higher standard if the company is to be successful. For example, in the automotive industry, we realize that there is a global standard for cars that all car companies need to reach. To be more successful, we have to achieve a higher level of production, of quality, of safety, of innovation, etc. Every car company in every country is pursuing this higher level and the learning process to be the best takes place at every level from people to tools to mobilizing the workforce to processes and so on.

*Do you think there is a downside to globalization, since it makes people more aware of the haves and the have nots?*

The downside to globalization is that people become frustrated when they don't reach a certain standard of living, and then they reject globalization and its benefits. Social tensions grow between those whose lifestyles are less and those who are better off. Today, people are finding that to maintain a higher standard of living, they have to keep working harder. If they don't, it deteriorates.

*What is one mistake you witness business leaders making more frequently than others? Can you give an example of such a mistake, particularly within your, you know sector, the car sector?*

Many global leaders don't realize that just because they were successful in one place, it doesn't necessarily prepare them to be successful in another place. Some people tend to be too cocky, confident, and arrogant. They don't listen; they think they know it all. Sometimes we just need to listen more, be humble, and recognize that we don't know everything when we come to a new place.

*Can you name a person who has had a tremendous impact on you as a leader? Maybe someone who has been a mentor to you? Why and how did this person impact your life?*

My father and my uncle have had tremendous impact on me as a leader. They were businessmen. My uncle helped start up Manpower. It was a fantastic vision. My father, along with being a businessman, also ran a high school. Running the high school, I think, was much more complicated than running a business. The kids need to be educated. Activities need to be managed. There is a small city of people who are part of the school who have health problems, social problems, and more. At the end of the day, his job was to ensure that in the midst of all this chaos, the kids received a high-quality education and had high test scores. I am also inspired by books like *The Fountainhead* by Ayn Rand. Ralph Waldo Emerson has had tremendous impact on my philosophy of life.

*Within the global economy, how important is it that a global business leader understands the key features of the Geoleadership Model?*

It's invaluable to have an academic framework to reference and to help global leaders think about the context. Everyone needs to study, learn, and think more broadly about their jobs and what they do.

*What do you like to ask other business leaders when you get the chance?*

Usually when I'm with someone in business, I don't want to talk about business. I want to try to get more into what makes this person a happy person and what makes them successful. I usually ask about their family, interests, and hobbies. I ask them about books and current events, but I avoid talking about business. I want to know the key attributes of a person that has made him or her successful. I want to understand the key tipping points in their life. Where did luck play a part? Where were they at the right place at the right time?

\*\*\*

Todd Fortner believes that learning how the systems of countries operate is a critical factor for global business leadership success. We agree. When communicating cross-culturally, whether the differences are slight or great, the culture of the receiver of the communication will act as a filter through which he or she interprets the message. And, this fact will be a determinant in the success of the project, team, and/or organization.

**Todd Fortner** is the president, CAIP Group, Ltd (Changshu Automotive Interior Parts Group, Ltd). CAIP Group is one of China's largest automotive interior and exterior systems suppliers. CAIP Group designs, engineers, and manufactures automotive instrument panels, cockpits, consoles, door panels, sun roof sun shades, luggage trim, and package trays for key automotive companies in China including BMW, Beijing Benz, Shanghai GM, Chevy Motors, Jaguar Land Rover, FAW VW, and FAW Audi. CAIP Group also have two joint ventures with Magna Corporation and Peguform Germany. Sales in 2012 are expected to be over 450 million USD.

Todd Fortner was born and raised in the metropolitan Detroit Michigan area. He is a graduate of Hope College in Holland, Michigan, and has graduate degrees from Thunderbird International Graduate School (MBA) and the Johns Hopkins School of Advanced Interior Studies Nanjing China Program. He pursued advanced graduate study at the Stanford NUS campus. Todd Fortner has worked as a Director for PricewaterhouseCoopers Consulting, a Business Development Director for Visteon Corporation, and has served as the President and part-owner of the CAIP Group in Changshu, China, for the past nine years.

By now, it may seem to the reader that we have characterized global business vis-à-vis globalization as a destructive force; in other words, the problem. On the contrary, we view global business as the potential unifier of societies. It is our conviction that people of diverse cultures can peacefully and creatively cohabit, indeed thrive, without altogether losing their unique character. To accomplish such a splendid transformation though, businesses and country governments must approach the process mindfully such as mentioned in Figure 4.3.

### *The art of communication*

Even though business leaders speak different languages around the world, the need to be understood is universal. Humor, for example, does not always translate well. Many U.S. firms have flat leadership structures wherein informal communications prevail and colloquial discussions take place daily. When you add in a global layer of staff who do not share the same verbal and non-verbal language cues, misunderstandings increase. Training can take place in order to teach the

A Geoleader can demonstrate the principle of Communication through the following practices and behaviors:

- Break out of your cultural comfort zone—Put yourself in a minority position within an unfamiliar culture—Engage with that culture on their terms.
- Volunteer your time with an organization that serves a culture with which you are unfamiliar.
- If you can afford it, travel to an unfamiliar country—Do not be satisfied with tourist experience—Meet people and summon all of your curiosity to find out about the worldview of this unfamiliar culture.

*Figure 4.3* The principle of "Communication" in practice.

meanings of different words and phrases in another language, but if a common tongue is chosen (i.e., English), there will be varying degrees of language meaning. For example, native U.S. English speakers may not understand the conveyed message of someone who learned English in England, India, or New Zealand. Exhibit 4.2 explores how communication can be challenging in the leadership process.

---

*Exhibit 4.2* **Interview with Jim Kouzes, co-author of**
**The Leadership Challenge**

Renowned leadership expert, Jim Kouzes, has been researching and teaching about the topic of leadership and communication for 30 years. He and his co-author (of *The Leadership Challenge*, Barry Posner) have studied this topic and been pioneers on the forefront of leadership study. Here we interview Jim and find that, not surprisingly, people across the globe want leaders who communicate the characteristics of honesty, integrity, and trustworthiness.

*What are the most important decisions you make as a leader of an organization of which you have been a part or with which you have consulted?*

My co-author, Barry Posner, and I have done research for over 30 years on what people look for and admire in their leaders and the behaviors that exemplify personal-best leadership practices. In one of our studies we asked this simple question: Imagine that someone walks into the room right now and says, "Hi, I'm your new leader." What questions immediately come to mind? The two top categories of responses were "Who are you?" and "Where are we headed?"

Based on these results, we'd say that the first important decision a leader has to make personally is around the question of "Who are you?" They need to wrestle with and make choices about "What do I stand for, what do I believe in, and what do I care about?" It's imperative that leaders be able to articulate the answers to these questions. And they have to be able to express them so that *others* clearly understand the leader's philosophy of leadership, his or her personal beliefs, and the values that guide his or her decisions and actions. These have to be so evident and transparent that when the leader isn't around, people still understand the guidelines for making decisions and taking action.

The second most important decision a leader needs to make is around the question, "Where are we headed?" Other ways to frame this question are: "What is our vision of the future and what will success look like when this project or initiative is complete?" This is true for leaders at all levels—business unit, department, team—and not just at the CEO level. Leaders need to make sure that they have so clearly articulated the answer to the question of where we're headed that others can see themselves in the final picture. They know the final destination, and they can envision themselves being there.

*How do you encourage creative thinking within your organization (i.e., given the type of industry in which you operate)?*

The most fundamental principle that supports innovation is trust. People in organizations won't create, innovate, or do things differently if they don't trust the leader and their team members. Innovation is about risk-taking; it's about taking initiative. If people feel that they will be punished if they step outside the formal boundaries or make mistakes or doing something different in the service of creativity and innovation, then they will not innovate.

The first thing leaders have to do is to create a culture of trust and mutual collaboration so people feel comfortable taking initiative. Building a culture of trust within which initiative is encouraged is one of the most important things a leader must do. One of my favorite quotes comes from the former Hollywood talent scout, Irving Paul (Swifty) Lazar, who said, "Sometimes I wake up in the morning and nothing's happening, so I make something happen by lunch." That's the kind of spirit needed if people are going to do things differently and make extraordinary things happen.

People who take initiative are seen by others as better leaders, and they are seen by others as more innovative and creative. It's important to keep in mind that challenging the process is not an end in itself. It is not challenge for challenge's sake: it is challenge for meaning's sake. We keep this alignment by knowing our values, our vision, and our purpose. Challenge with purpose is key.

According to a recent study from IBM, about half of an organization's innovations come from the outside, not from the inside! It's important to look outside the organization, not just inside, for new ideas and creative solutions. It's called "outsight," and it means looking beyond the formal boundaries of your department or organization in order to find creative ideas from other departments and/or best practices from other organizations. Encouraging "outsight" is an important way to stimulate creativity and innovation.

Lastly, creativity and innovation involve taking risks, and risks often mean making mistakes. The chances of getting it right the first time when innovating are nearly zero! Obviously in production mode, the organization should get it right every time, but when we're creating we nearly never get it right the first time. Experimentation, trial and error, and learning from mistakes are critical components of a learning culture.

*What is one characteristic that you believe every global business leader should possess?*

Our research, as well as other research by Project Globe, finds that the most important characteristics of global leaders are honesty, integrity, and trustworthiness. In our research, we use the word "honest" and such synonyms as trustworthiness, integrity, and so on. Exemplary global leaders are credible. They have high integrity, they are honest, and they are trustworthy. These are THE most important qualities that any leader can possess. Credibility is the foundation of leadership. If people don't believe in the messenger, they won't believe the message.

*What is the biggest challenge facing global business leaders today?*

The biggest challenge global business leaders face today is trust. Trust in business has been on a steep decline since the beginning of the Great Recession. As the economy improves, perhaps business leaders will be seen in a more favorable light globally; however, I believe the biggest challenge global leaders face today is regaining trust and confidence internally and externally. To the general public, business leaders are not seen as highly trustworthy.

Virtual trust is very difficult to establish. For people to feel fully confident in their leaders, they have to have some interpersonal interaction with them. While social media have enabled leaders to communicate more quickly and more deeply with people than ever before, we are much more likely to trust our leaders if we see them face to face.

*What effect do you think national culture has on business leadership decision-making? (This can also include how your own native national culture affects your decision-making.)*

One of my favorite examples of global leadership is a man named Titus Lokananta. Some time ago, Titus described himself as "an Indonesian-Cantonese, carrying a German passport, working for a Mexican company in the Czech Republic." Titus was a native of China, hence the Cantonese. His family moved to Indonesia when he was young. He changed his name to an Indonesian name in order to fit better into the local culture. He then went to school in Germany. Then went to work for a Mexican company with a factory in the Czech Republic. (He's since moved back to his native China where he's a manufacturing executive.) If you are Titus Lokananta, what is your national culture? Which culture do you pay attention to when you are leading people, theirs or ours?

In a global environment, our cultural backgrounds are certainly important. They are part of who we are. However, a single national culture should not dominate leaders' decision-making. What is important for my colleagues in the U.S. may or may not be important when leading a group in China. When making decisions that impact business in China, Mexico, the Czech Republic, Indonesia, or Germany, leaders need to be sensitive to multi-cultures, not just their own native culture. Another interesting question that this brings up is which leadership model does one use? Is it an Indonesian model, a Cantonese model, a German model?

We would suggest that there are universal principles that govern effective leadership around the globe. These are the principles that should guide your actions as a leader. People want leaders who set a good example, who have a vision of the future, and who treat people with dignity and respect. In every religion around the world, there is something akin to the Golden Rule, which is: Treat others as you would want to be treated yourself.

Let's say that we know that globally recognizing individuals for their exemplary performance is important. However, how I do that in China is going to be different than how I do that in the United States, the United Kingdom, Indonesia, or Argentina. As a global leader, I have to be sensitive to the specific "how" I execute, but the general guiding principle of encouraging the heart is universal.

*What are your thoughts on globalization and how important is it for leaders to develop their own self-awareness so as to adjust to the changing context(s) under which they operate in a given situation and/or organization? (This consciousness could include the leader's own cultural self-bias while operating with diverse constituents.)*

In addition to the universal truths about leadership we already talked about here are a few other thoughts.

I grew up near Washington D.C. in a family of immigrants to the U.S., my mother was Danish and my father was Greek. My mother was on the board of the local United Nations Association for years. Today, at 95-years-old, she continues to open her doors to people from different cultures. Over the last 50 years, she and my father hosted more than 100 people from other countries. These early life experiences motivated me to join the Peace Corps right after university. As you can see, my upbringing was to value multi-cultural views of the world. But what I learned from all these experiences was that I did not have to be someone other than I was. We were all allowed our different views, and we could work together, so long as we exhibited basic respect and openness for each other.

In addition to the common qualities of leadership that Barry Posner and I uncovered in our research—attributes such as being credible, forward-looking, competent, and inspiring—there is another truth that is vital to global leadership. It's the truth that "you can't do it alone." Successful global leaders are collaborative and team-oriented.

The work of Morgan McCall and George Hollenbeck[17] support this. They call it "the global mindset." In defining the global mindset, descriptors that made their list are: open-minded, flexible, adaptable, curious about others, interested in differences, empathetic, gets along well with others. These are key to effective global leadership. THE key differentiator is open-mindedness. My friend Claudio Fernandez-Araoz, a partner in the global executive search firm of Egon Zehnder International and author of the book called *Great People Decisions*, once said to me, "You have to be able to work with people as peers and see their differences not only as acceptable, but perhaps even preferable to your own." It's important to be able to think beyond your own culture. Claudio terms this, "Getting out of yourself." So, while global leaders have to be self-aware and know who they are, they also have to be able to get out of themselves in order to be effective in global leadership.

*Have you ever consulted with an organization that did or did not believe in facilitating an organizational culture capable of intercultural learning agility?*

A lot of my own work has been about being interculturally sensitive and having learning agility. Organizations do have their biases, but, particularly recently, I cannot say that I have worked in or consulted with an organization that did not believe in facilitating a culture of intercultural learning agility. Most of the organizations that I work with may be headquartered in the U.S., but they have plants and offices in Singapore, China, South America, and other countries around the world.

It's interesting to note that the lowest-scoring leadership behavior in our research is "asking for feedback." Feedback is an important part of learning, whether it is intercultural or your own learning from your own experience. We've found that the leaders who engage more frequently in learning activities—who devote more time to learning—are more effective at leading. When global leaders spend time learning and asking for feedback they are much more likely to be effective.

*What is one mistake you witness business leaders making more frequently than others? Do you think that some leaders make such errors due to their inability to be self-aware of their own national cultural bias, as mentioned above?*

If, as mentioned in response to an earlier question, open-mindedness is the key differentiator in successful global business leadership then not being open to the views of others will make it much more likely that a leader will be unsuccessful. Those who have done research on derailed executives, such as Morgan McCall, find that poor interpersonal relationship skills are generally the cause of failure. It's not strategic or technical knowledge, but interpersonal incompetence that causes leadership failures. If I had to put the answer to this question into one word, I would say "listening." Those who believe their job is to tell, not to ask, are going to be less effective than those who follow the dictum of "ask, don't tell." To be effective with people from different cultures, you have to spend more time listening than talking. You have to actively listen to others so that you understand fully what they are saying. Big mistakes are made when we assume we understood what the other person said, and didn't check our assumptions.

*Within the global economy, how important is it that a global business leader understands the key features of the Geoleadership Model?*

The Geoleadership Model is a good framework to use when thinking about leadership. Models are extraordinarily helpful in that they give leaders a frame of reference within which to make leadership decisions. Barry Posner and I have The Five Practices of Exemplary Leadership®. Other leadership researchers and scholars have their models. Anyone who wants to work globally needs to have a framework that applies in many different contexts and countries, and the Geoleadership Model does this.

*What do you like to ask other business leaders when you get the chance?*

There's a terrific scene in the movie *Invictus* about Nelson Mandela and the 1995 Rugby World Cup that comes to mind in response to this question. It's a scene in which Mandela asks Francois Pienaar to join him in his office. (The meeting actually took place, but the actual dialogue may be an adaptation of what transpired. Nonetheless, it's very instructive.) Francois Pienaar sits down. Mandela looks at him and says, "Tell me, Francois, what is your leadership philosophy?" I love this question. And, I love it of leaders. "Tell me, what is your leadership philosophy?"

***

In leading cross-culturally, a single national culture should not dominate a leader's communication. What is interesting about Jim and Barry's research though is that while leaders need to be sensitive to multi-cultures, not just their own culture, there are universal principles that govern effective leadership across the world. Jim mentions that these include setting a good example, having a vision for the future, and treating people with dignity and respect. These important aspects of how leaders "come across" are foundational to healthy, respectful intercultural communication.

**Jim Kouzes** is the Dean's Executive Fellow of Leadership, Leavey School of Business, Santa Clara University, and the co-author with Barry Posner of the internationally award-winning and best-selling book, *The Leadership Challenge*, with over two million copies sold. Jim and Barry have co-authored over 30 other books, including *The Truth About Leadership,*

*Credibility, Encouraging the Heart,* and *A Leader's Legacy,* as well as the *Leadership Practices Inventory* (LPI)—the top-selling off-the-shelf leadership assessment in the world. In 2009, they received the American Society for Training and Development (ASTD) 2009 Distinguished Contribution to Workplace Learning and Performance Award. The *Wall Street Journal* has named Jim as one of the ten best executive educators in the U.S., and in 2010 he was presented the Thought Leader Award by the Instructional Systems Association and in 2010 through 2012 was recognized as one of *HR Magazine*'s Top 20 Most Influential International Thinkers.

Diversity training is a start to build communication awareness, but it is a sustained commitment to understand that what is said is not always what is meant. For example, there is the classic example: U.S. business leaders have learned that in Japan, "yes" can actually mean "no." The topic of body language can also add in another layer of complexity. It is common that the issue of communication such as this does not cross the leader's radar until problems arise. Miscommunications can be minimized by initially having all those involved in the situation to actually meet each other face to face. In this era of virtual communications, misunderstandings increase because messages are mostly judged on their context and tone and not on the sender or his/her proficiency in all possible cultural connotations.

Given the spread of communication technology, it becomes imperative that situations above be taken into consideration. Simple things such as recognizing time differences can be the first step in realizing that any one firm contains a plethora of individuals with differing communication styles and tones. It is best not to readily judge a note from a foreign counterpart on the base level only if there is an initial negative reaction. Meeting those with whom you will communicate regularly will be integral to build a necessary foundation for future dialogues.

## The bottom line

The essential message in this chapter is that you must connect with people from other cultures to understand them. To understand people who are different from us, we must engage in meaningful communication. For the intercultural leader this means developing a keen general understanding of how communication works. Beyond this, however, the intercultural leader must learn the communication styles of other cultures so that s/he can know how other cultures operate and can learn how to discuss communication with other cultures. In other words, intercultural communication skill means being effective and appropriate within intercultural contexts. Working toward mutual understanding and agreement is a necessity. Being an effective communicator means having the ability to achieve desired outcomes. To do so, competent communicators should be able to influence their social environment to obtain those goals. This presumes that competent communicators are able to identify their goals, assess the resources necessary to obtain those goals, accurately predict the other communicator's responses, choose workable communication strategies, enact those communication strategies, and, finally, accurately assess the results of the interaction. Appropriate communication entails the use of messages that are expected in a given context, and actions that meet the expectations and demands of the cultural situation.

This criterion for communication competence requires leaders to demonstrate an understanding of the expectations for acceptable behavior in a given situation. Appropriate communication means the leader must recognize the constraints imposed on their behavior by different sets of rules, avoid violating those rules with inappropriate (e.g., impolite, abrasive, or bizarre) responses, and enact communication behaviors in a culturally appropriate (e.g., clear, truthful, considerate, responsive) manner. When communicators interact, they are co-orienting and coordinating their behaviors (verbal and non-verbal) to accomplish social functions, obtain personal goals, and conform to the normative expectations of the situation. To the extent that the communicators do these activities effectively and appropriately, they are considered competent communicators.

At a greater level, business leaders must adjust their mindset from simply trying to move into a new market to engaging with the culture for mutual benefit.

# 5   The principle of "Consciousness"

> "The ultimate value of life depends upon awareness and the power of contemplation rather than upon mere survival."
>
> —Aristotle[1]

We could fill up pages with clear and unequivocal messages from true sages all admonishing us that real knowledge comes from being aware of one's own ignorance. This sage advice is true for all people, and what is important for ordinary people is critical for extraordinary people; those people in positions of leadership.

In a recent study of intercultural specialists, researchers asked the experts to define the competencies needed by intercultural leaders and their top response was "self-awareness." Above all other competencies in the interpersonal competency category, participants reported that a business leader's ability to be self-aware of his or her culture, as well as that of others, should be of primary importance.[2] This finding reinforces the assertion that a leader arrives in a new cultural situation as ignorant, but then should move into the novice stage of awareness and should continue to evolve in knowledge through building awareness.[3] Building competence about a target culture means that leaders acquire a hands-on knowledge and skill base in combination with self-awareness. In sum, the quality and level of a leader's awareness largely determines his or her performance.

It turns out that a good number of studies have determined that competency occurs when an individual recognizes cultural differences and ultimately reconciles them by transforming conflicting values into complementary values.[4] Some researchers have concluded that the first level of interculturally skilled leadership is an awareness of the culturally learned starting points in the leader's thinking.[5] This intercultural awareness becomes the foundation of the leader's decision-making ability, through which the leader interprets knowledge and utilizes skills. However, the problem is that, until very recently, intercultural awareness has not been a subject for study in the generic leadership training.[6]

```
┌─ ── ── ── ── ── ── ── ── ── ── ── ── ── ── ── ──┐
│                                                 │
│           "CONSCIOUSNESS"                       │
│              DEFINED                            │
│                                                 │
│     Situational perspective with no judgment.   │
└─ ── ── ── ── ── ── ── ── ── ── ── ── ── ── ── ──┘
```

To Daniel Goleman, whose groundbreaking research led him to propose the concept of Emotional Intelligence, self-awareness is perhaps the most important of all EQ competencies.[7] As Goleman notes, and we agree, the higher a leader climbs in the organizational hierarchy the more important EQ, and therefore self-awareness, becomes. Self-awareness means being tuned in to one's own cognitive and emotional states, core values and beliefs, personal preferences, and biases. Self-awareness also means being able to assess how one's behavior affects other people; important in building trusting work relationships with subordinates, whether they are individual contributors or managers. In one recent study, the researcher found that emotional competence was a better predictor of leadership effectiveness than was IQ.[8]

The point of self-awareness is its use as a tool of exploration, receptivity, and compassion rather than as a device for self-judgment and self-loathing—it is not another channel for your internal critic. Self-awareness is a reflective practice meant to be a means to enhance your intentionality, higher order thinking, and interpersonal skills. Despite what you may think, interpersonal skill begins with learning how to interact effectively with *yourself*. Largely, self-awareness is an internal process; however, its effect is to both, relationship with self, and relationship with others. The objective is actually to become more, *you*. Paradoxically, the more you understand yourself, the more open and receptive you can be with other people. Only with a high level of self-awareness can intercultural leaders engage the trust and commitment of others that is necessary to sustain organizational excellence.

Interculturalists have identified several interpersonal skills associated with self-awareness, determined necessary for intercultural leaders. The list of skills and attributes include curiosity, observation, reflection, adaptability, empathy, and perspective taking. To these, we add mindfulness and, taken all together, we categorize this skill area as consciousness. Consciousness is the quality of *being* in a state of total awareness.

## Mindfulness

Mindfulness is not the same as concentration. Concentration is the willful extended focus of one's attention to something. It is the particularization of one's attention. Concentration is an important skill, but is not our focus. On the other hand, mindfulness is the fully opened and freely receptive quality of observation, and it is a vital skill.

Mindfulness is the state of complete awareness achieved through receptivity and observation. There are four areas of mindfulness: awareness of one's body and all of its functions; awareness of sensations and feelings; awareness of thoughts, beliefs, and attitudes; and, lastly, awareness of mental and emotional hindrances.

In many world religions and spiritual orientations, mindfulness is taught as a practice through such methods as meditation. While we are not making recommendations for religion or spirituality, we do note that neuroscientists have studied brain functioning of meditators and found that they are healthier than non-meditators because they are able to shift their mental focus from the stress-prone right frontal cortex to the calmer left frontal cortex. Additional and important information of such studies for leaders is that meditators (people practicing various meditation techniques including mindfulness meditation) were able to shift their mental foci more readily than those who do not meditate.

## Curiosity

Curiosity is a natural function of human consciousness and it can be developed. Quite simply curiosity leads people to consider both life within themselves, and life outside, themselves. Effectively, it is a process of inquisition, of questioning what, how, when, where, and why phenomena exist. Leaders require a certain level of skill in being curious about the world in which they live in order to be able to observe, assess, derive meaning, and envision a future. Psychologically speaking, curiosity is a primary driver of human motivation.

The success of a leader's influence in compelling others to follow is in their ability to question, which then leads the best leaders to the right answers. Good leaders take time to listen, engage, imagine, and investigate alternatives. They inspire others through their own curiosity.

Successful intercultural leaders set their curiosity loose in new cultural settings to satisfy a thirst to discover the possibilities. In the classic Bennis text, *On Becoming a Leader*,[9] the management guru discusses the virtue of curiosity in several facets of leadership from desiring to understand their own thinking process, to an insatiable desire to discover all that can be known.

Curiosity leads us to discovery and coupled with human compassion will compel leaders to engage people from different cultures from a place of genuine interest. Curiosity coupled with intelligence forms the cornerstones of vision. Curiosity coupled with discernment prepares a leader to evaluate and make ethical decisions. Curiosity coupled with imagination creates the fertile ground of innovation. Interculturally competent leaders develop a sense of wonderment. The capability and capacity for wonderment often dissipates in people after childhood; brilliant leaders, and interculturally competent leaders, enhance their sense of wonderment rather than lose it. Curiosity is an important element in adaptation skills. It prompts us to explore new frontiers.

## Observation

Closely connected to curiosity is the ability to observe. Leaders, in fact, have a lot to observe. They must build perceptual abilities that enable them to perceive behavior in their staff, consumers, and beyond; they must be able to perceive and scan what is going on in the marketplace; they must be able to perceive trends; they must perceive a complex array of data; and they must be able to accurately describe, analyze, and make meaning out of what they observe. Organizational members look to their leaders to help make sense of what is going on in the world around them.

Because meaning-making is an important aspect of leadership, leaders in intercultural contexts face greater complexity in deriving meaning from multiple layers of context (e.g., local, global, intercultural). The complexity lies in the layers of pan-cultural languages, norms, symbols, attitudes, beliefs, and laws. Facing such complexity, the leader must perceive issues, problems, opportunities, and threats from his/her own culture, the host culture, the regional, national, and global perspective. In such situations, leaders must be able to discern whether, for example, a threat is only perceived as a threat in certain stakeholder groups and not others due to naïveté, culture, or something else.

Observation skills require first that the leader has awareness of his/her biases and filters (generation, gender, ethnicity, orientation, profession, religion, etc.). Second, perfecting observation skills means learning how to observe descriptively and evaluatively. Descriptive observation (objective) means creating a picture of a situation in as neutral a manner as possible. Evaluative observation means being able to discern risk, danger, opportunities, and possibilities. It is a quality of astuteness.

## Reflection

Reflection is the ability to learn through careful consideration; often reflection means considering previous actions, events, or decisions. Two foci of reflective activity are important for leaders: external and self. In reflecting on external life, leaders should consider all aspects of their responsibilities, including financial responsibility, strategic purpose, structure, corporate culture, and stakeholder groups. Self-reflection is an introspective activity in which one poses and answers provocative questions towards examining one's values, attitudes, beliefs, and biases. Self-reflection must include the leader's sense of his/her job, so that positional power does not infect interactions. In Exhibit 5.1 is a self-reflection survey to assess your leadership effect.

*Exhibit 5.1* **Leader self-awareness assessment**

| Behaviors | Seldom | Sometimes | Often | Frequently | Always |
|---|---|---|---|---|---|
| | 1 | 2 | 3 | 4 | 5 |
| 1 I recognize the effect of my emotions on work performance. | | | | | |
| 2 I recognize the effect of my emotions on relationships with others. | | | | | |
| 3 I recognize my personal impact on group and team functioning. | | | | | |
| 4 I can describe my strengths realistically. | | | | | |
| 5 I can describe my weaknesses realistically. | | | | | |
| 6 I work to understand others' perspectives. | | | | | |
| 7 I take time to discern the dynamics of all stakeholder groups. | | | | | |
| 8 I listen to others actively, checking to ensure my understanding. | | | | | |
| 9 I discern non-verbal communication accurately. | | | | | |
| 10 I use a variety of techniques to inform my self-reflections. | | | | | |
| 11 I seek feedback from all relevant constituencies about my behavioral impact. | | | | | |
| 12 I show an interest in others who are different from me. | | | | | |

**Your score: Add together all of your circled values for a grand total and compare to the chart below:**
**51–60 = Excellence  41–50 = Constructive awareness**
**31–40 = Opportunity  21–30 = Behavioral and attitudinal change required**

## Adaptability

Adaptability has always been important for leaders and managers; however, in an increasingly complex global society and marketplace, adaptability is the crucible. Without adaptability a leader and his/her organization faces extinction. In an environment that is constantly in flux, leaders must be able to respond to, if not predict, change. Change brings novel situations, which in turn require leaders to understand that what worked before may not work again. In other words, novelty places people in learner mode where prior experience is tested. This means that a significant ingredient in adaptability is learning agility—being able to learn something new, adeptly and swiftly.

Several elements comprise adaptability: learning agility (cognitive flexibility, curiosity, memory, recall, synthesis); attitudinal adjustment; and behavior modification. In order for an adaptation to quicken, the person must align values, attitudes, beliefs, thoughts, and behaviors. Unless the leader aligns an adaptation in all of these areas, the resulting misalignment creates incongruent behavior. Often, organizational personnel will interpret the leader's incongruent behavior as lack of integrity. Such interpretations by personnel can create an atmosphere of mistrust.

In a global context, where leaders are responsible for intercultural enterprise, layers of culture create even more complexity to the leader's adaptive competence. In intercultural situations, the leader is adapting to or within a cultural context. In such cases, the leader's alignment of cognitive, attitudinal structure and behavior must take into consideration the cultural expectations.

## Perspective taking

One quality that has paradoxical consequences for leaders working in intercultural contexts is perspective taking: the ability to empathetically understand someone else's perspective and worldview. It is paradoxical in that, while this characteristic portends a successful performance of a leader working within an intercultural context, it also portends a negative rating of that leader by his/her domestic peers.

Perspective taking requires more from the leader than mere concern about other people. It requires that the leader tangibly recognize and understand the experience of other people. Through understanding perspective taking as a process are the abilities to consider and adjust to the thoughts and emotions of oneself and other people, to consider and contrast various religious and other beliefs, consider and adjust one's motives, and to elicit and consider prior experience. In Exhibit 5.2 is a brief perspective-taking assessment.

*Exhibit 5.2* **Leader perspective-taking assessment**

The following statements inquire about your thoughts and feelings in a variety of situations. In the space before each item, indicate how well it describes you by choosing the appropriate number on the scale at the top of the page. Read each item, reflect on it before responding, and answer honestly.

*Scale:*

*Describes Me Well*                  *Does Not Describe Me At All*

**1**       **2**       **3**       **4**       **5**

——— 1. Before criticizing somebody, I try to imagine how I would feel if I were in his/her place.

——— 2. If I'm sure I'm right about something, I don't waste much time listening to other people's arguments.

——— 3. I sometimes try to understand my friends better by imagining how things look from their perspective.

——— 4. I believe that there are two sides to every question and try to look at them both.

——— 5. I sometimes find it difficult to see things from the "other guy's" point of view.

——— 6. I try to look at everybody's side of a disagreement before I make a decision.

——— 7. When I'm upset at someone, I usually try to "put myself in their shoes" for a while.

There is no score for the leader perspective-taking assessment because it is meant to provoke reflection only. There is no right or wrong and no profile associated with it.

A Geoleader can demonstrate the principle of Consciousness through the following practices and behaviors:

- Practice mindfulness techniques—Meditate.
- Expand your awareness quotient—Periodically assess and review your awareness of your environment and yourself.
- Build and enhance your natural curiosity—Take critical thinking, or creative thinking courses.
- Develop your observational skills—Practice descriptive and evaluative observation.
- Consider the stakeholders as individuals and as groups—Learn the techniques of ethnographers.

*Figure 5.1* The principle of "Consciousness" in practice.

In the interview in Exhibit 5.3 with Maya Hu-Chan, the principle of Consciousness stated above can be seen in the juxtaposition of cross-cultural understanding and global leadership.

*Exhibit 5.3* **Interview with Maya Hu-Chan, president, Global Leadership Associates**

Rated a top Leadership Guru from Asia by Leadership Guru International, international management consultant Maya Hu-Chan is an expert who specializes in global leadership and cross-cultural business skills. Her book, *Global Leadership: The Next Generation*, has been translated into Chinese and Polish and greatly supports and is in alignment with *Global Business Leadership*. Maya's insights for global leaders include a strong emphasis on adaptability and self-awareness as keys to successful leadership.

*What are the most important decisions that a leader of an organization must make?*

The key decisions I find global leaders need to make are around developing themselves and their people. This is a critical differentiator and applies to not just their immediate teams, but also to their global talent. First, they have to have self-awareness. They are no longer working at a local level, they are global leaders. As they develop, they have to be mindful and ask themselves: How can I learn about the national culture (or cultures) I'll be operating in? How do I understand the corporate culture of this area? How do I adapt my leadership style to the fast changing and unpredictable global business environment? How do I build strategic relationships with my global customers, employees, and business partners? Just because a leader has worked at the same company for 15 or 20 years, does not mean that they know the corporate culture in another part of the world. So, how do they learn the corporate culture as well as the national culture? These are important decisions about self-development global leaders must make if they are to be successful.

Also important are decisions around developing people. Looking at people as the most important asset, a leader must decide how to recruit the best talent and then retain and develop them. What is the best strategy to develop global talent at multiple levels? How do they create a global talent pipeline? How do they develop local talent around the globe, rather than deploying "experts" from company headquarters to different countries within which they do business?

These are very critical decisions leaders must make if they are going to be successful in the global arena.

*How have global leaders you have worked with encouraged creative thinking within their organizations?*

Innovation is very important to companies if they are going to stay competitive in today's global environment. Every company is looking for ways to be more innovative, for ways to produce better products and services, and for ways to be leaders in their industries.

One of my executive coaching clients is the chief innovation officer of a Global Fortune 50 organization. The organization isn't in a highly innovative industry, like technology; however, it puts strong emphasis on innovation. This has helped them to be more successful. They make innovation a priority, and in doing so they encourage creative thinking. If an organization does not measure its teams by how creative or innovative they are, if they do not put emphasis on innovation, then people will not put forth the effort to come up with new ideas. They will stagnate in the attitude, "If it isn't broken, why fix it?" As a result the company will plateau and probably over time, die out.

The question then, how do you encourage people to make creativity a priority is answered in many ways. Some companies measure creativity by how many ideas (business, product, improvements, etc.) their people put forth every year or even every quarter. Companies will measure performance based on this, so people actively engage in innovating new processes and products.

Leaders not only have to make creativity and innovation a priority, but they also have to lead by example. Encouraging people to come up with and share their ideas, empower them to contribute their thoughts, even if they are not fully formed, and then build on those ideas. Also, it's important to include ideas from people in all functions and backgrounds at the organization. Encouraging everyone to participate, regardless their personal or cultural background or role in the organization, is very important. It is the global leaders' responsibility to give everyone a chance to be heard.

Finally, another very important piece in encouraging creative thinking and innovation is to actually turn the thoughts into tangible business ideas and/or business plans and then execute them. This makes a huge difference. People see that their ideas are not just talk, but that they add value to the business and become concrete products, processes, etc.

*What is one characteristic that you believe every global business leader should possess?*

One characteristic that every global business leader should possess is adaptability. To be a successful global leader it's not just about how many degrees you have, how many years of experience you have, or how many awards you have won, it's how adaptable you are as a global leader. A global leader truly has to walk the talk in terms of being flexible, adaptable, open-minded, inclusive, and appreciating diverse global talent. Working in the global arena is very challenging. Leaders who have adaptability are resilient and thus far more likely to succeed.

*What is the biggest challenge facing global business leaders today?*

My answer to this question ties back to adaptability. Global leaders today are faced with many challenges. They are constantly dealing with uncertainty and change. The global business arena today is unpredictable. It is a VUCA (Volatility, Uncertainty, Complexity and Ambiguity) world![10] The biggest challenges leaders face today are how to manage constant change and how to handle complex global business situations. And, there is no set answer to these challenges. Global leaders have to figure out new and creative answers as they go along, so they must be very adaptable, very flexible, and very creative if they are to succeed.

*What effect do you think national culture has on business leadership decision-making? (This can also include how your own native national culture affects your decision-making.)*

The effect that national culture has on business leadership is immense. It affects everything!

There are four sets of cultural dimensions or characteristics that have direct impact on how leaders make decisions. For example, one of these key characteristics is risk-oriented versus restraint-oriented. Some cultures are more risk averse, and some are more restraint averse. Neither is good or bad, but they are embedded in the culture and so have direct impact on how leaders make decisions. A second key cultural dimension is group versus individual. Leaders from individualistic cultures are more likely to take personal responsibility for their decisions. They own their decisions and are personally accountable for them. Group-oriented cultures often take longer to make decisions because they build a consensus and get buy-in from all the groups involved. In this way, everyone is part of the decision. This cultural dimension has a huge effect on how decisions are made. A third set of cultural dimensions is egalitarianism versus hierarchy. A culture that values equality values everyone's opinion. So, regardless a person's status, position, background, or tenure, everyone's opinion is valued when decisions are made. In a hierarchical culture, decisions are made at the top and everyone not at the top follows. A fourth set of cultural dimensions is task versus relationship. Many cultures are task-oriented. If a leader is task-oriented, he or she will look at the challenge from the standpoint of getting from Point A to Point B. What is the most efficient way to get to the goal? A leader who is more relationship-oriented will look at who will be impacted, who will need to be consulted, who might be offended or affected in a positive or negative way. Relationship-oriented leaders look at the people factors first and so can end up with a very different decision than those who lead from a task-oriented perspective.

*What are your thoughts on globalization and how important is it for leaders to develop their own self-awareness so as to adjust to the changing context(s) under which they operate in a given situation and/or organization? (This consciousness could include the leader's own cultural self-bias while operating with diverse constituents.)*

Self-awareness is extremely important as global leaders continually adjust to the changing contexts within which they operate in their organizations. Having self-awareness of one's strengths as well as weaknesses is extremely important as leaders navigate the global arena. Global leaders must know their own biases (the experiences, thoughts, and assumptions about people, places, and things that all people carry), if they are going to self-correct when their own ideas are holding them back. Another question is raised when thinking about self-awareness. How do you raise self-awareness? There are a few techniques that have proven very helpful. Having a 360-degree assessment is a very useful tool. Working with an executive coach is also very helpful in developing emotional and cultural intelligence.

In recent years, I've worked with a couple of leaders who have addressed this issue of self-awareness. One leader, born in Israel, lived and worked in the U.S. most of his adult life. Working at a global company, he has worked with leaders from around the world. When he was promoted to a country manager in South America, he needed to raise his awareness about how he came across to people there. He was extremely smart, but didn't realize that many of the people perceived him very negatively. He received feedback and did the work to change his behavior. He stopped interrupting people. He learned to listen. He acts with humility and empathy. These simple changes made a huge difference for him as a leader.

Another leader who is Asian is also extremely successful. When he started in a new global role, he was not aware that different cultures operate differently. He received feedback and from it came to the realization that his behaviors and the words he was using were being interpreted differently than he intended by those of different cultures. He started working on getting to know people. He let people get to know him. As a result, he was able to bridge the gap between himself and people in different countries. In both of these examples, the global leaders' successes really had to do with becoming self-aware about their behaviors, leadership and communication styles through honest feedback, and then working to change their behavior.

*What is one mistake you witness business leaders making more frequently than others? Do you think that some leaders make such errors due to their inability to be self-aware of their own national cultural bias, as mentioned above?*

Global leaders make the common mistake of assuming without having all of the facts. They make assumptions and draw conclusions too quickly. I've seen this many times, and it is particularly dangerous when work-ing in the global arena. There are many differences: People from differ-ent companies work differently. They operate differently. They have different business practices and build relationships differently. They buy and sell differently. In addition, their local environments, whether it be in regulations, customs, holidays, or customs, are very different. When a leader assumes too quickly, and does not ask questions and get a full understanding of what is happening, then they tend to make the wrong decisions based on wrong assumptions. This is not a good combination for successful global leadership!

*Can you name a person who has had a tremendous impact on you as a leader? Maybe someone who has been a mentor to you? Why and how did this person impact your life?*

Marshall Goldsmith has had a tremendous impact on me. He is my mentor, and has had a tremendous impact on me as a consultant, a parent, a coach, and a person. He has had such an immense impact on my life overall. Sometimes when I am dealing with tough situations, I will ask myself, "What would Marshall do?" And, his words will come to me: "Take a deep breath and let it go. Just let it go." He has taught me that although things are not always perfect, if I focus on the negative things are worse. If I focus on the positive, life is good. I have two autistic children, and they have tremendous challenges. It is difficult. But, I am very grateful for my children, who are so sweet and loving. I love them with all my heart. I also have a child who is typical and wonderful too. Nobody's life is perfect. We all have problems. Marshall has taught me to step back and look at the whole picture. I have a great family and a wonderful career! I get to work with wonderful people and do things I love every day. I remember every day that my life is good and I count my blessings.

*What do you like to ask other business leaders when you get the chance?*

I like to ask global leaders what are the biggest lessons they have learned? What are the most valuable lessons they have learned as global leaders? I enjoy hearing their stories. Whether the story is personal or related to their business success/failure, I like to hear about their "aha" moments.

\*\*\*

As we mention throughout this chapter, having self-awareness is key to adjusting to the constant changes of the global marketplace. We appreciate Maya's insights on this subject and also her suggestions as to how leaders can raise their own self-awareness and that of their teams.

**Maya Hu-Chan** is an international management consultant, executive coach, author, and sought after speaker. She specializes in global leadership, executive coaching, and cross-cultural business skills. Maya was recently rated one of the Top 100 Thought Leaders by *Leadership Excellence Magazine*, and Top Leadership Guru from Asia by Leadership Guru International. Maya has trained and coached thousands of leaders in

Fortune Global 500 companies throughout North America, Asia, Europe, South America, and Australia. She has worked extensively in China, Taiwan, Singapore, Hong Kong, Korea, and Japan, helping global companies to develop their senior executives and high-potential leaders as well as their teams. Maya has delivered many training programs in English and Mandarin Chinese. Her book *Global Leadership: The Next Generation* was chosen by Harvard Business School as one of their Working Knowledge recommended books. This book has been translated into Chinese and Polish.

It is not surprising that Marshall Goldsmith's interview should follow Maya Hu-Chan's. As a pioneer in the field of executive coaching and 360-degree feedback, Marshall is a mentor, teacher, and advisor to many executive coaches and global leaders, including Maya. From self-awareness, a leader can become cognizant of strengths and weaknesses and then take the necessary steps to make behavioral changes, which leads us to Marshall Goldsmith's area of expertise, as seen in Exhibit 5.4.

## Exhibit 5.4 Interview with Marshall Goldsmith, executive coach, speaker, and best-selling author

Marshall Goldsmith was a pioneer in the use of customized 360-degree feedback as a leadership development tool. His early efforts in providing feedback and then following up with executives to measure changes in behavior were precursors to what eventually evolved as the field of executive coaching. A writer and editor of leadership works since his first book, *The Leader of the Future* with Frances Hesselbein and Richard Beckhard, his works have since been translated into 28 languages and have sold millions of copies.

*What are the most important decisions that a leader of an organization must make?*

The most important decision that a leader makes in his/her organization is with regards to the mission of the organization and the organization's vision for the future. All other decisions should stem from this base.

*What is one characteristic that you believe every global business leader should possess?*

An interesting question, I don't believe there is just one characteristic every leader should possess. Here's why. A few years ago, as part of a multi-country research project aimed at helping global organizations understand the most important characteristics of the leader of the future, my colleagues and I asked leading companies to identify future leaders who have the potential to be the CEO of a global organization. Rather than the usual process of asking *today's* leaders (who will not be there) to describe the future of leadership, we decided to ask *tomorrow's* leaders. We received input from these future leaders through focus groups, interviews, and surveys. In total, we received input from over 200 future leaders who were nominated from 120 major companies around the world.

In comparing the desired characteristics of the leader of the future with the desired characteristics of the leader of the past we found both similarities and differences. Many qualities of effective leadership were seen as being important for yesterday, today, and tomorrow. Characteristics like vision, integrity, focus on results, and ensuring customer satisfaction were seen as factors that were critical in the past and will be so in the future.

Five key factors emerged that were seen as being clearly more important in the future than in the past include: 1) thinking globally, 2) appreciating cultural diversity, 3) demonstrating technological savvy, 4) building partnerships, and 5) sharing leadership.

*What is the biggest challenge facing global business leaders today?*

Globalization has a major impact on global business leaders today. In the past, major companies could focus on their own country or, at most, their own region. Those days are over. In the new world, a financial crisis begins in Thailand and spreads to Southeast Asia dramatically influencing the rest of the world. Globally connected markets mean that leaders need to understand the legal and political implications worldwide rather than just in their own backyards. Producers have to manage global production, marketing, and sales teams. Leaders who are stuck in local thinking cannot compete in a global marketplace. Leaders who make globalization work in their organization's favor have a huge competitive advantage.

*What effect do you think national culture has on business leadership decision-making?*

Global leaders have to get beyond their own national culture to understand economic and legal differences as well as the social and behavioral differences that are part of working around the world. Critical to business leadership decision-making is respect for differences in people and cultures. This is one of the most important qualities of a successful global leader, and it includes respect and appreciation of differences both big and small that make up a unique culture. For example, few Europeans or Americans who work in the Middle East have taken the time to read (much less understand) the Koran. It is clear that religion is one of the most important variables that impact behavior in the region—and perhaps the political climate of the world. Smaller issues, such as the meaning of gifts or the importance of timeliness also need to be understood.

*How important is it for leaders to develop their own self-awareness so as to adjust to the changing context(s) under which they operate in a given situation and/or organization?*

Self-awareness is the mark of a great leader. While leaders have always worked to understand others, today they must devote significant effort to understanding themselves. That is to personal mastery. Personal mastery essentially means having a heightened self-awareness, a deep understanding of one's own behavior, motivators, and competencies, and having "emotional intelligence," which allows one to monitor and manage rather than control or suppress his or her emotional state. This is critical if leaders are to be flexible and adjust to the pace of rapid change today.

*What is one mistake you witness business leaders making more frequently than others?*

Any human, in fact, any animal will tend to repeat behavior that is followed by positive reinforcement. The more successful we become, the more positive reinforcement we get—and the more likely we are to experience the success delusion. The one mistake I witness global business leaders making more frequently than any others is the belief that: "I behave this way. I am successful. Therefore, I must be successful because I behave this way." This is wrong! We all want to hear what we want to hear. We want to believe those great things that the world is telling us about ourselves. Our belief in ourselves helps us become successful. It can also make it very hard for us to change. By understanding why changing behavior can be so difficult for successful leaders, we can increase the likelihood of making the changes that we need to make, in our quest to become even more successful.

*Can you name a person who has had a tremendous impact on you as a leader? Maybe someone who has been a mentor to you? Why and how did this person impact your life?*

Passing in 2012, Dr. Paul Hersey was an icon in the world of leadership development. He, along with Ken Blanchard, developed Situational Leadership—a model that has helped millions of managers around the world become more effective leaders. Paul was also the co-author of *Management and Organizational Behavior*, one of the best-selling management texts in history. Along with all of this, Paul went out of his way to help lots of young people—including me—get started in their careers. When asked about his own success, he always humbly replied, "I am just standing on the shoulders of giants." As for whatever success I have achieved, I am clearly just standing on the shoulders of Paul Hersey.

*What do you like to ask other business leaders when you get the chance?*

I help successful leaders achieve positive, lasting change in behavior: for themselves, their people, and their teams. I ask them to get feedback from their most important stakeholders, pick important behavior to change, follow-up with stakeholders in a disciplined way and get better.

*** 

Isn't it surprising to hear that leaders' biggest mistakes are made in response to the behaviors that have made them successful? For global leaders, and humans in general, it is of the utmost importance to be aware of our tendency to repeat behavior that has been followed by positive reinforcement if we are to adapt to the changing times. A great insight and duly noted!

**Dr. Marshall Goldsmith** has recently been recognized as the Most Influential Leadership Thinker in the world at the Thinkers 50 Conference (sponsored by *Harvard Business Review*). He was also listed as the no. 7 Greatest Business Thinker in the world in the global bi-annual study sponsored by *Harvard Business Review*. Other acknowledgments include: *American Management Association*—top 50 thinkers and leaders who have influenced the field of management over the past 80 years; *Institute for Management Studies*—lifetime achievement award (one of two ever awarded); *Wall Street Journal*—top 10 executive educators; *Forbes*—5 most-respected executive coaches; *Economic Times (India)*—top CEO coaches of America; and *Fast Company*—America's preeminent executive coach. Marshall is one of a select few executive advisors who have been asked to work with over 150 major CEOs and their management teams. He is the million-selling author of 34 books, including *New York Times* best-sellers, *MOJO* and *What Got You Here Won't Get You There*—a *Wall Street Journal* no. 1 business book and winner of the Harold Longman Award for business book of the year.

## The bottom line

We live in a changing global culture in which there are two driving and ostensibly opposing forces: one is globalization, and the other is the counter-globalization fueled by political and religious factions. No one is sure what globalization will lead to; however, most authorities and theorists believe that globalization will continue. Some observers have speculated that globalization is an innate drive in humans from the basic motivation that propels people to connect with each other, to profit by trading, to spread their beliefs, to exploit resources, and the ambition to dominate others.

In the past, leadership theory and practice have tended to be from a universal, essentialist, one-size-fits-all strategy. However, it seems clear that working in global and intercultural contexts requires leaders of a different kind. While it may be impossible for individuals to be expertly prepared to lead across all cultures, some characteristics and skills do seem to fit in all cultural contexts.

The critical message of this chapter on leader consciousness is that leaders working in intercultural contexts must develop the skills of a sage individual. To build such a high level of sophistication in leadership requires that the leader becomes adroit in mindfulness, awareness, observation from a 360-degree perspective and from an objective perspective of self. Keen curiosity, observation, awareness, and mindfulness skills are mandatory for leaders to be able to deal with the "contrasts" and ambiguity of intercultural leadership. In the next chapter, we explore the topic of contrasts.

# 6   The principle of "Contrasts"

*Ambiguity*, from the Latin *ambigere*, which means, "to wander," does not just mean, "Having two or more meanings." It also means "doubtfulness or uncertainty as regards to interpretation" (*American Heritage Dictionary of the English Language*, Third Edition). In other words, ambiguity means that there is doubt, disagreement, tentativeness, or contrasting perspectives.

To say that we live in a world that is complex and seems at times rife with ambiguity would be an understatement. The fact is that our lives are lived amidst contrasts from the most mundane to the exotic. For leaders and managers, the modern business environment presents either routine or novel situations. While this always has been true to some extent, in the modern business world, leaders and managers face a changeable continuum in the ratio of novel to routine. As we have discussed in previous chapters, a leader faces ambiguity as a normal aspect of the role and intercultural leaders face increased ambiguity because of the complexity dealing with multiple layers of culture.

## "CONTRASTS"
### DEFINED

Cultural differences in leading and motivating followers.

What is ironic is that the more ambiguous the situation, the more leadership is needed. Consider your own experience in routine work situations: Do you feel confused? Chances are that you do not. Now consider what happens in novel work situations, when you encounter something you have never encountered before and you do not have an explanation for what is occurring: How comfortable are you in these situations, especially if you are required to make a swift decision? Chances are that you desire some type of assistance; most likely, you desire guidance. The more urgent the situation, the greater is the desire for relief. That is what leaders do, provide relief, meaning, and the path forward—from the front-line supervisor who answers a novel procedural question, to the enterprise president, who steps up to the podium to address personnel when two competitors merge, seemingly ending life as usual at work.

The truth remains that leadership is all about deriving meaning out of a *living* context and the capability to envision a plausible future. In order to derive meaning, a person must be able to discriminate one event or phenomena from another. Basic physics of Field Theory informs us that humans are in a constant state of discerning "figure" from "ground." This simply means that we perceive reality via a dimensional picturing during which we select, through our various sensory capabilities, that which we deem important against that which we perceive as unimportant. The "rightness" or "wrongness" of our interpretations may very well be reliant upon our ability to convince ourselves and other people of the reality that we perceive. Enter culture which, effectively, presents cultural members with "automatic" interpretations according to some previously estimated principle or truth.

Contrasts and ambiguity commonly occur in the eyes of the beholders, when multiple (cultural) interpretations are represented in the situation. The degree of effect of cultural differences on people depends on the level of cultural sensitivity and openness of the parties involved. The perceivers in any situation act based on choices determined through, albeit brief, interpretive exercises, where the perceivers choose the (figurative) lens with which they make their choices. Again, culture provides convenient solutions to the dilemma of deriving meaning. Choosing convenience too quickly presents the possibility that the chooser closes themselves off from greater potential, or opportunities.

Leaders face contrasts and ambiguity at multiple levels in their roles. While ambiguity typically feels uncomfortable for most people, the discomfort occurs because of uncertainty, of not knowing the outcome. What is helpful for people is realizing that ambiguity occurs because people recognize that there is more than one answer, more than one way forward. Rather than perceiving this as negative, effective leaders perceive ambiguity as an opportunity to create something new in the place of what used to be.

## Ambiguity zones

Values and beliefs undergird most of our perceptual experiences and, as discussed previously, culture plays a significant role in shaping our values and beliefs. In organizations, leaders face ambiguity in two main areas: role and values. Role elements refer to those aspects of leadership that involve the leader's role, the leader–follower relationship, vision, and results. Role elements are the *content* of

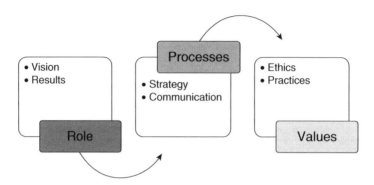

*Figure 6.1* Role, processes, values.

leadership. Value elements include values and operating principles, ethics, and corporate citizenship. Value elements are the *importance* attributed to life issues. These ambiguity areas are shown in Figure 6.1.

### Role elements

In Chapter 2, we briefly discussed the point that leadership is conceived of differently across cultures. How leaders, working in an intercultural context, conceive their *role* and how intercultural stakeholders perceive their leaders' role is a matter to be socially constructed rather than assumed. In any context, leaders must be aware of their role within the organization; how they, and their behavior, affect other organizational members. Leaders wear many hats in executing their jobs. They must understand that they do not have all of the answers and give latitude to other organization members to do their jobs. However, even this wisdom, as true as it is for leaders working in U.S. contexts, does not apply across cultures. In intercultural contexts, leaders must be aware that their perception of their role and how they developed their identity as a leader was constructed from a culturally based orientation. Working across cultural boundaries requires what sociologists refer to as "code shifting." Code shifting means that a person shifts their attitudes and behaviors when they enter a different culture. An intercultural leader's attention to cultural context also means that how they communicate aspects of their role to organization members require special attention. While an egalitarian or democratic leadership style may be appropriate in one culture, in another culture, the leader may need to take on a more authoritarian style to be congruent with the expectations of the host culture. Although, even when a directive leadership style is warranted to fit a host culture, a leader in such a context would need to be mindful to consider stakeholder groups and establish practices that would facilitate interaction with those groups, yet use decision styles and other support behaviors that would match the authoritarian style.

Since *vision* is a capability that requires leaders to foresee, scan, and interpret the environment around them, leaders must be aware of their own cultural and background biases that tint their perspectives. We do not mean to suggest that what is perceived, interpreted, and transformed by a leader is necessarily ripe for rejection by intercultural stakeholders simply because of a cultural bias. There is more that binds people together across cultures in the way of similarities than sometimes we bother to acknowledge and leverage. What we do mean to suggest is that leaders, by the nature of the delicate relationship between leader and follower, already have quite a significant challenge in communicating and inspiring followers to own and actuate a leader's vision for the future. The challenge is that what is interpreted as "good" or "bad," "right" or "wrong," "worthy" or "unworthy," "plausible" or "implausible," is in the eyes of the beholder. Hence, what the leader determines is worthy and plausible may seem off the mark to organizational stakeholders from different cultures. The outgrowth of a clearly articulated and executed vision in all organizations is *the result*; that which is achieved at a predetermined point in time. There are wide variances across cultures about what constitutes appropriate results for spent labor, although, there is less variance than during the Cold War era, when the worldwide economy was dominated by two opposing forces, capitalism and Marxism. Even within capitalist countries, there is variance in how the people of cultures perceive the concept of results. Achieving results involves values, beliefs, and worldview. The interview in Exhibit 6.1 with Alain Barbier of INTERPOL shows this variance in the perception of results.

---

### *Exhibit 6.1* Interview with Alain Barbier, INTERPOL, deputy special representative of INTERPOL to the European Union

Today's chiefs of police are confronted with the growing impact of several societal factors, including individualism, diversity, and economic austerity. In parallel, modern policing is facing the increasing internationalization of crime, political influence over police work, and community expectations. As a result, top police executives are evolving within a complex web of social, political, and community pressures, in other words, "contrasts."

Working for INTERPOL, Alain Barbier occupied several leadership functions, including head of the project office, advisor to the executive director for police services, and assistant director for forensic and technical databases. He is currently the deputy special representative of INTERPOL to the European Union.

*What are the most important decisions that a leader of an organization must make?*

Although the leader's capacities and capabilities are primarily developed to best lead a group of people towards common goals, I am using a general framework focusing on the types of decisions that a police leader needs to make. Those decisions can be clustered in six main categories: corporate strategy, human resources management, logistics, ICT, finance, and communication.

To answer the question, I suggest using these categories and explain for each of them what were the major decisions taken or what are the major decisions to be taken based on the so-far gained experience.

### Corporate strategy

The CEO is expecting its leaders to bring a new impetus to his/her position. Indeed, if the CEO preferred keeping the status quo, he/she would rather look for a good manager without the needed leadership skills to dare taking initiative and bring the organization into a new era. Every time I started in a new position, it was requested from me to bring something new, yet without pushing for a brutal organizational change which, in my mind, can never be profitable for an organization in the midterm.

My first decision was *to give 100 days* to present and explain the orientation and possible changes to be brought to the department. Why 100 days? Not because it sounds nice. Not because the media are measuring the first 100 days of politicians. Not because 100 days is sufficient to entirely assess the state of a department. But more pragmatically, because practice showed me that 100 days is the right timing: neither too short nor too long. This period of time is just enough to get people on board. Then, no longer than *18 months* after taking up the position, I make decisions on new initiatives to be taken, thus showing that I dare to take decisions and start new initiatives, while always building decisions on discussions in order for a critical mass of stakeholders to buy into the new initiatives.

My second major decision is to *challenge the status quo* through one-on-one meetings with the department's key figures and other key figures from other departments functionally linked to mine. All issues should be addressed within the 100 days in order to get the right picture of the department, its people, activities and difficulties.

The third major decision is to *foster open mindedness and creativity*, encouraging people to "think out of the box"(see next question).

### Human resources management

The fourth major decision is *choosing the key collaborators* to best advise me. It is not an easy decision and not one to be taken in a hurry. Indeed, every organization has its pace and systems that have to be understood in order to avoid major mistakes in the choices or breaking written or unwritten rules. Therefore, this decision should come as the result of a process taking up to three years. The process is relatively simple, but it requires patience, trust, and confidence. In a nutshell, the need for key collaborators should be identified early on (to be made within 30 days for at least the closer ones). After the 100 days, the needs should be identified and preparations start to identify the best profiles. It can take time to get internal colleagues transferred, but also time and money to recruit external collaborators.

The fifth decision is (since the completion of my University of Liverpool MBA and the subsequent exchange of best practices with fellow students also occupying key positions in their organization) *to encourage positive attitude and outcomes* and not to spend too much time on negative attitude and outcomes. It encourages people to focus on the positive rather than the negative. After a while, a critical mass of colleagues naturally seeks to be recognized, while others will either leave to other positions or be pushed to leave, using individual coaching and a dose of frankness. This is also part of building trust and confidence with colleagues, no matter whether they follow you or not.

## Logistics

The sixth decision is one that is applicable from the first until the last day. Anybody working under my leadership should be able to do her/his work with the required equipment. Because the work at INTERPOL is mostly a desk job, the tools must be modern and updated. PCs should be replaced after a maximum of five years. It clearly has a financial impact which should also be considered during the initial 100 days period.

## ICT

The seventh decision is not a decision as such but more a process of building the understanding that ICT spending will decrease. Therefore, teams should always seek the *best tailored solution for the best (cheap) price*. In the twenty-first century, ICT corporate strategy should be a lot more flexible and IT geeks should serve the core strategy of the organization. Therefore, I *ban the NIH virus* (Not Invented Here) when seeking for IT solution or development.

## Finance

The eighth decision is what I call with some sarcasm the *"WWD" (Wise Wife Decision)*: all finance issues, at least for the first 18 months, come under my full supervision. It enables me to study the nuts and bolts of the department and to get to know about all activities having a cost. This strong decision, sometimes brutal, makes it easier to understand all aspects of the department's functioning and to play the role of leader in identifying personal or group hidden agendas.

### *Communication*

The last decision is also more a way to proceed from the first day on than a decision per se, but it is still essential to the success of a leader: open and transparent communication. Of course, we all hear it everywhere and from all bosses. But communication (internal and external) is predominant in all the activities of a leader. Therefore, this decision means that several means of communication are used (including using social networks). In addition, within the first 100 days, I do the internal and external communication myself, using the appropriate terminology (adapted to the organization's culture) as well as new vocabulary. It gives greater visibility and helps staff understand the leadership style.

*How have global leaders you have worked with encouraged creative thinking within their organizations?*

The industry of public service is naturally a different breed than the private industry. Indeed, goals and objectives can largely differ from non-profit to profit organizations. However, the common parameter is the fact that both are composed of human beings with their education, motivation, career, and personal issues interfering in the daily business. Consequently, despite the fact the police's goals and objectives are not profit-oriented, creativity should be no less important (if not more), as corporate motivation varies a lot depending on leadership styles. In addition, by definition non-profit organizations do not have the same financial resources than the private sector. Therefore, to achieve goals with less resources, creativity is often the best source of achievement and corporate/personal satisfaction.

Without trying to be exhaustive, hereunder are some examples of how I have been encouraging creativity.

### *The role example*

From my perspective, a leader cannot expect his/her staff to be creative if he/she is not showing any interest for creative thinking and working. This does not come from books or my MBA studies but clearly from two important elements of my personality. The first one is my readiness to take the risk of using creativity and accepting innovation. The second one is the fact that I am curious and constantly observing, reflecting, comparing and trying creative tools with colleagues, friends, and even my children to devise new ways of achieving goals.

### *Crucial meeting introduced by a creative action or activity*

I start a meeting with a creative thinking introduction such as the ones on the Internet found when typing "out of the box" or "creative thinking." Those small films showed and briefly discussed, set people in a different mindset, allowing discussion to start in a fresher and smoother manner. One good example is probably Simon Sinek explaining how great leaders inspire action.

### *"No budget limit" way of thinking*

When confronted with a new concept or idea to be developed, most of the teams are stuck in their comfort zone and by several limits and boundaries nobody wants to challenge. Starting a meeting by announcing that the concept to be developed is a top priority and with unlimited or huge budget can completely change the perspective through which the team will think. The leader must then be both well prepared and convincing.

### *Bringing external views*

I had to deal with deadlocked situations where the team thought that INTERPOL was the only organization confronted with certain difficulties and thus thinking that the problem can only be solved internally. Leading through a problem-solving process requires the leader to be open, curious and in contact with other businesses than only the police. Problem solving requires the leader to identify comparable issues in other businesses and bring in external people to speak about their difficulties and the approaches to solve difficult issues. The result of external experience then has less importance than the process used to reach a solution. This experience helps the team to think about other ways to look at the current deadlocked issues.

### *"What if..." approach*

Generally speaking, although the "what if..." approach is used to define strategic objectives, trigger discussions, and exchange views within a team or a group of people, I use it in face-to-face discussions with key people from my team. When discussing about future perspectives, I suggest my counterpart physically takes my place in my seat and ask her/him what he/she would do if he/she were in my seat. When the discussion is open enough and producing new ideas, I suggest a step further by saying: "What if tomorrow you are appointed Secretary General of INTERPOL?" The initial reaction is always to be intimidated. But using leadership to bring the individual to a certain comfort level can generate brilliant and creative ideas. But let's not forget to wrap it up into some trust and confidence relationship guaranteeing some kind of discretion.

### The place of the meeting

For those who remember the film *Dead Poets' Society* with Robin Williams, being the captain of his class, he challenged his students to look at things through a different perspective by jumping on his desk and saying "Oh Captain, my Captain." Yes, I used it to break the ice in some brainstorming or creative sessions but what is important is to dare changing the place of meetings. First, it takes participants out of their comfort zone and allows more focus on the tasks. Organizing a meeting in a different place and/or in a different way has been regularly used to trigger creativity and it works although the budget for such activities could be quite limited in the public sector.

*What is one characteristic that you believe every global business leader should possess?*

Transactional leaders may not always have the required competencies to face the increasing pressures from the political sphere in the area of security and internal affairs. The increasing influence of the political sphere on chiefs of police and for sure on an international police organization such as INTERPOL has been amply demonstrated. I found out in writing my MBA dissertation that leadership requirements could be presented in a competency model limited to those best suited to cope with political influences. This limited competency model embodies five categories: personal character, strategic leadership, people/personal leadership, execution and results and stakeholders focus. Finally, the research as a whole concludes that the police leadership paradigm has shifted at least from a transactional to a transformational and/or servant-driven leadership.

In my MBA dissertation, I came to another important conclusion: Any police leader on national level should promote modern policing while being able to cope with ambiguity and complexity.[2]

*What is the biggest intercultural challenge facing a global business leader today?*

As a preamble, in order to bring everyone on the same page, let's discuss the meaning of "intercultural." Firstly, coming from Belgium, I have been, like all Belgians, confronted with three cultures in the same country (French, German, and Flemish). Thus, intercultural doesn't mean international per se. Secondly, in police services, one can find several cultures, such as the one from the frontline officers, desk officers, or forensic specialists. Therefore, the term "intercultural" does not necessarily refer to a profession, a language or geographical origin. "Intercultural relations" have many interpretations and can vary a lot when working at international level and where several cultures are embodied (country, language, profession, and region).

As a leader in a global business, my biggest intercultural challenge is to get things done in a way to meet citizens' needs, while having a common vision of what should INTERPOL do globally in an ever changing world and with the taxpayers' money! How can we translate this into leadership words?

I need to carefully observe the environment. Above any culture, at least in international policing, are the moral sense and the global ethic. These are globally accepted values irrespective of religion or faith. Any police (wo)man in the world, confronted with crime, will feel the same and approach the situation with the same objective: "catch the criminal and, using the rule of law, get him/her in jail using the judicial procedure." Thus there is a common understanding above individual cultural influences about what should be done in international policing.

Consequently, at INTERPOL, the challenge is to craft and execute a vision and strategy based on a common moral sense that has existed since much longer than globalization.

*What are your thoughts on globalization? How do you think national culture (if at all) affects the rate of acceptance of globalization in certain parts of the world?*

As indicated in the previous question, I believe there is a global moral sense and ethic, but what has changed for a leader in the international arena is the capacity to communicate instantly across borders. Today, we can find common ground with people whom we may never meet and exchange ideas and viewpoints using the Internet or any other modern means of communication. This aspect of globalization means that we can take collective action to deal with virtually any problem or situation of injustice. This makes our age a truly unique one in history. It is the forming of a global society where international policing will have a place it never had before. The power of global communication is limitless.

Globalization is *"en marche"* and should be seen as a great opportunity where the power of communication and of global morals could create a new era of internationalization seeing important change in world affairs. This provides today's international police leaders with the power of global ethics (fairness, responsibility) and with the power of communication to face global issues such as climate change and the financial crisis but also the challenges of transnational (organized) crime and terrorism.

The leaders of the twenty-first century can create a new world with more stability, economic growth, and security by working towards global solutions beyond the national level. How can it be possible to combat transnational crime when not integrated in the fight against the globali-zation of crime through the work programs of INTERPOL and the United Nations?

For this reason, as a police leader, I made the choice early in my career to serve an international police organization for the benefit of my country.

*How do you think leaders today deal with ambiguity? How have you found leaders in being successful in effectively tolerating working with contrast-ing perspectives, methods, and value systems? Do you think the ability to deal with such ambiguity requires a higher level consciousness in order to perceive multiple levels of meaning simultaneously?*

A leader today should accept that occupying a leadership position will never enable any kind of comfort zone. Indeed, the fast changing world, the fast speed of information exchange, the evolution of technologies and specifically for the police, the political importance of internal security (against crime, terrorism, etc.) create a permanently changing situation. There is no certainty apart from the fact that everything is always changing. For the leader, this brings the question of how to push forward a vision, craft a strategy and lead the team toward common objectives (and which ones?).

In the globalization era, a successful leader should manage ambiguity by:

- Developing a global vision and understanding of his/her environment (professionally and privately);
- Deploying her/his energy in crafting an agile strategy taking into account the permanent changing factors;
- Defining her/his personal values and the red lines never to cross. Therefore, no matter which factors are changing in the company or the society, (s)he will finally make up her/his mind at the end of the thought process based on those personal values. I personally find this extremely important when working in law enforcement, as we are serving the State and consequently politicians.

Dealing with ambiguity calls for a better understanding of the larger envi-ronment. Personally, as a potential leader in the twenty-first century, I decided to acquire an MBA degree as a challenge, but also to get additional tools to manage ambiguity. During the MBA, I studied the profile of police leaders and looked at the personal character leaders. My conclusions in 2010 where the following:[3]

- Need to cope with increased ambiguity[4] and complexity:[5] indeed "authority is no longer taken for granted, morality is fragmented, social

differences are more pronounced, citizens have become extremely assertive, media (including new media) play a leading role in shaping people's opinions, and declining confidence in governments";[6]
- Need to become a social leader;
- Higher political visibility for the police, meaning more frequent presence in political debates or in the media;
- Neutrality and being apolitical but also not silent;[7]
- Police executives should show leadership qualities in terms of confidence, anticipation and efficiency in providing the best rapid solution while striving towards sustainability and implementation of the strategy. It calls for having the perceptual intelligence[8] to balance short-term visible solutions and long-term proposals more suited to provide sustainable solutions to crime issues.
- Need to be transparent with the political authority, while also showing integrity and being an example in the function.

Police leaders, when coping with increasing conflicting situations, such as becoming a social leader while maintaining the order, are constantly dealing with ambiguity. Additionally, because they are close to the top decision makers, the politicians, facing ambiguity is for police leaders a second nature. This said, in order to survive, I believe that police leaders need to stay true to their values at all times and be ready to quit if they cannot be respected.

*What is one mistake you witness business leaders making more frequently than others within business organizations or governmental organizations? Can you provide an example of such a mistake, particularly one in which the leader did not understand the importance of appropriate intercultural cues?*

The mistakes I witness leaders make more frequently than any others are summed up in the following statements: "One size fits all," "In my former job," "In my country," "In my police organization."

These expressions have been used thousands of times by leaders working in international police cooperation. Although with a good intention, leaders refer too frequently to past experience to plan the future. Of course past experiences build knowledge, but a solution, although once successfully applied, is not always applicable. As a leader, you always think about your staff and would like as much as possible to reward them, knowing that it will be good for team spirit and motivation. But, while this is true, the question is how to reward my people in an intercultural environment. Would a Belgian have the same appreciation of a public handshaking as a Russian or an American or a Chinese? In fact, while the reason for rewarding is intercultural, the way to reward will vary with the culture. As a result, the leader is always at risk of making mistakes. Are there any solutions? Yes, an agile perception of situations, learning by doing and being ready to listen to your personnel will help building useful knowledge. This also applies to project approach, crafting a strategy, and for developing an organizational culture which takes into consideration those intercultural challenges.

*Can you name a person who has had a tremendous impact on you as a leader? Maybe someone who has been a mentor to you? Why and how did this person impact your life? Was this person from the same native and/or organizational culture as you?*

HB was my boss earlier in my career in Belgium. In order to avoid writing tons of good words about him, I will only say that, if he called me today and asked me to join him, unless a paramount private issue, I would quit and get in touch with him, whatever the job. It says enough about his leadership skills. He was not a mentor as such, but more an example to follow. He worked hard (over 14 hours/day). He knew not only the police environment, but also the political and international ones. He brought his directorate to a level and position in the Belgian police landscape never reached before. He was able to speak with you about your family, your work, your strengths and weaknesses in the most pleasant way. His strong character and some-times explosions were predictable, but also well managed by him after the fact. He taught his first line managers all the aspects of investigation management, from strategy crafting against a phenomenon such as traffick-ing in stolen vehicles to the way and possible approach for an investigation coordination meeting. Intellectually very strong, he never showed superior-ity and always had enough patience for most of us. His humility was remarkable. While being Belgian like me, his origins were from the Dutch speaking side of Belgium, which was not a problematic issue, as the direc-torate was a mixture of languages, origins, and education. It was hard work-ing with him but probably one of the best learning moments of my career.

*Within the global economy, how important is it that a global business leader understands the key features of the Geoleadership Model?*

This question will be answered following the Geoleadership Model starting with "Care" and finishing with "Capability."

*Care*: At INTERPOL, the international police cooperation is by defini-tion not calling for profit, and therefore, the leaders of the organization have no difficulties considering the expectations of the citizen, the politi-cians, and any stakeholders for a safer world. However, the social respon-sibility is probably the orientation an international leader at INTERPOL should further clarify and convince the followers and the stakeholders about although there is no profit orientation.

*Communication*: This is a MUST! As a global policing leader, attention to communication is not only paramount, but also essential. The different cultures matching international policing are calling for intercultural understanding and integrate them into any communication. INTERPOL is a mix of several cultures in terms of languages, countries, professions, educations. Hence, an international police leader will strive towards adopting the tailored communication depending on the staff members or stakeholders (s)he is communicating with.

*Consciousness*: In line with communication, the global leader in policing should never stop acquiring knowledge in policing, international police cooperation and police culture. Developing a large cultural knowledge will enable the leader to cope with any situation by being better aware of the counterpart expectations.

*Contrasts*: International policing is by definition a mix of opposite interests, "nationalism," diverging political views, whatever the bottom line street officer is needing. Thus, maybe unfortunately for the sake of the work to be achieved against organized crime, the global police leader will have such as his/her counterpart on national level to cope with the ambiguity of the position. Indeed representing the power while trying to serve the society could simply be impossible but calling for keeping the right balance.

*Context*: Contextualization is facilitated through the development of the consciousness.

*Change*: Bringing change, getting people out of their comfort zone is what is expected from a post-modern leader. Unfortunately as studied in my MBA dissertation,[9] most of the leaders in the international police arena are merely transactional leaders not yet having the agility to combine it with intercultural skills in order to achieve major changes. The current leaders are a lot more flexible with people management in order to keep the workforce in place whatever the time to bring change.

*Capability*: Finally, although known, today the international police leadership skills to be developed to better face intercultural challenge are not really part of a structural exchange. Indeed, internationally among high level colleagues or part of any international public leadership schools, global police leaders do not have yet a structural learning process or center where all of them come together. Only the initiative on "Pearls in Policing" tries to meet this objective. On its side, INTERPOL started this year some programs for global leadership development.

*What do you like to ask other business leaders when you get the chance?*

In a few years, most of the businesses will have to deal with three generations (X, Y, digital) of staff. It will be a challenge for businesses themselves, but also for the culture and the type of leadership. My questions to some international business leaders will be: "How are you going to deal with the different generations working together in your company?" "What about the next full digital-minded generation and their motivation in a company?" I would also ask: "With the decrease of interest for work, as opposed to leisure, how do you manage talent?" And, finally, I would ask: "What do you expect to achieve tomorrow? And the day after?"

*\*\*\**

In his interview, Alain Barbier discusses the challenge of leaders in international policing, which according to Alain is by definition a mix of opposite interests. This balance of contrasts—representing the powers that be while serving society at large—calls for strong leadership and extraordinary navigation. This may only be possible for highly adept global leaders.

**Alain Barbier**, from his past experiences with police and intelligence organizations, gratefully accepted the opportunity to participate in the development of a new EU Office for INTERPOL as deputy to the special representative to the European Union. His former tenures in the police and private sector help him to liaise with EU institutions as well as to position INTERPOL as an important partner for the external security policy of EU. Alain previously worked for the Belgian police (2009) and also worked for a year to reposition his career (2008). Before, he was appointed by the Secretary General as an assistant director within ICPO-INTERPOL from 2003 to 2007, he served at the General Secretariat in Lyon, France. There, Alain had responsibility for the development and implementation of the second INTERPOL core function related to the international police data management and the forensic support. Alain's work has taken him worldwide and he has worked closely with many foreign police services/forces from the 190 INTERPOL member countries and their respective representatives in the police and in governments. Alain holds a Master'sdegree in Criminology from the University of Liège and a Master of Business Administration from the University of Liverpool.

### *Value elements*

A lot of what informs people's decisions and actions are their beliefs and *values*. Values are the principles by which people live, they indicate the worth and importance we place on aspects of life. They capture our attention and motivate us toward goals. No human being reaches adulthood without having formed values. Culture plays a significant role in the values people adopt. Values are either implicit or explicit, depending on the person, group, and culture. Leaders typically demonstrate their values through their behavior. When values are known and followed between people, they form the basis of trust. When values are unclear, or incongruent, mistrust occurs. Some organizational researchers concluded from their comparative studies the possibility that successfully performing organizations tended to have a leadership style based on values.[10] The common element of high-performing organizations is that values are prioritized over purely profit.

## What can go wrong

It appears that people who are comfortable with higher levels of ambiguity are also more interested and comfortable with contexts that feature diverse groups of people. People with low tolerance for ambiguity, who find themselves in intercultural situations, can make costly mistakes.

*Risk aversion* occurs when leaders are inexperienced or ineffectual; however, several potential causes underlie ineffectual issues. One issue, previously discussed, is the difference in how people of different cultures conceptualize a situation as a problem, or not a problem. This can become problematic in situations such as personnel performance evaluations, where culturally bound behaviors are interpreted as "good" and "bad" by the different cultures present at the table. Another issue is that people can perceive something as a problem, or not, based on the amount of uncertainty that is created (potentially) by perceiving something as a problem. For that matter, the same issue comes up in intercultural assessments of opportunities. A last issue that can occur is when people, such as a group of leaders within an organization, unconsciously and subjectively narrow the potential solutions because of fear of uncertainty, which raises the risk factor in the minds of the participants.

*Auto-pilot decision-making* occurs when leaders seek to govern and direct from a place of operating by precedent. In such cases, a leader may perceive the complexity inherent in a particular situation and seek to avoid their own discomfort and will make a decision based on something they did in the past. These types of decisions typically conform to cultural norms.

*Decision paralysis* occurs when leaders in intercultural contexts face their own inexperience with the good intentions of acting with integrity and based on the desire to accommodate local culture, but without the benefit of other intercultural competencies in place to support their efforts.

*Over complicating* occurs when inexperienced leaders have the desire and intention to act in consideration of all stakeholders, but perceive that the situation has no solution that will be appropriate. Usually, this occurs when the leader lacks the skills necessary to bring all parties to the table and negotiate solutions.

*Reactionism* occurs on both the emotional and/or the behavioral level when novice intercultural leaders have built little or no self-awareness, and little or no awareness and appreciation of and for other cultural perspectives. A high performing career professional has many competencies. Above all, the global leader has to have managerial and technical competencies. In addition, here are three areas of competence to cultivate.

## Competencies

*Regulating emotions* is critical for leaders. We do not mean to suggest that leaders should not ever show their emotions, because at times allowing a window to one's feelings helps normalize situations for followers. The challenge for leaders is to know their own sensitivity areas as well as where they may have emotional blinders. Emotionally intelligent leaders can identify what emotional state they are in at any time and understand the effect this is having on their perceptions of a situation, their behaviors, and their cognitions. Leaders with less emotional intelligence are more likely to be at the mercy of their emotions in that they will color and change their perceptions of reality, their behavior, and the way they think and think about their thinking and emotions without being aware of this.

*Monitoring behavior* is closely related to regulation of emotions, since behavior is the outgrowth of thoughts and feelings. It is unrealistic to think that leaders will never behave in a way that they regret, or in a manner that causes some type of negative reaction or response from followers. However, and to extend the point made above, when leaders are able to build awareness of their emotions and know their own biases and emotional triggers, they have a better chance of acting from an informed rather than impulsive frame of mind.

*Cognitive flexibility* means that leaders perceive "reality" as something co-created rather than fixed by precedent. Hearken back to our earlier discussion about mindfulness and flexibility. Leaders working in intercultural contexts must be able to tack back and forth between their own perspectives and taking in the perspectives of other stakeholders.

## The leader ambiguity aptitude continuum

Leaders who are able to cope well with situations of high contrast and ambiguity without undue stress also tend to value a diversity of people to challenge and inform their thinking. Conversely, leaders with low tolerance for ambiguity, those who prefer the comfort of more stable environments tend to prefer to work with people who are like them. They tend not to like being challenged by different thinking and ideas that do not accord with their own. For the ability to accept and value diversity, read the ability to accept and value a diversity of thinking.

Essentially, there appears to be a link between cognitive broadbanding, tolerance for ambiguity and an understanding that diversity can help to extend one's thinking and help with problem solving. Table 6.1 provides a description of levels of ambiguity comfort and approximates the behaviors one could expect from leaders working at each level. However, this schematic is culture-bound to the extent that the underlying assumption is that high ambiguity tolerance is valued.

Dealing with ambiguity in the fields of global mediation and negotiation is a valuable skill. In Exhibit 6.2 an interview with Senator George Mitchell provides a perspective into how diplomacy can clarify ambiguity in different situations.

*Table 6.1* Ambiguity tolerance overview

| Basic | Intermediate | Advanced | Proficient |
|-------|--------------|----------|------------|
| Copes with change and novelty, shifting when necessary and with support | Copes with change and novelty, shifting with relative ease | Perceives effects of change and novelty on self and others, prepares to shift responsively | Anticipates effects of change and novelty, directs self and engages others in effortlessly shifting emotions, behaviors, and cognitive patterns |
| Suggests solutions, plans, and acts without having considered stakeholder/other perspectives | Decides and acts to compensate with some consideration of stakeholder perspectives | Uses creativity to adapt useful alternatives in collaboration with stakeholders | Predicts and communicates the opportunities from a stakeholder-aware perspective, engages stakeholders in co-creating new and mutually agreeable realities |
| Tolerates and reacts to risk and uncertainty after some disruption | Handles risk and uncertainty with minimal disruption | Embraces risk and uncertainty | Prospers self and others by maximizing benefits and lessening effects of risk and uncertainty |

---

**Exhibit 6.2** **Interview with George J. Mitchell, former U.S. senator; chairman emeritus, DLA Piper LLP**

A former U.S. senator and chairman emeritus, DLA Piper, George J. Mitchell served as U.S. special envoy for Middle East Peace from January 2009 to May 2011. Prior to that, he had a distinguished career in public service. His interview, which follows, reveals how this inspiring leader was able to manage high contrast and ambiguous situations throughout his career.

*What are the most important decisions that you make now or that you have made as a leader of an organization of which you have been a part?*

I think among the most important decisions of leaders in public or private organizations is to choose wisely the people who will assist them. It's very important to give these people sufficient flexibility and authority to act and make decisions and then to hold them appropriately accountable for their decisions as well as for the results. Except in individual endeavors, such as if one is for instance an artist, an author, or a marathon runner, most human efforts are team efforts. Global leaders, particularly of large organizations, have as a very important part of their duties to assemble the best team members, to motivate them, to establish clear goals and objectives that can be measured by widely understood and accepted metrics.

Even the most impersonal and large of organizations are moved by individual action. People who are properly motivated and compensated, both in financial and psychic terms, will do well and feel good about themselves and their work. I've found in my own experience that selecting the right people to assist, implanting of a culture of fairness and high motivation, and having a meaningful goal and an appropriate way to measure progress toward those goals, are perhaps the most important duties of leaders.

*What is one characteristic that you believe every global business leader should possess?*

I think there are several. Certainly, a clear understanding of and a commitment to the goals and objectives of the organization is essential. You can't build a roadmap to success unless you know where you're going. It is the duty of the leader to understand, and in many cases establish, that objective, to determine what it is that the organization is seeking to achieve and to make certain that all decisions that are made are consistent with and further progress toward that objective.

*What is the biggest challenge facing global business leaders today?*

I think the biggest challenge facing global leaders in corporations and in every aspect of human activity, including government, is to keep pace with the rapid changes in technology and communications and in the rapid increase in the volume of information that is available. Further to this challenge is to integrate all of this information and technology into tools for progress for the organization which one is serving. It is not easy to do. For instance, I travel extensively. It's hard to keep up with what's going on in just my own occupation. I'm the chairman emeritus of the largest law firm in the world. With 4,200 lawyers across 25 countries, simply keeping abreast of the changes that are occurring in life generally and in the profession I serve can be difficult. Finding ways to accept and harness those changes to the benefit of an organization seeking to achieve its objectives is an enormous challenge.

*What effect do you think national culture has on business leadership decision-making at Fortune Global 500 organizations? (This can also include how your own native national culture affects your decision-making.)*

All human beings are to some extent the product of their environments, of their homes, their communities, and the societies within which they live. Not all people react the same way to events, but all people are influenced by these factors. These factors play a role in decision-making throughout our lives. This is just a fact. There is no escaping it. It has nothing to do with intelligence, skill, or lack thereof. To people leading multinational organizations, it is of critical importance to recognize this. These leaders have people working for them and reporting to them from more than one country, and must be very aware of the impact of cultural decisions on performance.

While I think this is an important factor, I don't think it ought to be exaggerated. People can and do change. They do adapt to new cultures and societies. Sometimes they relocate precisely because they will be in a different culture. In fact, we Americans ought to recognize that people around the world want to come here in part because of what they see as freedom and opportunity existing together in greater degree than where they presently are or where they have been. So, while I think national culture does play a role, it is a factor and will continue to be one, it is not necessarily the only or the most important determinative.

*What are your thoughts on globalization and how do you think national culture affects the rate of acceptance of globalization in different parts of the world?*

First off, globalization has to be defined. Different people have different definitions of it. I would certainly take it to mean increased trade and exchanges between people of different societies across national borders. Certainly, part of the issue of globalization, I think, is that it is inevitable and will continue. The most successful societies and people will be those who harness those forces to their benefit, as opposed to resist them by trying to build walls to prevent increased trade or increased exchanges of information or persons or data out of their societies. I think it is important for all leaders, national and international, to be aware of this. If global leaders want their organizations to succeed, it's important to once again look for the factors that they can harness to the benefit of their organizations that will help them achieve their goals and to work to both expand those opportunities, while mitigating the undeniable disadvantages that follow from globalization in certain areas.

*What is one mistake you witness business leaders making more frequently than others in Fortune Global 500 organizations? Can you provide an example of such a mistake, particularly one in which the leader did not understand the importance of appropriate intercultural cues?*

I don't know that I can identify one mistake that I see global leaders make most or respond with a specific example out of my own history. I would go back to what I said before; I think it is important for global leaders to have an understanding of the many different forces now at work in changing our societies, almost all them which can provide benefits to people, and to try to harness those benefits to their advantage. I think if there is a mistake, and I'm not sure how widespread it is, it is in failing to understand this and in wanting to resist it because of fear of change and uncertainty. This holds global leaders and their organizations back as opposed to embracing and harnessing these changes to their benefit.

*Can you name a person who has had a tremendous impact on you as a leader? Maybe someone who has been a mentor to you? Why and how did this person impact your life? Was this person from the same native and/or organization culture as you?*

The two most influential people in my life were firstly my mother, who was a very strong, able, energetic, and loving person. Who I am and what I've done are largely the products of her influence on me. The second most influential person in my life was a former United States Senator from Maine, Edmund Muskie. He was my predecessor in office, and my personal hero, mentor, and friend. He was perhaps the greatest environmental legislator in our nation's history, and one whose integrity and principles had a major impact on me in the forming of my own principles, values, and objectives.

*What do you like to ask other business leaders when you get the chance?*

I like to ask them to tell me about their experiences. What were their successes? Why were they able to succeed? What didn't work for them? Why didn't it work? How would they propose to change this? Also of course, as any inquiring or curious person would, I want to know about their personal history. How did they get to the point that they are at currently? What were the turning points in their life? And, of course, who were their influences?

\*\*\*

As former senator Mitchell states, "most human efforts are team efforts," and global leaders have the great responsibility of assembling strong teams whose members come from a variety of cultural backgrounds. They must establish clear goals and objectives and then grant individual members the authority to act and make decisions as they see fit. A great feat for global leaders tasked with managing multi-cultural teams is to then manage the ambiguity that is a natural consequence of doing business in the global arena.

**George J. Mitchell** served as U.S. Special Envoy for Middle East Peace from January 2009 to May 2011. Prior to that he had a distinguished career in public service. He was appointed to the United States Senate in 1980 to complete the unexpired term of Sen. Edmund S. Muskie, who resigned to become Secretary of State. He was elected to a full term in the Senate in 1982 in a stunning come-from-behind victory. After trailing in public opinion polls by 36 points, Sen. Mitchell rallied to win the election, receiving 61 percent of the votes cast. Sen. Mitchell went on to an illustrious career in the Senate spanning 15 years. In 1988, he was reelected with 81 percent of the vote, the largest margin in Maine history. He left the Senate in 1995 as the Senate majority leader, a position he had held since January 1989.

Sen. Mitchell enjoyed bipartisan respect during his tenure. It has been said "there is not a man, woman or child in the Capitol who does not trust George Mitchell." For six consecutive years he was voted "the most respected member" of the Senate by a bipartisan group of senior congressional aides. He was a leader in opening markets to trade and led the Senate to ratification of the North American Free Trade Agreement and creation of the World Trade Organization.

Mitchell served as Chairman of the Global Board of the international law firm DLA Piper; Chairman of the Board of Directors of The Walt Disney Company; a member of the Board of the Boston Red Sox; and a director of several companies, including Federal Express, Xerox, Staples, Unilever, and Starwood Hotels and Resorts. In 2008, *Time Magazine* named Senator Mitchell one of the 100 most influential persons in the world.

All leaders and managers who are considered for positions within intercultural contexts should be assessed for their level of ambiguity tolerance. Those who may have the desire but who do not assess at higher ambiguity tolerance levels should be given the opportunity to expand their ambiguity tolerance through coursework and special mentored assignments. Those who demonstrate the flexibility to develop higher ambiguity tolerance could be considered for further development. Those who are not comfortable with ambiguity and do not demonstrate an interest and flexibility to develop this ability should be considered for stable environments only. Please see Figure 6.2 for more information about contrasts in practice.

A Geoleader can negotiate the principle of Contrasts through the following practices and behaviors:

- Deflate stress: Analyze what makes you anxious, and short-circuit the process before it takes hold. Drop the issue for a short while if you get emotional.
- Embrace change: Be willing to let go of one way of doing things to try something new. Invite new ideas, and experiment until you are comfortable with change.
- Manage a temporary group of resisting people in an unpopular project.
- Assemble a team of diverse people to accomplish a difficult task.
- Take on a task that you have never done before.
- Teach others something you do not know well. Pick something new, different, and unfamiliar.
- Be a "researcher" of other people. Study their behavior and what they do differently from you. Adapt what you learn to change your behavior.
- Be alert to your behavior and emotions when faced with transitions. Review what is similar and what is different before transitioning between old and new situations.
- Monitor yourself more closely and get off your autopilot. Look at each situation from a fresh perspective. Ask yourself questions consistently, and try new solutions for old problems.

*Figure 6.2* The principle of "Contrasts" in practice.

**The bottom line**

Change, transitions, differing contexts, and novel situations all require that leaders possess the requisite skills to negotiate the inherent ambiguity. Intercultural leaders must be able to do this with the added layers of complexity associated with intercultural contexts. In all organizations, there are particular areas where ambiguity occurs.

Leaders in intercultural contexts must develop the requisite awareness, knowledge, and skills. Awareness of self and others enables leaders to appreciate difference and similarity toward creating mutually acceptable agreements and relationships. Knowledge of a leader's own cultural bias and a willing and active pursuit of knowledge of other cultures are necessary. A skill in languages and in the practices of other cultures allows leaders to optimize mutually set goals and objectives. Four essential practices can enable leaders to prepare and navigate the terrain of intercultural relations as shown in Figure 6.3.

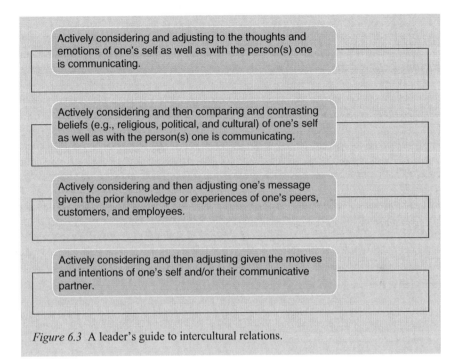

*Figure 6.3* A leader's guide to intercultural relations.

# 7   The principle of "Context"

Normally, humans are effective at conveying ideas to each other and responding fittingly. This is due to many factors: the richness of the *language they share*, the *common understanding* of how the world works, and an *implicit understanding* of everyday situations. When humans interact within cultures, they enjoy a higher degree, or capability, to use implicit situational information (context) to increase the level of comprehension. However, this ability to interact becomes complicated when humans interact across cultures. In such intercultural circumstances, social actors endeavor interactive exchanges with an impediment, the lack of common understanding. Consequently, individuals from differing cultures, trying to interact, are unable to use context as an expedient channel to comprehension. By increasing each person's understanding of the other's cultural context (language, norms, rules, etc.), in other words increasing their access to context, we increase the richness of communication interaction and enable mutual success.

*Context* means the surrounding circumstances and conditions in which something unfolds. It can be understood as the frame within which phenomena exist. It provides the staging, the backdrop, the props, and the script with which we interpret and derive meaning. In other words, we use context to make sense of what we observe happening around, or to, us. For example, normally, we understand birds flying as belonging to the context of air, and fish swimming as belonging to

## "CONTEXT"
### DEFINED

Self-awareness of own cultural background and bias.

the context of some body of water. However, as convenient as contexts are to us, human social contexts can be complex.

Not only are contexts complex, but they emerge, evolve, dissipate, develop, and change. While context may influence, it does not necessarily determine decisions and action. We argue that humans and context interact. Contexts exist within the minds and memories of people, and they consist in the external world, of culture, nation-states, regions, the geo-political climate (government, religion, war, agreements, and law), technology, resources, and naturally occurring phenomena in the biological world.

Effectively, "a context" has three essential aspects: (1) the objective reality—that which is created in form; (2) the relational—the exchange of energy between individuals and other entities; and (3) the transcendent—the individual's essence or group essence, which is always in a state of creativity. What this means is that context, as does "reality," exists in multiple dimensions, simultaneously. Context may be unambiguous or veiled.

Clear contexts need little explanation. For example, an email coming from your manager communicates a request for your attention, superficially. However, veiled contextual clues are those which either we must already know, or we must have trained ourselves to identify. Often, such training is made difficult because we commonly do not recognize that we have missed something. Veiled contexts, such as when cultural cues are sent, may be almost impossible to perceive. Also, they are generally the most essential for us to perceive for mutual understanding between individuals (or groups).

Frequently, deeper contexts will carry the most important clues to understanding what we are to do. For example, an email from a manager may just be intended to indicate that the company's CEO will be in for a visit. The meaning you take from this information, as an American engineer working in a high tech company in Silicon Valley, however, includes understanding that the project you were going to finish over the weekend must be ready by Friday morning and that the usual "casual Friday" blue jeans will be frowned upon. The manager's goal of gaining more resources for the department and your desire to exude professionalism are two contexts with which you interpreted the manager's email. In such ways, our success is often directly related to how well we learn to understand our organizations and ourselves. Understanding how to perceive contextual clues is the difference between understanding and confusion.

Contexts, which are unclear to us, present challenges. What happens if you miss the subtle or unspoken culturally-bound social cues in a message? For example, what if you, as an Indian engineer, are a relatively recent arrival to the U.S., now working in the Silicon Valley high tech industry, and receive the same memo (as we described above) that your American engineer colleague received. What if you had been told, just the day before in a team orientation, that it was company policy and the "way we do things around here on Friday" to dress yourself in blue jeans to come to work? Further, what if you had been told that on the second Friday of the month, the team comes to work an hour later and gathers for a relaxing "team-building" activity? The salient point about context is that it is inseparable from those who constructed it. Unless you participate or are somehow privy to, or made aware of, constructed context, how would you know the essential information? How would you know how to behave?

## The intersection of culture and context

At its best, culture (with its elements of language, norms, artifacts, practices, and beliefs) is something humans use to make sense of the evolving world around them. At its worst, culture is something humans use to habituate decisions and actions based on outdated information. In other words, both culture and context have dual qualities of stasis and motion given by their creators. Here again, we emphasize the relational dimension between culture and context and between the creators of culture and context. We know and acknowledge of course that both culture and context have certain stabilizing characteristics also given by their creators.

The point is that leaders, as users and creators of culture and context, must account for both the stability and the motion of culture and context, with the primary focus being on the relationship between the two in the immediate moment. By focusing on the immediate relationship between culture and context, between stasis and motion, the leader (along with others) is constructing context, what can be thought of as the enactment of context. In this relationship, we can perceive that context exists in the internal, as personal thoughts and feelings, and in the external, as other people, objects, artifacts, and settings. What happens when the focus is not on the relationship between culture and context in the immediate present?

## Cultural misunderstandings vis-à-vis the intersection of culture and context

The following factual stories provide the reader with clear examples of how misunderstandings at the intersection of culture and context occur. Each story involves leadership failures not at top levels, but at all levels where real-life action takes place; where leadership competence is most necessary.

### *Armed with guns rather than understanding*

In the memoir of his distinguished career with the United Nations, Sir Brian Urquhart tells the story of the first night in 1957 when a contingent of the United Nations Emergency Force was deployed to Gaza. That evening, hearing from the minarets the muezzin's call to prayers, but not understanding Arabic or the meaning of this as a religious act, the UN troops thought it was a call to civil disorder and they fired in panic on the mosque.[2] Through this tragic story of meaning lost, we can visualize the intersection of culture and context at play. Freshly deployed UNEF troops never before exposed to Arab or Muslim custom, in keeping with their internalized role context behaved lawfully. By lawfully we mean they behaved in a manner congruent with their training, having internalized the role of the UNEF in entering Gaza as a "conflictual context." The failure to perceive, interpret, and discern the distinction between the "context of religious practice" and the "context of geopolitical conflict" caused irrevocable harm. At a base level, in this example, we can perceive the failure to focus on the relationship between culture and context in the immediate moment. Fittingly, perhaps, are the words of Aga Khan, a Muslim spiritual leader, who recently said, "The supposed 'clash of cultures' is in reality nothing more than a manifestation of mutual ignorance."[3]

### Yours, mine, and ours

Some years ago in Nigeria, in a Catholic seminary, letters written and sent in or out to the seminarians were always opened and read before they were released to the addressees or sent out respectively. On one particular occasion, a letter arrived for a young seminarian (who was preparing to be a priest and as is custom should have been celibate). The letter was sent from his village and was written in the Yoruba language. The priest in charge of the seminary at the time was a European missionary who could not read the letter in the native language of Yoruba, so he called someone else who read the letter to his exact understanding. One passage of the letter said, "Your wife has just given birth to a child." The priest in charge on hearing this news summoned the young seminarian and sent him away from the seminary, unceremoniously. The seminarian arrived home and learned that his elder brother's wife had just given birth and that a letter had been sent to inform him, which was the reason he was sent away. A delegate had to be sent down to see the priest in charge and explain to him that in the Yoruba culture (actually most Nigerian cultures) your brother's wife is called your wife. It turned out that it was the young seminarian's elder brother who had a wife, who had just given birth to a child, and that the seminarian did not have a wife, but as was the custom, the letter was addressing the brother's wife as *his* wife. The priest understood his mistake and misunderstanding, in which case if he was correct, the expulsion would have been justified, but since he was not right, his action was based on a misunderstanding of the culture of the people. The seminarian was rightfully restored to the seminary and today he is a bishop in Nigeria. In this example, we can see clearly the effect of context on understanding.

### Hearing is not necessarily believing

Several years ago, a British manager was in China for the signing of an important railway contract. The details and pricing had all been finalized and the manager only needed to endorse the contract with one of the Chinese ministers. The business location was in a small town in the northern part of China where people, by custom, speak loudly. Their business culture norm also is not to negotiate business deals on the first day they meet; instead, they first have a casual meeting followed by dinner and karaoke. On the following day, business deals are closed and then contracts are signed. The British manager being quite new to Asia (only five months into his assignment) and not knowing the Chinese culture, let alone specific regional cultures within China, *mis*understood that his Chinese counterparts were not happy when they first met because they spoke quite loudly and dismissed his attempts to engage in signing the contract. Feeling frustrated, annoyed, confused, and bewildered, the British manager departed the following day without a signed contract and with having left without what the Chinese considered to be the vital stage of cementing their working relationship. Because of the British manager's abrupt and perceived rude departure, another manager, familiar with the local Chinese customs, was sent to salvage and close the deal.

## Durable structures at the intersection of culture and context

When leaders focus on the immediate moment and relational motion between culture and context, they should not exclude attention to the durable structures of culture and context. Durable structures are the artifacts, institutions, and values existing within constructed reality.

### *"Learning culture" is different from "learning* about *culture"*

How do we learn culture? Learning *about* a culture often means learning facts about its history, art, government, taking language instruction, learning what social scientists (sociologists, anthropologists, folklorists, etc.) report, and learning a few obligatory "dos and don'ts." Most often, however, such superficiality will serve you only if you plan a typical weeklong tourist trip. While our understanding of ways to learn about cultures improves, we are still trying to understand culture through cross-cultural comparisons and reductionistic methods. The truth is that such superficiality ignores important considerations and can actually cause more harm than good for everyone involved. The point is that if you are a Caucasian European-American, can you ever expect to "know" the experience of an African Kenyan by taking two courses in language and customs of West African countries? The answer is, no, you cannot, not even if you took ten courses.

With the realization that both context and culture are inseparable from those who constructed them, the problem becomes how to know which culture one should learn. We will reframe this last statement just a little to ensure your comprehension because we do not mean, should you learn about German culture or should you learn about Thai culture. We mean that one important consideration concerns the tendency to "stereotype" cultures. While we have discussed stereotyping previously, here we mean the tendency to assume that because one studies a culture generally, one can know the culture. When we identify and categorize general tendencies in efforts to compare and contrast cultures, we reduce and oversimplify. The problem being that within cultures, we also find significant variation. What is important to remember is that while one can draw certain generalizations, which can be helpful, since generalization includes flexibility for variation and evolution, stereotypes enforce rigidity. We recommend keeping three concepts in mind as shown in Figure 7.1.

It is especially important that those in technical occupations, such as engineering or information technology, learn more about the behavioral science approach to management, such as culture.

## Leadership and the intersection of context and culture

Leadership, *the action of leading a group of people or organization*,[4] is a social construct. We construct leader and follower relationships as we interact with each other and the environment to create our future through our visioning and actions in the present. The truth is, everyone is born with potential to lead, and everyone must choose when and where s/he will take the initiative, step forward, and lead. Human activity and social interaction creates choice points for the people involved. Social interaction creates relationships between the involved parties. The choices individuals make create the potential of leader–follower relationships. In this way, social interaction creates context. In other words, and most relevant to our discussion, the leader–follower relationship creates context.

The residual of human social interactions, beyond the immediate circumstance, is what we call culture. More importantly, reality is perceptually based and constantly in a state of flux. This means that leaders and followers are always in the position to affect and change their circumstances. Some of what we perceive as reality is actually residual from our former experiences. Experience can be beneficial or deleterious. Experience influences how leaders make decisions and how followers react to leader-initiated decisions. Outcomes depend largely on how effectively leaders and followers can create clear expectations. Expectations

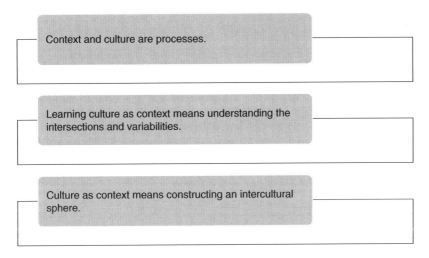

Context and culture are processes.

Learning culture as context means understanding the intersections and variabilities.

Culture as context means constructing an intercultural sphere.

*Figure 7.1* Three cultural concepts to keep in mind.

can be problematic, however, when either the leader or follower create expectations based upon inaccurately anticipating certain behavior.

Currently, organizational leadership is influenced notably by two interrelated social phenomena: globalization, and the resultant diversity. The leader's challenge is the competing tug between global standardization and local differentiation. As we have said previously, a leader's experience is vital to outcomes and performance. However, here, we are not speaking about leaders' *experiences* from the past. Here, we are speaking of the leader's ability to be present, fully, in all situations and in his or her ability to draw upon current experience to co-create and co-construct a workable, emerging reality for all stakeholders. The following interview with Jean-Christophe Bas of the United Nations illustrates these abilities.

---

### *Exhibit 7.1*  Interview with Jean-Christophe Bas, senior advisor strategic development and partnerships, United Nations

As the senior advisor of strategic development and partnerships at the United Nations, Jean-Christophe Bas has a unique vantage point from which to view world leaders. With his focus on creating and inspiring an environment of respect and inclusiveness in which people work as a team and take into account different cultures and expertise, he is a great model of global leadership.

*What are the most important decisions that a leader of an organization must make?*

In my successive job incarnations, being with the United Nations, the World Bank, or the Aspen Institute, I had the responsibility to spearhead corporate efforts in the field of strategic development, policy dialogue and innovation. These are all tasks that can be very sensitive and somewhat risky for the image and the reputation of the organization.

I have observed how important and difficult it is, when you are developing a new and significant initiative, to combine the risks inherent to innovation while preserving the integrity and the image of the organization. Particularly when the reputation and the image are so vital for the organization. Being creative means taking risks, but you have to define the notion of "measurable risk." How far you can go in your endeavor without taking the risk of harming the image and the reputation of the organization if ever you fail in your attempt?

Another very important decision, at least in my position as a developer and "incubator" of projects, is to be able to identify and hire the right people to handle the project when the implementation phase starts. With nearly thirty years of experience, I realize that the level of comfort and potential for extraordinary development of any project is based on the talent and capacities of those involved in the implementation. Once the innovation phase is complete, implementation begins. Finding the right person who can handle the inception and implementation is absolutely key.

*What is one characteristic that you believe every global business leader should possess?*

The capacity to inspire, communicate trust, passion and vision. These are fundamental ingredients for leadership.

Vision and passion are indispensable to motivate people, to give them a sense of a common goal and willing to give the best of themselves; to challenge their own creativity.

Equally important, the leader must inspire trust in his or her capacity to accomplish the vision; to achieve successfully the goal, to deliver.

There is a third characteristic: inspiring respect and inclusiveness. A global leader should create an environment where people feel ownership and work as a team. Having the capacity to listen and take into account diverse knowledge, expertise, and cultures is crucial.

Global leadership is three-dimensional: vision and passion; trust and capacity to accomplish your goal; valuing diversity and inclusiveness.

*Would you say that the capacity of accomplishment applies to both success and failure, so this refers to not only the capacity to fail but also the capacity to learn from failure?*

Yes, this can also be the capacity to fail as well. But even more so, accomplishment is the sense that the leader will not just come up with great ideas and an inspiring vision, but he or she will also be able to reach the objective, to create the framework necessary to succeed. So, it's not just to have a great idea, but to have a plan for the organization to reach the goal. That is also why I mentioned in the previous question that one of the most important decisions a leader has to take is to identify the right people who will succeed in the implementation phase. There is indeed a critical time period or transition between the phase of creation and the phase of implementation that requires extreme attention from the leader.

*What is the biggest challenge facing global business leaders at the United Nations or any organization of which you've been a part?*

The United Nations is confronted with a double challenge. The first challenge is about its governance structure: the UN is a "Westphalien"-type organization, predominantly led and governed by member states. This old and somewhat rigid form of State predominance is hardly compatible with the goal and the mission of the international community and the UN to solve issues that are increasingly global—therefore borderless and stateless—and common to most of humanity. The complexity of these global issues—global warming, spread of disease, biodiversity, poverty eradication, conflict prevention—indeed requires lots of flexibility and creativity and the involvement of a wide range of non-State actors, i.e., the corporate sector, academia, civil society organizations, religious groups, social media... and the public at large. It requires going beyond strictly the national interest and going towards the interest of all. This becomes very difficult in a world increasingly fragmented, characterized by the emergence of new players and unchallenged powers.

The second challenge is actually related to the first one: it is about values, how people around the world see today the notion of universal principles in a world that is dramatically changing. Until recently, the Western model and principles—democracy; human rights; gender equality; freedom of expression—were somewhat dominant and associated to universal, there was not much space left for other cultures and world views. Today, with the emergence of new economic powers in the world, but also with major demographic shifts and the resurgence of religions in many parts of the world, we are witnessing a profound change in terms of values, and new players who are claiming a seat at the table. This is the irony of the contemporary world: on one hand, it is increasingly globalized; on the other hand, people are increasingly entrenched in their identity, in their own values. There is still a long way to go until peoples and cultures become easily compatible and coexist together peacefully.

This is a huge challenge for the UN which must continuously steer a global conversation among State and non-State actors in order to set up altogether workable mechanisms to ensure cohesion, inclusion, stability, and a sense of common destiny shared by all. This is actually one of the main goals of the UN Alliance of Civilizations that was created in 2005 at the initiative of the Secretary General of the UN.

*What effect do you think national culture has on business leadership decision-making? (This can also include how your own native national culture affects your decision-making.)*

Bottom line, national culture should not affect the decision-making process of a leader at the UN. Though we cannot deny the importance, for any human being, of our own culture, education and traditions, here at the UN, and in other inter-governmental organizations, our responsibility and our duty is to embrace multiple perspectives, to "transcend" our national vision and national thinking in order to find the appropriate responses.

With regards to whether where the organization is headquartered has an impact on the given organization, again, I would say bottom line it should not, but the reality is that it often does. For instance in the 1990s, the World Bank and the International Monetary Fund (both headquartered in Washington D.C.) were criticized as being influenced by an American market-based approach coined as "the Washington consensus."

The UN, based in New York, a city characterized by the diversity of people, cultures and religions living in this small territory, with its rule at the General Assembly of "one country, one vote," may be seen as the defender of the diversity in the world, an equal voice for all.

UNESCO, based in Paris, is the champion in the promotion of cultural diversity, very much in line with the French call to protect the "l' exception culturelle."

The last example is the European Central Bank, based in Frankfurt. It represents the tempo of the orthodoxy of finance and the Euro policy, very consistent with Germany's agenda.

If we take these examples, it shows us that whether it is the cause or the effect, the location of an organization is not totally disconnected from its environment.

*How does national culture affect the rate of acceptance of globalization in certain parts of the world?*

Globalization is profoundly affecting the fabric of the society and the notion of identity in all parts of the world, and we are witnessing the emergence of growing gaps within and among countries. This includes demographic gaps, with radically opposed trends between countries and regions around the world. There are growing gaps between the increasingly rich and the poor on the planet. There are gaps between people and countries either increasingly religious or increasingly secular. There are growing gaps between the winners and the losers of globalization. This includes those who have an increasingly global perspective and capacity to navigate successfully the global work and those who feel threatened and unable to be part of the process and therefore reject it radically. There are also growing gaps between corporate rules and country legislation, particularly due to new media and the Internet.

All of these gaps generate tensions, fear, anxiety, and stress. It is urgent and vital to address these issues if we want to make globalization work and be accepted by all. We are entering a radically new world that requires serious explanation, awareness raising and open conversation if we want to have people accepting the differences and agreeing with the objective of living together under the motto "Unity in Diversity." Building an inclusive society is one of the major challenges of our time. That is the role of the United Nations Alliance of Civilizations.

*Is there a difference between how inter-governmental organizations (IGOs) and non-governmental (NGOs) organizations view leadership?*

I am not sure if there is a major difference between how leaders in NGOs and IGOs view leadership. It is more a matter of personality. The difference rather lies more in their mandate, their goal.

Most NGOs are focused on one major goal, being climate change; health; education for all; gender equality; fighting corruption. I appreciate that they have been instrumental in mobilizing public support and in influencing the way most of the inter-governmental organizations work today. For instance, the world movement advocating canceling the debt of the poorest countries had a major effect at the turn of the millennium.

IGOs by nature have a slightly different approach: their role is to promote change "from the inside" in engaging with governments. Their role and their responsibility are to develop a comprehensive approach, looking at all these issues together, and not just one in particular. This is, in my view, the major difference between NGOs and IGOs. But their goal is the same—to promote stability and development—and they can be very complementary if their respective leaders manage to create trust and common views.

The reality is that the leadership skill that is needed today, being in non-governmental organizations, the corporate sector, and the government sector is this capacity to look beyond strictly their field of work, their own sector, to put themselves in the shoes and the mind of other stakeholders, and to understand that their role and their responsibility is not just limited to their own success. Sustainability, successful results, innovation, this all requires leaders to be inclusive and to embrace multiple and sometimes conflicting perspectives. This is what I call "hybrid leadership."

*What is one mistake you witness business leaders making more frequently than others? Do you think that some leaders make such errors due to their inability to be self-aware of their own national cultural bias, as mentioned above?*

There is sometimes a tendency within the UN, like in most inter-governmental organizations, of overestimating the role and the capacity of governments, of *the State*, to solve problems affecting people. We may call this "the bunker syndrome."

I have observed this phenomenon in lots of large organizations, being governmental or multinational companies. They are so big and powerful that their employees become "bunkerized." They see the world strictly through the lens of their organization and have a tendency to forget that there are multiple players, partners, and dynamics globally that can make a difference.

It is very important for inter-governmental organizations like the UN or the World Bank to take better into account the capacity of non-State actors in finding responses to challenges affecting people. They need to look carefully at how working *truly together* at solving problems operates. This is different than pursuing the same goal but working in silos, as it happens too often.

I see this as a major challenge more than national cultural bias. In my view, the true leader is the one who has this capacity to create the real synergy, to establish a climate and mechanisms that will optimize the potential contribution of each partner and player.

*Can you name a person who has had a tremendous impact on you as a leader? Maybe someone who has been a mentor to you? Why and how did this person impact your life?*

I had the privilege throughout my whole life to collaborate with amazing people who inspired and influenced me profoundly. And I'm proud to say that I have learned a few important things with each of them. Two had a special impact on me.

The first actually is a tandem composed by Jim Wolfensohn and Jean-François Rischard, respectively president and vice president of the World Bank. They both have very creative minds, looking continuously for innovation, with an amazing capacity to think out of the box and to inspire those working with them to give every day the best of themselves and to work with passion. This is quite unusual in this kind of environment. They represent typically this kind of "hybrid leadership" that I mentioned above. And actually both of them have developed successive experience, being in public and private sectors, the arts, and academic research. That is what gives them this capacity to think big, to understand the multiple dynamics in any given issue and to engage comfortably with a wide and diverse range of interlocutors.

The second is my grandfather. Coming from a modest family of farmers at the border with Switzerland, he was in both World War I, and in World War II as a resister. He actually spent ten years of his life at war with Germany. After World War II, he was elected as a member of the Parliament of the French Congress. He dedicated the thirty years of his life after World War II, to promoting dialogue and reconciliation between France and Germany. He spent the remainder of his life focused on strengthening the peace among Europeans and the creation of the European Union. I'm very proud of him; I have learned from him the extraordinary virtues of dialogue and respect among people and cultures.

*Within the global economy, how important is it that a global business leader understands the key features of the Geoleadership Model? http:// www.geoleadership.com/model.asp*

The Geoleadership model provides a very useful compass for action and global leadership. It has encapsulated some of the most crucial characteristics of global leadership. Many elements are part of what I mentioned, which are very much in line in terms of creating inclusiveness and ownership. I think the model should be shared and discussed with others.

*What do you like to ask other business leaders when you get the chance?*

I would love you to bring together the people interviewed for this book, *Global Business Leadership*. I would like to have them discuss together their key messages, and validating or challenging their point of view.

I would be interested in their opinions about the growing gaps that globalization is generating. Do they feel the same way? Also, I would ask them how they see this notion of "hybrid leadership" from their own perspective.

More directly related to my work at the United Nations Alliance of Civilizations, I would welcome their views on how to create strong public support for diversity and inclusion. I have indeed the conviction that it is indispensable to make a better world for all and more sustainable.

\*\*\*

An interesting point made in this interview is that large organizations, governmental and multinationals, are becoming siloed. Leaders and employees often view things through the lens of just their own industry and/or organizations. We, along with Jean-Christophe Bas, would love to bring the people interviewed for *Global Business Leadership* together. By pooling our knowledge we might bridge the gaps between organizations and people that globalization is creating.

**Jean-Christophe Bas** is senior advisor of Strategic Development and Partnerships at the United Nations secretariat of the Alliance of Civilizations. Jean-Christophe is the author of L'EUROPE A LA CARTE (Editions du Cherche-Midi), a book of reflections on Europe published at the occasion of the 20th anniversary of the fall of the Berlin wall.

From 1999 to 2008, Jean-Christophe served as development policy dialogue manager at the World Bank and set up innovative mechanisms of strategic dialogue between the World Bank and key constituencies around the World on Development and Poverty eradication challenges. He is a former executive director of the Aspen Institute in France (1994–1999), and is now serving as vice chairman of the advisory Board of Aspen Institute in France. Jean-Christophe started his carrier as head of staff of the president of the Committee on External Economic Relations (1984–86) at the European Parliament.

Please see Figure 7.2 to understand how context influences a leader's behavior.

*The principle of "Context"* 159

A Geoleader can negotiate the principle of Context through the following practices and behaviors:

- Practice setting intentions for your actions.
- Practice asking other people with whom you interact for their understanding and interpretation of your meaning and your intention.
- Practice evaluating your motives for your actions to see whether they are outdated or important for your future.
- Practice evaluating your mental models for their appropriateness to your now actions.

*Figure 7.2* The principle of "Context" in practice.

In Exhibit 7.2, an interview with former governor Michael Dukakis, lays the foundation for how context can be interpreted depending on both the goal and perspective of any leader.

### *Exhibit 7.2* **Interview with Michael Dukakis, former governor Massachusetts**

Former governor of Massachusetts, Michael Dukakis, is a role model for the principle of Context. Throughout his interview you will read his description of his personal style of leadership, which is to continually ask other people with whom he interacts for their understanding and interpretation of his meaning and intention as well as solutions, ideas, and input on challenges facing the team, organization, and/or public sector in general.

*What are the most important decisions that a leader of an organization must make?*

As a leader, the first thing you have to do is put a team together. Picking team members is as important as anything you will do as a leader. A colleague of mine, Gordon Chase, used to say that there are three important things when it comes to managing in the public sector: people, people, and people. Picking people who have a good combination of intelligence and political skills, and then molding the team so that it works well together is absolutely crucial. If you make a mistake, maybe one or two are not as good as you thought, you will end up spending an inordinate amount of time fixing the situation that you would probably much rather spend elsewhere. I've picked people who I thought would be stars, who turned out to be less than that. I've also picked people who I thought were a bit of a risk, who turned out to be stars. There is no question that the leader's ability to be effective has everything to do with the people he or she is surrounded by.

In the public sector, this means people with more than "talent." They must have plenty of intelligence and political skills, which make it possible for them to work effectively in the public environment. You don't necessarily need these skills in the private sector, but you must have them in the public sector. Choosing people who have the ability to work with other elected officials, with constituencies and advocacy groups, to handle the press on an almost daily basis is of the utmost importance to the leader's success and to the success of the people with whom he or she works. Without these skills, there will be problems.

One major difference between the public and private sector is in to whom the leader reports. If you're a governor, you have to work with your legislature. The legislature is your board of directors. In the private sector, most boards of directors are handpicked by the CEO, by the leader. As a public leader, you have to work closely and effectively with a board which has been picked by your constituents, not by you. It is a different operation all together than working in the private sector. Another part of daily life as a political leader is dealing with the media. On a daily basis, political leaders show up to the office with 25 people with cameras, tape recorders, and notebooks, trying to find out what they are doing and what they did wrong. Most private sector leaders do not have to deal with this. And of course, we wouldn't have it any other way. The press is ideally the public's watchdog, but this is a group that private sector leaders rarely have to face.

Building coalitions is also very important. Particularly at the state and local level, bringing people into the process is crucial. I believe in creating working groups in which people may disagree with each other, but at least they agree that there is a problem. Say for instance, with healthcare. If the people in the group agree that there is a problem, you are halfway to the solution! Bringing people together and working with them to find solutions is very important, and if you are in the position of political responsibility, people will usually respond favorably to an invitation to participate in the group. Americans want to be part of the solution, and it is amazing what happens when you get them together. The skill here—yours or someone who works for you—is to make it possible for people to gather together and start thinking constructively about a problem even when they have been arguing about it for years.

*As a global leader, how have you encouraged creative thinking within your organizations?*

While I encouraged my people to be creative, I also appointed people who were in fact creative thinkers. This is one of the reasons I wanted them to serve. Some public CEOs, mayors, governors, and presidents hire a flock of special assistants to be around them. I am not a big believer in hiring a lot of staff to be between me and my cabinet. I wanted as few people between me and my top policy people as possible. They knew they could walk into my office anytime. No appointment necessary. I challenged them to be innovative. I encouraged them to look at what could be learned from other governors. I had a very strong cabinet of secretaries deliberately because I wanted them to feel that they were encouraged to come up with new ideas and that I would be responsive to them.

*What is one characteristic that you believe every global business leader should possess?*

Passion for what you are doing. If you are going to lead, you have to feel a very strong sense of commitment to your vision and convey this to the people who work for you.

*What is the biggest challenge facing global business leaders today?*

This depends on which stage you are playing on—in the broadest possible sense, I would say it is: how to build a world in which force is increasingly ruled out as a means [for] settling disputes between and among countries. This to me is the single most important goal as a world society we should have. Invading Iraq doesn't serve that goal: Strongly suggesting to China and Korea and Vietnam and Japan that the International Court of Justice is the place to resolve these island disputes does meet that goal.

We ought to be building the credibility of international peacekeeping organizations. The World Court is there to solve these problems that are basically property disputes. When we skirt around Nicaragua, financing Contra operations, mining the harbor illegally and in violation of international law, because we have decided not to accept the jurisdiction of the World Court because it ruled against us, we are hardly an example for the rest of the world, are we? The UN, imperfect though it is, is the one institution that can step in to deal with challenges like Syria, for instance. It's important that global, political, and business leaders not engage in these issues unilaterally, which too often both we and others do. Predictably, it never seems to work and always seems to turn out disastrously. No one appointed the U.S. the world's policeman. Not only are we not doing it very well; we can't afford it.

This needs to be everywhere, intervening, is a hangover from the Cold War, and now is the time when we can change it. In my view, building international institutions whose decisions will be accepted by all countries is very important. I think we have this opportunity today.

*What effect do you think national culture has on business leadership decision-making? (This can also include how your own native national culture affects your decision-making.)*

My parents were Greek immigrants. They came here when they were 15 and 9, so while Americanized there was a lot of Greek culture in my upbringing. This is where my interest in politics came from. Greeks are very political and take politics seriously.

In terms of American culture and its impact on business leadership or for that matter political leadership, this is a country that opens up the door of opportunity in a remarkable way to millions of people. Immigrants believe coming to the U.S. gives them and their children an opportunity that they wouldn't have had in their home countries. There is also no question that the extent and level of charitable giving and work in the U.S. far exceeds any other place in the world. As a governor of Massachusetts, the fact that there were so many people willing to come into public service because they cared was a great example of this.

There are downsides. When I grew up, the U.S. was racist. It was anti-Semitic. It was inconceivable in 1962 when I first went into the legislature that a Greek-American could be elected Governor of Massachusetts. Twenty years later, we had a Greek in the governor's office, in the U.S. Senate, in Congress, and we were all sons of immigrants. Now, the political culture is much more open and encouraging of diversity and the election or appointments of people are from a very broad ethnic and racial background.

*What are your thoughts on globalization and how important is it for leaders to develop their own self-awareness so as to adjust to the changing context(s) under which they operate in a given situation and/or organization? (This consciousness could include the leader's own cultural self-bias while operating with diverse constituents.)*

Globalization is here to stay, and it can have an enormous impact for the better if we do it right. To me this means ensuring that as we globalize, the international community sets standards for the conduct of countries that are part of this globalized economic system. The question is: What do we expect of countries if they're going to be part of this globalized economy? I think we've got to insist that every country meets certain important standards when it comes to worker occupational safety and health. Every country ought to be expected to pay a reasonably decent minimum wage. These issues should be determined by the World Trade Organization (WTO), and should be a requirement for membership and participation in the benefits of the WTO. There are other aspects as well, such as expecting countries that participate and benefit from this global economy to meet certain responsible standards to their workers and to the environment. We aren't there yet, but there is a growing movement in this direction.

*What is one mistake you witness business leaders making more frequently than others? Do you think that some leaders make such errors due to their inability to be self-aware of their own national cultural bias, as mentioned above?*

Often, global leaders don't listen until they've got a bee in their bonnet. Then they go off half-cocked, determined to do something, but they haven't listened to others, they haven't picked others' brains to get a sense of whether or not their particular idea/solution makes sense in the context of what they are trying to do. A degree of confidence helps in a leadership position, but you've got to listen to understand what people are saying and a lot of leaders don't do this well. This applies in all sectors, domestically, globally, private, and public.

*Can you name a person who has had a tremendous impact on you as a leader? Maybe someone who has been a mentor to you? Why and how did this person impact your life?*

Obviously it wasn't a close relationship, but one person who particularly inspired me and served as a model in my young political life was Jack Kennedy. He was a Massachusetts guy, born and raised a mile from my house. He was very important in that sense. I only met him once personally and heard him speak a few times, but he was proud of public service and had the ability to reach out to young people and encourage them to get into public service. His leadership and ability to touch hundreds of thousands of people was a gift.

My high school basketball coach was more of a mentor to me, though at the time I'm not sure I realized it. He was a wonderful guy named Johnny Grinnell. In fact, he was my wife, Kitty's, homeroom teacher. I used to ask him, "Why didn't you tell me about her?" He'd say, "You wouldn't have been interested. You were a senior; she was a freshman." He hated Joe McCarthy, couldn't stand him. Every night, he'd drive me and one of my teammates to the southern part of town on his way home to Newton, Mass, and we'd have conversations about McCarthy. He'd say to me, "You ought run for elective office someday." No one else had ever said that to me. He subsequently became the Director of Guidance at Brookline High School. The night I was nominated in Atlanta, he was sitting next to my mother in our family box, watching his two students, Mike and Kitty Dukakis, accepting the nomination.

*Within the global economy, how important is it that a global business leader understands the key features of the Geoleadership Model?*

We've talked about all the features of the Geoleadership Model, and I think they're all important. I don't know if consensus building is part of it, but it is certainly implied. As I've said, consensus building is extremely important in both the private and public sectors, but especially in the public sector.

*What do you like to ask other business leaders when you get the chance?*

I like to ask them: What do you do, and how do you do it? I ask them if I can pick their brains about what they do, how they do it, and the challenges they've faced. It's interesting and helpful, so I appreciate the opportunity to ask them these questions. I'm particularly interested in how they interact with the public sector. If they are in the private sector, who do they work with in the public sector, what is the relationship like, what things can public sector people do to make it possible for them to do more, to be better, etc.

***

With his emphasis on building coalitions to bring people together, former Governor Michael Dukakis made a significant impact on the state of Massachusetts with an unprecedented three-term period of service. His style of leadership, to create working groups in which people may have disagreed about the solution but at least were in agreement that there was a problem, brought people together. His optimistic outlook that if people agree there is a problem, they are halfway to the solution is undoubtedly a prerequisite to being a global leader whose high context skill makes it "possible for people to gather together and start thinking constructively about a problem even when they have been arguing about it for years."

**Michael Stanley Dukakis** was born in Brookline, Massachusetts, on November 3, 1933. His parents both emigrated from Greece to Massachusetts before marrying and settling just outside of Boston. Dukakis graduated from Brookline (1951), Swarthmore College (1955), and Harvard Law School (1960). He served for two years in the United States Army, sixteen months of which he spent with the support group to the United Nations delegation of the Military Armistice Commission in Munsan, Korea.

Dukakis began his political career as an elected Town Meeting Member in the town of Brookline. He was elected chairman of his town's Democratic organization in 1960 and won a seat in the Massachusetts legislature in 1962. He served four terms as a legislator. Dukakis won his party's nomination for Governor in 1974 and was re-elected to an unprecedented third four-year term in 1986 by one of the largest margins in history. In 1986 his colleagues in the National Governors Association voted him the most effective governor in the nation.

Dukakis won the Democratic nomination for the presidency of the United States in 1988, but was defeated by George Bush. Since June of 1991, Dukakis has been a distinguished professor of political science at Northeastern University. Additionally, since 1995, he has served as a visiting professor at UCLA's School of Public Affairs. His research has focused on national healthcare policy reform and the lessons that national policy makers can learn from state reform efforts. Dukakis was nominated by President Clinton for a five-year term as a member of the new Board of Directors of Amtrak.

Former Governor Dukakis exemplifies a leader whose skill was to facilitate connections between people even those of highly disparate opinions. This high context focus is of significant importance to the success of global leaders as one of their most critical responsibilities is to forge relationships across the globe. While important to the success of the global leaders, this skill is even more important to the sustainability of global society. Gone are the days when leaders could be more short-sighted and task-oriented to just the bottom line of their organizations. Today's interconnected web of global business requires that leaders learn about context.

## The bottom line

In summary, we described context as being both helpful and a hindrance to us as leaders within intercultural situations. Every culture can and has been categorized as either high or low context. High context refers to societies or groups where people have close connections over a long period. Many aspects of cultural behavior are not made explicit because most members know what to do and what to think from years of interaction with each other. Countries like China, Japan, India, and some parts of Spain and Italy fall into this category. Inversely, low context refers to societies where people tend to have many connections but of shorter duration or for some specific reason. In these societies, cultural behavior and beliefs may need to be spelled out explicitly so that those coming into the cultural environment know how to behave. Countries like the United States, the United Kingdom and some other Western nations qualify as low-context cultures.

In China communication tends to be very efficient because of their information-flow at work and in private. They discuss everything in advance and consider meetings as an official "ceremony" where the already commonly agreed decision will be announced. This is important in the way of "giving and keeping face." The Americans and Germans in contrast inform the participating attendants in a meeting about the hard and necessary facts. We have observed times when an American company hires employees from India or China; they tend to ask too many questions and are always inquisitive. Indians tend toward this and some have the habit of wanting to know it all before they commit to something. Americans might sometimes find that behavior intrusive and unnecessary; placing great importance on ambience, decorum, the relative status of the participants in a communication and the manner of message's delivery. In France, it might be hard to feel fully accepted for outsiders within their culture because of their big diffuse connections. In comparison members of individualistic cultures using low-context communication like Germans, Americans, and Finns sometimes ignore those differences from high-context countries cultures.

In case of a meeting where members from low- and high-context cultures would have to work and discuss matters together, the French and especially the Chinese would not interact and express their disagreement or reservations. For Chinese issues, circumstances and relationships are as important as work so they would comment only in a more private or appropriate occasion. Additionally, people from high-context cultures (Indian, Chinese employees) tend to form min-groups at work where they would talk in their native tongue and discuss everything in detail. In contrast, the American employees would keep work and friendship away from each other as far as possible. Discussions at work in a professional environment would be to the point and concise. High-context cultures are often misunderstood as being too relationship-oriented. The fact is that these cultures tend to value relationships more than the task. These differences in cultures create misunderstandings and miscommunication.

# 8 The principle of "Change"

"There is nothing permanent except change."

—Heraclitus[1]

Change has several meanings, including: to become different or render something or someone different, to replace or substitute something for another, and to pass from one state of being to another. In North American cultures (U.S. and Canada), it is cliché to say that the only constant is change. However cliché, the fact remains that people working in global business contexts face an evolving state of affairs. We devoted several sections of Chapter 1 discussing the various challenges apparent at the time of this writing. Now, we address the effects of external change on the efforts of leaders and what change means to these individuals in terms of what is required of them.

A discussion about change commonly is paired with discourse on adaptation. In terms of adjusting to foreign cultures, adaptation describes a person's response to a new social environment. Aggregate patterns of adaptation are called modes of incorporation. Whether as individuals or as members of social groups, people entering foreign cultures typically modify old behaviors and beliefs and learn new ones as they adjust to new institutions and new situations different from their native environment. A person's ability to participate fully and effectively in a "host society" is diminished until such adaptation occurs.

Prominent in adaptation literature are discussions on the theory and model of acculturation. Acculturation strategies refer to the planned methods that individuals use in responding to new stress-inducing cultural contexts.

## "CHANGE"
### DEFINED

Flexibility in adapting to dynamic cultural environments.

According to several models, acculturation strategies can be categorized into four classifications, which include "assimilation," "integration," "separation," and "marginalization." Assimilation strategy occurs when individuals decide not to maintain their cultural identities by seeking contact in their daily interactions with a dominant group. When the individuals from the non-dominant group "place a value on holding on to their original culture" and seek no contact with the dominant group, then these individuals are pursuing a separation strategy. When individuals express an interest in maintaining strong ties in their everyday life both with their ethnic group as well as with the dominant group, the strategy used is "integration." The fourth strategy is marginalization in which individuals "lose cultural and psychological contact with both their traditional culture and the larger society."

Integration implies both the preservation of the home culture and an active involvement with the host culture. Central to integration strategy is the assumption of universality. This perspective assumes that although there are substantial variations in the life circumstances of the cultural groups that experience acculturation, the psychological processes that operate during acculturation are essentially the same for all the groups. In other words, an individual's acculturation strategies reveal the underlying psychological processes that unfold during their adaptation to new cultural contexts. Other psychological processes such as "behavioral shifts" (changing behavior), "culture shedding" (eliminating traditions), "culture shock" (sudden exposure to an unfamiliar culture), and "acculturative stress" (stress related to adapting to different cultural expectations) are also experienced in varying degrees by an individual undergoing acculturation.

Another adaptation strategy, "segmented assimilation" describes three contrasting acculturation patterns characteristic of some individuals and groups as they cope with cultural shock. The first is linear acculturation and assimilation whereby the assimilating individual or group advances effectively and is integrated socially, culturally, and politically into the host culture. In other words, an individual or group becomes effective in their strategies to integrate and has been welcomed by the host group. The second pattern is selective assimilation where individuals and groups develop bonds with other expatriates and deliberately preserve their native culture behaviors. In this strategy, incoming individuals are less effective in being welcomed by a host culture. Conversely, the third pattern is descending assimilation where entire expatriate groups fail to adjust and disintegrate. Ostensibly, the acculturation process is highly influenced by structural and contextual factors in the host culture. In other words, some cultures, at certain times in their history, are more or less welcoming of strangers into their midst.

## The key? Learning agility

We begin by stating that people when faced with change have choices. They can refuse to participate, they can resist and sabotage, they can blithely go their merry way and see how they will fare (letting events dictate their fate), they can stubbornly adapt, they can adapt fittingly, or they can lead the way by setting a shining example. We would posit that the latter two choices are the only choices for leaders, potential leaders, and nearly everyone else who envisions a satisfactory future. The question, then, is not about shall we adapt, but how shall we adapt. The answer should come as no surprise. We must be *learning agile.*

Before we consider learning agility, though, we will first discuss the idea of learning about culture within culture. How people learn, the nature of learning, is culturally diverse, although learning is universal (found in all human cultures). The ways in which people learn to think, perceive, build beliefs, behave and feel, capture and comprehend, and derive and create meaning, have an intimate connection to their own cultural context. In other words, you cannot understand learning without considering the specific cultural terrain within which it occurs. Most of us tend to think about learning in ethnocentric ways, in accordance with our own cultural preferences; although there is, naturally, variation within cultures. The challenge is that we need to develop the capacity to stand outside our own cultural conditioning in order to appreciate and invite a variety of cultural perspectives into our own learning atmosphere. The idea that people learn through the lens of the relationships between living things and their environment is relatively new.

The time was that the words *learning* and *agility* seldom were found within the same sentence, let alone as its subject and predicate. In recent years, however, one contributory factor to business success for intercultural leaders and their organizations is building *learning agility*. To be agile, means to move quickly and easily. The inference here is that to be successful in a global economy, one must be agile at learning.

Research suggests that people who are quick learners, and therefore have a greater capacity to adapt, are not necessarily smarter than other people are. What they possess are superior (and quantifiably more) learning strategies. Figure 8.1 presents how individuals can build learning agility.

## Link between emotions and learning

### *Have you ever been told not to let your emotions rule your thoughts and actions?*

If you are like many adults, the answer is yes. Throughout the history of Western civilization, people have been in conflict about the connection between emotion and thought. In general, the wisdom was not to allow emotion to rule the "rational" mind. Recent research conducted by neurologists and educators shows an inextricable, if not *healthy*, link between emotion and reason—perhaps finally putting to rest the maxim that emotion is the antagonist of reason. Learning is identical in process to any other cognitive brain function in that the circuits that control and link reason with memory connect emotion and decision processes as well.

- Critical thinking skills—a repertoire of thinking skills including analysis, synthesis, evaluation, etc.
- Self-knowledge—including awareness of one's own learning styles and building access and usage of alternative styles and under which circumstances each is best utilized.
- Comfort with ambiguity.
- Comfort with taking risks and making mistakes—including being willing to experiment in public forums.
- Confidence.

*Figure 8.1* Building learning agility.

## *Consider just the brain's process for digesting information*

First, everything is processed through a kind of switchboard called the thalamus, located at the base of the brain.

Second, the information is then routed automatically to different sections of the brain. Initially, the information goes through the brain's emotion-arousal systems for evaluation to determine whether the information is perceived as benign, beneficial, or threatening.

The evaluation involves a number of feedback loops originating in long-term memory. If we perceive the incoming stimuli as threatening, we automatically engage in a series of reactions, which sometimes remain unconscious, to help us process the information. This process illustration is the "flowchart" of *sense making*.

In other words, our brains must decide whether to admit or reject all incoming information (or stimuli). During this process, when unconscious emotional awakening reaches a certain point, it pushes into our conscious level and is experienced as *feelings*.

## *So, what do emotions have to do with learning?*

Memory and problem-solving processes that develop a solution to a situation are activated when we *attend* to risk and/or opportunity. Attention then locates the risk or opportunity and provides useful information about it to the person, who then acts on the information.

It turns out, that emotion activates attention, which is our focusing system and root of learning. Once again, emotion drives attention, which drives learning, memory, and problem-solving behavior.

## *In other words, it is an emotional structure that stimulates us, not a logical structure!*

Here we will apply this more explicitly to learning. Simply put, learning cannot take place when there is no emotional stimulation. Now let us also be clear that emotional stimulation does not necessarily result in learning! Here is why.

As a reminder, basic human emotions include just six: surprise, happiness, fear, anger, disgust, and sadness. No doubt, you noticed that several of these basic human emotions represent, what is generally perceived as, negative experience. *However*, people do not always experience emotions in the purist form.

For example, a person who has just received a promotion to a challenging position may experience surprise, happiness, and fear all at once. This combination of emotion may create a sense of exhilaration and may be perceived as excitement and considered positive by the person. Another person, in the same situation experiencing the same combination of emotion may perceive their reaction as anxiety, and feel overwhelmed by all of the new things they will have to face. Global leaders need to be capable at both the cognitive and feeling levels of analysis. "I think" is not enough without "I feel." The blending of both leads to emotional maturity, and better use of "intuition."

At this point, we want to introduce the principle of *Learning Trajectory*. All learning has a trajectory. This means that may be learning occurs in *continuous motion*.

This motion sometimes follows a linear path in its progression, but more often occurs along a circuitous route. At times, it is quite planned and structured, while at other times a learning trajectory can occur serendipitously, almost coincidentally.

Along all learning trajectories, there are moments when there are naturally occurring rewards. These types of rewards belong to the learner and are those special moments when there is a feeling of exhilaration on the learner's part at having achieved something they perceive as important. Other moments along the learning trajectory provide opportunity for managers (and organizations) to recognize and reward the result of individual learning. In Figure 8.2 these opportunities are listed.

Ostensibly, the organization's executive leadership decides the compensation and benefits policies for the enterprise. Managers have the responsibility to support these policies within their units. However, managers can influence policy decisions as well as the espoused and practiced values of the enterprise.

---

- At the moment the learner takes a risk to try something and makes a mistake and learns from that mistake.
- When the learner is observed utilizing learning to acquire a skill for the first time.
- At the time when a new skill is used to perform at a higher level.
- When that same skill generates an innovation.
- When a particular skill makes the individual an important resource.
- When the individual attains a new level of certification.
- At the time when the individual is perceived as an expert by others and becomes a mentor.

---

*Figure 8.2* Learning trajectory.

## Developing learning strategies

*Have you ever observed an accomplishment of someone and wondered to yourself: How did s/he do that?*

Perhaps you have wondered the same thing about yourself and your own accomplishments. If so, you are in good company! Two theorists entered into answering this question several years ago and one said to the other: "If you teach me to do what you do, I'll tell you how you did it." In this way, the second theorist was providing a "model" for understanding the underlying patterns used by the first theorist to accomplish a task, expertly. Of course, most of you will recognize this as inductive reasoning—identifying and describing patterns from the behavior of something. This is one fundamental process for model building. Such an example is simply one way of codifying knowledge and competence so that it may be replicated at will. The result of these two theorists' work is one meta-model that allows people to find out *how* they do something so that they can repeat their successes and transfer their learning and doing process to other endeavors or communicate it to other people.

*Therefore, what does this all have to do with learning strategy, you ask?*

To begin with, a learning strategy is the pattern and process people (unconsciously) use to learn. Everyone has a learning strategy! The question, then, is not *whether* adults have learning strategies, so much as *how effective* is a person's learning strategy in meeting (their) objectives! Research indicates that some people develop very effective strategies while other folks, for various reasons, do not. The implication for modern global organizations is that to optimize intellectual capital, global workers must possess *both* content expertise as well as learning agility. Now, let us focus attention on the meta-model we discussed earlier and how managers can facilitate effective learning strategies.

To review, we said that a learning strategy consists of the patterns and process a person uses to learn. We also said that there is a way of modeling a person's expertise such that their knowledge and expertise are codified. What we are saying, then, is that the modeling process is identical for describing patterns and processes someone uses for doing and learning. The objective of modeling is to identify outstanding patterns of doing and learning, which provides workers with the data they need in order to replicate their most effective learning and doing patterns. The simple steps to the basic modeling process applied to learning are given in Figure 8.3.

## Implications of learning strategy for intercultural leaders

In modern global organizations, managers must first build their self-awareness related to their learning strategies. This process will include conducting modeling exercises like the one described above and by adapting and building

Step One: Select a relevant learning experience – Identify three learning experiences in which you felt good and successful.

Step Two: Identify the characteristics of the learning environment in each situation – identify what was important in each learning experience as far as the setting, the support, your state of being, under what conditions did each occur?

Step Three: Identify the steps you took – describe the process. How did you begin? What did you do to motivate yourself? What kinds of things did you tell yourself about what you were doing and what you expected to do?

Step Four: Now, compare the process by identifying commonality in the patterns in the three situations.

Step Five: Identify one additional learning experience in which you felt you were not successful – compare the two patterns to discover what was missing in the unsuccessful experience.

*Figure 8.3* The five basic steps in the modeling process.

*learning agility.* In this way, managers will increase their own capability and provide needed role modeling for associates. However, this is only part of the story. In Exhibit 8.1 Garry Ridge will discuss the relationship between learning and leadership.

---

### *Exhibit 8.1* Interview with Garry Ridge, CEO/president/director, WD-40 Company

President and CEO of WD-40 Company, Garry Ridge is also adjunct professor at the University of San Diego where he teaches leadership development, talent management, and succession planning. This knowledge and experience, plus his multi-cultural background, make him a perfect exemplar and teacher of learning agility, as you'll read in his interview.

*What are the most important decisions that you must make as a leader of an organization?*

To me, there are three main areas. The first area is the decisions that must be made around the vision of the organization. The vision must be clear and easily understood by people in the organization;here at WD-40 we call them "tribe members", so that followers/employees can adopt the vision and embed it as something they want to achieve.

The second area is to make sure that values of the organization are truly reflective of what and how we want the organization to be. Values are the written reminders of not only acceptable behavior in an organization, but also values are a key driver and guide to decision-making in the organization.

The third area has everything to do with people. Who do we hire, who do we develop, and who do we let move on to other opportunities. People are such a vital part of the organization that we need to make sure as leaders that we are really engaged around the important decisions that apply to and affect people.

*How do you encourage creative thinking within your organizations?*

For leaders it's important to reduce the paralyzing nature of fear. At my organization, mistakes are learning moments. We've changed the terminology within the organization, and then let people be seen and heard *not* being punished because of a negative learning moment. This is really important. Also, as leaders we have to show our vulnerability. If we want people to think creatively and bring new and interesting ideas to the table, they need to be sure that the ego of the leader is not going to get in the way. For instance, if the leader "knows all" why would anyone try to think differently?

*What is one characteristic that you believe every global business leader should possess?*

Every global leader should possess patience. Global leaders who lead across so many different cultures and geographies need to be patient with people from different places doing, thinking, and being differently. It's important for leaders to be patient enough to listen, to learn, and to understand, and also very important to be tolerant. I think these are very important when a leader is acting in a global arena.

*What is the biggest challenge facing global business leaders today?*

The biggest challenge facing global business leaders today, without any doubt to me, is uncertainty. As leaders, we can face and handle many challenges, but uncertainty can really hold us back because it impacts our ability to take and/or not take risk. It impacts our ability to invest. It affects our ability to want to hire. Around business, there is so much uncertainty in the world today that it is a challenge. And, it's not helped by the fast track of communication, which fuels uncertainty as so many different scenarios are put in front of us all the time.

*What effect do you think national culture has on business leadership decision-making? (This can also include how your own native national culture affects your decision-making.)*

The effect national culture has on business leadership decision-making is huge, particularly given something as simple as whether the culture you're dealing with is an indirect or direct culture. The U.S. is a very direct culture. Spain and Mexico are indirect cultures. Global leaders have to be aware of this difference. National culture also impacts our systems and hierarchies. If you try to execute a Western style in China, for example, without respecting the family or tribal relationships of the Chinese, you will fail. First, you have to win their trust, not do business. If they don't trust you, you won't be successful.

*What are your thoughts on globalization and how important is it for leaders to develop their own self-awareness so as to adjust to the changing context(s) under which they operate in a given situation and/or organization? (This consciousness could include the leader's own cultural self-bias while operating with diverse constituents.)*

In my experience, I recognize that I would not be effective in my role as a global leader if I had not immersed myself in so many different cultures and countries around the world. I travel extensively to many countries, and the main reason for this is to develop my self-awareness of those areas to know what to do and what not to do. I think developing self-awareness and also experiencing different cultures and countries are crucial for leaders today.

*What is one mistake you witness business leaders making more frequently than others? Do you think that some leaders make such errors due to their inability to be self-aware of their own national cultural bias, as mentioned above?*

Business leaders today are pressured, especially in the U.S. because of the pressures of Wall Street, to make short-term decisions. Rather, we should be making decisions to build companies and organizations that endure over time. Yet, we're pressured to make the 90-day number. This is a major conflict. There is pressure to make short-term decisions, even though a business plan or strategy is solid. Bumps in the road are to be expected, but short-termism often wins out as people focus on the short term. This is not the way to build enduring businesses.

And we should be making decisions to build enduring companies or organizations over time.

*Can you name a person who has had a tremendous impact on you as a leader? Maybe someone who has been a mentor to you? Why and how did this person impact your life?*

The person who has had tremendous impact on me as a leader, and who I have probably spent the most time with, is Ken Blanchard. Ken and I met a number of years ago at the University of San Diego. Ken taught me the gift of trusting people and allowing them, within certain guidelines, to make decisions. He taught me to encourage people to do great things. We wrote a book together, *Helping People Win at Work*. A lot of the learning in the book is about empowering people around a set of clearly identifiable and measurable goals and then recognizing them for their achievements.

*Within the global economy, how important is it that a global business leader understands the key features of the Geoleadership Model?*

All the features of the Geoleadership Model are vital. Each attribute helps leaders have a better understanding of different cultures. I think each one of the key features is very important and should be considered by global business leaders.

*What do you like to ask other business leaders when you get the chance?*

I like to ask them: "What have you learned today?" I'm a learn-a-holic. A long time ago, I came to the conclusion that I learn more if I am consciously incompetent. If I can keep in this state of mind, it is amazing how much I can learn from others. And, why bother getting older if you can't get wiser?

As a self-professed "learn-a-holic," Garry Ridge has much to teach us about learning from others, about facing uncertainty, and about building enduring businesses. Most specifically in the context of this chapter on the Change Principle, we find that Garry's focus on building learning agility within his organization is paramount to its sustainability.

**Garry Ridge** is president and CEO of the WD-40 Company headquartered in San Diego, California. WD-40 Company is the maker of the ever-popular WD-40® multi-use product lines and also markets a wide range of homecare and cleaning brands. Garry has been with WD-40 since 1987 in various management positions, including executive vice president and chief operating officer and vice president of international. He has worked directly with WD-40 in 50 countries.

A native of Australia, Garry has served as national vice president of the Australian Marketing Institute and the Australian Automotive Aftermarket Association. Garry received his Master of Science in Executive Leadership (MSEL) from the University of San Diego, CA, in June 2001. Garry is now an adjunct professor at the University of San Diego, where he teaches leadership development, talent management and succession planning in the MSEL program. Garry has been the recipient of a number awards, including: Director of the Year for Enhancement of Economic Value by the Corporate Directors forum in March 2003; the Arthur E. Hughes Career Achievement Award from the University of San Diego in April 2004; the Ernst & Young Master Entrepreneur Award in 2006.

In 2009, Garry co-authored a book with Ken Blanchard titled *Helping People Win at Work: A Business Philosophy called "Don't Mark My Paper, Help Me Get an A."*

As we have noted, everyone has a learning strategy. How we develop these strategies, and how we apply them, has a direct correlation to whether or not an organization, team, or leader will meet their objectives. Global leaders whose strategies optimize learning and develop learning agility within their organizations are better able than those who do not to meet their objectives. The interview with Harry C. Triandis in Exhibit 8.2 looks at how learning behaviors differ across cultures.

---

### *Exhibit 8.2* Interview with Harry C. Triandis, Department of Psychology, University of Illinois

Harry C. Triandis, Professor Emeritus of Psychology (1997–) at the University of Illinois, has focused his research on the links between behavior and elements of subjective culture and on the differences between individualistic and collectivist cultures. Very interesting and pertinent to our chapter on the Change Principle, Professor Triandis believes the global leader's greatest challenge is jumping to conclusions without all the facts— that is making changes without having a fully developed strategy.

*What are the most important decisions that a leader of an organization must make?*

The most important decisions that a leader of an organization must make are around the following issues:

- How to hire people, how to promote people, how to evaluate people.
- How to invest the resources of the organization.
- How to find new sources of revenue for the organization.
- Whether to collaborate with other organizations.

*How have global leaders you have worked with encouraged creative thinking within their organizations?*

The global leaders I have worked with have encouraged creative thinking by:

- Becoming aware of multiple perspectives. Multilingual people are able to see the world from different perspectives.
- Having free discussions with colleagues.
- Exploring new ideas in the literature (magazines, books, journals).
- Attending conferences.

*What is one characteristic that you believe every global business leader should possess?*

I believe every global leader should possess the ability not jump to conclusions, in other words to suspend judgment until they have all the relevant information.

*What are the biggest challenges facing global business leaders today?*

The biggest challenge facing global business leaders today is developing cultural intelligence. For more about this see *Cultural Intelligence: Individual Interactions Across Cultures* by P. Earley and Soon Ang (2003, Stanford University Press).

*What effect do you think national culture has on business leadership decision-making? (This can also include how your own native national culture affects your decision-making.)*

When it comes to business leadership decision-making, national culture is like a set of lenses. For every decision in each culture, the leader needs another set of lenses.

*What are your thoughts on globalization? How important is it for leaders to be culturally competent wherein they build on their own cultural strengths and build where there is a deficit?*

Globalization increases gross national product but it also alienates people from their culture. Alienation is bad for their mental health.

We know that well-being increases with income, up to a point, and then increases in income make very little difference for well-being. I use four criteria for judging cultures: Do they promote health (both physical and mental), well-being, longevity, and do not destroy the environment (for details see my book *Fooling Ourselves*).

Globalization improves the health of the rich in most societies, but the poor become less healthy. It helps well-being in some societies (e.g., China for some social classes), but again it helps those who are relatively rich. It may help somewhat the longevity in a society. It generally is not good for the environment. So, it is a mixed bag.

*Have you ever consulted with an organization that did or did not believe in facilitating an organizational culture capable of intercultural learning agility? Can you provide an example of how this facilitation took place and whether or not it was successful?*

I consulted the U.S. Navy and developed culture assimilators, so that its personnel would become more culturally sensitive. Culture assimilators help people feel more at home in other cultures, but many people do not bother to work through them, so they do not improve. There is a literature on culture assimilators that can be consulted to see whether they do the job.

*What is one mistake you witness global business leaders making more frequently than others?*

Mistakes I witness global business leaders making more frequently than others are:

- When they do not know the language of the host culture they make many mistakes.
- Multilingualism is very good, but very few leaders are multilingual.

*Do you think that some leaders are not capable enough to successfully understand the necessity to be flexible while operating within the dynamic global business arena?*

Many leaders are not flexible, especially if they have not had multicultural experiences.

*What do you like to ask other business leaders when you get the chance?*

I like to ask other business leaders:

- How well do you speak the languages of the host country?
- Do you understand how cultural identity works?

\*\*\*

If globalization alienates people from their cultures, as professor Triandis states, then it is an absolute imperative that learning agility be elevated in its importance as a skill of global leaders. Cultural isolation inhibits growth, development, and connection to others, while learning agility— gathering facts, sifting through immense amounts of information, interpreting current and past events—is the key to envisioning a global future.

**Harry C. Triandis** is Professor Emeritus of Psychology at the University of Illinois. He received his Ph.D. from Cornell University in Ithaca, New York, in 1958, and an honorary doctorate from the University of Athens, Greece, in 1987. He was Chairman and Secretary General of the Society of Experimental Social Psychology; he was President of the International

Association of Cross-Cultural Psychology (1974–76), the Society for the Psychological Study of Social Issues, the InterAmerican Society of Psychology, and the International Association of Applied Psychology (1990–94), as well as of Divisions 8 and 9 of the American Psychological Association.

He received the Eminent Scholar in International Management Award from the Academy of Management, in 2009. He was a Master Lecturer at the meetings of the American Psychological Association in 2009. His 2009 book *Fooling Ourselves* received the William James Award from Division 1 of the APA. The Society for Personality and Social Psychology gave him its Lifetime Contributions Award in 2012.

His research interests concerned (a) the links between behavior and elements of subjective culture and (b) differences between individualistic and collectivist cultures. His work focused on the implications of these links for social behavior, personality, work behavior, intergroup relations, prejudice, attitude change, and cultural training; and applications to intercultural training for successful interaction in other cultures. He is currently writing a book on self-deception, which discusses the relationship between culture and religion.

His 200+ publications include *Attitudes and Attitude Change* and *Analysis of Subjective Culture, Interpersonal Behavior, Variations in Black and White Perceptions of the Social Environment, Culture and Social Behavior* and *Individualism and Collectivism*. He was the general editor of the six-volume *Handbook of Cross-cultural Psychology*, and editor of the fourth (international) volume of the *Handbook of Industrial and Organizational Psychology*.

---

A Geoleader recognizes opportunities for learning and change within differing cultural comfort zones, including:

- Accepting that certain changes cannot be controlled
- Identifying those variables that can be controlled and acting upon them accordingly
- Recognizing one's own reasons for feeling fearful or angry at changes to be imposed
- Looking for the positive benefits of the change rather than concentrating on the negative implications
- Remembering that change will occur whether one embraces it or not

*Figure 8.4* The Principle of "Change" in practice.

### The bottom line

Rarely do we find learning agility to be the top of the list of leadership skills in texts on management and leadership. The truth is, in order for a leader to be a brilliant visionary and an adroit communicator, that leader must be able to scan and interpret what is going on in the world, and imagine a compelling future as seen in Exhibit 8.4 above. The undergirding cognitive structure in all of this is the capability to learn. All people must and do learn, or they experience the consequences of not evolving.

Encountering a new culture is a learning experience, one that can be rich and rewarding. When that encounter is an integral aspect of our work life, especially as leaders and managers, our approach often dictates the quality of our experience and the quality of that encounter by the other parties involved. Our suggestion throughout this book has been that to enhance the experience one must have an honorable intention, a well-prepared and integrated strategy, a sense of adventure, courage, and determination.

# 9 The principle of "Capability"*

> "A hero is born among a hundred, a wise man is found among a thousand, but an accomplished one might not be found even among a hundred thousand men."
>
> —Plato[1]

By now, the concepts of "learning organization" and "organizational learning" are becoming commonplace. Still, however, there is a tendency to confuse these terms and for our purposes here, it is important to clarify the difference between these two related but distinct concepts since our discussion will focus on one more than the other. "Learning organization" is a concept of an organization in which humans cooperate in dynamical systems to continuously learn and adapt using particular processes and systems.[2] Organizational learning, which is our interest in this chapter, refers to the natural process through which an organization acquires new knowledge and adjusts in order to adapt successfully to external and internal environmental changes and to maintain sustainable existence and development. Implicit in this definition is that organizational learning consists of two dimensions (individual and social), and occurs at three levels of functioning: cognitive (acquiring new knowledge), behavioral (adjusting to change), and system (cultural and structural). While there is much debate about what constitutes a "learning organization," it is not our interest in this chapter.

All organizations, to some degree, engage in learning, or they do not survive. Arguably, organizations that become proficient at learning have a greater chance of not only surviving, but thriving in their environments. Some gifted theorists such as Argyris and Schön[3] have speculated that the reason why organizations overall have such difficulties learning is simply that they still behave in ways that obstruct learning, such as stifling communication patterns and power-politics. The good news is that neither the organization theorists nor organizations have

---

* The authors would like to acknowledge the significant scholarly contribution of Edgar Schein and his book, *Organizational Culture and Leadership* (fourth edition), to this chapter.

> # "CAPABILITY"
> ## DEFINED
>
> In order for a leader to be effective in intercultural situations, there must be development of sufficient personal and organizational capability. Intercultural competence requires that leaders are able to assess their own and others' capability and build it where there is deficit. Organizational-level learning, agility, and understanding how modern organizations operate are essential skills for intercultural leaders and managers.

given up. The truth is, all organizations learn and have distinct patterns and strategies of learning. As posited by Edgar Schein, the most agile companies are sensitive to various levels of emerging changes internally and externally.[4] They are sensitive to internal shifts and evolution as the organization as a whole and as a collective of individuals develops. Whether the organization builds its wealth and capability on knowledge (e.g., technological innovations) or on natural resources (e.g., lumber and oil), an agile organization thrives in harmony with its environment, and/or responds synergistically with its milieu.

Take, for example, how some global organizations have done this successfully in their expansions into regions of China. Procter & Gamble sends employees to live with average Chinese families to acquire information on their laundering behavior. McDonald's is investigating the shifts in Chinese food culture to adapt its services to the needs and tastes of Chinese consumers. On the other side of the same intercultural engagement, China's Legend Computer Company assigns certain employees to research the Internet for data and other benchmarks that may influence the development of the company.

General Electric is famous for having established a learning culture called "learning from your employees." However, its chairman and CEO between 1981 and 2001, Jack Welch, was well known for fostering an organizational culture that learned the technologies of other organizations for the intentional purpose of improving technology and advancing into the competitor's market. Organizations now in a highly competitive global marketplace face both tremendous opportunity and temptation and must make decisions agilely to avoid costly mistakes. In other words, it is not enough just to figure out what other companies are doing. It is not enough to amass a group of brilliant innovative employees. Schein contends that organizations must become capable.[5] Figure 9.1 depicts the characteristics of agile organizational learning.

*Capability* is a person's or group's core competence and potential plus the ability to learn and adapt to the changing environment. Core competence is the essence of an organization. In a sense, it is organizational DNA. In effect, it is what distinguishes one company from any other. If you are a software company your core competence is probably the invention, development, and distribution of proprietary software (programs) that serve some specific purpose (i.e., financial software). However, even within this identity, there is a lot of room for differentiation. For example, you may really be specialists in research and development and not really focused on manufacturing nor marketing and distribution. In this case, your organization may have built alliances with other organizations that have become part of your value network (similar to value chain).

As with domestic organizations, all global organizations must continually question their business and their place in that business.[6] Answering this question requires that global organizations go about the process differently than their domestic cousins. In a world before globalization, an automaker that developed a new model vehicle, for example of a type they had not previously built, would re-tool a local factory. Now, in a global and highly competitive economy, where brand name is not synonymous with products being exclusively homegrown, an automaker wishing to enter a new-to-them market may acquire that segment of a foreign-owned automaker's firm, and place their brand on a product which is made in another part of the world. In the case of a global software company that needs to expand its strategic position by development of a new software product, it is not about re-tooling factories. Rather, that company may choose to invest in the acquisition of an organization that has already developed the software, acquire additional intellectual capital and cut costs in the bargain

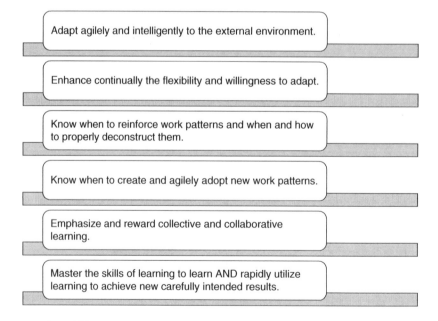

*Figure 9.1* Skill attributes of organizational learning.

by acquiring a small design firm in another country, where innovation is high and labor cost is low. In any case, building organizational capability is a new game compared to decades past and organization-level learning agility is requisite.

The keys to building core competence and branding organizational DNA (at the strategic level) are: valuing and measuring intangible assets (intellectual capital); developing capability acquisition strategies; creating a tangible knowledge base and knowledge centers; creating intercultural collaborative cultures; and building or purchasing supportive collaborative infrastructures.[7] This is seen clearly in the germinal work regarding organizations by Edgar Schein.

## Optimizing structure

If you take a moment to reflect on what it means to be a global organization operating in a highly dynamic global environment, and on what it means to be learning-agile, a picture should emerge of a very different looking structure than an industrial era organization. In the last decades, we have seen organizations constitute themselves into new architectures. Some of the more notable designs include the network, the web, the lattice, and the holonic.

Does this mean that bureaucratic designs are dead? No, not entirely. It does mean shifts in how we grant authority, how we integrate units, how flexibly we construct boundaries, and how we view social work units. The benefits of designing these new types of structures are that they enable innovation, inherently demand resilience, and foster autonomy. The drawbacks of such structures *when* they are poorly constructed and/or mismanaged are confusion (about vision or standards), lack of boundary integrity (disembodiment), breakdowns in resource control, and instability. Although these drawbacks may seem formidable, they are manageable and no more a challenge than are the drawbacks of hierarchical bureaucracies.

The key principles of new organization designs are establishing flexible boundaries and interdependencies, constructing to the velocity of the business, creating renewable social agreements, and embedding learning in work.

## Optimizing organizational renewal systems (learning)

Various models have been postulated for building and maintaining learning agility. We favor models that include the following important processes of building agility and maintaining capability: discovery, reflection, selection, mining, transfer, execution, innovation, contribution, and memory. When studying these systems and processes, it is important to keep in mind the various culture dimensions we discussed in our chapters on contrasts and context (i.e., power distance, uncertainty avoidance, gender egalitarianism, performance orientation, future orientation, collective versus individualist orientation, social orientation, and ambiguity tolerance).

*Discovery* processes enable the organization to sense and monitor changes, problems, challenges, and opportunities in its internal and external environment, and that provides early warning signals to shifting trends. Through conscious and systematic monitoring and analysis and sense-making, the organization can maintain its engagement with its environment. This is particularly important when an organization embarks on global expansion. It will require establishing local relationships in the foreign countries.

*Reflective* processes facilitate the organization's ability to learn from its experience. The reflective process is perhaps the most challenging for organizations because there can be the tendency to reflect upon one's successes, learn from them, and assume that through precise replication, one can achieve the identical results. The fundamental problem with this type of thinking is that nothing in our environment actually stays the same through time. Therefore, the prevailing conditions of the past do not necessarily portend the same results in the future. Numerous theorists have given attention to this problem and none more astutely than Argyris and Schön, whose single-loop and double-loop learning theories and Issacs's triple-loop learning have provided viable means for organizations to avoid the classic mistake of assuming that past success is the best council for decisions in the future. Single-loop learning occurs when the problem is corrected by altering behavior or actions to meet organizational norms, goals, values, and assumptions. It involves detecting problems without questioning underlying policies and methods. Double-loop learning occurs when the underlying values are changed and new actions follow. It involves questioning and changing governing conditions or values and testing the assumptions underlying what is being done.

One practical example is a model called After Action Review (AAR), which is used to analyze the result of every action. In certain situations, reflecting and reviewing can lead to improvement for next time. A typical discussion during an AAR process revolves around four questions as listed in Figure 9.2.

Additionally, these processes can be used to reflect on the successes and mistakes of other organizations, which is particularly important in global ventures. Benchmarking results of other organizations should be part of the reflection processes.

*Selection* processes allow an organization to make the right choices about innovative ideas or external intelligence that is mined. An organization must develop a variety of selection and decision methodologies, processes, and activities, so that optimal business decisions can be achieved. Selection methodologies, according to Edgar Schein, include both accepting in and starting new, as well as unlearning old habits and practices.[8] Only when there is an internal selection system for optimization, can an organization build the capacity to adapt to external environmental selection and maintain competitive advantage. In a global organization, selection methods must be congruent with local customs, laws, and needs.

*Mining* processes allow an organization to remain open as a system with a continuous exchange of energy as well as information and knowledge between

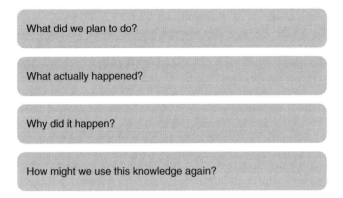

What did we plan to do?

What actually happened?

Why did it happen?

How might we use this knowledge again?

*Figure 9.2* After Action Review process.

it and its environment. This acquisition system is crucial for an organization's ability to learn faster and build competitive advantage, especially in a new environment. The acquisition system should provide channels for the recruitment of people, foster social networks of employees (localized to the area/areas in which an organization has operations) and cooperative interactions with other institutions. We emphasize the importance of not only getting information and knowledge from outside, but also the organization's ability to assimilate and apply learning for intended purposes.

*Transfer* processes allow the organization to harness individual and team learning so that it can be transferred and utilized throughout the organization. Best ideas, practices, and experience obtained by individuals, teams, or departments should be transferred to the rest of the organization. This area is one of those that Argyris proposed is likely to cause problems because of the human tendency for turf and politics. In order for learning to be shared in an organization, its people must develop and foster trust and psychological safety. It has been suggested that processes that foster dialogue between individuals and teams provides the requisite assistance for transfer of learning to occur. In a global organization, the interface between "global" structures and "localized" structures is one critical element for success.

*Execution* processes allow the organization to move that which is incorporated cognitively into behavior. In other words, learning about something intellectually is only productive if it can be translated into manifest form. Organizational learning not only includes changes of perception and thinking (such as discovering, innovating, and selecting), but also changes of behavior. No action means no real learning. Transferring knowledge into action is sometimes a challenge for people and without processes, intentionality, motivation and courage, knowledge typically becomes shelved. However, leaders and managers must be aware of the cultural differences in their particular locales to make the proper tactical plan.

*Innovation* processes allow an organization to renew and maintain its core competence, even if that core competence shifts over the organization's lifespan, as related by Edgar Schein.[9] It is not enough for an organization to discover various kinds of changes: it has to find new ways to deal with them. It is not enough to perceive opportunities and envision brilliant ideas: the organization must continually recreate itself from concept to manifest form. Adjustments must be made, of course, based on local customs, since, for example, people's future orientation can affect how they go about innovative thinking. Future orientation (the extent to which a person perceives the horizon in imagining and envisioning the future) can change the types of innovations people generate.

*Contribution* processes enable an organization to participate in the circulation of life by putting back into the environment. Not only should organizations acquire knowledge from outside, but also they should contribute to the outside. For some organizations, such as universities, schools, consulting companies, and so on, providing knowledge service is the reason for their existence. Other organizations such as manufacturing firms do this, too. Contributing knowledge can improve an organization's reputation, and, from the perspective of learning, can give the organization chance to receive feedback from outside about its own management and performance. An organization will never be a real learning organization unless it can contribute learning and knowledge to society.

However, few Western literatures address how an organization can enhance its learning capability through contributing knowledge to environment. Chinese traditional philosophy, however, emphasizes that one must first contribute something (including knowledge) to other people before taking it from them. Therefore, if an organization wants to acquire knowledge from outside continuously, it should have the willingness and ability to contribute. Although the subject of corporate social responsibility is beyond the scope of this book, we do believe that it is an even more important consideration for global organizations, particularly in terms of maintaining caring and conscious relationships with local cultures.

*Memory* processes facilitate an important organizational function: knowledge management. There are two kinds of knowledge management methods. One is codification, which means knowledge is carefully codified and stored in a database, where it can be accessed and used easily by anyone in the company. The other is personalization in which knowledge is closely tied to the person who developed it and is shared mainly through person-to-person contacts. Just as a computer cannot solve complicated problems without a memory, a person cannot absorb intricate knowledge without a brain (memory). Similarly, with the growing complexity of the environment, organizational memory increasingly is needed for continuous learning. While knowledge generated by the eight processes is stored in organizational memory, the stored knowledge will also affect the eight processes. If an organization fails to establish organizational memory to retain knowledge, the loss is great—organizational learning cannot be constantly upgraded and further learning cannot occur. Good experience cannot be exploited and failure may be repeated. Future orientation and uncertainty avoidance are two cultural dimensions that will weigh heavily in a global organization.

## Leading collectives

Over the past several decades, in Western business cultures we have observed the rise of the team as a focal point of people management. The movement toward embracing the team concept, once fueled by the influence of Japanese management practices and later with flattening of hierarchies, continues. Much has been written about what constitutes an effective, high-performing team. Globalization has again brought attention to team performance given the increase in diversity and in geographically dispersed membership.

There are some important differences and similarities between teams and collectives for a global organization. A collective by its nature is a group, as is a team. It has been argued that teams are more effective than workgroups. However, for the global organization, especially those that are highly networked, teams can be problematic without some redefinition. The conventional wisdom, espoused in management literature, has urged managers to transform their workgroups into teams. The reasons for this are that while groups are loosely bound aggregates of people interacting during the course of their work, teams consist of members who influence one another, after having forged certain agreements, toward the accomplishment of organizational objectives.

The field of Organizational Development (OD) has influenced management practice by having introduced the concept of team building, a process whereby team members diagnose their effectiveness and plan changes to improve. In-and-of-itself this is not bad practice. What can become problematic is that teams can develop such a state of cohesiveness that their effectiveness is diminished. In these situations, the over-cohesive team may develop goals that are in conflict with the organization's goals.

One of the major contributors to team effectiveness is team membership, as seen in the work of Edgar Schein.[10] In order for a group to become first a team, second an effective team, and potentially over time a cohesive team, the members must have certain attributes (based on several tangible and intangible elements) and must have relative stability (of members and environment).

Alternatively, the team must be constituted with the explicit understanding that its membership will be ever-changing and that its environment will be unstable and that, more than likely, it will have a brief lifespan. The global economy demands that leaders and managers have a keen awareness of and skill at organizing and/or facilitating the work or purpose of collectives. Specifically, managers must know the different types of collectives and for what each is best suited.

## Team effectiveness and the intercultural leader

We observe that many specialists in intercultural team effectiveness preface their work with the disclaimer that intercultural teams begin with an inherent

- The **workgroup**, people working interdependently on a variety of loosely related objectives.
- The **team**, people charged with specific objectives related to the same result, sometimes time-bound and having the same reporting relationship.
- The **network team**, people working across internal and/or organizational boundaries working on related objectives, sometimes time-bound.
- The **community**, people either formally or informally organized around non-task related objectives, sometimes time-bound (e.g., communities of practice or communities of learning).

*Figure 9.3* The four types of social units managers encounter.

disadvantage by virtue of the cultural differences between members. Please see Figure 9.3 for more information on managers and teams. We have worked on intercultural teams, consulted to intercultural teams, composed and led intercultural teams and, in our opinion, cultural difference is neither advantageous nor disadvantageous. Legitimately, you may ask why we make this statement. The answer is simple. We have observed intercultural teams over the past 15 years, and find that such teams are no more or less likely to be effective than their culturally homogeneous cousins. Having said this, we recognize that intercultural teams require additional assistance and different basis of approach. Whereas standard practices could/can be used when constituting and developing teams with less differentiation among the membership, intercultural teams require more tailored approaches depending on the membership and context.

However, our experience is that when people can focus on the universal similarities across human cultures there is a great potential for building strong working relationships. The truth is there are three levels of relationship between human beings. We are all individuals and completely unique—there simply are no nor have there ever been two human beings alike. As individuals, we all have our unique personalities, experience, and perspective. At the next level, we all share some common experience, perspectives, and behaviors with particular others—that which links us together in social groups and subgroups through culture (language, ethnicity, etc.). At the most fundamental level, all humans share the presence of the identical life force, or manna. Although, at the two lesser levels, we find wide variance, we also find similarities and universal characteristics. At our most fundamental level, we are all identical, as living human life forms.

In our experience, there is a relationship between intercultural teams and the performance of a global organization as explained in Exhibit 9.1. Intercultural teams develop intercultural competencies in order to perform. They then contribute to the organization's performance and capability because the organization's ability to learn and achieve is enhanced. Intercultural interaction among the intercultural team membership through interaction, care, and resolved conflict characterize global teams, which builds capability within the organization.

*Exhibit 9.1* **Interview with Linda D. Sharkey, global managing director and partner, Achieveblue Corp**

A proven leader with experience in Fortune 10 companies building teams and driving talent development initiatives, our interview with Linda D. Sharkey explores her thoughts on globalization, leadership, and building talent. Interestingly, we found that Linda purports establishing organizational values that support the organization's strategy and then turning those values into aligned behaviors as essential to success in building intercultural inter-action and global teams.

*What are the most important decisions you make as a leader of an organization of which you have been a part? (This can also be answered from the perspective of what is the most important decision a leader/client makes in his or her organization.)*

As a leader, who you hire and promote speaks volumes about you and what you value. The people you surround yourself with signal the type of culture that you think is important. These leaders then become the role models for the type of leadership that you expect. Poor choices in this regard can create cultures and behaviors in organizations that can either help the organization "spiral up or spiral down."

Too often time is not spent on clearly articulating the values of the organization, what those values look like in the behaviors of the leaders, and how those values support the strategy of the business. Not paying attention to the leadership behaviors that you want defining your organization has consequences. You can create a toxic organization before you know it, and turning around a toxic organization can be exhausting. I have inherited toxic organizations and coached many leaders who have either created or inherited toxic organizations. The time, resources, and energy required to build a more constructive culture can be personally and organizationally debilitating.

Spending time upfront on organizational values that support the strategy and turning those values into aligned behaviors is essential. Articulating those behaviors in ways that everyone can understand is a critical step. Using these behaviors and values as an anchor for the hiring and promotions you make as a leader is probably one of the single most important things you can do. Ensuring that everyone role models the behaviors is so important. It requires diligence to ensure that the wrong leadership behaviors do not get rewarded because of expediency or the achievement of short-term results. In my mind and in my experience, it is all about the people you surround yourself with and your ability to develop others and help shape a culture of high performance.

In the research for our recent book *Winning with Transglobal Leadership*, we found that the very best global leaders were those who focused on their people. These leaders worked hard at getting the people requirements right from a cultural and behavioral perspective.

*How do you encourage creative thinking within a/your organization (i.e., given the type of industry in which you operate)?*

Creative thinking comes about through driving fear out of your organization. Developing an organization that allows people to take reasoned chances, express ideas, and not be punished or criticized for thinking differently is the key. You might think this is self-evident, but you would be amazed at how many leaders don't realize that their subtle behavior engenders the exact opposite response in others. What they reward and how they react to new ideas can shape a culture that causes people to be creative or shuts them down. In the extreme, seeing followers take risks, fail, and be punished for failure, causes people to hide mistakes and go "underground."

Valuing diverse thought is harder than you would think, because we all have hidden biases and perspectives that if not understood can shut down creativity in others. Bias limits open thinking. While we will never likely eliminate our personal bias, it is important to understand your personal bias. Without understanding your own bias, you will make judgments about others' ideas through a filter that can limit progress. The first step to eliminate bias is to understand yourself and what bias you have, so that you can recognize when you are stifling creative thought and disrupt that pattern. This does not mean that you have to accept every idea that comes across your desk! The truth of the matter is that leaders will say they want and value creativity, but in reality when all is said and done they value ideas that fit their view of the world and support their personal yet often hidden bias.

*What is one characteristic that you believe every global business leader should possess?*

It is very difficult to boil this down to one characteristic. In the recent book that I co-authored with Nazneen Razi, Peter Barge, and Robert Cooke, we set out through research to answer that very question. Based upon extensive survey, interview data and analysis, we found five critical characteristics of highly successful global leaders or as we call them Transglobal Leaders: Team Connectivity, Uncertainty Resilience, Pragmatic Flexibility, Perceptive Responsiveness, and Talent Orientation. These Transglobal Leadership dimensions are defined as follows:

1. *Team Connectivity*: Transglobal Leaders connect people around the world to create innovation. They are not concerned with traditional organization structures. They create opportunities for people to collaborate on innovative ideas and approaches regardless of who or where they are.

2. *Uncertainty Resilience*: Transglobal Leaders manage ambiguity and in some cases chaos. Leaders who possess Uncertainty Resilience don't need lots of data and process to know the way forward. They are inspirational and aspirational. They are uniquely able to understand the environment and intuit the vision for the future. They help others see the way forward and how they can contribute.

3. *Pragmatic Flexibility*: Transglobal Leaders understand and appreciate the values of others. These are leaders who do not impose their values on others. They are clear about their own personal values, understand their bias, and allow others to live their values. They are highly respectful and don't feel threatened by what others see as personally important. Leaders who demonstrate Pragmatic Flexibility are not afraid to have open discussions about values and organization culture. In fact, they encourage it to create understanding and alignment. They are the ultimate inclusive champions. They are not unethical. They always act with integrity.

4. *Perceptive Responsiveness*: Transglobal Leaders recognize how others are reacting to them and pick up on clues when others are uncomfortable or not understanding their point of view. They have honed their ability to perceive others non-verbal cues. They do not just "forge on" believing everyone is onboard with what they as a leader are saying and doing. They actively explore differences and seek understanding before they move forward. They don't assume acceptance.

5. *Talent Orientation*: Transglobal Leaders are more focused on the development of their people than on themselves. They are stewards of their people. Their focus of interest and action is not about making themselves look good or ensuring that the work of others supports their work. Rather their focus is on supporting those who work with them to achieve organization excellence. They lack hubris and are focused on developing others to achieve organization success. They define organization success as achieving constructive goals that do not destroy the communities in which they operate, but rather sustain these communities.

Because our research was so clear on these five dimensions, it is difficult for me to pick just one trait. Our research shows they are all important. However, if I were forced to sum up the key points, I would say leaders should have an ever-widening appreciation of others and focus on their people rather than themselves.

*What is the biggest challenge facing global business leaders today?*

The biggest challenge facing global business leaders today is appreciating that the world is small and getting smaller. Every day there are more ways to connect physically and virtually. Yet differences abound; not everyone thinks the same way. Opposition to your ideas as a leader is not necessarily resistance, but possibly a lack of understanding of how they might play out in someone else's context and culture. If you have the patience to allow others to explore an idea or approach to see how they can make it work in their environment, you will be much more successful. Letting go of "it's my way or the highway" is paramount. The world is moving so fast and communication of ideas and issues is at lightning speed—being able to show tolerance, patience, and appreciation for others is a must.

Also, because of this shrinking world, unexpected events in one part of the world can have significant and swift impact on other parts of the world. Resiliency in the face of adversity and change relative to issues and events you cannot control is a must. We do not live in a predictable world and the likelihood of the world becoming more predictable is slim. The Black Swan Theory developed by Nassim Nicholas Taleb makes this point eloquently. Running business in environments that are increasingly less predictable, where unforeseen or unimaginable events can change the course of history in a moment is a huge challenge. We live in a world where something can happen in Dubai and have immediate repercussions in China and the U.S. Being resilient in the face of these immediate disruptions and flexible in the swiftness of our interactions presents a significant challenge for any leader.

*What effect do you think national culture has on business leadership decision-making? (This can also include how your own native national culture affects your decision-making.)*

While there has been a great deal of research on the role of national culture on leadership decision-making, it all goes back to bias and values. What a culture values and the perceptions and bias it engenders shapes how a leader from that culture makes decisions about others. This is the ultimate shift in diversity. We used to think that diversity was accepting people who were, for instance, different from us physically, socially, in sexual preference, or religiously. We have an unconscious code that says certain people are different in certain ways based upon differences in their values. This is the heart of what drives the lack of acceptance of others.

I have done a great deal of research on this topic using a valid and reliable cultural assessment test, such as the Organization Culture Inventory (OCI) created by my co-author Robert Cooke, CEO of Human Synergistics. We discovered that people generally want the same things from the workplace. For example, whether you are in China, the Middle East, India, Europe, or the United States, you want a workplace that is constructive, where people can achieve their goals, are treated with respect and fairness, can collaborate with others to create innovation, and work free of fear. However, how these workplace values play out in other countries takes on different forms. This is the influence of country cultures. In Japan, work–life balance looks different than in the U.S. In the Middle East respect for religious differences takes on a different form. Because the context of the workplace is influenced by the country cultures, leaders must be flexible in how they make decisions. This relates to one of the Transglobal Leadership dimensions discussed earlier: Pragmatic Flexibility—understanding and appreciating the values of others and how those values impact decisions and how decisions will be carried out.

I started this answer with a point about diversity. In the past we viewed diversity from a more superficial perspective, e.g., appearance, religion, sex, but the real difference is in understanding the values of others and the values that bond us together, because they are common across borders. It is a unique individual who can transcend borders, appreciate values, and see the common threads in all of us no matter how differently we manifest those values in our particular countries.

*What are your thoughts on globalization and how important is it for leaders to develop their own self-awareness so as to adjust to the changing context(s) under which they operate in a given situation and/or organization? (This consciousness could include the leader's own cultural self-bias while operating with diverse constituents.)*

If ever there was a time for a call to leadership it is now. We have talked about many of these facets of leadership throughout history. They are not new. However, in this global world—self-awareness and being able to adjust to others is essential. "Peeling back the onion" and taking an honest look at yourself is a non-negotiable for leaders to be successful going forward. Self-awareness is critical, and incredibly difficult. We all want to rationalize our behavior, even when it's wrong. If you are not comfortable with your own bias and values, you cannot accept others'. Transglobal Leaders as we have found in our research are deeply aware of who they are at their core, and they are not threatened by those who are different. These leaders can truly flex to the values of others and appreciate and embrace them.

We use self-awareness tools like 360-degree feedback frequently in leadership development programs and exercises. We use coaching and mirroring to help leaders see how they impact others and how they are seen by others. However, these tools only scratch the surface. Developing self-awareness requires leaders to face their bias, get out of their comfort zones, and be honest about how that feels. We need new ways to develop leaders that builds on Chris Argyris's double-loop learning and takes leadership development to a very personal level. Understanding who you are will be essential to the renaissance of leadership in the global world.

*What is one mistake you witness business leaders making more frequently than others? Do you think that some leaders make such errors due to their inability to be self-aware of their own national cultural bias, as mentioned above?*

The biggest mistakes that leaders make are being power-focused and arrogant. As they are promoted and make more money, many leaders begin to believe that their success was because of them. Arrogance and hubris are by far the biggest derailers of leaders. I think national cultures have very little to do with it. As Marshall Goldsmith, a mentor to me, often says, it is the tendency for leaders to believe that their success is because of them rather than as is often the case in spite of them.

Having power breeds the belief that without you, the leader, there would be no progress, no success. In fact, it is quite the opposite. Real leadership is bringing out the best in others, but so many leaders forget this fact. From our research, we found that the truly successful leader, the Transglobal Leader, is not self-absorbed, but concerned about the development of others. Unfortunately, in my coaching and leadership development practice, I still very often see leaders who predominately focus on their own personal success to the exclusion and/or expense of others. Command and control leadership is still alive and well. It is an easier style than that of engaging others. In my research and experience, I have not found that country culture is the primary driver of this phenomenon. When leaders are under enormous pressure to deliver or are threatened, it is more expedient to use the "command and control" style. History has shown however that over the long term this style does not work.

*Can you name a person who has had a tremendous impact on you as a leader? Maybe someone who has been a mentor to you? Why and how did this person impact your life?*

While there have been many people who have had a great impact and influence on my life in this context the person who had tremendous impact on me was my college roommate, Dale Mason Cochran. Dale is an African American woman, and we met at a predominately white college. We grew up at a time of great prejudice, and she exposed me to events where I was the only white person in the room. I understood how she felt every day in our all white college. This helped me realize that our differences were physical, not values-based. When I met her friends and family, I realized we were the same and wanted the same things out of life. Appearance and preconceived perceptions can be so blinding. Getting out of your comfort zone and experiencing people for their aspirations and values is tough to do, but so essential for personal growth. When you share common values and beliefs, superficial differences that are not important melt away. My roommate gave me this great gift. We are dear friends to this day. It is a gift that I have carried through my life. The older I get the more I appreciate it.

*Within the global economy, how important is it that a global business leader understands the key features of the Geoleadership Model?*

In reviewing the Geoleadership Model, I find it supports the research that we have done relative to Transglobal Leadership and what it will take to lead in this increasingly global world. Leaders need to understand the people they lead, be able to communicate with them, and understand the context and contrasts within which they lead. A compelling point is the notion of the bottom-line focus of Americans, in particular U.S. companies, to the exclusion of key stakeholders beyond shareholders. This notion that organizations have more to contribute than just to the bottom line is, and will continue to be, essential as the world gets smaller and we become more connected. Workers' expectations will be for a better community and better life for themselves and their families. Organizations will need to put values front and center of their corporate activities to succeed in this next century. Contributing to creating better lives for people who are part of a corporation community will be essential. I think the Geoleadership competencies embody these notions. Now we have to ensure that we are able to nurture and develop leaders who can build these corporate communities that are not only successful financially for shareholders but for the community as well—not at the expense of the community.

*What do you like to ask other business leaders when you get the chance?*

Here are the questions that I like to ask. In fact in some environments, like GE, I have been able to ask these questions and have learned many inspiring things. Here are my questions:

- Deep down, what are your biggest fears?
- What is the real meaning and purpose of your life?
- Why is it that you want to lead others?
- Through your life what have been your core leadership lessons and why are they important to you?
- What is the legacy you want to leave in the organizations you lead and with the people you lead and love?
- How can you move beyond your fears to create the great hope of your legacy?
- What is the "privilege" your life has provided you and how can you help others achieve their "privilege" and dreams?

When I have been able to discuss these questions with leaders I know and have worked with, I have learned amazing and wonderful things about them. I hope we can create workplaces where these questions and the answers to them are not seen as a weakness but a great strength for the organization to use to build powerful and sustainable businesses. Where organizations have truly self-reflective leaders, these leaders will create organizations that will move us forward and these leaders will be the renaissance leaders of the twenty-first century.

***

As we've read, Linda D. Sharkey espouses the need for leaders to bring out the best in their people. In fact, based on the research for her book (*Winning with Transglobal Leadership*), Linda and her co-authors found similarly that truly successful leaders focus on the universal similarities across human cultures, develop their people, and build strong working relationships cross-culturally.

**Dr. Sharkey** was born on Long Island, New York, and attended Nazareth College in Rochester, New York, and received a B.A. in History and Political Science. After completing college, Dr. Sharkey went to work in Washington DC to experience politics firsthand. Dr. Sharkey has worked for the New York State Government and completed a Master's in Public Administration. In the private sector, Dr. Sharkey worked primarily in financial services and this is where her first real experience working globally began. Dr. Sharkey worked for Chemical Bank overseas and then moved to Paine Webber where she started a Ph.D. in Organization Development from Benedictine University in Lisle, Illinois. Halfway through her dissertation studies, Dr. Sharkey was recruited to GE as the head of executive development where she worked with and coached developing leaders all around the world.

After a successful run at GE, Dr. Sharkey joined Hewlett Packard as their chief talent officer worldwide. Again, she had the privilege of working with leaders and talent from all over the world. Dr. Sharkey then decided to pursue her passion after three years with HP to write about her experiences and co-wrote *Winning with Transglobal Leadership* (with Nazneen Razi, Robert A. Cooke, and Peter Barge, 2012).

## Managing the organizational culture

Organizations all have a culture. Culture reveals itself through the language, customs, and traditions of the individuals within the organization. The culture also finds realization through the standards and norms that the group demonstrates on a daily basis. Culture also arises from the shared history of a group of individuals placed together for a specific mission, as asserted by Edgar Schein.[11] This integration of shared beliefs serves to lessen the ambiguity of the organizational environment in order for goals to reach fruition. Each culture features its own unique substance and form. An organization's ideologies create the substance of the decision-making process for the group in question. These ideologies are emotionalized, shared sets of beliefs, values, and norms that both impel people to action and justify their actions to themselves and others. Once the ideologies become an ingrained part of the group's activities, these thought patterns morph to form to create the organization's culture. Each new member who joins the organization learns how the organization operates based upon this intangible entity known as the culture's substance.

The cultural forms of an organization seek to give credibility to its substance. Examples of cultural forms include metaphors, myths, and symbols. Every organization must survive, and often strength derives from the usage of such metaphors. Metaphors find basis in experience and usually include personal elements. An example of an organizational metaphor arises when a group's formation and activities receive comparison to a team and a game. The cultural forms resident within an organization allow for greater simplification of concepts often too complex to understand. The role of a leader remains to recognize and leverage the organization's cultural substance and forms for the benefit of everyone.

An effective leader distinguishes between the various cultures and even subcultures existent within the organization. A leader must manage the culture efficiently or risk being managed by the culture itself. A leader conscious of the organization's structure grasps the various levels of culture that require management. Anyone involved with the organization, whether new or old, insider or outsider, adapts to the culture as it directly receives direction from the leader. Three levels of culture that occur within any organization include artifacts, espoused values, and basic assumptions.

Attempting to decipher the espoused values of an organization can be challenging. The learning of a group mirrors individual values. When a leader emerges in the group, the values of the leadership prevail among the group itself. Over time, these shared values evolve into shared assumptions. As group values appear more regularly, the members of the group seek to validate these values within the social context of the organization. The original values of the leader thus grow into the culture of the organization itself and members of the group gradually become acclimated to this shared set of values.

The key point to remember here remains that individuals possibly espouse certain values, however their actions sometimes demonstrate the antithesis of these values. Individuals desire to know that identical actions provide identical results. Theory evolves into practice. Assumptions serve to attach rationality to different situations. For example, if an individual fails to be a "team player" within a group culture, then the leadership of the group may relegate this individual to outside of the sphere of information. Individuals require a consistent pattern of decisions and results in order to function effectively within an organization. Acting only upon one's own assumptions, and not those of the group, distances an individual from the organization as a whole.

A cohesive strategy and common mission remain two characteristics important to an effective organization. Individuals require a road map to follow in order to act accordingly within the culture of this organization. These individuals also provide the willingness to contribute their individual efforts to the cooperative system.[12] Culture simply exists when a shared identity emerges that all individuals embrace. This sharing then provides for the goal-setting atmosphere necessary in an organized venture.

Goal-setting most effectively occurs when the organizational culture provides for shared language and shared assumptions. The mission of the organization (i.e., sell the best widgets in the world) needs continuous acceptance. However, the goals of the organization (i.e., reach $1 million sales in current year) must exist for a specific time. This idea of goal-directed, rational decision-making exemplifies more closely the mechanistic metaphor of the organization. The culture of the group defines the path to reach such goals and characterizes such variables as the division of labor and the bonus system.

## The management of results

Reaching goals entails the measurement of results. Does the organizational culture possess a system whereby evaluation appears fair and impartial? If errors occur in the measurement process, what mechanisms exist to correct these problems? When change takes place within the culture, there exists the opportunity for growth. The culture of the organization survives as the group's experience in learning to cope with change.

The internal dimensions of culture face similar analysis. Such internal issues include shared language, power distribution, and reward incentives. How do the members of the culture communicate? Does a common vocabulary exist, either relevant to the organization or to the industry? An inclusive organization is one in which communication and information flow from all directions, in all directions, and across all levels of responsibility. Once the group members possess a similar vocabulary, what decisions receive acceptance in terms of influence and authority?

The organization functions according to the power plays acted upon by the leadership. Does the power structure receive acceptance by the members of the group? Comparably, does the power granted appear valid and actionable by the group's members?

Any organization desires to reach certain goals. Rewarding accomplishment remains a major issue among the group's members and determines the cultural undertones of daily decisions. A clear path to performance and punishment motivates the individual to seek the most effective manner in which to succeed within the organization and accomplish common goals. The reward system perhaps appears logical only to an insider. However, each organization and its relevant members understand how success finds measurement in their own environment.

## Intangible entities: reality, truth, time, space, human nature, and relationships

An organizational culture finds basis in how its members view the intangible aspects of their environment. For example, how does the organization determine what reality to believe? A fundamental part of every culture is a set of assumptions about what is real and how one determines or discovers what is real. Each aspect of reality appears influenced by external, social, and individual factors that remain difficult to manage, particularly in a cross-cultural scenario. Combining these cross-cultural influences within the relevant context demonstrates more clearly the organization's words and actions.

Once the sphere of reality appears understood, the quest for the truth ensues. Truth is impossible to represent as an absolute. Does the culture recognize the truth purely as dogma, rational thought, or the result of continuous debate? The scientific analysis and acceptance of the truth appears similar to dogma. The group must agree upon what constitutes information and then derive the truth accordingly.

The value of time within an organization determines the importance of past, present, and future activities. Do monochromic or polychronic time intervals prevail within the organization? The authors know of a firm that allows workers only one piece of paper on their desks at a time. The management believes that a worker can only concentrate on one matter at a time. Each organization perceives time differently also according to their industry (i.e., sales cycles). The function of time imbues a certain type of order to the organizational culture.[13]

In conjunction with the value of time, how does the organization view spatial concepts? For example, how closely aligned do cubicles reside within the office landscape? Does the corporate culture call for management to dwell on a separate floor than the regular workers? We choose and operate in environmental domains according to how we construct conceptions of who we are and what we are trying to do. An organization's attitude towards space often symbolizes more than just a design sensibility.

Individuals may prescribe to Maslow's hierarchy of needs; however, leadership normally does not appear within this structure. Does the organization's culture evolve to recognize that the leadership individuals require at one point in their lives does not remain static as time passes? Leaders who give credence to the Being Orientation model of human activity state that humanity remains subservient. The individual may then choose to adapt to the organizational culture, or decide to leave it.

Individuals rarely act within a vacuum. Individuals within an organization interact with others within a dynamic environment. Does the organizational culture then stress the role of the individual or the group as more important? Do organizational relationships function more for utilitarian or moral purposes? The manner in which the organization recognizes its relationships signifies its value system.

Every variable that influences an organization's culture directly relates to its leadership foundation. The assumptions, beliefs, and values of the leader set the original tone for the organization's intangible culture. As more members join the group, the culture adjusts. When the original leader leaves the organization, then the culture also morphs into a different entity. For example, Wal-Mart today does not promote the same exact culture as when founder Sam Walton directly managed the corporation.

Leaders such as Sam Walton and others lend their own ideas to the organization, and thereby teach their followers. The acceptance of these ideas derives from such variables as charisma and socialization. Would the Rainbow Coalition still be as successful if Jesse Jackson stepped down from power? The leader creates an environment wherein the values of the leader remain paramount. Myths and stories abound then about the leadership as time passes. The effective leader realizes that the organizational culture changes according to the mechanisms implemented by the leader.

Every organization passes through a life cycle on its way towards fulfilling its mission. The leader of the organization both consciously and unconsciously shapes the culture of the group by instilling personal assumptions, beliefs, and values. Critics often suggest, "Money is culture." However, culture seemingly finds foundation also in such variables as geographical, industrial, and strategic differentiations. In addition, the existence of organizational subcultures greatly commands attention. Every organization undergoes dynamic changes throughout its existence. The most natural reaction to change is to challenge its validity, particularly if we are unable to explain the change. An effective leader efficiently manages organizational change and the relevant cultural paradigm shifts that ensue.

The assessment tool (see Exhibit 9.2) seeks to outline a checklist of variables useful to any individual questioning the culture of a prospective (or even current) organization. The assessment allows an individual and the organization to match each other in terms of assumptions, believes and values. As each individual completes this assessment, the higher percentage of affirmative responses reflects more of a cultural fit between the individual and the organization.

---

### *Exhibit 9.2*  **Cultural inquiry within an organization**

|  | Yes | No |
|---|---|---|
| Do you perceive agreement between your assumptions, beliefs, and values and those apparent in the overall mission of the organization? | | |
| Do you require the organization to match closely your own idea of what makes an effective organizational environment? | | |
| Do you agree with the espoused values and practices of the organization's culture? | | |
| Would you be (are you) comfortable working according to the various cultural norms of the organization? | | |
| Do you understand how the various levels of culture operate? | | |
| Are you willing to accept a greater sense of cultural ambiguity in return for higher rewards? | | |
| Are your personal and professional goals in line with the organization's culture and structure? | | |
| Are your perceptions of the variables such as reality, truth, time, space, human nature, and relationships in line with the organization's espoused and perceivable culture? | | |
| Does the perceivable leadership culture match with your own cultural value system? | | |
| Are you willing to accept less of a personal cultural fit in return for a stable position within the organization? | | |

## The changing practice of management

Review any basic textbook on management and you will notice that the body of knowledge about this profession has been divided into four functions, known as planning, organizing, monitoring, and leading. Within these four functions, there are essential responsibilities that fall into either strategic or tactical tasks and that occur at differing levels of management. In our opinion, management and leadership are much more than these four functions reveal. For convenience sake, though, we have employed the four-function rubric and have described the changes that are evolving or need to evolve within the profession of management to accommodate the demands of an increasingly global economy. However, before we begin to discuss the changes relative to each function of management one important preamble must be stated first.

In our experience, no business leader has the universal capacity and capability required for the job because of the sheer complexity, scope, and magnitude. Rather, global organizations need to develop skilled leaders and managers with highly specialized skill sets, some of which are focused on "localization" and some of which are focused on "globalization" of strategy and operations. Arguably, this replicates a pattern of organizational structure from the past. The difference is that the requirements and the skill sets have changed dramatically. It is also our experience that great leaders and managers develop over time, and with time, after having developed through successive and increasingly more demanding roles from the bottom, up.

### *Planning*

The traditional management function of *planning* has included the tasks and responsibilities associated with the strategic and tactical preparations of the normal business cycle. Such responsibilities as analysis of physical and material assets and forecasting of sales, profit, and capital expenditures based on business strategy occupied a significant portion of management time. Presently, we see the need for management and leadership specialties at global, regional, country, business, and functional (Marketing, Accounting, Human Resources, Legal, Information Technology, etc.) levels.

Increasingly though, managers now have to refocus their analysis and forecasting activities based on new requirements, not the least of which is the sourcing and allocation of resources. Chief among those resources is skill and knowledge. Now, organizations are no longer in competition with the factory down the lane; they are in competition with companies and countries all over the planet. Nowadays, when companies are begun they are often already multinational or global. Some of this is due to the types of business, such as information, knowledge, or creative based; and the other factor is because some businesses begun from third world, developing, or small countries cannot find enough market base in their home regions. The solution to this is to compete in the global economy.

Commonly, Human Resources (HR) was called upon—in some organizations relied upon—to provide projections of "people needs" based on the headcount needed to, for example, work on an assembly line. Now, HR has shifted from being focused on enterprise talent management to global workforce planning and talent sourcing.

While the HR function will always have a role in people development, in a high-velocity, networked, multinational, or global organization, it is "local" business managers who assume a major role in determining people needs within their regions. Localized business managers must coordinate efforts with local-ized HR staff because they have the knowledge of local law. HR will assume the role of asset procurement and disillusionment based on their expertise in hiring, personnel law, etc, and will share a greater link with the accounting function whose role it is to "valuate" the organization's intellectual capital. HR is now seen as a collaborator with business and functions.

However, it is localized business and regionalized functional managers (Marketing, Accounting, Legal, etc.) who will analyze and determine capability needs for local business managers. Business managers continually will be focused on building the capability to achieve organizational objectives. Building capabil-ity means managers will be ever focused on learning and the link between learn-ing and performance.

A high-velocity global economy will operate with a smaller number of metrics than do more traditional economies; although, a strong argument can be made for traditional organizations to do the same. Global companies operate in dynamic environments where it is necessary to establish the "critical few" measurements that will ensure that the company is on track to meet its business objectives. However, having said all of that, increasingly, in our opinion, there is a need to remove the institutionalized greed that has taken hold of American business. Business performance metrics must be properly and ethically balanced in accom-modation of all stakeholder needs, not just of shareholders.

Never before has there been such a need to ensure a strong infrastructure than there is now in the global economy. In order to optimize technology, other resources and intellectual capital, organizations need to prepare, maintain, and upgrade infrastructure. Over the last few years we have witnessed a signifi-cant shift from information processing to knowledge processing, which includes the concepts of learning tools, intelligent electronic coaching, decision-making systems, and collaboration tools. Tools such as these are vital to the successful global organization. As the marketplace becomes more dynamic, organizations become more networked, people become more autonomous, and processes become seamless, these same organizations will become more reliant upon the infrastructure that supports them.

Infrastructure and technology augment intellectual endeavors at different stages of information flow. For instance, they can support human thinking, facilitate information access, help the human interpretation of complex data, and provide decision support.

We all bear witness to the rapid evolution of incredibly sophisticated new technologies. For example, we have seen the advance of data warehousing; discovery tools such as data mining, and parallel processing systems; knowledge-gathering tools such as intelligent agents and text retrieval; guidance systems such as case-based reasoning and business simulators; thinking aids and colla-borative technologies. This of course is in addition to the World Wide Web and Internet. The problem is that all of this is wasted unless it actually serves business goals, through human endeavors. Technology is marvelous when it supports people; otherwise, it is but a nuisance or a nightmare.

Modern technological advances are employed to optimize the flow and exchange of energy through the enterprise infrastructure. These processing systems accelerate the development exchange and application of useful knowledge required for distributed social interaction. They also integrate all business strate-gies, plans, and operations into a coherent assessment of situational positioning at any point in time.

At the beginning of this section, we stated that management specialties in global organizations should probably be at global, functional, regional, country, and business levels. Those leaders at the global level are the few and are at the top of the organization. These specialists must be the most strategic and be the most synergistic, synthesizing, forward thinking of the organization. The functional specialists will have the most integrative role of all the management groups because their reach will cover the enterprise. The regional manager specialist must own the best collaborative and analytical skills among the group to maximize the organization's strategic potential in the marketplace, and with the keenest eye on allocation of resources. The country management group will be the true local specialist who can truly translate between the local culture and the organizational culture.

These leaders must know their consumer and employee pool base intimately; however, they must be able to manage the ambiguity and tension between competing needs between local and global stakeholders. The business manager's role has to be balanced between strategic and tactical foci. Chief among the stra-tegic roles of localized business managers will be tracking market trends, design-ing market strategy focused on both the country, regional managers, and in coordination with functional roles.

### *Organizing*

The organizing function of management has traditionally included the task of structuring the organization in a way that facilitates the accomplishment of strategy and objectives. This process occurs at the executive level of the organi-zation first and then cascades through each region, country, business unit, and function.

One of the basic rules of design is that form follows function. To operate in a high-velocity environment organizations need flexibility to adapt quickly to change. Therefore boundaries and resource allocation will be primary elements to give due attention along with creating and managing alliances and partnerships with other organizations. The essential element is coordination, rather than centralization.

Working relationships between organizational members (employees and managers) as well as contractors and allied organizations must be built upon mutual respect, responsibility, and commitment rather than following orders. To build collaborative and respectful relationships, politics and turf wars must end. Politics and turf wars are built on an antiquated mental model of lack and limitation. In our experience, politicking and turf battles demonstrate a failure of imagination.

Whereas traditional organizations relied on formal communication and information structures, global companies must support the use of both formal and informal channels—even strengthening and emphasizing the informal communication and social network—in order to provide the latitude people need to succeed at the appropriate pace.

Perhaps the slowest transformation, and the one most needed, is toward building structures that enable what we refer to as "embedded learning." It must be a required element in all organization designs. There must be time allotted to and processes and systems developed for both individual and collective learning occurring on a daily basis. In a global organization understanding how people of local cultures live, learn, communicate, consume, and make decisions is imperative.

### *Monitoring*

It makes sense that an economy that has shifted from domestic, to international, to global requires new ways of measuring and monitoring progress. The field of accounting has undergone a period of renewal as it has redefined new appropriate methods to assign value to and measure intangibles such as patents, copyrights, trademarks, licenses, and intellectual property. Within the management function of monitoring, there are new metrics and standards such as the balanced scorecard to use to measure organizational and individual performance. There are new and appropriate classifications for dividing intellectual capital.

These categories divide intellectual capital into four categories as outlined in Figure 9.4.

Increasingly, global organizations have begun to develop a greater awareness and understanding of the nature of intellectual assets and the role of knowledge in their strategic portfolio. Managers within globalized industries must operate with a common framework and language to bring meaning and clarity to an already high ambiguity economy. This meaning and clarity must extend to the development of coherent measurement models and systems with matching reward systems all of which must be congruent with the local cultures of countries in which a business operates.

More importantly, though, is the change in how businesses monitor performance. To begin with, and as we have already stated in multiple ways, it is time to move away from the tendency of leaders and managers, on behalf of businesses,

Human Capital—the minds of individuals employed or allied with the organization, including their competence, knowledge, experience, and know-how.

Structural Capital—all of the infrastructure left once the Human Capital is removed, such as databases, knowledge centers, processes and repositories.

Intellectual Property—your patents, copyrights, trademarks and licenses.

Customer Capital—the relationships and contracts with customers, brands, and trademarks.

*Figure 9.4* Intellectual capital categories.

of hyper-focusing on profit above all else. Business leaders and managers must care about the ultimate well-being of all stakeholders. The implication of holding this intention in a global business requires leaders and managers to understand their local culture's customers and norms related to performance and to their ethical practices.

On a practical level, monitoring and leading (discussed next) are management aspects that directly involve working with people. In Figure 9.5, we provide some suggestions for managers working in intercultural situations related to understanding the employee's perspective and related to motivation, reward, and performance. Motivation is closely related to the performance of human resources in modern organizations. When considering motivation in the context of intercultural work contexts, management must remember that although the motivation process may be similar across cultures, what motivates people often is culturally based.

What motivates employees in the United States may be only moderately effective in Japan, France, or Nigeria. Therefore, although motivation is the concept of choice for analyzing employee performance, an international context requires

- Identify multiple but conflicting culturally-learned viewpoints in the employee's context.
- Explain the actions of employees from their own cultural perspectives.
- Listen for information about cultural patterns that leaders can share with the employee at an appropriate time.
- Learn to shift topics in culturally-appropriate ways.
- Reflect culturally appropriate feelings in specific and accurate feedback.
- Identify culturally-defined multiple support systems for the employee.
- Identify alternative solutions and anticipate the consequences for each cultural context.
- Identify culturally-learned criteria being used by the employee to evaluate alternative solutions.
- Generate accurate explanations for the employee's behavior from the employee's cultural context.

*Figure 9.5* The principle of "Capability" in practice.

country-by-country, or at least regional, examination of differences in motivation. Even more importantly, motivation, while influenced by culture, is also influenced by age and health, and differs based on personality. However, some solid research has found that, as they approach their goals in life, people apparently take into consideration their psychological needs (intrinsic), their physical survival and pleasure (physical), their desires for rewards and praise (extrinsic), and their existential quest to have a meaningful place in the broader world (self-transcendence). These influences on goals might be considered as four occasionally overlapping but sometimes-conflicting motivational systems that people must negotiate as they make their way through life.[14]

Culture and national laws will affect the management not only of people but also of processes. Some processes that work in some regions in the U.S. may not work internationally. Cultural awareness can facilitate the translation of management of people and processes and there are many questions to ask. For example, is time perceived differently in the production environment? In many Latin American countries, for example, promptness is not normally practiced. Is the work ethic driven or more casual? In Japan, typically, the work ethic is stricter than in many European countries. What are the attitudes toward risk?

The stage of technology in a country also affects culture. Where technology is limited, product demand and production capabilities are limited. Greater technology exposes people to greater products made and consumed. Greater technology increases educational opportunities, and thus the skill level of the labor force. This affects culture as we have mentioned previously because more material possessions are available and sought in the culture. Consider the effect of increasing materialism on the cultural values of the United States.

### Leading

In this knowledge culture, the managerial responsibility of leadership has and will undergo the most significant change in its history. A global economy based on knowledge, creativity, technology, and information requires that organizations possess a level of leadership and management sophistication far above anything previously seen. Old practices like "supervision" and "training" will be transformed into practices like "facilitation" and "embedded learning." Managers will now need to be competent in both their "technical" profession, in performance learning, and in building proper social relationships. Leaders and managers must now know (1) how to learn, (2) how they, themselves, learn, (3) how to teach others how to learn, and (4) to teach others to *know* how they learn. Opportunities for learning must be embedded in every work practice. Leaders and managers must possess emotional, social, and cultural intelligence in order to establish strong long-term and short-term relationships with a variety of people.

Global organizations cannot afford to have work cultures burdened with politics and power conflicts where learning is obstructed and where managers have no idea about social organization. Since intelligence, knowledge, and expertise resides within the minds of individuals, it is incumbent upon managers to accept that their primary role is to cultivate a learning-rich intercultural work environment in which social interaction is optimized and where people flourish. Managers need help in this because they need the tangible support of their companies which must provide appropriate compensation and reward systems that reward the right behaviors and that are anchored and based in local customs, which have been coordinated with the organization's strategic objectives. Lastly, it is incumbent upon the leaders within global organizations to set new and high standards of ethics, which truly are congruent with local cultures.[15]

In summary, leading and managing global organizations is different in many ways from how domestic organizations are operated as we have detailed. In one very important way, successfully operating a global organization is precisely the same as successfully operating a domestic operation. Aside from e-business and a few business types, all successful businesses rely on establishing and caring for customer, employee, and partner relationships. Doing so is a localized effort. Global businesses rely on localized efforts.

The way we think about leading and managing has changed or, at least, it should change. For a number of decades we have put too much energy and effort into perceiving and treating management as a "science" when it is actually a "science" and a "social art" of and within specialized domains. By this, we mean the following about these three management and leadership dimensions. First, leading, and managing are inseparable; you simply cannot do one without the other. Second, there are methods for accomplishing many management and leadership tasks; this is the science dimension. Third, leading, and managing require knowledge, skill, and expertise in social relationships, what we call the social art dimension. Fourth, all business and organizational pursuits fall within some domain or profession, therefore leading and managing within a domain area requires skill and expertise in that domain; this we call the "technical" dimension. Now, when we add global marketplace intentions to business endeavors, we add layers of complexity within all three of the leading and managing dimensions.

Given all of the changes needed in being practicing leaders and managers, how we go about preparing and developing leaders and managers must also change. Arguably, how we develop leaders and managers should have changed long ago. However, we are now in the place in our history as humans that our ways must change to avert potentially dire results. The interview in Exhibit 9.3 provides an example of this need for capable change.

---

**Exhibit 9.3** Interview with Ulziibayar Vangansuren, associate professor, National Academy of Governance, Ulaanbaatar, Mongolia

Dr. Ulziibayar Vangansuren provides us with a unique look at global leadership from her point of view as an associate professor of the National

Academy of Governance in Ulaanbaatar, Mongolia. She deftly points out that not all global leaders are put into their positions because of their capabilities or adaptability. She warns of nepotism and corruption, which still affect decision-making in Mongolia.

*What are the most important decisions you make as a leader of an organization of which you have been a part?*

As a manager of international projects, I make decisions about work plans, budget, domestic/international procurement, and project monitoring and evaluation. As a leader of the lecturers' team teaching the same subject/s (i.e., team leader of an International Management class, etc.), I make decisions on course content, schedule and division of labor among lecturers. As the leader of research teams, I make decisions about substantive and organizational matters of surveys, including research methodology, fieldworks, reviews, and report development. As a lecturer, I make decisions about the content and organization of my courses while conducting lectures and seminars. As a leader of ad-hoc and working groups in my institution, I make decisions about different tasks assigned by the administration and supervisors.

*How do you encourage creative thinking within your organization (i.e., given the type of industry in which you operate)?*

For one thing, I encourage my students to brainstorm and express their opinions freely. Secondly, I encourage my young colleagues to take initiative and lead the team or tasks.

*What is one characteristic that you believe every global business leader should possess?*

The one characteristic that I believe every global business leader should possess is adaptability.

*What is the biggest challenge facing global business leaders today, particularly female leaders?*

I believe the greatest challenges facing global business leaders today, especially female leaders, to be navigating cultural differences and the discrimination and/or underestimation of female leaders in some cultures.

*What effect do you think national culture has on business leadership decision-making? (This can also include how your own native national culture affects your decision-making.)*

Some cultural aspects that have an effect on decision-making are nepotism, corruption, and cultural biases (stereotypes, prejudices, religious beliefs, etc.)

pertinent to that culture. In Mongolia, for example, most business leaders consult with Buddhist monks prior to setting launch dates for important business activities, such as grand openings of buildings/branches. They are guided by their religious belief that there are good days for certain activities and rituals. Also in Mongolia, nepotism is seen in the relations of extended family members, classmates/school ties, political affiliations, and people from the same province or people sharing the same birthplaces. These relationships sometimes affect the leaders' decisions.

*What are your thoughts on globalization and are women more or less affected by the global effects of market fluctuations depending on their cultural context?*

I think women are more affected by the global effects of market fluctuations. For example, in the process of downsizing, women tend to be fired first. Also, as more men become unemployed, women shoulder more family burdens. Poverty affects the quality of life of women and children. Women work harder both domestically and officially (personally and professionally). More women become victims of family violence and so on.

*What is one mistake you witness female business leaders making more frequently than others?*

One mistake is being very hyper-sensitive in the workplace. The other is they put too much concern, care, and worry into unimportant details.

*How long do you think it will take before there is 50 percent representation of female CEOs at Fortune 500 companies as well as at academic institutions, both domestically and globally?*

I think it will be less than 20 years before there is a 50 percent representation of female CEOs at Fortune 500 companies and academic institutions.

*Within the global economy, how important is it that a global business leader understands the key features of the Geoleadership Model?*

I think it is vital for a global business leader to understand the key features of the Geoleadership Model. The cultural aspects embedded in the Geoleadership Model are keys to the success of global managers.

*What do you like to ask other academic and/or business leaders when you get the chance?*

I like to ask foreigners to Mongolia what their perception of Mongolia was prior to their arrival and how are their expectations different than the reality they found. I also want to know how they value essential aspects of management like change, human resources, organizational culture and leadership. This is usually a more in-depth conversation, not just one question.

***

The characteristic that Dr. Vangansuren believes all global business leaders should possess is adaptability, which as we've discussed is an integral part of capability. Adaptability, along with continually developing its core competencies, is essential to the organization's survival and success.

**Dr. Vangansuren** lives in Ulaanbaatar, Mongolia and has been teaching in the Academy of Management since 1997. Dr. Vangansuren teaches management subjects, including general and strategic management, international management, leadership, organizational development and change management. Dr. Vangansuren was born in Zavkhan province, Mongolia, and grew up in Ulaanbaatar, capital city of Mongolia. After secondary school, Dr. Vangansuren studied in the Institute of Foreign Languages, Ulaanbaatar, Mongolia, majoring in French and Russian (1990–94). Dr. Vangansuren holds an MBA degree (1997) from the Institute of Administration and Management Development and Master of Public Affairs degree (2002) from the School of Public and Environmental Affairs, Indiana University, Bloomington, U.S. Dr. Vangansuren defended her Ph. D. degree in the Academy of Management, Ulaanbaatar, Mongolia (2010), and her thesis was about Changing Pattern of Leadership among Public Service Executives of Mongolia. Dr. Vangansuren spent time as a visiting scholar at the University of California, San Diego (2008), and also Columbia University in the City of New York (2011–12).

**The bottom line**

All organizations must learn and continually build capability in order to survive and thrive. Furthermore, cultural intelligence is a prerequisite of global leadership and for global organizations. Global competition has intensified as new organizations enter into global expansion activities and as new globally birthed organizations arise. In such an environment, it is critical for organizations to establish strong intercultural relationships with culturally diverse groups of employees, inter-organizational partners, and consumers in local contexts. In order to manage these relationships effectively, organizations need a means to understand and improve their capability. The complexity of intercultural business requires leaders and management to understand the nature of domains of global relationships and the level of complexity when attempting to communicate with multiple partners having unique national and organizational cultures. While organizations are gaining in expertise and cultural sensitivity, some initiatives founder as people fail to consider fully culture's impact in context-specific situations. Focusing on understanding differences is important; however, we also state that focusing on similarities and universal human goals and needs is a powerful way of building bridges toward mutual benefit.

# 10 Gender and leadership*

"There are two sides to every question."

—Protagoras[1]

According to the CIA *World Factbook*, there is nearly a one-to-one ratio of men and women on this earth.[2] With a nearly equal split, gender and leadership have been ongoing areas of study and discussion. Where exactly do leadership and gender meet? How do the gender-based situational and biological instances we encounter every single day impact us on an individual and global level? Using the Seven Key Geoleadership Principles, we can begin to see how the model applies to gender, a specific variable within leadership.

Although the term "gender" indicates a biological designation of man or woman, among other dimensions, for the purpose of this chapter we will adopt the term "sociodemographic gender" as a working definition.[3] Operationalizing gender as a sociodemographic trait, as many authors and researchers do, allows for a deeper investigation of behaviors, assumptions, and status of men and women, leaving biological designation as a self-reported factor, rather than the center of the study.[4] Now let us view gender through the lenses of the Geoleadership Model, beginning with the concept of Care.

## Gender viewed through the Seven Key Geoleadership Principles

### The principle of Care

The bottom line for Care, discussed in Chapter 3, addresses sensitivity, concern, and appreciation for other cultures as primary requirements for an intercultural leader. Care indicates a balanced interest and value for profit and stakeholders. How do gender and leadership apply to the principle of Care? Gender and leadership are important to view together because a line is often drawn between men and

* The authors would like to acknowledge the significant scholarly contribution of Maureen A. Guarcello to this chapter.

women; this line is both visible and invisible. Men and women possess different ways of approaching leadership, and viewing these differences as they pertain to the principle of Care provides insight for both genders to consider.

When the line is visible, sometimes it is boldly painted across a city street. On October 1, 1972, six women sat down on the white, painted starting line after the gun fired to begin the third annual New York City Marathon. The line was positioned several feet in front of the men's starting line. The women sat in peaceful protest against the rules preventing them from competing among men during the marathon. Although the women were permitted to run, they were instructed to begin the race ten minutes before the men, due to health and morality concerns upheld by the Amateur Athletic Union (AAU). Neither of these factors was on the minds of the young women that October morning; instead they wanted the opportunity to compete among men in a race they knew they could endure, and pave the way for future female runners.[5]

The illustration above highlights the principle of Care in a couple of ways. The women were less concerned about their own race times than they were about creating a chance for women to compete as equal participants in the marathon. A sit-in protest was a future-oriented strategy, rather than an attempt to immediately benefit the competitors. Additionally, the protest did not slow the men's competition in the marathon. The women stood up and began the race at the men's starting gun, each incurring a ten-minute penalty on their race record.[6]

Research and statistics assist in making invisible phenomena clearer. When evaluating the similarities and differences between genders, there are benefits and drawbacks within each group. For example, fewer women than men reach top-tier leadership positions, across profit-generating corporations to the government sector. In the United States, women represent more than 50 percent of leadership roles in nonprofit organizations, but this number diminishes to a mere 3 percent when looking at Fortune 500 CEO positions.[7] Women are also underrepresented in the global leadership realm. In 2011, only 19 women represented the total of elected heads of countries throughout the world.[8] The principle of Communication helps outline the ways other countries recognize gender and culture within leadership.

### *The principle of Communication*

Effective intercultural leaders must connect with people from other cultures to understand them. Communication within the Geoleadership Model articulates the importance for business leaders to connect with diverse individuals and groups in order to see outside of their own cultural assumptions and biases. Imagine trying to market to a culture wholly different from your own. What do other cultures value, and how do they respond to advertisements? Who are the assumed decision-makers? Hofstede's index measuring dimensions of national culture is a good place to begin. The dimension of individualism versus collectivism (IDV) in the

United States focuses primarily upon the individual and receives a high score, 91 out of the 120 possible points on the index. Chapter 2 displays a list of countries that fall on both ends of the IDV continuum. The differences between cultures make it difficult for people accustomed to an individualist background to understand collectivist principles enacted in other cultures. Similarly, when two or more of the principles are combined, they could yield entirely different dynamics regarding gender and leadership.

When a high IDV score is combined with a low power distance (PDI) score, some cultures yield what are described as egalitarian power structures.[9] Egalitarian cultures do not focus upon the assignment of specific characteristics to gender roles.[10] These scores, coupled with low masculinity/femininity (MAS) scores, as is the case in a number of Scandinavian countries, presents a new challenge to outsiders trying to communicate within those markets. Denmark's scores, for example, are significantly lower than those of the United States. When thinking about business and leadership within different cultures it is imperative to conduct the research necessary to operate within the culture and communicate effectively with diverse constituents.

Though data alone will not paint a picture of Danish culture, the information in Figure 10.1[11] provides a strong indication that individuals are regarded over the collective in Denmark, the power structure is more balanced than in other hierarchical cultures, and the country's dominant values pivot around caring and quality of life above achievement and success.[12] As a result, it could also be assumed that Danish culture is more egalitarian than within the United States.

This brings us back to the question of advertising within a culture that may not hold the same values as the one creating the campaigns. Studies now scrutinize a country's culture, gender dynamics, and media before putting one word on paper. Research can extend as far as analyses to select a male or female voice for the background of a television advertisement.[13] Although market research has been conducted for nearly a century, this level of detail raises an important question. How were these decisions made initially? The principle of Consciousness sheds some light on how we arrived at our current destination and where we may be headed.

### The principle of Consciousness

Some characteristics and skills do fit within a majority of cultural contexts. Consciousness challenges leaders, again, to be aware, reflective, and intentional.

|  | IDV | PDI | MAS |
|---|---|---|---|
| Denmark | 74 | 18 | 16 |
| United States | 91 | 40 | 62 |

*Figure 10.1* Hofstede's dimensions of national culture comparison.

When leaders enact intentional and reflective behavior it increases trust and capacity within the organization. Sometimes it is difficult to know where the Consciousness process begins and ends, but an important aspect of the principle is remaining aware of personal, cultural background and biases. The very emergence of leadership theory was constructed without full consideration of Consciousness. Two early leadership theories were proposed by, and benefited, the same individuals, raising some questions around bias.

The great man theories were popular in the nineteenth and twentieth centuries, with the assertion that leadership qualities were inherited, passed down from one generation to the next. The theories focused almost entirely upon wealthy men.[14] Now, think for a moment about the principle of Consciousness. Would these theories have been as clear to upper class men if they reflected and considered the other members of society at the time? For example, who was building the railroads and the skyscrapers; didn't those tasks require leadership *and* extraordinary labor?

When great man theories lost momentum, trait theory came into the forefront. Trait theory does not assume leadership as a genetic predisposition; rather that certain traits serve as a precursor to business leadership success.[15] After a century of research on trait theory, coupled by a resurgence of the concept, a single list does include specific but hardly inherited traits, for leaders to hone or acquire as listed in Figure 10.2.[16]

Consciousness brought leadership practice to the hands of people who under the great man and early trait leadership theories were not authorized as leadership practitioners. These individuals included men of color, those from low socioeconomic classes, and women. Now, as leadership and the world change, multiple congruencies exist between women, transformational leadership style, and the emerging global business structure. Although only 19 women sit at the helm of entire countries, studies surrounding how men and women interact within the business environment are rapidly changing.[17] Let us investigate this concept further by looking at gender and leadership in Exhibit 10.1.

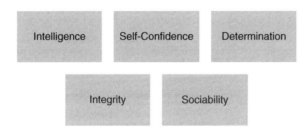

*Figure 10.2* Leadership traits.

***Exhibit 10.1*  Interview with Marye Anne Fox, chancellor emeritus, distinguished professor of chemistry, University of California, San Diego**

Marye Anne Fox was the first woman to be appointed permanent chancellor to the University of California, San Diego. In this role, she epitomized a Geoleader and led the university through extraordinary growth and financial challenges. With a diverse leadership team, she improved the campus climate, increasing the number of students and expanding the school to a billion-dollar research enterprise. Former chancellor Fox leads from the female perspective and she illustrates in her interview how women can be great global leaders.

*What are the most important decisions you make now or have made as a leader of an organization of which you have been a part?*

Decision-making at the chancellor level typically involves more than one of the sub units of the university (sub units are essentially colleges from an academic perspective). There's also the operation of the hospital. So a decision that affects the physicians, perhaps won't affect other parts unless they are doing research in which case the chancellor has to mediate and prioritize the setting for those opportunities.

*How do you encourage creative thinking within your organization (i.e., given the type of industry in which you operate)?*

We encourage all thinking and collaboration by looking at the skills of all of our employees and how their skills potentially can overlap in a new way. So, when we set priorities, we always put the highest priority on those things that are interdisciplinary. We've tried to do this and I think have had some success.

*What is one characteristic that you believe a global business leader should possess, whether it be in academia or an organization, today?*

I think being open-minded and inclusive of different cultures, different religions, basically being inclusive of differences.

*What is the biggest challenge facing global business leaders today, particularly female leaders?*

I think the major challenge we face today is the economic decline. Countries around the world need to act in collaboration as we move forward with opportunities. This isn't as much a gender issue as it is a creative issue. There may be a bright side of this economic downturn in that women's ideas, because we are in such desperate need for new ideas, will be regarded more positively. I hope that's the case.

*What effect do you think national culture has on business leadership decision-making at Fortune Global 500 organizations? (This can also include how your own native national culture affects your decision-making.)*

There certainly is a national culture. I think in the United States it's *exceptionalism*. There are those who believe strongly that the infrastructure available in the United States leads to a more positive result. I think the work ethic is strong in the United States and that this is a cultural imperative. This feeling of inclusiveness that I mentioned before I think is an important part of our national psyche.

*What are your thoughts on globalization and are women more or less affected by the global effects of market fluctuations impending on their cultural context?*

Culture has a major effect on leader and organization success as well as the global economy. Women, as they affect that culture, can have a very important role in how it's played out in the economic progress. I believe women are very important in setting the cultural norm that dictates the success of economic progress.

*What is one mistake you witness female business leaders making more frequently than others?*

None come to mind. I think women make mistakes equally or more frequently to men. Maybe you would say that women stick to a problem longer than men do, whereas men are often willing to more quickly recognize that something hasn't been optimally successful. In other words, the ability to fail quickly is for both men and women, I think, part of the American psyche.

*How long do you believe it will take before there is 50 percent representation of female CEOs at Fortune 500 companies as well as at academic institutions, both domestically and globally?*

I don't think that it ever will be, unless there's a dictate by law. And that's facing the reality that women have to participate in childbirth. But, I do expect that women are going to be very active in business development. And just because I don't think it'll ever be complete equity, that doesn't mean there won't be a lot of women participating in leading organizations in the future.

*Within the global economy, how important is it that a global business leader understands the key features of the Geoleadership Model?*

The points raised within the Geoleadership Model seem to me to be very significant components. I think if you stick to the seven areas of the model, it will be very exciting and useful.

*What do you like to ask other business leaders when you get the chance?*

I am interested in their thoughts about similar questions to what we've discussed in this interview. For instance, the pressures for support and new models that can be conceived of intellectually that would maintain the quality of research but deliver higher education at a less expensive value. Please see Figure 10.3 regarding the gender line.

\*\*\*

Though recognizing that we all make mistakes, Marye Anne Fox believes that women stick with a problem longer than men, who are more likely to recognize a project as unsuccessful more quickly. Marye Anne has an optimistic outlook that there may be an upside for women in leadership due to the global economic challenges we face today. She thinks that, because of the drastic need for creative ideas, collaboration, and change around the world today, women's ideas may be invited, accepted, and regarded more positively than ever before.

**Marye Anne Fox**, the seventh chancellor of the University of California, San Diego (2004–12), and the first woman to be appointed as permanent chancellor, led the university during a historic era of extraordinary campus growth and unprecedented financial challenges. She assembled a diverse leadership team and set a visionary course for UC San Diego's next 50 years and beyond. Under her leadership, UC San Diego successfully completed a billion-dollar capital campaign, celebrated the campus's 50th anniversary, improved campus climate, and expanded at a record-setting pace to accommodate increasing numbers of students and a billion-dollar research enterprise. Fox previously served as chancellor and distinguished university professor of Chemistry at North Carolina State University, a post she held since 1998. Before going to North Carolina, Fox spent 22 years at the University of Texas, where she advanced from assistant professor of Organic Chemistry to vice president for research, and where she held the Waggoner Regents Chair in Chemistry.

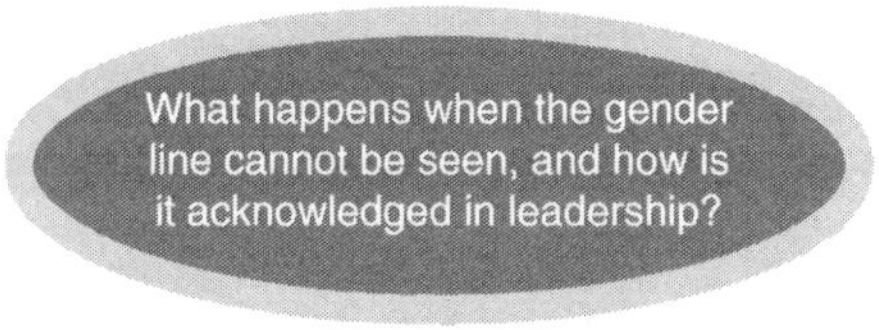

What happens when the gender line cannot be seen, and how is it acknowledged in leadership?

*Figure 10.3* Gender line question.

Fox has held over 50 endowed lectureships at universities around the world and has published more than 400 refereed scientific articles. She also has served as visiting professor at Harvard University, the University of Iowa, the University of Chicago, the Université Pierre et Marie Curie in Paris, and the Chemistry Research Promotion Center in Taipei. At the conclusion of her tenure as Chancellor, Fox returned to the UC San Diego Department of Chemistry and Biochemistry to teach and conduct research.

### The principle of Contrasts

Intercultural leaders face increased ambiguity because of the complexity involved in dealing with multiple layers of culture. Viewing the evolution of early leadership theory illustrates the ambiguous nature built into our leadership perspectives and needs. From an early adaptation of great men as the genetically predetermined leadership class, to this current place where many men and women can now vote, lead, and take charge of change worldwide, it is ultimately the ability to work through ambiguity that makes these strides possible.

Think back for a moment, to the three principles we have covered thus far, Care, Communication, and Consciousness. Consider how many factors balance upon these three key leadership factors alone. The addition of Contrasts, essentially a concept of ambiguity management, removes the predictable factors from the leadership scenario. Until this point, strategy, planning, and research set a foundation to exercise intercultural leadership. Contrasts present impenetrable layers of culture that require a different skill set to navigate.

Contrasts exist in the ways leaders motivate followers. Going back to the specific role of gender, biology does not dictate *how* men and women choose to lead, but there are connections between gender and the ways men and women approach leadership. Using the study of leadership and gender, we can begin to make sense of differences within the leadership realm and some of the ways motivation is utilized. Though there are many leadership styles, the two discussed here are transactional and transformational leadership. These styles are widely studied within organizations, and their application has been linked to gender.

Social psychologists and leadership scholars propose several reasons why men are counted as the dominant population in the leadership sphere, but increased attention points toward the different ways women approach their respective leadership roles.[18] As the globalization of business increases, so does the call for different leadership styles. Transactional and transformational leadership are both proven to be effective, but transformational leadership qualities are considered more closely aligned with the needs of a flattening global leadership structure.[19]

Much like the future-oriented stance adopted by the 1972 New York City Marathon runners, transformational leadership is an approach that allows for a participatory experience, one with the potential to empower followers.[20] Studies show women are often transformational leaders, although both men and women employ both leadership styles.[21] Transformational leadership is collaborative, bringing forward communication of the organization's values, purpose, and the importance of the mission. One hypothesis for women adopting a transformational leadership style, points to the investments in the community women often make to overcome organizational assumptions and attitudes accompanying their leadership roles.[22]

Researchers found by combining and analyzing 45 studies in a meta-analysis, there are indeed connections between gender and leadership style preference. Women exercised transformational leadership more than men, who instead took a transactional leadership approach.[23] Transactional leadership emphasizes task-oriented behaviors and rewards for meeting objectives.[24] To the very core of the principle of Contrasts, each leadership style depends upon the situation. Contrasts help support our understanding of the ambiguous and deep multilayered nature of culture, but the concept also frees us from assuming that there is a right and a wrong way to lead.

In addition to having a diverse group of potential leaders, each individual has a toolbox from which to choose a leadership style. Although we may gravitate toward one leadership style or another based upon our gender, the ultimate choice is our own. Next, the principle of Context will expand upon leadership style options of the gender settings global business is increasingly navigating.

### *The principle of context*

Context presents itself when it is least expected, like a speed bump in the middle of our fast-paced global workplace, or the frame within which phenomena exist. In China, as explained in Chapter 7, meetings serve as a ceremony to wrap up the final dealings of an agreement that took place behind closed doors. To a businessperson outside of this low-context culture, standing up to present a new proposal or offer alternatives to the existing arrangement could destroy a business deal.

Gender makes the concept of Context even more difficult. There is a historic high of women participating in the global business context. The *Global Gender Gap Report* (Figure 10.4) was introduced in 2006 and has continued as a longitudinal analysis and comparison of countries' gender disparities in the areas of economics, politics, education, and health. The 2012 report includes data from 135 countries; 111 of those have been part of the report since its inception.

Three concepts set the *Gender Gap Report* apart from other global analyses of gender issues. The report focuses upon measuring gaps within countries, rather than the levels of available resources.[25] If it is illegal for women to drive in Saudi Arabia, there is little benefit to have healthcare available 20 miles away from her home because the woman cannot access the resource. Outputs are measured instead on the ways policies are managed in the different countries.[26] This measure would be counted as all male and female university students, not the differences they may pay in tuition, or the type of institution they attend. The third concept measures the relationship between the genders rather than who is ahead. For example, when women and men are reported to hold an equal number

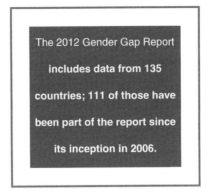

The 2012 Gender Gap Report includes data from 135 countries; 111 of those have been part of the report since its inception in 2006.

*Figure 10.4* Gender gap report.

of mid-level governmental positions, the country receives a point on the report, but the country is not rewarded if women outnumber men 2:1 in governmental job placement.

Saudi Arabia possesses a mean score of 131 of the 135 countries measured appearing in the report. This indicates that of the 135 countries included in the report, Saudi Arabia presents some of the largest gender gaps between men and women. The countries that follow in the 2012 report include Syria, Chad, and Pakistan, with Yemen ranking last.[27] It is important to use resources like the *Gender Gap Report* to understand how gender fits within the context of a culture. In one example, four United States congresswomen encountered an embarrassing scenario at the Saudi Defense Ministry. The Ministry does not have a women's lavatory. Due to the gender gap in the country's political realm, women do not visit the Saudi Defense Ministry. Additionally, it is not a priority for Saudi officials to install facilities for international visitors.[28]

Just as it is difficult to imagine the cultural infrastructure of other countries, it is equally important to consider the assumed cultural principles we adopt and practice over time. When we work with other cultures these are the social cues that can spell success or disaster on either side of the relationship. The principles of Change and Capability provide the final two Geoleadership lenses for us to examine the construct of gender and leadership. While the entire Geoleadership Model works as a system with interlocking components, Change and Capability are extraordinarily interdependent concepts, so we will view them together within this final section.

### The principles of Change and Capability

Intercultural leaders are challenged to shift from old mechanistic mindsets of the industrial era to the adaptive perspective of organizational life as a complex sociocultural system. The principles of Change and Capability assist in making this transition possible. Change primarily addresses the individual, while Capability addresses the organization, and both principles are necessary competencies for intercultural leaders moving forward.

Technology, global work teams, and fewer boundaries between the professional and private spheres have all emerged in a relatively short time span.[29] With rapid change, some issues are overlooked or set aside for future review. As a result, decision-makers may employ technical solutions to help assuage the discomfort associated with change. Technical solutions are not the elements called for in the principles of Change and Capability.

Technical solutions are generally applied by authority figures, and involve a high concentration of know-how already present within the organization.[30] The following is an example of a technical solution within an organization dealing with gender and culture issues. In order to bolster espoused family values, an organization offers employees *paid* family medical leave, an elusive benefit among many businesses. A male manager of the company becomes a new father and exercises his compensated leave benefit. However, when the manager returns to work, he is discouraged from talking about his newborn and new family responsibilities. The man learns that staffers view him as weak when he talks about his new family dynamic, and his commitment to work and overall authority have been called into question.

In this case, paid family medical leave represents a technical solution to a larger problem surrounding the organization and family values. The real issue resides deep beneath the surface, and it can only be resolved with participation and flexibility on behalf of the individuals and the organization. This deeper issue represents an adaptive challenge.[31] Learning agility described in the Change Principle is required on an individual level in this case. Change, coupled with a team dynamic and Capacity to think outside of the box are essential factors when addressing an adaptive challenge.

It is possible in this case that the organization does indeed value family, but the underlying issue is that of gender stereotyping. The assumption that men and women should behave a certain way is interfering with the way the manager is being perceived by his team. By talking about his new role as a caretaker, the team believes their manager has grown soft, and they assume he will not exercise leadership in the same ways as he did before his leave.

Throughout this chapter we discuss the one-to-one ratio between men and women. It can be inferred that men and women will be working together, managing one another, and evaluating each other both formally and informally well into the foreseeable future. So, what would happen if men and women took a cue from the opposite sex and adopted the leadership *characteristics* each gender tends to deliver effectively? Masculine and feminine leadership roles are loaded with stereotypes, making it extremely difficult for either gender to be perceived as effective without violating gender assumptions.

By taking the manager's case on as an adaptive challenge, the individuals within the organization have an opportunity to pose the following solution. The agentic and stereotypically male attributes of self-confidence, power, determination, and independence would pair well with the stereotypically female and communal attributes of softness, sensitivity, empathy, and affection.[32] A study conducted to learn how this approach would impact manager–employee perceptions, identification between and among genders, and overall leadership efficacy, yielded promising results for the future of "androgyny" and transformational leadership styles.[33]

Since masculine and feminine behaviors are socially constructed, it is not out of the question for an organization to reorganize gender role assumptions and train members to enact and follow androgynous leadership attributes. Now, imagine what this discussion would look like if individuals within the organization were not capable of breaking out of the stereotypical masculine and feminine mindset? Androgynous leadership roles and adaptive challenges each come with a warning label for highly combustible outcomes. Women who employ an androgynous leadership style with too much agency could fall into the realm of masculine, and risk prejudice. Similarly, any leader working through an adaptive challenge, gender-related or otherwise, must proceed with care, caution, and the principles of Change and Capability.

---

### Exhibit 10.2 Interview with Jane Roberts, co-founder, 34 Million Friends

A political activist and champion of women's rights, Jane Roberts is co-founder of 34 Million Friends. Jane has dedicated herself to this organization for more than a decade. As you'll read in her interview, Jane is herself beyond a masculine or feminine stereotype of a leader. We may try to stereotype her, but she remains focused on her cause.

*What are the most important decisions you make as a leader of an organization of which you've been a part?*

I am in the "business" of persuading people of what I think in the long term is the most important "cause" one can adopt and the most noble "calling" one can have. That would be the cause and the calling of gender equality in all realms of civil society. The money raised for the United Nations Population Fund (UNFPA) by 34 Million Friends ($4.2 million by May 2012) has certainly contributed to this message. However, my vision for 34 Million Friends has always been much larger. On page 1 of my book, I state: "My ultimate goal is a worldwide grassroots movement dedicated to ensuring the full humanity and individual rights of women and girls. This is too important an issue to leave to governments alone. Many are doing a terrible job. The outcome will affect us all. We all must do our part. It's time to take a stand!" I view myself as a leader, yes, but not of an organization but of a movement. There are tens of thousands of "leaders" related to various aspects of this movement, but I truly think I have a unique vision. My vision is that all that we talk about regarding gender comes down to one subject: gender inequality. Gender inequality is the root cause of maternal mortality, of the lack of access to family planning, of the 20 million unsafe illegal abortions every year, of female infanticide, of child marriage, of female poverty and illiteracy, of sex trafficking, of gender-based violence in ALL of its permutations, of legal, cultural, and religious barriers to participation by the female sex in governance, in economic activity, in peacekeeping, and in peace negotiations. It's all one subject!

On Valentine's Day 2007, I read a "column left" article in the *Los Angeles Times* entitled "Movies Shoot for Change." Paraphrasing, it said that millions of dollars were there for the taking for movies that would change the world. I raced upstairs and wrote a nine-page proposal for the project I had been dreaming about, i.e., a major motion picture documentary that would tie all these subjects together under the gender inequality rubric. The title of this documentary would probably be "The Stories Women Don't Tell" and would make clear to everyone in the world that gender inequality is the moral scourge and challenge of the age, that the price the world is paying for gender inequality is incalculable, and that gender equality in all realms of civil society is the only hope for people, the planet and peace. The proposal funded by the Packard Foundation is done. The executive producer, Linda Harrar (of www.lindaharrarproductions.com), is ready to go. We have searched for "these millions of dollars" everywhere. No takers YET!

Regarding 34 Million Friends, my most important decision came at 3:00 a.m. on July 23, 2002; the morning after the Bush administration's decision was announced not to release the $34 million Congress had approved for UNFPA. Intuitively I knew that the idea of this grassroots movement would have great appeal to many. My second important decision was to say "All the way forever" when in October 2002, UNFPA asked how serious I was about a long-term commitment. My third important decision was to write a book. Having a book in print means media attention. A media interviewer can find legitimacy by being able to say: "Her book, *34 Million Friends of the Women of the World*, is now available." Another decision which has had countless ramifications has been a willingness to leave my "comfort zone." In 2007, I flew to London from California for the Women Deliver worldwide conference, which was attempting to draw the world's attention to high rates of maternal mortality. Returning to the U.S., I landed at JFK, rented a car BY MYSELF! and drove to New Jersey where I gave 11 talks in 5 days in different places, and then drove back to JFK to take a flight home. I felt high anxiety, had sleepless nights, and worried so much, but I made it. My basic decision I suppose is to do anything to further this cause, comfort zone or not.

*How do you encourage creative thinking within your organization (i.e., given the type of industry in which you operate)?*

I have amazed myself by my own "creative thinking." The thought of asking 34 million Americans and others for one dollar (instead of asking $34 from a million people) was the reason this movement took off. Lois Abraham, I call her my partner in crime, had the same quixotic idea and for three years we both gave this our all. It was she who came up with the name "34 Million Friends." For personal reasons she was not able to continue her efforts but it took both of us to get 34 Million Friends well established.

Dogged determination quite frankly counts as much if not more than "creativity." I can say that I have not been lazy once, nor not kept records once, nor not written a letter to the editor once, nor not made a phone call once, nor not commented once on the Internet, nor not written an article once, nor not gotten technical help once when I thought some Internet technology was needed. When you wake up every morning with a mission and a vision for that mission, you are a lucky person. That's me.

Thai social entrepreneur Mechai Viravaidya is my idea of a perfect leader both for creativity and dogged determination. (Please look him up: www.mechaifoundation.org and study him.)

*What is one characteristic that you believe every global business leader should possess?*

Vision and integrity are the two characteristics that business leaders, political leaders, "movement" leaders, and leaders of any stripe must possess. They must believe in what they are doing. This is absolutely critical. I think many of the business leaders in today's world pay no attention to the long-term effects of where they are leading people and the planet. Having followers is kind of fun. But where you are leading them is the most important question. Moral dilemmas faced by "leaders" are often shunted aside to please constituents, stockholders, the unaware, and the ignorant. We need leaders of leaders! I was struck by the Foreword to the first edition of Dr. Wibbeke's *Global Business Leadership* book, which says that leadership is involved with vision, motivation, and trust. I possess the first two in spades and that's why people trust me.

*What is the biggest challenge facing global business leaders today?*

The biggest challenge global business leaders face today is sustainability of their businesses. The biggest challenge for 34 Million Friends is how to sustain it here in the U.S. and how to take it global. 34 Million Friends has joined with Women Deliver, with the Partnership for Maternal Newborn and Child Health, and with the Global Strategy (Every Woman Every Child) of Ban Ki-moon. I have partly sustained 34 Million Friends by writing. (You can find some of my best works at www.rhrealitycheck. org.) I wrote "Let's Envision Gender Equality—Nothing Else is Working" for *The Solutions Journal*. I also have had several op-eds published over these ten years. "Jane Roberts and Her 34 Million Friends" is in the Table of Contents under Chapter 8 of the international best-seller *Half the Sky: Turning Oppression into Opportunity for Women Worldwide* by Pulitzer Prize winning journalists Nicholas Kristof and Sheryl Wu Dunn. They trusted in the worthiness of this cause to feature 34 Million Friends in their book. This has resulted in emails of interest from around the world. Andrew Revkin has written about this in his "Dot Earth" blog in the *New York Times* (www.tinyurl.com/dotpopulate). Lately Foussénou Sissoko has blogged about my book and 34 Million Friends on several Internet sites in Africa and Alassane Sy has written a song in French recorded in Senegal about 34 Million Friends. The song and the images are haunting. (And you can see it at http://www.youtube.com/watch?v=3BcHkX7AiLg&featu re=related) I offered lots of encouragement to these two individuals. I've also, with practice, become an effective spokesperson, both on radio and television.

*What effect do you think national culture has on business leadership decision-making? (This can also include how your own native national culture affects your decision-making.)*

The UN Population Fund is always seeking to incorporate culture into the services it offers in more than 150 countries. Hence it appeals to village leaders, to imams and pastors, and to women's committees to gain support for its reproductive health programs. You cannot dictate in these matters the way, frankly, I might want to with my down-to-earth "get-it-done" personality. For instance, in a rural Senegalese UNFPA clinic, I met a woman who, at 22, had just had her fourth baby. Both she and the baby were suffering from anemia and UNFPA was going to call the husband in and explain what needed to happen, i.e., iron supplements and family planning to delay the next pregnancy. What, may I ask you, should UNFPA do if, in this patriarchal society, the husband refuses to cooperate? What should UNFPA do if the husband is relying on God's will for whatever happens? UNFPA has to deal with difficult situations like this every day. Luckily, 34 Million Friends lets UNFPA furnish the expertise to do its job. Financial support is what 34 Million Friends is all about as well as educating the world's peoples about the centrality of reproductive health, education, and the human rights of women and girls to any chance at all for people and the planet to thrive.

*What are your thoughts on globalization and how important is it for lead-ers to develop their own self-awareness so as to adjust to the changing context(s) under which they operate in a given situation and/or organization? (This consciousness could include the leader's own cultural self-bias while operating with diverse constituents.)*

My thoughts about globalization can be found in my book *34 Million Friends of the Women of the World*: "We have to imagine a world where all people, men and women, in equal partnership, with no artificial legal, cultural, religious, or economic barriers, work together for the greater good. We must imagine a world where all people, regardless of their gender are judged, as Dr. Martin Luther King might have said, only by the content of their character." That is the vision that must go global. That is why I want 34 Million Friends to go global. This would be a new worldview. Individual governments would be held accountable for furthering this vision. Education and health would be the cornerstones of public policy. Budget priorities are a picture of policy. Governments, be they national or local, would be judged on the resources they allocate. The UN would be judged on the resources it allocates. I know there are 34 million people who would take a stand for this vision, who would lead the world toward this vision. This vision if realized would change the world.

Ban Ki-moon, Secretary-General of the United Nations, has said: "In women the world has the most significant but untapped potential for development and peace." He has, to his great credit, established his Global Strategy "Every Woman Every Child." But if he truly believes what he says, then his entire life's work, his entire energy and commitment should go toward this vision. He has the biggest bully pulpit he will ever have. Every person on the planet should know of his vision. They don't! Margaret Chan, in her second term as head of the World Health Organization has said she will concentrate on women's health. I like to say that when the world takes care of women, women take care of the world.

*What is one mistake you witness business leaders making more frequently than others? Do you think that some leaders make such errors due to their inability to be self-aware of their own national cultural bias, as mentioned above?*

One mistake I see business leaders making more frequently than others is not putting enough emphasis on accountability. This is probably the major mistake of business leaders, of political leaders, and of leaders of international organizations, and of leaders of non-governmental organizations (NGOs). Accountability is hard to measure. Measuring results is costly and in some cases might not be cost-effective. This is a conundrum. Another mistake that is so easy to make is not involving the "local community" in decision-making and in "ownership" of what needs to be done. It is easy to think that "YOU" are the expert. But sometimes you have to sacrifice efficiency for the slow work of showing and convincing that your project will have long-term effects after you leave.

*Can you name a person who has had a tremendous impact on you as a leader? Maybe someone who has been a mentor to you? Why and how did this person impact your life?*

In 1964, at the age of 23, I was hired as an instructor in French at the University of Redlands. Dr. Robert Morlan, a giant in the political science department, took me under his wing. In 1968, he got me involved in the Redlands Democratic Club. At that time I was a registered Republican. Soon I was President and "leader" of the RDC. At that time, he also suggested that I be a faculty advisor for a brilliant senior, Sue Thomas, who wanted to put together a course on women as an honors project for her graduation. Sue and I did a great job, and I taught the solidly academic course for four January interims with more than 100 students enrolled each time. It is pretty clear that the late 1960s cemented me as a strong supporter of women. There is a straight line of 48 years between Robert Morlan, Sue Thomas, political activism, and 34 Million Friends.

*Within the global economy, how important is it that a global business leader understands the key features of the Geoleadership Model?*

The importance of the key features of the Geoleaderhip Model particularly that of communication, is significant.

The epigraph to Chapter 4 of Dr. Wibbeke's *Global Business Leadership* (first edition) is a quotation from Nelson Mandela: "If you talk to a man in a language he understands, that goes to his head. If you talk to him in his language, that goes to his heart." Since my teenage years, I have had a love of the French language and taught the language for many years at varying institutions in the U.S. I have also lived in France for a total of perhaps four years during my lifetime. So, when I knew I was going to visit Senegal and Mali as a guest of UNFPA in February 2003, I asked UNFPA to send me their French version of the 2002 State of World Population report so that I could read through the entire publication for all the reproductive health vocabulary I would need. UNFPA asked me about four times if I wanted a translator along on the trip, but I said that I didn't need one. I do speak fluent French. I gave press conferences and radio and television interviews *en français* and received wonderful publicity for UNPFA and for 34 Million Friends in those two countries. The people I think were doubly impressed with this American woman who was countering the policy of her own government, who was touting the work of UNFPA, which is so appreciated by these two very poor countries, and who could do it in French. I wore slacks and long-sleeved blouses so as not to appear uncovered. I listened attentively for hours as people shared with me their stories.

You can see that I had a great desire to communicate. I still have that desire. And to a very small degree, I have talked to the world.

*What do you like to ask other business leaders when you get the chance?*

I like to ask them: How did you get to your position of leadership, i.e., your biography? What sacrifices, if any, have you had to make? Do you ever get burnout? What kind of "reward" besides pecuniary do you get from your work? Nearing the end of your life, will you think that it was a life well lived?

*\*\*\**

Within the Geoleadership Model, Jane Roberts is focused on communication. We find this made apparent in her description of her global leadership style, her focus on the website, and her style of email and written correspondences. Her drive to communicate her vision to the world, to help women around the world, is her focus.

**Jane Roberts** was born in 1941 to a general science teacher mother and a professor of English father in San Diego, California, U.S. Jane spent her sophomore year in college in Grenoble, France, learning French with the help of a French friend and hard study. This was a pivotal year as it opened her eyes to the world. An M.A. from Middlebury College Graduate School of French in France allowed her to become an instructor of French at the University of Redlands. In 1965, Jane married Jay of the chemistry department. They adopted Jeff in 1974 and our surprise Annie came along in 1976. Jane was always a political activist and a champion of women's rights. In 2002, President George W. Bush did something so extreme that in response she found herself dedicated to countering this political act by founding 34 Million Friends to donate at least one dollar to the UN Population Fund (UNFPA) in order to counter the administration's decision to withhold the Congressionally approved $34 million. More information can be found at:www.34millionfriends.org.

In leading globally, gender is a significant issue that has been addressed in varying ways over the years. Viewing it as we have here, through the lens of the Geoleadership Model, is useful in grasping the enormity of this challenging opportunity for growth, collaboration, and cooperation.

## The bottom line

Viewing Geoleadership, business, and gender in one place helps put the magnitude each of these topics holds into perspective. Theory, research, and practice underscore the approaches men and women have taken throughout the years in an attempt to enact leadership. Remember that culture and gender are both visible and invisible constructs, and to be cognizant of each. Employ a conscious and balanced perspective when weighing culture and gender issues on a global scale. Utilize research and reflection to thoroughly examine gender issues relating to leadership and culture. Embrace change responsibly, creating a space for others to work through the discomfort and uncertainty accompanying our rapidly evolving global marketplace. Consider the opportunities within adaptive change, and the potential it holds for both genders and our future leaders.

# 11 Technology and leadership*

> "Give me a lever long enough and a fulcrum on which to place it, and I shall move the world."
>
> —Archimedes[1]

As technological devices and developments permeate every sector from big business to small-town bakeries, it is tempting to assume each of these advancements connects to a power cord. This is not the case for many of the most notable technological advancements in our history. The advent of the printing press by Johannes Gutenberg in the mid-1400s forever changed the way mankind experiences the printed word.[2] While many technological solutions have developed throughout the past 600 years, this chapter focuses upon advancements taking place over the last 30 years. Just as the topic of gender provided us with a closer analysis of the Seven Key Principles of the Geoleadership Model, we now have the opportunity to take a critical look at technology through the Geoleadership lenses.

Technology is a broad term, which includes the application of knowledge in specific areas.[3] This chapter will refer to technologies as computers, tablets, mobile phones, military advances, and communications—including social media and Web 2.0. When we think about computers, tablets, and mobile phones, these wireless devices stand out with visible popularity growth. Estimates project there will be more than one mobile device for every human on the planet in a few short years.[4] So where do we begin to understand how technology and the ways we communicate work as both an enormous benefit and a risk in our global society? Let us start by reading an interview with Peter C. Farrell, an innovator in the medical sciences field in Exhibit 11.1.

* The authors would like to acknowledge the significant scholarly contribution of Maureen A. Guarcello to this chapter.

## *Exhibit 11.1* Interview with Peter C. Farrell, chairman and CEO, ResMed Inc.

As the founder and CEO of ResMed, Peter C. Farrell has been its chairman and a director of the company since its inception in June 1989. His vast knowledge in the field of technology and global experience makes for an interesting interview full of insights for those who desire to be great global leaders, beginning with "business is a team sport" and the life sciences are about "helping people."

*What are the most important decisions you make as a leader of an organization?*

The most important decisions revolve around strategy. Put simply: You can't saddle up all the horses in the barn and expect to be successful. You've got to pick the horses you want to ride and saddle only those. Strategy is vital because it tells you where to focus your time and effort in order to achieve the desired business goals. Then, you have to build a structure that will support achieving the strategy. Next, you have to put in place metrics so you will know whether or not you're moving in the right direction and will get to the goal in a reasonable timeframe. Lastly, you've got to populate the structure with the right people. Of course, people are also critical. And in that regard, we have developed a template, which I've developed over many years, of the characteristics of people who do well and stay with the company versus those who don't do so well and stay only for a short time. In short, we have a good grasp on the key qualities that we see in people who should do well and will likely stay with the organization.

Business is a team sport, and you're not going to "win" with a B-grade team. You want to have the best people. So, when hiring people, first we look for the right skill set for the position, and then we look for a series of character core values that define a person's character. I like the comment which Warren Buffett made about people selection; he said you need people with integrity, intelligence and energy, and without the first, the others don't matter.

So we start first with ethics and integrity. We want our people to have these, and you can't teach them. If you haven't learned them by the time you're seven-years-old, you will never learn them. We also value initiative. If you like, this means asking for forgiveness rather than permission. I think people also need to have a sense of urgency. Another characteristic we value is resourcefulness. Basically we like people who can put together the team they need to get the job done. Creativity is important. Being proactive in communicating with people even if you think people are in the loop is important to making sure everyone is on the same page and everyone has their say. Self-esteem is another important characteristic. If you don't like yourself, who will? Being conscious of value, being fiscally responsible—this is important not just personally and professionally, but also to the customer. In the end it is the customer who writes the check, so we want people whose focus is on service towards and the satisfaction of that end customer. Finally, we like our people to have a concern for their co-workers, because business, as I suggested earlier, is a team sport. So, you have to have skills to play a certain position, but you need to be conscious of all of your teammates. It cannot be all about you—it is primarily about the team.

*How do you encourage creative thinking within your organization given the type of industry in which you operate? How is encouraging creative thinking within the biomedical field different than within another industry, for instance, the manufacturing field?*

The life sciences are about helping people. So, we encourage people to think about how we can do things differently to help more people. And, more importantly, we aren't prescriptive. We don't mandate. We ask people for their ideas, we share ideas, we encourage people to think, if you like, out of the box. We ask people to turn challenges on their head, and to look for different solutions. In order to encourage this creativity, you have to have a culture that is open to new ideas and to doing things differently. You don't punish failures. Failure is a way of learning and moving forward. To engender such a creative approach to solving problems, it is important to have an open door policy in which everyone is approachable, nothing is off the table, and there is no killing of the messenger.

*What is one characteristic that you believe every global business leader should possess?*

One characteristic that I believe every global business leader should possess is moral courage. In other words you cannot please everybody, and if you try to you will likely make some very bad calls. Leadership isn't about being liked. It's about doing the right thing. Sometimes it's uncomfortable and not everyone is behind it. But, again, it's not about getting votes; it's about doing the right thing.

It's also helpful to have a sense of humor. In general, people take themselves too seriously. As one wag put it: one should laugh at life since no one gets out of it alive. And mistakes are inevitable. No one sets out to make bad calls, but it happens. When it does, admit your mistake and move on. One of the worst characteristics of leaders is not being able to admit mistakes. This isn't conducive to creativity, and it's not conducive to teamwork. Of course, one doesn't ever want to fail but that is an unrealistic expectation. You want to increase your odds of success by learning from your failures. That is absolutely crucial. Over the last 30 years,

I've developed a template for making decisions based on the lessons I've learned from both successes and failures. And this template helps me make much better decisions.

On my template for investing in an existing business or making a mergers and acquisitions decision or simply beginning an expensive project, there are six areas which I address before doing a robust financial analysis. These are as follows:

1.  Is there a market which is not only big, but accessible? If you don't have a way to get into the market, the business will never be realized.
2.  Do you have access to world-class people? This doesn't necessarily mean having world-class people in the organization (though that is very helpful). This is about bringing together a group of experts for a day to use their experience, background, education, and ideas to gauge what they think about your idea, plan, and/or strategy.
3.  What is the likely timing for realization of results? I call it the 4–2 Rule, which means that even with a robust business plan, it generally takes four times as long as you think it will take and costs you twice as much money, or it costs four times as much and takes twice as long. Either way, things rarely go to plan when there are significant unknowns and one needs to consider that.
4.  Do you have the finances for the end game? As you de-risk the project or business, the value of it increases. You start with a concept, develop a few prototypes, which should be tested and proven to work, and then people will pay a lot more money for it, if you plan to sell it. And if the project is for internal consumption, it is important to make sure that there will be enough funds to complete the exercise. So, it's finance for the end game that counts. Don't start something where you can't actually afford to get the job done.
5.  Consider whether the product or idea is something really new and whether or not you are likely to get a patent for the intellectual property. Consider also whether or not you fully understand the technology and have the right team to work on it, the right mix of skills. In short, can you be really good at it? Can you really get the job done?
6.  Do you have a high tolerance for bad news? This is what I call the "Alpha Factor"—it's not taught in business schools. Even when the business is not going well, you need to be able to get up in the morning and say, "Things might be bad right now but I love this business. We are going to get through this!"

Not many things get held up on the filter when you ask these questions. The final step is to do a robust financial analysis. If you find there's a negative net present value, that's a bad sign. If you don't hit a breakeven point, that's a bad sign. And so on. In short, you might love the technology or the product, but it also needs to pay the rent. And the end game is innovation where the idea gets paid for.

People often say innovation when they mean creativity or imagination. Innovation only happens when someone writes a check. If there is no economic transaction, there is no innovation. It could be creative or imaginative, but it is not innovation until the product, service or the idea is anointed financially.

*What is the biggest challenge facing global business leaders today, particularly for those in the technology areas of life science, biomedical, or biotech?*

Currently, the biggest challenge facing global leaders is the global economic environment. Debt is a significant problem. We cannot spend our way to prosperity, and I see the U.S. losing fiscal rectitude with annual debt over a trillion dollars. It is nonsensical. People, including politicians, need to have financial responsibility and accountability. I also worry about the lack of financial understanding that young people have today. They are just not rigorous enough about the way they handle finances. The expectations are out of kilter with reality. All governments are spending too much money irresponsibly. We should not spend what we do not make; we shouldn't spend what we aren't collecting. The massive level of debt throughout the Western world is a huge challenge because it negatively impacts the business environment. There are too many lawyers in political office—their career is politics. They don't really know how the economy works. They tend to be too Keynesian in approach and their focus is too often wrong. In short, they tend to do more harm than good. Arnold Toynbee, the twentieth-century English and historical philosopher said: "Civilizations die from suicide not murder." And I think we're on suicide watch in a lot of Western democracies, including the United States.

*What effect do you think national culture has on business leadership decision-making? (This can also include how your own native national culture affects your decision-making.)*

I think it all goes back to basic values. You've got to be honest with yourself and with other people. Do the best you can, and don't let people down. Strive for excellence, but don't push people into a corner. As a leader you have to be very conscious of the impact of what you do and how you act on the people around you. When it comes to cross-cultural issues, the key is to make sure everyone involved has signed off on the idea and is on the same page. It doesn't matter to me what culture you've been brought up in. The fundamentals are the same. If you're in business, you're in it to make a contribution. If the contribution is good enough you will make money. For instance, I set up Baxter's research and development in Japan in the mid-1980s. I understand well that there are vast cultural differences, but you just have to get on with it while being appropriately culturally sensitive. You have to ask yourself and be clear about what you are specifically trying to achieve. The culture is a second order effect after you clarify your expectations. It's the way you present things; it's the way you engage people. But fundamentally in business, what you're trying to do is the same no matter what culture you're in. You are trying to make a good enough contribution. And, if you make the right contribution, people will pay you for it. So, first you look at business fundamentals; these count above all. Then the cultural overtones and potential hurdles come after you have clarified what objectives you are trying to achieve.

*What are your thoughts on globalization and how has technology affected market fluctuations depending on their cultural context? Is technology accepted more readily in certain markets depending on how that culture views technology and globalization?*

Technology and globalization are very interconnected. The ease with which we can digitally communicate globally via the Internet, email, cell phones, iPads is a great tool. Information travels much more quickly than it ever has before. If one examines the basis of economic growth in places like Africa, India, and China, a lot of it is due to improved ease of communication, particularly via cell phones. Technology makes things cheaper. Cell phones for instance, save money as they eliminate the huge costs of optical fibers, copper wires, and so on that was incurred with landlines.

A danger I see is that people are almost too well off in the more advanced economies and become complacent. Free enterprise has made us what we are today. It is freedom to choose which is important, as Milton and Rose Friedman emphasized. It is about people being able to make individual decisions choosing for themselves. One of the dangers today is losing our liberty, our law-governed liberty. We should be very cautious of voting in changes that take away this liberty. As Hayek warned, almost seven decades ago, too much government and centralized power can send us on the road to serfdom.

*What is one mistake you witness business leaders making more frequently than others?*

One big mistake that business leaders make frequently is not thinking things through properly, thinking that you can get away with things without proper circumspection and due diligence. Again, it really boils down to fundamentals. It is a huge mistake for leaders to think they can get away without abiding by the fundamentals, or thinking rules and laws don't apply to them, or that they can avoid doing their homework. Even the best ideas benefit from pilot studies before the boat is pushed too far out.

In general, leaders take too much risk without understanding the level of risk they are taking—the danger always looms that they are leading beyond their level of expertise, hoping everything will turn out all right, without examining the fundamentals. This is more likely to happen in the technology arena than other industries, because in the tech arena, people really benefit from having a technology background and if the decision-makers don't have it, the challenge is much greater. In short, technically trained people are more likely to be data driven and make fewer mistakes.

In the tech industry, another serious danger I see for leaders is excessive hubris. Narcissistic thinking suggesting that the fundamentals don't apply to them because they've already been so successful is an inherent danger. We all need a large dose of humility.

*Can you name a person who has had a tremendous impact on you as a leader? Maybe someone who has been a mentor to you? Why and how did this person impact your life?*

Over the years, I've been greatly influenced by the writings of various business strategists. For example, Peter Drucker's book: *Innovation and Entrepreneurship*, published over 25 years ago, had a big impact on me as well as his prior books, *Managing for Results* and *The Effective Executive*. Andy Grove's *High Output Management* also had a great influence on me. Reading and contemplating the works of these business strategists and others has certainly impacted my thinking about business and my subsequent actions. More recently, it was Charles Koch's *Science of Success*. The wisdom these books imparted, particularly those of Drucker, saved me a lot of trial and error and, no doubt, unnecessary mistakes.

*Within the global economy, how important is it that a global business leader understands the key features of the Geoleadership Model? How important do you think having a model such as this is?*

Having templates is extremely useful. If you go to the supermarket, it's helpful to have a list. It's the same in business. A set of reference points or a template to ensure that you're on the right track is essential to thinking things through properly. Fundamentally important, I would say.

*What do you like to ask other business leaders when you get the chance?*

Life has become too complicated for a simple question like, "What's the reason for your success?" Let me digress. Charles Koch, a highly successful engineer and businessman who has a net worth over $30 billion, wrote *The Science of Success* a few years ago about how he and his team built the world's largest private company, Koch Industries. The book was highly relevant to me and my team as Charles reviewed his business career in a warts and all fashion to delineate the lessons he learned in building Koch. Charles pointed out that he and his team would regularly ask themselves "How do we make sure that we do not make the same mistakes again?"

What actually resonated with me, albeit a little too late in my career to be a big help, was the introduction to the main contents of the book.

Charles and his brothers, David and Bill, like their father, Fred, were engineers; in fact, they were all educated as chemical engineers at MIT. (As an aside, my son, Michael, and I also graduated as chemical engineers from MIT but I can say categorically that's not what made the introduction to *The Science of Success* so impactful.) What was significant to me was Charles writing about what his father had taught him. He said that his father had drummed into him the following fundamentals: the importance of hard work, the importance of integrity, the importance of humility, and the importance of continuous learning. These characteristics may not guarantee success, but one might argue that these traits represent a truly excellent springboard. It certainly worked for the Koch brothers and I would be happy to employ people with these traits, provided it was also coupled with, as Warren Buffet has suggested, intelligence and energy.

****

With his focus on ethics and moral courage, and his template for choosing his employees, Dr. Peter Farrell has a one step at a time approach to global leadership.

**Peter C. Farrell** is founder and CEO of ResMed and has been chairman and a director of the company since its inception in June 1989. From 1984 to 1989, he served as vice president of research and development at various subsidiaries of Baxter International, Inc. From 1978 to 1989, he was foundation director of the Graduate School for Biomedical Engineering at the University of New South Wales (UNSW), where he currently serves as a visiting professor. He holds a B.E. in Chemical Engineering with honors from the University of Sydney, an S.M. in Chemical Engineering from MIT, a Ph.D. in Bioengineering from the University of Washington, Seattle, and a D.Sc. from UNSW for research contributions regarding treatment with the artificial kidney. He was named 1998 San Diego Entrepreneur of the Year for Health Sciences, Australian Entrepreneur of the Year in 2001, and US National Entrepreneur of the Year in 2005 for Health Sciences. He is chairman of the executive council of the Harvard Medical School division of sleep medicine; and is a member of the Visiting Committee of the MIT Harvard HST Program. He is a director of NuVasive, Inc., a NASDAQ-listed company involved with the surgical treatment of spine disorders and is the non-executive chair of QRxPharma, a clinical-stage specialty pharmaceutical company. He is a fellow of several professional bodies, including being a member of the National Academy of Engineering, and is active in philanthropy.

# Technology viewed through the Seven Key Geoleadership Principles

## *The principle of Care*

This section expands upon these concepts and how technology accelerates the outcomes in either direction. Care calls for the balanced interest and value for profit and the stakeholders. How does the concept of Care intersect with technology?

Military technological advancements have made way for robots, the size of bumblebees, to monitor communications or attack on command. Despite being a perceived asset on the battlefield, military drones, or unmanned aerial vehicles (UAV) are also the topic of debate. Specific concerns surround the devices' ability to cause harm.[5] The Geoleadership principle of Care comes into play as the stakeholder value is weighed. On one hand, UAV's are remote, allowing operators to keep a safe distance while flying the devices. On the other hand, and still weighing stakeholder value, the new military technologies and leadership strategies must be fully evaluated, including the perspectives of those affected by drone technology on the ground.

Viewing the drone technology through the Care lens reveals the following. Since drones are robotic, the level of *responsibility* attached to the activities the devices enact is called into question. Where does the responsibility reside, with the operator, or the robotic device? Similarly, the devices could malfunction altogether and act autonomously, inciting unplanned events. Research to assign a moral framework to the technical devices is currently underway, in an attempt to keep the drones from becoming the bearers of blame for wartime actions, either intentional or accidental.[6] Next, the principle of Communication shifts focus to help demonstrate the ways technology moves people.

## *The principle of Communication*

No matter your language or cultural background, the sound of a ringing cellular phone is now nearly universal. The phenomenon seems counterintuitive. How do countries with little to no infrastructure and few economic resources have access to mobile phones? The answer is simple. Mobile communication is the ideal solution for countries with little to no infrastructure, requiring cellular towers and minimal electricity to charge the device. Community members possess personal phones, share handsets among family, and switch out subscriber identity modules (SIM cards) for community phone use.[7] Africa is the world's fastest growing cellular phone market, with an impact reaching far beyond friendly chatter.[8] The principle of Communication highlights the importance of engaging with, understanding, and appreciating a culture and its people. This principle is exemplified through Africa's mobile phone phenomenon over the past 14 years.

In a rural Western Kenyan village a census was deployed to understand how residents utilized mobile phones. The census inquired into which households possessed mobile phones and who primary users were. The survey went on to learn whom callers chose to contact most often and what topics of conversation typically entail. The results of the census were both surprising and a reflection of early telephone adoption in the United States during the 1930s.[9] Similar rural surroundings were the same reasons early American women adopters began using household telephones.[10]

Kenyan women use mobile phones for a variety of reasons, one being to cut down on the travel time required to learn a piece of news, or exchange important information. This could be classified as a convenience, but within the rural farming community using a phone is a cost–benefit consideration. The phone also helps families access help in case of illness, village intruders and violence, and to activate the networks within and between villages.[11] Kenyan men generally own the newest phone in the rural households and women and children receive the older devices. Men and women use the phones for different purposes, as the culture is shaped so men stay nearby the family unit and women typically relocate for marriage. As a result, women phone family and friends back home, while men use the phones to make business calls and to contact religious figures and friends from outside of the region.[12]

Cultural difference shapes the ways Kenyans utilize cellular phones, but the availability of the mobile technologies opened up new opportunities and advantages for African people. Farmers, nonprofits, and healthcare workers fighting the battle against HIV and AIDS now use cellular phones to communicate and congregate. The rapid rise in mobile phone use created a tremendous communications infrastructure within a former void, in fewer than two decades. This new mobile community presents emerging opportunities for the future of business, banking, and communication throughout Africa.[13] The next principle of Consciousness brings us back to the smartphone and the social networks that seemingly follow us everywhere.

### The principle of Consciousness

Consciousness as a tool of exploration, receptivity, and compassion, coupled with a self-awareness of our own cultural backgrounds and biases makes perfect sense within the Geoleadership framework. One place where the work of developing our internal self-awareness and our relationships with others is occurring on a grand scale is within social networking systems. What happens when our personal social networks have the same readership as some small-town newspapers? Mindfulness, curiosity, observation, reflection, adaptability, and perspective are all elements built into the LinkedIn and Facebook networks. Please see Figure 11.1 for more information.

It is tempting to have keys in-hand to access LinkedIn, a no-cost space granted the title of the world's largest online professional network with more than 175 million users. LinkedIn users represent more than 200 countries and territories and account for more than five billion searches on the network.[14] The network is intuitive, and promotes the names and profile images of people who indicate they attended similar schools, worked within the same companies, or those who have high concentrations of the same connections.[15]

The challenge for leaders during this time is learning how to use these networks as tools rather than crutches.

*Figure 11.1* Challenge for leaders.

So how does the principle of Consciousness intersect with the wide world of social networks? We can take the elements apart to take a closer look. For example, mindfulness is a state of complete awareness achieved through receptivity and observation. Well, how would a member of the LinkedIn network remain mindful with millions of searches, connections, and communications occurring each day? Remain calm and consider your own intentions. Why are you in the space? What do you intend upon accomplishing it? From that place, you can build your profile to reflect your intentions. University professors help guide undergraduate students through the complicated social networking world by setting benchmarks for them to accomplish one step at a time. By approaching the LinkedIn network with intentionality the students reported higher levels of comfort and connection utilizing the networking tool.[16]

LinkedIn is designed for professional networking, while Facebook represents the social side to social media. Here we will use Facebook to dig a little deeper into the opportunity for observation as a part of the Consciousness competency. In October 2012 Facebook reached a total of one billion, monthly, active users, 81 percent of whom reside outside of the United States and Canada. Users are increasingly mobile, with 604 million active users who used a Facebook mobile product.[17] A leader's ability to *observe* is extremely important within the principle of Consciousness. Sorting through the Facebook advertisements, friend's status updates, friend suggestions, and your own photos, location tags, and status updates, how is there space for observation?

Observe the Facebook atmosphere by remaining as neutral as possible. This tip does not indicate that opting out of Facebook is optimal. There are many levels to the world's culture infused within the crowded, social space. Facebook users make nearly all things visible through the content they post. A streaming newsfeed displays user whims, prejudices, complaints, celebrations, where people place value and esteem, all alongside popular culture, trends, fashion, news, and charitable outreach efforts. The job of a neutral observer is to peel away the cultural layers within the Facebook sphere, and use the pieces to help construct a small portion of the Geoleadership puzzle.

The power of these networks lies in the hands of the consumer. There are fewer differences between news and gossip because they now increasingly reside within the same venue. Communication technologies make it possible to remain in real-time constant contact with people all over the globe. What are we forgetting during this process? Is there time for thoughtful preparation and reflection when technology allows us to move so quickly? Maintaining intentional practice, careful observation and reflection will serve as reminders to slow down to make the most of our newfound global efficiencies. While social networks are growing, education is also moving into the virtual space. The principle of Contrasts addresses how leaders within the higher education realm are working with the uncertainty surrounding the rapid change.

### *The principle of Contrasts*

Throughout this text we discuss and analyze the complex layers of culture within organizations and the ways global leaders work through the challenges. How do global leaders work within entirely ambiguous environments? The principle of Contrasts deals with the ambiguity accompanying many leadership processes and the anxiety held by those involved with change. Education is typically the medium utilized to train leaders. Whether you are reading this text on a tablet, computer, or as a physical book, is an indicator that the delivery of education is changing. Education is changing worldwide in a variety of ways, and technology is once again front and center. Massive open online courses (MOOCs) are one example of a technological educational phenomenon sweeping traditional higher education within the U.S. and abroad, as related in Figure 11.2.

MOOCs are online courses offered by universities, generally tuition free, to anyone who has access to the Internet.[18] The courses are taught using a video of the instructor(s) and the content is presented in a live or pre-recorded format. Sometimes you may see the instructor's hands drawing sketches if the course has design elements, or a PowerPoint presentation guides you through the lesson. There are assignments and readings, but the courses do not generally qualify for college credit. One of the major draws to MOOCs is their often-prestigious home base. Universities counted among those offering the courses include Harvard, Yale, Stanford, and MIT. Course content varies from philosophy to engineering, and each course has the capacity to host thousands and sometimes more than 160,000 students logging in from 190 countries, at one time.[19]

Students in China are especially excited about access to the course content, which they utilize to augment their current class materials. Due to the relevance and accessibility of the course content, Yale Professor Shelly Kagan is cited as one of the most recognizable American professors in China, and he receives thousands of web hits for his course videos each week.[20] Chinese student volunteers dubbed Mandarin subtitles onto the videos, making them even more accessible to

---

> The change of venue from brick and mortar institutions to the Internet is enormous, with an instant, global audience.

*Figure 11.2* From brick-and-mortar to Internet.

Chinese students.[21] Many institutions do not know where MOOCs will lead, but they are planning them nonetheless.

Stanford University took a step towards planning and investing in the future by appointing a vice provost for online learning, the first for the university.[22] Change is also on the horizon in terms of course credit for MOOCs. The American Council on Education agreed to evaluate five to ten courses for recommended college credit.[23] College credit eligibility for MOOCs could reduce the cost and the time required for students to complete a college degree. The models are experimental and no two MOOCs are alike, but university leadership including administrators and faculty are trying to get their arms around the concept of making education in this form available to everyone.[24] Students are reciprocating with attendance, participation, and feedback on courses they are not earning credit to attend.

The principle of Contrasts is woven throughout the MOOC trend. Students are not guaranteed success or credit, faculty risk critique on a global scale, and universities offer the service without charge, while each participant within the massive open online course model has overcome a level of uncertainty and moved on to see what collective potential lies ahead. Once the uncertainty subsides, one thing remains very real. The principle of Context helps us learn what happens to technologies when they are no longer operational.

### *The principle of Context*

Situational perspective lends us a frame to view our technological world and interactions. Pull yourself away from the smartphone, tablet, desktop, email, and social media and what do you see? Where are these devices going when they are no longer cutting-edge or operational? Electronic devices that reach the end of their useful life are defined by the United States Environmental Protection Agency as e-waste. U.S. e-waste weighed in at 2.37 million tons in 2009 alone.[25] E-waste is then exported, often to developing countries, whose workers and systems are ill-equipped to manage the incoming, and potentially hazardous, materials.[26]

In recent years, leaders stepped back to view the conditions and concerns surrounding e-waste. Agencies from the governmental sector, academia, nonprofit, and international organizations collaborated to learn more about the impact of e-waste and how to manage the issue together. The mission of one group, who produced a 100-page report entitled, *Characterizing Transboundary Flows of Used Electronics: Summary Report*, was to create a vision for the future of our global technology discards.[27] The report takes the problem of e-waste into account in a number of ways, exemplifying the Context Principle. Trade data, surveys, country-specific e-waste discard projections, financial motivation analyses, e-waste tracking data, and legal policy articulation all reside in the same space to contextualize e-waste in our world. Each subject area is further deconstructed to highlight details from technical, elemental, and chemical levels, denoting the composition of e-waste, beyond the general device identity (cellular phone, flat screen television, etc.).

Building a thick context around the issue, highlighted gaps that may not have been apparent looking only through a scientific lens or from an economic perspective.

*Figure 11.3* Building context.


Cadmium, arsenic, zinc, copper, and flame-retardants appear on lists enumerating priority items and those posing harm to potential handlers and the environment.[28] In addition to chemical underpinnings, the report takes a high-level process perspective, dissecting the phases of current activities and gauging what is and is not known about e-waste transactions. Qualitative and quantitative data collection measures also appear within the report, as proposed methods to understand the motivations and mechanisms underscoring the export of e-waste.

Context illustrates how technology, though everyday becoming smaller and more efficient, can also prove to be an enormous burden (see Figure 11.3). Viewing technological device disposal through the Context lens provides cultural, economic, scientific, and geographic insights to paint a more holistic picture of the e-waste process.

By approaching seemingly mundane processes differently, behavioral changes have the potential to make a significant impact within the individual and the organization. The principles of Change and Capability provide the final two lenses for us to point in the direction of technology.


### *The principles of Change and Capability*

Change and Capability come into the technology discussion at every turn. Technology has altered the way we learn, where we go for news and information, how we connect with one another, and our charitable activities. Although technology is a part of our daily lives, it would be naive to assume infusing technology into a business is the secret ingredient for success. Understanding and adaptation are the elements business leaders require on an individual and organizational level.

Tales of horror from modern industry pivot around the collision of human and technological errors. Take, for example, the oversight of computer aided drafting platforms utilized in two different countries to engineer the Airbus A380 aircraft. The measurements were so mismatched that components designed in France would not fit into the fuselage designed in Germany. This error occurred even though every element of the process was the same, save for the software version employed by each group, separated by one generation.[29] On one hand, it is conceivable that the world's largest passenger plane, built in multiple countries, on two continents, may encounter some cultural and operational misalignment. On the other hand, the issue could have been identified earlier in the process if the *technological* influences of the project were weighed as a part of the *business* planning before the project launched.[30]

The principle of Change addresses building and adapting learning patterns as a leader, and modeling learning agility for the organization. The Airbus A380 project eventually recovered and took flight, but the lesson is how leaders can learn from these examples, and how a project, much like the e-waste report, has the capacity to be theoretically constructed and reverse engineered in order to view the components *and* the environments where they reside. Kiva.org provides an example of an organization working through Change on an individual level, while leveraging and strengthening community through the principle of Capability.

The statistical makeup of Kiva.org sounds as though it would be impossible to maintain. Kiva, meaning "unity" or "agreement" in Swahili, is an online network for global lenders and borrowers to interact. A lender provides a loan minimum of $25 and has the ability to view borrower profiles from all over the world.[31] Profiles generally include a photo of the individual or group of borrowers, the borrower's gender, location, and business or product, and total amount the borrower needs to realize their loan as funded. Kiva was founded in 2005 and has fostered the following explosive growth. Kiva.org has nearly 1.3 million users in 221 countries, with more than $370 million dollars in loans to 902,796 borrowers, and the nonprofit boasts a 98.97 percent repayment rate.[32]

The term Web 2.0 denotes an amalgam of traditional Internet components and user-contributed content.[33] Kiva.org allows users to view the website and borrowers, but also has a space for those involved as lenders, to log in and view the loan portfolio and the profiles of the other individuals who helped fund the same loans. This community is furthered through the mechanism that allows users making Kiva loans to broadcast their goodwill on their respective Facebook user profile with one simple click. The Capability of this particular organization remarkably lies, in part, within the hands of nearly 845,000 Kiva lenders.

Now consider the individual and organizational requirements of the Geoleadership principles of Change and Capability. Kiva is unlike most all of the nonprofit organizations we know. The organization empowers the individual and uses technology as a component of their enormous organizational structure. However, even Kiva, on the cutting-edge of philanthropy and technology, must continue to learn and reshape their intercultural expertise on an individual and organizational level.

In Exhibit 11.2, a Google executive discusses how technolgy and change are clearly linked.

---

### *Exhibit 11.2* **Interview with Osama Bedier, vice president of global payments, Google**

The interview that follows is with vice president of Global Payments at Google, Osama Bedier. Osama, like our previous interviewee Dr. Peter Farrell of ResMed, has a strong awareness of risk-taking. These global leaders of life sciences and technology are on the forefront of our "new world" and are setting the tone for what the world will be like in the not-so-distant future with the visions and goals they set for their people today.

*What are the most important decisions you make as a leader of an organization of which you have been a part? (This can also be answered from the perspective of what is the most important decision a leader/client makes in his or her organization.)*

First and foremost a leader has to articulate a vision. Leadership is not possible without a following and vision is a leader's primary tool to persuade people to follow. A well-defined vision inspires action at scale, fueled by passion, towards a common focus or direction—All necessary components for success. Many leaders go through the motions of creating a vision, but don't realize its importance—this often comes through as lack of direction. Lacking clear direction, leaders seem indecisive—not sure of what to do, and they go after too many things at once with bad results. Second, people decisions—hiring, growing and managing out. This stuff takes time, lots of time to get right. At least 30 percent of a leader's time should be spent on people. Not a lot of attention is paid to chemistry and makeup of the leadership team. Bringing in the right people is important, but making sure they work well together is critical. It can mean the difference between normal and super productivity.

Finally, decisions around taking risks. Corporate America has become risk averse and created a generation of middle managers that fear failure. Middle managers have been conditioned over the course of their career with an unrealistic expectation never to fail. They have been conditioned over time to play it safe as opposed a healthy risk-taking environment of learning from failure. This at the core of why large companies find it hard to innovate. I love being in the Valley, because employees here are not afraid to think big and embrace failure on the way there. When I think about my early days at PayPal, we started with a vision of being the global online currency and changing the future of money, never mind we only had 30 engineers in the company. When eBay acquired PayPal, a culture clash became very noticeable around the willingness to fail. PayPal's culture early on was "fail fast, fail often." When the two companies came together, they almost hit a brick wall because the philosophy at eBay at the time was "failure is not an option." Leaders are often left to make the most important risk decisions, often with the future of the company at stake.

*How do you encourage creative thinking within your organization (i.e., given the type of industry in which you operate)?*

In a word, by *democratizing* it. Unfortunately, we've been taught to believe that creative thinking is the responsibility of specific roles or levels, and that it's not the responsibility of every individual in the organization. If you survey the most successful products or ideas of our time, you'd notice that good ideas come from just about anywhere. And the best technology ideas are often a product of persistent solution iteration against a common problem as experienced by the consumer or employees closest to the consumer. Rarely does the first attempt work but the lessons from the first failure are critical to finding success. As a result of fearing failure, most organizations unintentionally block this type of creative thinking through process or structure intended to increase productivity.

So, how do you democratize it? Two culture changes are key—Freely sharing information on opportunities that only top management might have had access to in the past and empowering anyone across the organization to do something about it. How do you get over the fears that this is sensitive or confidential or should only be in the hands of a few? Google, Facebook, and others have a successful record of broadly sharing sensitive information with thousands of employees and keeping it within the walls. This is accomplished by making the privilege clear.

If you allow everyone in the organization to understand the opportunities to be addressed and give them tools to solve them—innovation will thrive at scale. Different organizations have found successful ways to empower employees. At Google, everyone in the company has 20 percent of their time to do what they want to do, as opposed to what their manager is asking them to do. This is an outlet for them to creatively solve the problems that they understand exist. So, first it's giving them access to the information and then empowering them to build on it. Other examples of this are the hack-a-thons at Facebook and PayPal that the company allows time for in certain time periods. Then there is the culture of open-door management where any individual at any level can walk into the president, CEO, or CGO's office, and tell them their ideas. An example of a hack-a-thon is when an organization puts forth a list of problems they want solved and gives employees a certain period of time to focus their attention on them without constrictions, rules, or other obligations to detract from the focus on solving the problems. Often there will be monetary and/or acknowledgment incentives for the top ideas.

*What is one characteristic that you believe every global business leader should possess?*

Being decisive. Decisiveness is often the difference between success or failure. Even if you make the wrong decision at first, you're more likely to get to the right answer more quickly than if you get stuck in analysis-paralysis. We've seen many, many examples of this. Over years sometimes, an organization will form committees and groups of committees and they ponder whether they should enter a space. Eventually, by the time they decide to enter, the cycle of implementation is so long that it's too late. Decisiveness, even at the risk of being wrong, is critical. A favorite mentor of mine used to say the best answer is the right answer, the second best answer is the wrong one and the worst answer is no answer.

*What is the biggest challenge facing global business leaders today?*

Two answers—accelerating pace of change and the platform paradigm shift. The pace of change has so accelerated in the last ten years because of the Internet that companies are at risk of complete failure to understand their customers and their needs. Digital netizens—those born in the digital/ Internet age have a different set of norms than generations before them. The divide is so wide in thinking and behavior that they often seem counter-intuitive to one another. This new generation are always connected to the Web, put out their "computing device" close to 100 times a day, use touch screens instead of keyboards, proudly share all their activities with the world and have a deeper understanding and expectation of technology than the industry can support; sometimes to the point where they expect to be involved in defining future versions of their product. As a result, innovation cycles are getting shorter and shorter while reaction times are getting longer. By the time a company has applied itself to solving a new problem or technology driven consumer behavior it becomes irrelevant, several additional change cycles have passed and they fall behind. For this reason, small companies are significantly out-innovating larger companies.

We're entering a platform era where a company is not necessarily defined by the number of its employees, but rather by the size of its eco-system or developers. Developers, external third-party developers, are taking on large parts of the innovation responsibility that companies used to have. This leads to a paradigm shift in both the pace of change, as well as the scale of innovation. The best examples of this are in device ecosys-tems (iPhone and Android) and social networking (Facebook). Both wouldn't be where they are if it wasn't for the platforms and the developer ecosystems that they created. If you look at the iPhone or the Android ecosystem, there are about six or seven hundred thousand apps each. They've redefined how we think about the mobile phone. Today, the phone is a multipurpose, computing device. On their own, Apple and Google could never have created the seemingly unlimited ways that we use the cell phone. This had to happen through developer ecosystems in which many, many developers are competing to build amazing ways to use the phone. If Apple or Google had to build 600,000 applications by themselves, the cost would be in the $100,000,000,000 range. With the developer ecosystems, you are delegating the risk of innovation to a much broader community that can handle a pace that could never be managed internally. This is changing the game as it relates to the old rules of management. How do you manage an ecosystem? How do you inspire them? How do you incentivize them? How do you motivate them? How do you punish them? What are the rules that you create? How do you generate a healthy ecosystem that continues to grow? These new norms are new and being defined now as the new physics for business.

*What effect do you think national culture has on business leadership decision-making? (This can also include how your own native national culture affects your decision-making.)*

Given that the U.S. is such a melting pot, it's hard to pin down a specific culture across the country. For me, it is hard to decipher between my own native culture and the national culture. However, two things I grew up with that affect how I make decisions. First, the immigrant mentality. We who are immigrants to this country don't take the opportunities offered here for granted. Growing up in Cairo and then moving here, the magnitude of the opportunity is not lost on me. As a result, I'm a lot more likely to use it effectively and not waste it. Immigrants are more aggressive and competitive in taking advantage of all the tools and opportunities available to us. For instance, my first job at 8-years-old was a paper route. At 13-years-old, I had three jobs: one at a Kmart, one at an insurance agency, and one at a Chinese restaurant. Each one of these jobs taught me very early on how to excel in the workplace. They taught me how to deal with people. I learned that anything is possible … I think that's one big cultural difference here in the U.S., the feeling that anything is possible. I learned a healthy disregard for boundaries or the limits to how far I could go. Americans grow up believing that they can be whatever they aspire to be.

The second thing that affects my decision-making is the idea of fairness. Growing up with four brothers, I focused on staying down-to-earth regardless of my position at work. I concentrated on things like: How do I interact with almost anybody in the organization? How do I make sure that I'm treating everyone fairly, whether it's during promotion time, raise time or annual performance reviews? For me, I have a strong sense of making sure I am fair. There is a strong sense of fairness that I have in telling people very early on, before it gets out of control, they are not performing. Sometimes it is necessary to part ways. There is a sense of fairness in helping the person find their next role.

*What are your thoughts on globalization and how important is it for leaders to develop there own self-awareness so as to adjust to the changing context(s) under which they operate in a given situation and/or organization? (This consciousness could include the leader's own cultural self-bias while operating with diverse constituents.)*

Ten or fifteen years ago, globalization was seen as an opportunity. Today it is a risk—if you don't do it, you won't succeed. Because of mobile technology, everyone is connected in real time. While the Internet reached a billion people quickly, mobile has reached five or six billion people in parallel. When we connect the Internet to mobile, everything is seen as it happens in real time. When an event occurs in China that the government doesn't want us to know about, they can't stop the information flow, it also enables people to organize in ways that weren't possible before. Take my own country of Egypt. The revolution there was caused because of social media enabling real-time communication to inform and get support from the rest of the world. One of the things I really enjoyed about working at PayPal is enabling a sole proprietor, someone who might have worked part-time at his home to sell his product like a multinational—to all the countries around the world. The individual became global! With mobile smartphones, cameras and global payment systems, a basket maker in a remote African village can sell her product directly to a consumer in the U.S. So, with this in mind, the whole concept of "globalization" is about to change. It is not optional anymore.

Digital is setting the precedent for everything else. The fact that digital goods have far fewer middlemen, and the author can sell the product to the consumer with only one middleman, the marketplace, is a precedent for all other goods in the future. Kids today grow up thinking the world is global from day one. It's not an option—it's the new way. Last year, I hired a 14-year-old from Toronto as an intern because he was one of the best developers in the Android market. At 14, he already had an app in the app store that has been downloaded by more than a million people, had made more than a million dollars. This is the new norm.

*What is one mistake you witness business leaders making more frequently than others? Do you think that some leaders make such errors due to their inability to be self-aware of their own national cultural bias, as mentioned above?*

Details. Knowing when to dig in and when to delegate. Executives sometimes get so enamored with their own success that they distance themselves from the average employee or customer. As opposed to keeping your ear to the ground at scale, they delegate everything and rely on everyone else's judgment to make decisions. This approach worked well when change was more rare. Because a bit part of corporate culture is pleasing your boss, the result is often telling them what they want to hear. A dangerous environment for tough decisions that requires risk-taking or unpopular steps including admitting failure. Not being intimate with the details also makes leaders seem out of touch with reality, unauthentic and their words are less inspiring. Digging very deep on one thing every quarter keeps a leader in touch with reality and inspires the organization as only leading from the front lines can.

*Can you name a person who has had a tremendous impact on you as a leader? Maybe someone who has been a mentor to you? Why and how did this person impact your life?*

First, my dad. He's the smartest person I've ever known and also the most spiritual. He's instilled values and work ethic through patience and repetition from a very young age that I still abide by today. Lessons like—if you start something, finish it. Do your work well or don't do it at all. And be the best at anything you take on. He was a walking example of all his lessons.

I've been fortunate to have some really good people help me grow along the way with key timely lessons. Maynard Webb taught me that I had to earn my way back onto the team every day. Scott Thompson at PayPal taught me the importance of communication to any successful leadership role. John Donahoe at eBay taught me how to be a thought-leader and many others stretched me to grow fast along the way. I appreciate all their support more and more every day.

\*\*\*

As Osama Bedier states, digital is setting the precedent for everything else. While the Internet connected billions of people quickly, mobile technology connected to the Internet connects billions of people in real time, as it happens. Children today cannot fathom a non-global, non-digitally connected world. The new way isn't an option anymore, it is the happening now.

**Osama Bedier** is the vice president of Payments at Google. He joined Google in January 2011 after seven years at PayPal and eBay. Most recently at PayPal, he was vice president of platform, mobile and new ventures. Earlier, he was responsible for PayPal's open global payments platform, as well as product development for all consumer- and merchant-facing products. Osama received a Bachelor's degree in Computer Science from the University of California, Berkeley.

## The bottom line

From Gutenberg's advent of movable type, to a world of knowledge and opportunity held within the confines of a 2 by 3 inch cellular smartphone, technology has taken global society through the paces at lightning fast speed. Viewing technology through the Seven Key Geoleadership Principles helps guide us through the impact it has upon culture, systems, and organizations from the military to the classroom, to the environment. Viewing technology through the Seven Key Principles of the Geoleadership Model helps illustrate the depth and breadth of a global leader's scope of work, while highlighting so much we cannot know without stepping out and practicing leadership as informed and invested members of our own global society.

# 12  Geoleadership and the community

Globalization is not an option; it is an imperative. U.S. business leaders no longer have the luxury of ignoring potential revenues from large markets such as China and India, as well as newly developing opportunities in countries in Africa, Asia, and South America. Outsourcing is only the tip of the iceberg. More and more skilled workers are immigrating to the United States, which makes cultural understanding a domestic, not global, agenda item.

The purpose of this book on Geoleadership has been to identify the vital intercultural competencies needed by U.S. business leaders working in global situations. Throughout this book, we presented each of the seven dimensions of the Geoleadership Model, explained their importance, and provided case interviews with prominent thought leaders. We have also shown how the influence of gender and technology are now affecting how leaders must adjust their thinking in order to reach all followers across virtual borders.

The seven Cs of the Geoleadership Model highlight how moving U.S. business leaders to a place of cultural competence is a several-tier process. A certain amount of energy, effort, and time are required to achieve such intercultural competence. The implication for U.S. leaders and organizations is that the process of internalization of the various components of intercultural competency requires a multifaceted approach. However, Hofstede (2004)[2] asserted that the United States reflected a more short-term orientation in its business environment. Such short-term orientation appears antithetical to the longer-term personal investment by the U.S. business leader.

The tiered learning process began in the first chapter of this book with an overview of the multitude of challenges in the global marketplace faced by leaders and organizations. Leadership emerged as a universal concept occurring in all contexts, yet it retained its own cultural perspective. The second chapter of this book highlighted that the concept of culture remains one of the most misunderstood constructs within organizations. A thorough overview of how culture and leadership are interconnected followed. The concept of care was discussed in the third chapter to show leaders who need to find value beyond economic indicators, meeting objectives, and spreading the *American Way*. Rather, caring about individuals in another culture and understanding how they view leadership emerged as important. In terms of leading others, the book showed that those leaders who paid attention to the concerns of employees and looked at problems in new ways were more effective in their intercultural business dealings.

Chapter 4 talked about the importance of effective communication among diverse business constituencies. The unspoken ways of communication remain just as important as the spoken ones, and the written modes of communication are taking on vital significance due to the advent of online messaging systems. Chapter 5 discussed that if business leaders are not often able to communicate face to face with their colleagues, then such leaders must become self-aware of both their own and other's cultural mindsets. Chapter 6 showed how contrasting approaches to leadership emerge when leaders hold differing expectations and values. Chapter 7 focused upon the context of leading, which is similar to the idea of situational leadership.

Chapter 8 spoke to the dynamics of organizational change globally and how competent leaders must be adaptive to such opportunities. Chapter 9's central message was that an interculturally competent leader is capable of operating in a multitude of diverse situations for the benefit of an organization. Chapter 10 walked us through the issue of gender in the global business workplace using the lens of the Geoleadership Model and showed us some of the great opportunities for innovation, collaboration, and teamwork being open to different genders can provide. Chapter 11 discussed the challenges, risks, and opportunities of technology. Because of the changes and growth of technology, global leaders are challenged to navigate into the unknown at a rapid pace.

Two important questions remain and they relate to practical application and scholarship, and are the topics of this final chapter. First, how do we recognize intercultural leadership within our global and local communities? Second, what is the future for global leadership research? The interview in Exhibit 12.1 with Tom Carson, CEO of the Rovi Corporation, will assist in answering this question.

---

### *Exhibit 12.1* **Interview with Tom Carson, president and CEO, Rovi Corporation**

Tom Carson is president and CEO of the Rovi Corporation. A global leader in digital entertainment technology solutions, Tom Carson leads a global team focused on creating and distributing home entertainment solutions. As you will read in Tom's interview, he, like many of our other leadership interviewees, believes that global leaders have to be able to look beyond their own native cultures to be successful today, especially as they enter and develop into new geographical areas.

*What are the most important decisions you make as a leader of an organization of which you have been a part?*

I think one of the most important things a leader needs to decide is the direction of the company and the goals it is going to try to achieve. The mission and goals of the company drive the focus of the people and determine the areas in which the company will invest its resources. So much of what the company works on, and shouldn't work on too, is determined by the mission of the company. Without a very clear direction, employees will lack focus on what they need to deliver, resources will get diluted, and external constituencies won't be clear on what the company is doing either.

   Another thing that is very important is the talent that is recruited into the company. While it sounds trite to say, people are the most important asset of the company. They are the ones that get things done and without the proper type of talent, a company can flounder. Continuing a consistent flow of talented individuals into a company will ensure the skill and energy of a company stays at a high level.

   Finally, the structure of the organization is very important. Rovi, as an example, has the historical reputation of being a functional company. However, being a company that has grown via acquisition, it has been problematic to use this type of structure. We grew to a size and product complexity where it was not a practical structure for people to manage both the number of people and the complexity of multiple product lines within their function. There had been loss of focus and communication, and people were given responsibility for things that were new to them to manage. As a result, I felt it was important to change the structure to be more business-unit driven to ensure clarity of mission, focus, accountability, and communication.

*How do you encourage creative thinking within your organization (i.e., given the type of industry in which you operate)?*

This is a hard one and one of the most difficult things I see for our company now. When I first started as CEO, one of the first things I did was add "Innovation" as a key value for the company. I believe that it is innovation that fuels a company via the development of products and services. It is hard for a company to grow and survive without creative and innovative products and services. The concept can also apply to administrative procedure within a company, improving things like process flow and procedures can also significantly help in delivering the goals of any enterprise.

   While this is still a work in process within our company, here are some of the things we are doing:

- We initiated "Blue Sky" sessions around the company. The idea is to get a group of 10 to 15 people together from various parts of the company, and let them talk about ideas that could be good for the company to explore. We did this within Rovi and it has resulted in a number of business ideas we are exploring, plus a significant increase in invention disclosures that will eventually turn into patents.
- We established an "Innovation Council" within the company, with the idea of having it as the forum for people to bring new ideas and to seek funding for non-budgeted projects.
- We are establishing an innovation pool within our budgeting process. One of the biggest complaints I get is that people often get pushback from managers on new ideas because of a lack of funds within the budget. The concept of the innovation pool is to have the money available for people should they come to the business with a great idea and sound business plan.
- The other thing we are trying to do is to push the idea of innovation down into the organization so that everyone feels the responsibility to innovate.
- The other reality is that it is important, at times, to buy innovation; both for the value it can bring to the company in the form of a product, but also for the talented individuals it can bring into the company to create new ideas.

*What is one characteristic that you believe every global business leader should possess?*

Every global business leader should possess a clear vision for the goals that are trying to be achieved and the determination to deliver results. Many organizations go astray because of lack of clarity around what they are really trying to achieve. Without that clarity, resources are not deployed consistent with the mission trying to be attained. I have seen time, energy, and money wasted, because people work on things that don't matter.

*What is the biggest intercultural challenge facing global business leaders today?*

I think one of the biggest intercultural issues has to do with the ability to look beyond your native culture for businesses opportunities and people skills because these areas may not be familiar. I have often seen a desire, for example, of companies wanting to expand their business to international territories. They talk about it and may even put resources on it, but it takes a lot of time to develop a new geography. You need to understand the market and the people. You need to see how your product or service fits. There may be governmental regulations to manage and the like. Understanding the time element involved and the cultural differences of the market are important, as is patience.

*What effect do you think national culture has on business leadership decision-making? (This can also include how your own native national culture affects your decision-making.)*

I think national culture has a lot to do with how a business is driven. A company's approach to how they do business is driven by the company's headquarters, which has a lot to do with the country in which they are located.

Having worked for a French company and a U.S. company, plus having done extensive international travel and business, I have experienced this personally.

In France, for example, there was a mandate for a 35-hour week for employees to work. This type of approach, when compared to many Asian countries, makes it hard for France to be competitive in the world market. I have also seen some crazy decisions, like keeping factories open in areas of France that should clearly have been closed. The factories were kept open for strictly social and political reasons.

I have also worked in or around the television manufacturing industry for a lot of my career. When a country like China sets a business/political mandate to be a leader in a particular field, they take a longer-term approach than many countries in the West. While all companies ultimately need to be profitable, there is very much more a short-term, quarterly, results-driven focus in many U.S.-based companies than what I have seen in other areas of the world.

*What are your thoughts on globalization and how important is it for leaders to understand and embrace the rapid pace of technology? How has it changed the global landscape for business as a whole?*

Business is global and will stay that way. Many companies rely on international markets for both revenue and employee talent and that will certainly continue. Business leaders need to understand that their business growth and resource pool will likely not just come from their domestic market.

In terms of technology, it does move quickly. The pace of innovation is fast and can quickly make a technology obsolete. There need to be champions in every company for technological change related to their business and industry. I worked for Thomson in the traditional CRT (cathode ray tube) display business. While there wasn't much desire to stay in the consumer electronics industry anyway, the management knew there was a move to LCD (liquid-crystal display) and plasma displays, but never invested to build the technology, thus a $1.2 billion business died. There are lots of stories like this in business. Managers need to be less myopic, particularly when it comes to technology that may impact their business.

*What is one mistake you witness business leaders making more frequently than others? Can you give an example of such a mistake, particularly within the technology realm?*

I think one of the biggest mistakes I have seen made in the technology world is the development of products without a clear business model around how the technology will be monetized and without a clear path as to how you are solving a customer's problem. Often, companies get enamored with technology because of the "coolness" factor that surrounds it, but often people either don't ask, or dig deep enough, about how money will be made with the technology. I like to think of it as people chasing the "Shiny Object."

*Can you name a person who has had a tremendous impact on you as a leader? Maybe someone who has been a mentor to you? Why and how did this person impact your life?*

The person who had tremendous impact on me as a leader is my father. He instilled a discipline of hard work and not giving up on me.

*Within the global economy, how important is it that a global business leader understands the key features of the Geoleadership Model?*

The key features of the Geoleadership Model are very important. The comments I made in this interview touch on a number of the facets of the model.

*What do you like to ask other business leaders when you get the chance?*

Particularly to those who are in our company, I like to ask the following:

1. What are the goals you are trying to deliver?
2. How do you measure success related to those goals?
3. What keeps you up at night?
4. What opportunities are we missing that we need to work on?

\*\*\*

With his view that business is global, and will continue to be so, Tom believes that business growth and an organization's resource pool will not just come from its domestic market. Relying on international markets for revenue and talent, global leaders must put in the time and effort to develop relationships, manage ambiguity, and communicate cross-culturally if they are to be successful in the global marketplace.

**Tom Carson** was born in Pennsylvania; his father was a pathologist and his mother was a nurse. Tom spent most of his time growing up in the Philadelphia area. He is one of eight children in the family and number seven of eight in the pecking order.

Tom attended Catholic grade school and high school before attending Villanova University to pursue a business degree. He graduated with a BSBA, but concentrated in marketing and finance. After graduating in 1981, Tom went to work for RCA and then went to night school a few years later, while still working, to get an MBA from Villanova, which he received in 1989.

Tom now works for Rovi Corporation as the president and CEO. Prior to his current role and joining Rovi, he worked for Thomson and held positions in three key areas. First, Tom held various positions in sales and marketing with the most senior role being the head of worldwide sales and marketing for consumer electronic products. He also held operational roles in manufacturing, with the most senior role managing the North American manufacturing operations for the Display Division. Finally, he managed the intellectual property and licensing business at Thomson.

In looking at the future of global leadership, and, in broader terms, in looking at the future of humanity, there is much research to be done and discussion to be had if we are to work cross-culturally towards solutions that benefit the greatest number of people—and organizations. We will discuss a little later in this chapter what are some interesting areas of exploration, and recommend possible research studies that would help in the quest to understand global leadership in the future. An interview with a global business leader follows in Exhibit 12.2 with chairman and CEO of ViaSat, Mark Dankberg.

## Exhibit 12.2  Interview with Mark Dankberg, chairman and CEO, ViaSat Inc.

Chairman and CEO of ViaSat Inc., Mark Dankberg epitomizes an inquisitive global leader. Rather than making decisions across the board without input, Mark encourages people to do what he does, which is ask a lot of questions. He believes that one of the biggest constraints to organizational growth is applying assumptions that were relevant in the past, but now are not necessarily so. He encourages his people to challenge the basic assumptions that led to success in the past. Unlike many, Dankberg, inherently knows the dangers of the Success Delusion, which Marshall Goldsmith discussed in his interview in Chapter 5.

*What are the most important decisions that you make as the leader of an organization of which you've been a part?*

The most important decisions I make as a leader are the people decisions. For instance, who is responsible for what, etc. These types of decisions probably have the most impact overall.

*How do you encourage creative thinking given the type of industry within which you operate (aerospace and telecommunications)?*

One thing that I do is ask a lot of questions. I also encourage people to ask questions. Basically, we challenge all the assumptions that we start with. One of the most constraining things is to apply assumptions that at one time may have been relevant, but now don't necessarily hold true. Encouraging a lot of questions and try to think as abstractly as possible are the main things that I try to do to encourage creative thinking.

*What is one characteristic that you believe every global business leader should possess?*

Every global business leader should possess empathy: the ability to understand whoever it is you're dealing with and what their perceptions are. If you can't do this, it's really hard to get the value out of the other skills you might have.

*What is the biggest intercultural challenge facing global business leaders today?*

The biggest intercultural challenge facing global business leaders today is probably that they start with the assumption that other people think the same way they do. They don't! Overcoming this mindset is really hard. It's one thing to deal with people from different cultures *in* the U.S., and it's definitely different dealing with people from different cultures who are on their home territory because then their rules apply, and they are often very different.

For instance, they likely think and deal differently with regards to their work, their employees, their view of markets, their customers, the role of government and regulatory organizations, and other factors that we may take for granted. Leaders in some places try to impress much more with who they know than what they know. In other places it's the opposite. Leaders shouldn't assume that leaders in different cultures are going to think like they do. This is where empathy comes in—you have to understand what they are thinking, not what you think they should be thinking.

*What effect do you think national culture has on business leadership decision-making? (This can also include how your own native national culture affects your decision-making.)*

National culture has a big effect on business leadership decision-making. To me, culture is similar to values, and different cultures have different values. Culture is, to me, all those things that you do without thinking about them.

For instance, in different parts of the U.S., there are different sorts of cultures. The Silicon Valley is different than other parts of the U.S., and certainly the U.S. is different than China. The Chinese are generally very good at low-cost manufacturing, and one of the things they look at is whether they can manufacture a product less expensively than anyone else. There's a business model there, which informs their thinking. In the U.S. many companies don't think that way, many Silicon Valley companies don't. They'd rather design something and depend on design differentiation, or software differentiation, instead of manufacturing advantages. This is a pretty fundamental view of competitive advantage. Company and leader decisions stem from these cultural bases.

*What are your thoughts on globalization and how important is it for leaders to understand and embrace the rapid pace of technology—how important is it for leaders to keep up with the innovative technologies? How has technology changed the global landscape for business as a whole?*

To me, globalization is about company competition on an international level. On the one hand, you have access to other markets. On the other hand you've got organizations competing with you in ways that are profoundly different from yours.

We are in the technology business, and certainly technology is a huge enabler of globalization. For instance, the advance of technology means that companies can design things like computers and telephones from mixing and matching different parts. A few years ago, you wouldn't have been able to do that. You have to understand technology from a lot of different dimensions. As a leader, you can't avoid it.

*In terms of technology, do you find pushback or a certain perception from foreign markets because ViaSat is a U.S. company? Does the technology have a certain cache?*

Yes, I think there are a number of developing countries that want the best technology. It can represent a level of sophistication and/or advancement. I don't think "American" is sought as the best technology in all domains, but there are some areas where it is. In a lot of space technology, it largely is, not completely, but largely.

*What is one mistake you witness business leaders making more frequently than others? Can you give an example of such a mistake, particularly within the technology realm?*

One mistake I see business leaders making more frequently than others is clinging to the status quo. Leaders tend to cling to business models, even more than technology!

For instance, Kodak, which pretty much invented the digital camera, is now in bankruptcy because they couldn't figure out a business model that didn't depend on film and chemicals for processing. It wasn't that they couldn't make digital cameras; they just couldn't figure out a business model they liked as much as the one they had successfully used for so long. Nokia is another example. Nokia dominated the world in phones, but because they thought the most important thing about the phone was that it was a phone, they've lost their advantage when that's no longer the case. It turns out the most important thing about the phone for many users now is that it is a little handheld computer. It depends on software—so this is a totally different model.

It's hard to let go of a business model that has worked and move on to a new one, but sometimes markets force you to do that. You might say failure here is a mistake. I'd say it is the hardest thing about being a leader. It's not that people fall into this trap because they are dumb. It's that they do things that look smart step by step, which cause them to resist fundamental changes to their business models. The resistance to changing the business model is huge when the business model has thus far been very successful. Many leaders just aren't willing to let go of a business model that has worked so well.

*Can you name a person who has had a tremendous impact on you as a leader? Maybe someone who has been a mentor to you? Why and how did this person impact your life?*

One person who has had a lot of impact on me as a leader has been Irwin Jacobs, founder of Qualcomm. From him I got a first-hand view of a business and leadership style that I really liked. He was really successful. It encouraged me to use a somewhat similar style of leadership that I'm comfortable with.

*Within the global economy, how important is it that a global business leader understands the key features of the Geoleadership Model?*

The Geoleadership Model's 7 Cs are very similar to the foundation of skills that we try to develop in our leaders so that they can work with each other, our customers, and our partners. To me, the "Cs" of the Geoleadership Model are examples of skills leaders need today. What we try to do internally in leadership development is develop a number of skills, and a lot of these are described in the model. For instance, we try to develop consciousness, care, and communication in our leaders and we also look at the cultural aspects of leadership.

The other thing we try to instill is domain-level understanding of the technology. You have to have that, as well as the other skills, or you can't lead effectively. And of course you have to have basic business skills like strategy and game theory.

*What do you like to ask other business leaders when you get the chance?*

When I get a chance, I like to ask leaders how they think about business and how they got to where they are. Did they make it step by step or did they get lucky with a fantastic insight? What was the thought process that got them to where they are? I'm always curious to understand how business leaders, whether they are in a good or bad position, got to where they are.

With years of experience in leading in the high-tech field, Mark Dankberg points to three Geoleadership principles in particular: ViaSat develops consciousness, care, and communication in their leaders. These skills result in improved cooperation across the company, with customers, and with partners. This is a great testament to the usefulness and importance of the principles of the Geoleadership Model.

**Mark D. Dankberg** is a co-founder of ViaSat, Inc. and has served as CEO and chairman of the company since its inception in 1986. As a start-up, ViaSat was selected to the Inc. 500 list of fastest growing private companies three times. After listing on the NASDAQ exchange in 1996 ViaSat has been recognized multiple times by leading business and industry publications including *Business Week, Forbes, Fortune, Red Herring, Space News*, and *Defense News* for its exceptional performance and growth. Mr. Dankberg is an acknowledged industry expert in aerospace, defense, and satellite communications, and is the leading visionary for a new generation of high-capacity satellite systems. He has co-authored several military standards on satellite networking, and holds a number of patents in communications and satellite networking technologies. He has participated on Department of Defense advisory panels and was invited to testify before a Congressional committee on high technology growth companies and IPOs. In addition, he has been invited to serve as a judge several times at the local and national levels for the Ernst & Young Entrepreneur of the Year program.

As we have seen in earlier chapters, the study of global leadership began in large part with Hofstede's groundbreaking work in developing the model of cultural dimensions researchers still use today. Current research focuses in large part on what affects success across cultures in business. What then is the future of global leadership and intercultural leadership research? We propose that there are several interesting areas to explore. Recommendations include exploring how cultural immersion and the *American Way* of conducting business can effectively coexist. In addition, a study highlighting how leaders understand the concept of caring for their global employees would further global leadership topics. Another proposed research study could include one that examines the concept of leadership (to lead) in other cultures and would prove valuable in determining situational leadership strategies on a select per country basis. Determining intercultural leadership competencies remains a situational and diverse endeavor.

In regards to diversity, many U.S. companies have designated training programs to teach employees and leaders about working with diverse colleagues in a company. While diversity initiatives are to be applauded, they inherently begin a discussion on a negative note. We would propose that the opposite type of training begin to take place in order to build cultural synergy. This idea of *cultural similarity training* deals with what people have in common and starts interactions on a positive tone. To liken it to a colloquial idea, it is akin to dating. People want to know what they have in common with one another so that they can then build relationships from there based on like foundations.

When individuals realize that there are certain things everyone has in common, particularly not having any control over where, when, or into which culture someone is born, then a dialogue can become more relevant. Companies that deal internally and externally with diverse constituencies can start focusing on what values are similar and then leverage this information to bridge the differences. Cultural synergy is created when leaders realize that a particular mindset must be adapted to deal globally, however many inherent similarities exist among individuals which can serve to make cultural adaptation easier. In addition, according to the book *World on Fire* by Amy Chua[3], ethnic minorities are the market dominant majorities in many countries of the world. Leaders who step back and realize the cultural values and norms of such cultures and subcultures can then initiate effective strategies to take advantage of more global opportunities. This book by Chua also is highly recommended, as it is the first book of its kind that links culture to economics and provides inventive and landmark insights.

For us, the possibility of actualizing human potential so that leadership can be culturally relevant is the paramount issue for global business leaders in this millennium. If we were to develop an action plan for business leaders operating within the global arena moving forward, we would stress the points listed in Figure 12.1.

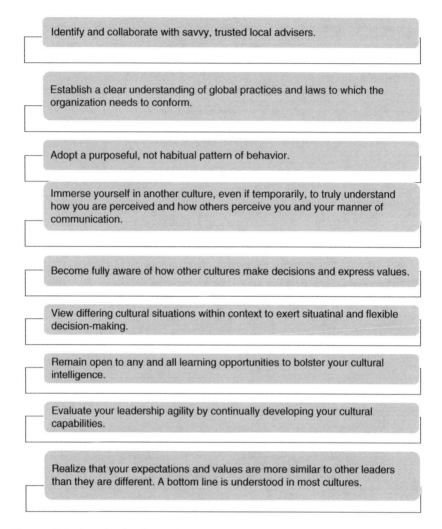

Identify and collaborate with savvy, trusted local advisers.

Establish a clear understanding of global practices and laws to which the organization needs to conform.

Adopt a purposeful, not habitual pattern of behavior.

Immerse yourself in another culture, even if temporarily, to truly understand how you are perceived and how others perceive you and your manner of communication.

Become fully aware of how other cultures make decisions and express values.

View differing cultural situations within context to exert situatinal and flexible decision-making.

Remain open to any and all learning opportunities to bolster your cultural intelligence.

Evaluate your leadership agility by continually developing your cultural capabilities.

Realize that your expectations and values are more similar to other leaders than they are different. A bottom line is understood in most cultures.

*Figure 12.1* Plan of action for our leaders of tomorrow.

# Appendix A

## The research behind the Geoleadership Model

The term "global leadership" has been variously defined as meaning the ability to work together effectively with other people anywhere in the world.[1] Although we have presented an argument that no individual can be fluent in the language, customs, laws, and ways of all cultures, we do believe that leaders who work within globalized organizations can become interculturally perceptive in multiple cultural contexts. We have also argued that there is no one best way of preparing leaders for intercultural work contexts; however, from our empirical research and experience in the field, we created a model that encompasses our best collective knowledge to date about what the important considerations are for such contexts. Through the preceding chapters, we presented what we call the Geoleadership Model consisting of seven dimensions found to be most important for leaders who work within intercultural contexts. The Geoleadership Model is the essential product of a year-long study conducted with the participation of intercultural experts from around the world. In other words, this book reflects the collective effort of many people. In this Appendix, we provide a detailed summation of the research study, which undergirds the Geoleadership Model. It is our hope that the information presented in the preceding chapters will assist leaders in developing intercultural leadership competencies.

### Research design

The purpose of the research study was to determine intercultural leadership competencies vital to U.S. business leaders. In the study, we gathered the authoritative feedback concerning needed intercultural competencies of U.S. business leaders from a diverse group of participating intercultural experts. Our approach was to maximize certain characteristics of both qualitative and quantitative methods, yet we required more than most common mixed method approaches afford. A qualitative research methodology, specifically a Delphi methodology using three sequential rounds of data gathering, provided the means to access, explore, capture, and analyze what ideas and approaches currently existed and/or potentially could be employed to assess intercultural competence in U.S. business, as well as the specific nature of intercultural competence. A Delphi study served as the means to gather expert opinions on cultural and social phenomena.[2]

Dalkey and Helmer pioneered the Delphi method at the RAND Corporation in the 1950s. The method is qualitative, exploratory, and utilized where high complexity and uniqueness prevent quantitative methods from being used.[3] Delphi methodology involves a series of focused and structured questionnaires that seek to reach agreement from a group of participating experts. The utility of Delphi methodology aided our efforts to explore and gather data from qualified participants over a global area because the method has been established previously as not requiring participating experts to interact in face-to-face communications.

The Delphi methodology also is a communication structure geared toward producing detailed critical examinations and discussions, rather than a simple compromise.[4] In addition to reaching group agreement, Delbecq, Van de Ven, and Gustafson found that the Delphi technique facilitates additional objectives.[5] Another of our objectives was to determine or develop a range of possible solution alternatives. A third objective was to explore and expose underlying assumptions or information leading to different judgments. A standard Delphi research study generally consists of three progressive rounds of data gathering.

### *Pilot study*

Before conducting the actual data-gathering rounds with the selected panel of experts, we conducted the first round of the pilot study using the same Internet-based survey delivery service intended for use in the research. An advantage of conducting a pilot study is that it might give advance warning about where the main research project could fail, where research protocols may not exist, or whether proposed methods or instruments are inappropriate or too complicated. To avoid bias, the researcher utilized different pilot participants than actual study participants.

Participants enrolled in the pilot study via electronic mail invitations. Seven intercultural experts responded to the eight-item open-ended questionnaire. The questions posed were:

1. How can U.S. business leaders recognize the concept of culture?
2. How can U.S. business leaders utilize the concept of culture in understanding their own cultural background and bias?
3. How can U.S. business leaders analyze and evaluate intercultural situations?
4. How can U.S. business leaders negotiate and make decisions within intercultural situations?
5. How can U.S. business leaders communicate in intercultural situations?
6. How can U.S. business leaders motivate and lead in intercultural situations?
7. How can U.S. business leaders develop intercultural teams?
8. What intercultural competencies can U.S. business leaders learn to compete globally?

In addition to the theoretically based set of questions, the pilot participants commented on the delivery medium and question content and clarity. The feedback received from the first round of the pilot indicated themes and patterns, and although it was a small group, the answers provided sufficient data to formulate the questions for the second pilot round.

The second round utilized the same question set as Pilot Round 1; however, we then formulated a questionnaire using a five-point Likert-type scale and the analyzed data from Pilot Round 1. We asked the pilot participants to rate items for each question. The results of the second pilot yielded data related to the degree to which participants agreed or disagreed with factors associated with the posed question.

We analyzed data from the second pilot round and calculated the means and standard deviations for each item. We retained items that received a mean of 2.5 for the final pilot round and then eliminated data that did not for the third pilot round. Additionally, due to participant feedback, we made certain modifications in wording for clarity.

In the final pilot round, we asked participants to accept or reject each item for each question. The objective of this action was to discover areas of convergence and divergence.

Since the goal of our pilot study was to ensure that the data-gathering instrument or protocol was viable, it was important to test the delivery mechanism as well as to ensure that the questions were as free of bias as possible. Although the pilot study was small, it did allow for the rewording of some questions for more clarity in later rounds.

### *Rounds of the actual study*

The first round took place to select and enroll the participating experts in the study. These participating experts received an invitation to participate based on their contributions in the intercultural leadership arena and their publication of relevant research in peer-reviewed and refereed journals. These participating experts also had worked in the field of global leadership for at least ten years. We selected participants based on their publication history, education, and work experience.

Only those experts selected to participate and who agreed to participate took part in the study. Similar to the pilot study, the first round also involved sending out a structured questionnaire, already approved by the pilot participants, to the participating experts and asking for their opinion regarding future events. Participating experts received an invitation to speculate on the future of intercultural leadership. The participating experts returned the initial questionnaires, with the data consolidated into a summary document describing the participating experts' feedback.

The second round involved sending out a second questionnaire to the same participating experts and asking them to rank and comment on the priority issues that emerged from the initial feedback. The second questionnaire asked the participating experts to rank the probability and magnitude of effect of these issues. The participating experts then submitted their rankings to the second questionnaire with the rankings then measured using a Likert-type scale. Next, a document summarizing the rankings of the feedback statements emerged. This revised summary document went to the participating experts for the third round.

The third round involved a third questionnaire that focused on reranking feedback statements given the results from the second round. The participating experts reviewed their feedback from the second round and identified where they saw both convergence and divergence of opinion. A document emerged that compiled these highlights of the agreement, disagreement, and uncertainty. In a Delphi study, each subsequent questionnaire builds upon responses to the preceding questionnaire. The process normally stops after the specified three rounds when agreement occurs among the expert panel. Each panelist also had the opportunity to construct additional trends, events, and analysis for contribution to the study.

## Research question

What intercultural leadership competencies are essential for U.S. leaders to develop in the era of globalization?

### *Population*

We selected our panelists based on whether they matched our established criteria and research intent. Each participant was a recognized and published expert in the intercultural leadership field and possessed a minimum of ten years of experience in either university-level academics or the consulting industry. The participants did not fall under the federal guidelines for vulnerable subjects. They also had Internet access to participate since the rounds of data collection were delivered through a web-based platform. Lastly, the participants possessed written English fluency since the Delphi survey appeared in U.S. English.

Researchers have conducted Delphi studies with a range in the number of participants; however, the median group size is 15–20 participants. For our study, we determined that a sufficient number of participants would be between 20 and 50 participants since an international expert group was gathered from Africa, the Americas, Asia, Europe, and the Middle East. Although we contacted 50 potential participants, the eventual number was 26 experts who took part in all three rounds of the study. We considered that adhering to a rigid group size was less of a determinant in conducting the study than participant expertise and response rate. Our sample proved to be large enough, yet not so overwhelming as to not allow us to perceive patterns in responses.

We conducted our study during the spring of 2005 over a period of eight weeks. This period included the initial contact of participating experts to the final feedback analysis. The survey utilized purposive sampling since the selected participants were representative of the intercultural studies field. Purposive sampling was nonprobable in nature. The study participants received initial contact through personal networking and industry association memberships.

*Geographic location*

The selected participants resided or worked in various countries, including nations in Africa, the Americas, Asia, Europe, and the Middle East. All participating experts accessed the survey electronically, which allowed individuals from geographically disperse locations to participate and interact without any required face-to-face communication. The Delphi method allowed for improved communications across geographies in an inexpensive and effective manner. The Internet served as the mechanism for this global interaction.

## Instrumentation

We developed a questionnaire delivered through an Internet platform. The questionnaire posed questions based on our central research questions regarding the intercultural leadership competencies necessary for U.S. business leaders and inquired how these leaders could develop such skills. These questions remained open-ended for full and free comment by the Delphi participating experts. NVivo software (QSR International, 2005) provided further analytical analysis of the data results.

Each Delphi expert had Internet capability to access the questionnaires online. Each individual received a separate electronic mail invitation and feedback to protect anonymity. Participating experts received notification that the study data gathered remained confidential. Participants had a specific period in which to respond to each questionnaire in order. An advantage of the Delphi process included the logical progression of participating experts focusing on a selected topic, providing answers, and then viewing descriptive statistics from the group. This process in the Delphi study spanned three rounds after the pilot study was complete.

The first round consisted of exploration of the subject under discussion through open-ended questions. The questions generated data that received coding and categorization. The participants then received these edited data. The second round provided an opportunity to understand how the group viewed the initial issues. The participants provided data through closed-end questions in the second round, usually through a Likert-type scale via the website. The third round repeated the process to gather specific feedback on individual responses and rankings from Round 2.

## Validity and reliability

Researchers in several fields previously utilized the Delphi method to identify a variety of competencies such as computer competencies,[6] competencies for distance education professionals,[7] and international business skills.[8] The Delphi method focuses on how a researcher chose participants to provide their opinions and beliefs regarding a specific set of questions. In our study, data collection included rounds of questionnaires, compilations of data, tests of validity, and reports of participant feedback between successive rounds.

The development of methodologies and their subsequent legitimization in qualitative methods have resulted in a better-formed research practice. We relied on three categories to determine the effectiveness of our qualitative methodology: a focus on understanding the nature of a lived experience, cultural, or social phenomena, and a language communication. The validity of qualitative methodologies such as Delphi is now well established. Our Delphi study consisted of quantifiable data as well as qualitative data collection and was valid in studying the phenomenon of intercultural leadership competencies.

The Delphi method utilizes the iterative process to produce a stronger result based on anonymous feedback. Typically, controlled statistical and aggregate commentary feedback to the participants and the results are statistical group responses. The stability of participants is critical in the value of the data collected and the ability to establish a summative knowledge base. A thorough understanding of each expert's background signals an individual's judgment abilities.

The effectiveness of the Delphi methodology lay in its technique to ensure anonymity, collect and report accurate data, and allow for a flow of communication between participating experts to solve a particular problem. The reliability of the Delphi technique is unique when compared to experiments with traditional group discussions and other interactive activities to obtain knowledge from a group of individuals. In addition, a theoretical assumption by researchers remained that informed group judgments, achieved through controlled methodologies such as the Delphi method, are more reliable than individual judgments. Objectivity and truthfulness remained critical to the qualitative research method and particularly to the Delphi technique. Trustworthiness and verification signified the Delphi method more than the traditional validity and reliability methods. Our research project utilized the Delphi process within the confines of a descriptive research study.

## Data collection

Data collection involves boundary setting and collecting information from varied processes. The boundaries we set in our Delphi study through the questions and manner of data collection allowed feedback and controlled interaction among participating experts regarding the intercultural competencies necessary for U.S. business leaders. Through repeated interrogations, solicitations for feedback began with the first round of a set of open-ended questions. The second and third rounds focused on closed-ended questions derived from the data collected and analyzed from the previous rounds.

## Data analysis

Our data analysis was an ongoing activity of obtaining and organizing emerging themes from the data collection process through the three sequential rounds of questioning. Using inductive analysis, repeated Delphi data emerged allowing us to discover developing themes and patterns. We analyzed collective and individual data from each participant and across participants. We eliminated any response combined after its submission through the website report and duplicate responses from the first round's feedback.

A Likert-type scale of 1 to 5 made it possible to score the final list of specific second-round rankings. A total score for each response ranking emerged from the statistical analysis we performed. The initial data report provided the responses and their occurrence percentage. Since the data may not have been continuous, the median emerged as a statistical indicator. We reserved only those responses receiving a median score of four or higher for the third round. NVivo software (QSR International, 2005) provided further analytical detail to this qualitative feedback.

Third-round rankings emerged in order of importance; numerically from one to *n*. *N* was equal to the total number or responses to that particular question. Round three data analysis concentrated on the total score received for each response. The response to the original research question receiving the lowest score ranked as the most important intercultural competency of a U.S. business leader. The qualitative data lay in the descriptive statistics generated by this Delphi study. We employed descriptive statistics for demographic and frequency data.

We determined that consensus occurred when an interquartile range score of less than 1.2 existed. This process of analysis provided a rationale for strong similarities among the participants. A second component of analysis allowed us to evaluate the perceived importance of each item. To accomplish this, the five-point scale divided into different levels of importance or relevance. These items received categorization based on an analysis of feedback combined with importance. The five-point scale provided an equal interval between high, medium, and low importance of the items as scored by the participants.

## Analysis, results, and findings

In this section, we present the data analysis approach used to evaluate the results and summarize the main themes discovered in our research. The themes were associated with the seven areas of inquiry. The questions that guided this study included: (1) How U.S. leaders utilize the concept of culture in understanding their own cultural background and bias, (2) How U.S. business leaders can recognize the concept of culture, (3) How U.S. business leaders can analyze and evaluate intercultural situations, (4) How U.S. business leaders can negotiate and make decisions within intercultural situations, (5) How U.S. business leaders can communicate in intercultural situations, (6) How U.S. business leaders can motivate and lead in intercultural situations, and (7) How U.S. business leaders can develop intercultural teams. These seven questions enabled the answer to the fundamental question of what intercultural competencies U.S. business leaders can learn and possess to compete in intercultural contexts of global economies.

In sum, in our study we utilized expert feedback using three sequential questionnaires to determine the intercultural leadership competencies deemed necessary for U.S. business leaders in the era of globalization. The Delphi approach served as a means to gather expert opinions on cultural and social phenomena.

Through industry and professional networking, participants who fit the intent of the study emerged. Each participant was a recognized and published expert in the intercultural leadership field and possessed a minimum of ten years of experience in either university-level academics or the consulting industry. These participants did not fall under the federal guidelines for vulnerable human subjects. The participants also had Internet access to participate in this web-based Delphi study. In addition, the participants possessed written English fluency since the Delphi survey appeared in U.S. English.

To analyze the round one pilot data, we took the following steps to ensure proper rigor. First, from the database created containing all of the text from the panel participant's responses, segments of text that relate to single concepts received tagging. For example, in answering the question of "how U.S. business managers can become aware of the concept of culture," if a response repeated, creation of a new tag or "node" emerged. One such node was "training." Then, after this first procedure of categorization according to themes, the next phase was to reduce further the data by searching for cross themes. For example, under training, two categories emerged as "self-education" and the other was "formal training." This step led to creation of a hierarchy of categories.

The themes that emerged from the qualitative data provided content items for the question set prepared for the second round of data collection. Although the first round instrumentation presented open-ended questions to generate breadth and depth of input (divergence), the second round initiated the process of convergence.

The second round utilized the same question set as Pilot Round 1; however, a formula emerged of a fixed alternative questionnaire using a five-point Likert-type scale and the analyzed data from Pilot Round 1. Each pilot participant then rated items for each question. The results of the second pilot round yielded data related to the degree to which participants agreed or disagreed with factors associated with the posed question; factors that the panel members generated (see Table A.1).

*Table A.1* Pilot Round 2 question data tables

|  | Mean | Standard Deviation |
|---|---|---|
| How can U.S. business leaders recognize the concept of culture? |  |  |
| Through understanding its effect on profit and loss. | 3.00 | (0.82) |
| Through experiencing culture first-hand. | 3.67 | (0.82) |
| Through self-awareness and education. | 4.33 | (0.81) |
| Through seeing cultural differences in getting work done in organizations. | 4.33 | (0.81) |
| How can U.S. business leaders utilize this concept of culture in understanding their own cultural background and bias? |  |  |
| Through the utilization of professional consultants, reading, viewing appropriate videos/films, and developing a heightened sense of self-awareness. | 3.75 | (0.81) |

*Table A.1* (Continued)

|  | Mean | Standard Deviation |
|---|---|---|
| Through understanding what the concept of culture means. By defining culture, business leaders can understand their personal assumptions that may be completely different for people from outside the U.S. | 5.00 | (1.63) |
| Through realizing that leaders are not interested in a concept of culture and do not care about understanding their own cultural background. They want to learn enough practical moves to avoid disasters and to propagate their own ideology. | 2.00 | (0.57) |
| Through seeing that leaders only understand one's culture better when it is reflected in the mirror of another culture. | 4.50 | (0) |
| How can U.S. business leaders analyze and evaluate intercultural situations? | | |
| Through training that is pertinent to their perceived needs. | 3.00 | (0.81) |
| Through collecting information about their employees/ partners/clients/etc. and understanding their cultural background. | 3.00 | (0.57) |
| Through hiring someone who knows about these things and could listen to them. Mostly they will simply react to threats and conduct damage control. | 3.00 | (1.54) |
| Through being in the culture and by reading and studying and learning the language of the culture. | 3.00 | (0.57) |
| How can U.S. business leaders negotiate and make decisions within intercultural situations? | | |
| Through utilizing cultural awareness and skill training. | 3.00 | (0.81) |
| Through realizing that leaders will function to the degree that they can conduct in their own language and in their own framework of what they believe a negotiation to be and what it should produce. | 3.00 | (0.57) |
| Through understanding the other culture and the ways contracts and issues are negotiated and the ways decisions are made. | 3.00 | (1.54) |
| How can U.S. business leaders communicate in intercultural situations? | | |
| Through realizing that no matter how different the cultures are, if communication is made in a respectful way bearing in mind that we are indeed different, negotiation can be successful. | 5.00 | (0) |
| Through realizing that largely from the CEO of the nation down to the corporate leaders, leaders do not and cannot communicate within intercultural situations. They are dependent on others to do this for them if they recognize a problem. Usually they do not communicate well enough to know that there is a problem. They see communication as selling, convincing and winning hearts and minds. | 2.25 | (1.52) |
| Through communicating preferably in the language of the culture and by being aware of norms and mores associated with the host culture. For example, do not show the bottom of your shoe to another person when seated in Indonesia. | 3.67 | (0.57) |

*Table A.1* (Continued)

| | Mean | Standard Deviation |
|---|---|---|
| How can U.S. business leaders motivate and lead in intercultural situations? | | |
| Through understanding that leading in an intercultural situation is more about knowing the differences of the participants than technical skills. Leaders can motivate others if leaders know what is important for a person and what makes that person to be willing to invest energy and time in a project. | 3.50 | (0.57) |
| Through seeking to understand the host culture. By behaving in ways that are acceptable in the other behavior as long as it does not break either the host country law or U.S. For example you cannot use a bribe to motivate someone in order to get a contract. | 4.25 | (0.57) |
| How can U.S. business leaders develop intercultural teams? | | |
| By staffing correctly and/or by the use of external professionals. | 3.75 | (0.57) |
| By giving people of a different background a chance to lead an intercultural team. | 4.00 | (0.57) |
| By sending leaders out of the country and make them answerable to someone not of their culture. | 3.50 | (1.73) |
| By ensuring that the modus operandi of the team is consistent with other cultural concepts or if the team is multicultural, then by putting into place a team philosophy that does not violate other cultural norms or values. | 4.25 | (0.57) |
| What intercultural competencies can U.S. business leaders learn to compete globally? | | |
| Knowledge of language. | 3.75 | (0.57) |
| Knowledge of history. | 4.00 | (0.57) |
| Knowledge of ethics. | 4.00 | (0.57) |
| Patience. | 4.00 | (0.57) |
| Ability to listen. | 4.00 | (0.57) |
| Awareness of other culture's ability to solve problems. | 4.00 | (0.57) |
| Host culture empathy. | 4.00 | (0.57) |
| Negotiation skills. | 3.75 | (0.57) |
| Debase the currency, exercise selective protectionism, make others see that their culture is best and enforce its adoption. | 1.50 | (1.53) |

*Note.* Total respondents for each question are four.

We analyzed the data from the second pilot round and calculated means and standard deviation for each item. Items that received a mean of 2.5 were retained for the final pilot round; those that did not were eliminated for the third pilot round (see Table A.2). Additionally, we made some modifications in the wording of certain questions for clarity due to participant feedback. In the final pilot round, participants were asked to accept or reject each item for each question toward the objective of discovering consensus.

Since the goal of a pilot study was to ensure that the data-gathering instrument or protocol was viable, it was important to test the delivery mechanism as well as to ensure that the questions were as free of bias as possible. Although the pilot group was small, it did yield interesting data considered important and incorporated in the administration of the actual Delphi rounds with the expert panel.

*Table A.2* Pilot Round 3 results tables

|  | *Accept* | *Reject* |
|---|---|---|
| How can U.S. business leaders recognize the concept of culture? | | |
| Through self-awareness and education. | 100% | 0% |
| Through seeing the cultural differences in behavior in getting work done in organization. | 100% | 0% |
| How can U.S. business leaders utilize this concept of culture in understanding their own cultural background and bias? | | |
| Through understanding what the concept of culture means and how to define it. By defining culture, business leaders can understand their personal assumptions that may be completely different for people from outside the U.S. | 75% | 25% |
| How can U.S. business leaders analyze and evaluate intercultural situations? | | |
| Through hiring someone who knows about these things and could listen to them. Mostly they will simply react to threats and conduct damage control. | 50% | 50% |
| How can U.S. business leaders negotiate and make decisions within intercultural situations? | | |
| Through utilizing cultural awareness and skill training. | 75% | 25% |
| Through understanding the other culture and the ways contracts and issues are negotiated and the ways decisions are made. | 100% | 0% |
| How can U.S. business leaders communicate in intercultural situations? | | |
| Through realizing that no matter how different the cultures are, if communication is made in a respectful way bearing in mind that we are indeed different, negotiation can be successful. | 50% | 50% |
| How can U.S. business leaders motivate and lead in intercultural situations? | | |
| Through seeking to understand the host culture. By behaving in ways that are acceptable in the other behavior as long as it does not break either the host country law or U.S. For example, you cannot use a bribe to motivate someone in order to get a contract. | 75% | 25% |
| How can U.S. business leaders develop intercultural teams? | | |
| By giving people of a different background a chance to lead an intercultural team. | 75% | 25% |
| By ensuring that the modus operandi of the team is consistent with other cultural concepts or if the team is multicultural, then by putting into place a team philosophy that does not violate other cultural norms or values. | 100% | 0% |
| What intercultural competencies can U.S. business leaders learn to compete globally? | | |
| Knowledge of history. | 75% | 25% |

*Table A.2* (Continued)

|  | *Accept* | *Reject* |
|---|---|---|
| Knowledge of ethics. | 100% | 0% |
| Patience. | 100% | 0% |
| Ability to listen. | 100% | 0% |
| Awareness of other culture's ability to solve problems. | 100% | 0% |
| Host culture empathy. | 100% | 0% |

*Note.* Number of respondents for each question was four.

## Data analysis and results

This section presents answers to the above research and includes the results from data collection of the three-round Delphi study conducted over a four-week period from April to May 2005 to gain consensus among the intercultural experts.

### *Demographics of Delphi Study participants*

Questionnaires were sent to 40 intercultural experts who had been invited to participate in the study. Of those 40 experts, 37 participated in Round 1, a 95 percent response rate. Thirty-seven questionnaires were sent to those who had participated in Round 1, and 31 (82 percent) responded for Round 2. Thirty-one questionnaires existed for Round 3, and 26 responded, for an 87 percent response rate.

Of the experts who participated in the Delphi rounds, 62 percent were male and 48 percent were female, and all but one held advanced degrees. Twenty participants identified themselves as being from the United States, eight identified themselves as being from a European country, three identified as being from India, one reported being from China, one from Taiwan, one from Australia, and two identified themselves as being from countries on the African continent.

### *Questionnaire data*

The purpose of the questionnaire was to determine what competencies U.S. business leaders need to possess in order to compete in a global marketplace.

*Table A.3*  Age of Round 1 panel participants

| *Age* | *Number of Respondents* |
|---|---|
| 20–30 | 1 |
| 31–40 | 3 |
| 41–50 | 15 |
| 51–60 | 11 |
| 61–70 | 7 |

## Rounds of the Delphi Study

Round 1 of the Delphi Study began by posing 13 open-ended questions to the participating intercultural experts:

1. How can U.S. business leaders become aware of culture as a factor in conducting their business?
2. Can you give an example of a business leader from any country that is truly conscious of the reality of culture? What did this leader do and what was the result?
3. How can U.S. business leaders utilize this concept of culture in understanding their own cultural background and bias?
4. What school of thought, paradigms, and tools can U.S. business leaders use to analyze and evaluate intercultural situations?
5. Can you give an example of how a U.S. business leader analyzed and evaluated an intercultural situation?
6. What school of thought, paradigms, and tools can U.S. business leaders use to negotiate and make decisions within intercultural situations?
7. Can you give an example of a U.S. business leader who negotiated successfully within an intercultural situation?
8. How can U.S. business leaders motivate and lead in intercultural situations?
9. Can you give an example of a leader in any country that motivated others and led successfully in an intercultural situation?
10. How can U.S. business leaders develop intercultural teams?
11. Can you give an example of a leader in any country that was successful in developing intercultural teams?
12. Please list and describe the three most important competencies that U.S. business leaders need to deal within intercultural situations.
13. Can you give an example of a leader in any country that was successful in learning and implementing these competencies globally?

## Round 1 of the Delphi Study

Thirty pages of raw data emerged from the first round. We extracted data from the electronic delivery system, exported it to spreadsheets, then coded and categorized using qualitative software according to the same procedure as the Pilot Round 1. Next, text data from the panel participant's responses were tagged and nodes were created once a single idea was repeated. This step concluded once data saturation was reached, in other words, once there were no new themes.

In the coding and categorization process, common themes emerged through recurring terms, phrases, and words. From this analysis, we developed and prepared a seven-item questionnaire for delivery through the Internet.

## Round 2 of the Delphi Study

In Round 2 of this study, participants rated all items on the Round 2 instrument, which was a reflection of the data collected in Round 1 and contained many of the recurrent words and phrases from the raw data. The Round 2 instrument consisted of seven items involving definitions and statements about intercultural competence, specific components of intercultural competence, assessment methods, and other issues raised by the participants about assessing intercultural competence. The rating process for the items in Round 2 used a Likert-type scale of 1 to 5 as follows: 1 = Most relevant/important, 2 = Relevant/important, 3 = Neutral, 4 = Somewhat relevant/important, 5 = Least relevant/important to intercultural leadership competence.

Participants had the opportunity to add items under each question, but formal modifications were not allowed. Ten participants added items under questions and several other participants made general comments; however, the nature of the comments was in support of the respondents' question response, rather than additional information. Data collection occurred through the Internet delivery system. Downloadable data assisted in creating reports and importing them into spreadsheets. The next step included determining the standard deviations (Tables A.4–A.12).

*Table A.4* Relative to how U.S. leaders can become aware of culture as a factor in conducting business, rate each of the following for its importance

|  | 1 | 2 | 3 | 4 | 5 | Mean | Standard Deviation |
|---|---|---|---|---|---|---|---|
| Formal training/ education (Higher education and training programs) | 19% (5) | 37% (10) | 19% (5) | 22% (6) | 4% (1) | 2.56 | (3.02) |
| Self-education (Reading, observation, research, language tapes, interviewing people) | 26% (7) | 41% (11) | 26% (7) | 0% (0) | 7% (2) | 2.22 | (4.39) |
| Cultural immersion (Living in the culture) | 59% (16) | 22% (6) | 15% (4) | 4% (1) | 0% (0) | 1.63 | (6.38) |
| Coach/consultant/ mentor (Using the services of a person from other culture, or who has worked within another culture for some time) | 41% (11) | 48% (13) | 7% (2) | 4% (1) | 0% (0) | 1.74 | (6.10) |

*Table A.5* Relative to how U.S. business leaders can utilize the concept of culture in understanding their own cultural background and bias, rate the following in terms of importance

|  | 1 | 2 | 3 | 4 | 5 | Mean | Standard Deviation |
|---|---|---|---|---|---|---|---|
| Recognition (Awareness of own culture, perspectives, differences between cultures) | 48% (13) | 33% (9) | 11% (3) | 0% (0) | 7% (2) | 1.85 | (5.41) |
| Engagement (Meaningfully interacting with other cultures) | 59% (16) | 30% (8) | 7% (2) | 0% (0) | 4% (1) | 1.59 | (6.69) |
| Intentionality (Purposefully seeking to broaden perspective and knowledge) | 67% (18) | 22% (6) | 7% (2) | 0% (0) | 4% (1) | 1.52 | (4.93) |

*Table A.6* Relative to which schools of thought, paradigms, and tools* U.S. business leaders can use to analyze and evaluate intercultural situations, rate the following in terms of importance

|  | 1 | 2 | 3 | 4 | 5 | Mean | Standard Deviation |
|---|---|---|---|---|---|---|---|
| The use of intercultural assessments and inventories | 22% (6) | 48% (13) | 22% (6) | 4% (1) | 4% (1) | 2.19 | (5.44) |
| The use of intercultural models | 15% (4) | 52% (14) | 19% (5) | 11% (3) | 4% (1) | 2.37 | (5.03) |
| Adopting a "global–local" perspective | 22% (6) | 26% (7) | 33% (9) | 15% (4) | 4% (1) | 2.52 | (3.05) |
| Using general communication and interpersonal relations models | 19% (5) | 30% (8) | 33% (9) | 4% (1) | 15% (4) | 2.67 | (4.04) |

*Note*: *Paradigm* refers to an example serving as a model; *School of thought* refers to a belief system; *Tool* refers to a product utilized to understand a certain concept.

*Table A.7* Relative to which schools of thought, paradigms, and tools U.S. business leaders can use to negotiate and make decisions within intercultural situations, rate the following in terms of importance

|  | 1 | 2 | 3 | 4 | Mean | Standard Deviation |
|---|---|---|---|---|---|---|
| Values-based perspective | 52% (14) | 26% (7) | 19% (5) | 4% (1) | 1.74 | (5.44) |
| Ethics-based perspective | 30% (8) | 19% (5) | 30% (8) | 22% (6) | 2.44 | (1.50) |
| Context-based perspective | 59% (16) | 26% (7) | 11% (3) | 4% (1) | 1.59 | (6.65) |
| Ambiguity tolerance | 44% (12) | 33% (9) | 11% (3) | 11% (3) | 1.89 | (4.50) |

*Table A.8* Relative to how U.S. business leaders can motivate and lead in intercultural situations, rate the following in terms of importance

|  | 1 | 2 | 3 | 4 | 5 | Mean | Standard Deviation |
|---|---|---|---|---|---|---|---|
| Engaging the culture and its people | 52% (14) | 33% (9) | 7% (2) | 4% (1) | 4% (1) | 1.74 | (5.86) |
| "Self–other" awareness and appreciation | 37% (10) | 41% (11) | 19% (5) | 0% (0) | 4% (1) | 1.93 | (5.03) |
| Global perspective | 26% (7) | 30% (8) | 22% (6) | 7% (2) | 15% (4) | 2.56 | (2.40) |
| Build intercultural understanding/sensitivity/ communication effectiveness | 56% (15) | 33% (9) | 7% (2) | 0% (0) | 4% (1) | 1.63 | (6.43) |
| Culture is integrated and part of business practices (Feedback/rewards/goal-setting) | 41% (11) | 48% (13) | 7% (2) | 4% (1) | 0% (0) | 1.74 | (6.11) |

*Table A.9* Relative to how U.S. business leaders can develop intercultural teams, rate each of the following for its importance

| | 1 | 2 | 3 | 4 | 5 | Mean | Standard Deviation |
|---|---|---|---|---|---|---|---|
| Shared or joint leadership | 22% (6) | 44% (12) | 19% (5) | 4% (1) | 11% (3) | 2.37 | (4.16) |
| Cultural preparation prior to assignment | 48% (13) | 33% (9) | 11% (3) | 4% (1) | 4% (1) | 1.81 | (5.36) |
| Select people with cultural understanding to staff the team | 48% (13) | 37% (10) | 11% (3) | 0% (0) | 4% (1) | 1.74 | (5.77) |
| Use processes, systems, and business models that are appropriate to the culture | 30% (8) | 48% (13) | 11% (3) | 4% (1) | 7% (2) | 2.11 | (5.02) |

*Table A.10* Relative to the most important competencies that U.S. business leaders need to possess to work within intercultural situations, rate each of the following in terms of its importance

| | 1 | 2 | 3 | 4 | 5 | Mean | Standard Deviation |
|---|---|---|---|---|---|---|---|
| Self-awareness (including knowing one's own biases) | 74% (20) | 19% (5) | 4% (1) | 0% (0) | 4% (1) | 1.41 | (8.38) |
| Curiosity, learning | 56% (15) | 41% (11) | 0% (0) | 0% (0) | 4% (1) | 1.56 | (7.09) |
| Flexibility and adaptability | 81% (22) | 15% (4) | 0% (0) | 0% (0) | 4% (1) | 1.30 | (9.42) |
| Imagination/creativity | 26% (7) | 59% (16) | 11% (3) | 0% (0) | 4% (1) | 1.96 | (6.50) |
| Tolerate ambiguity | 44% (12) | 44% (12) | 7% (2) | 0% (0) | 4% (1) | 1.74 | (6.06) |
| Patience | 63% (17) | 22% (6) | 11% (3) | 0% (0) | 4% (1) | 1.59 | (6.87) |
| Mindfulness | 44% (12) | 33% (9) | 15% (4) | 4% (1) | 4% (1) | 1.89 | (4.93) |

*Table A.11* Relative to the most important competencies that U.S. business leaders need to possess to work within intercultural situations, rate each of the following in terms of its importance (interpersonal dimension)

| | 1 | 2 | 3 | 4 | 5 | Mean | Standard Deviation |
|---|---|---|---|---|---|---|---|
| Perspective taking | 33% (9) | 26% (7) | 22% (6) | 19% (5) | 0% (0) | 2.26 | (3.36) |
| Nonjudgmental | 15% (4) | 44% (12) | 26% (7) | 15% (4) | 0% (0) | 2.41 | (4.45) |
| Empathy/ compassion | 19% (5) | 15% (4) | 44% (12) | 15% (4) | 7% (2) | 2.78 | (3.85) |
| Bridging/ synthesizing | 30% (8) | 15% (4) | 7% (2) | 48% (13) | 0% (0) | 2.74 | (5.17) |

*Table A.12* Round 2, Question 9: Relative to the most important competencies that U.S. business leaders need to possess to work within intercultural situations, rate each of the following in terms of its importance (cultural dimension)

| | 1 | 2 | 3 | 4 | 5 | Mean | Standard Deviation |
|---|---|---|---|---|---|---|---|
| Sensitivity/ appreciative of difference | 67% (18) | 26% (7) | 4% (1) | 0% (0) | 4% (1) | 1.48 | (7.57) |
| Effective communication | 70% (19) | 15% (4) | 7% (2) | 4% (1) | 4% (1) | 1.56 | (7.70) |
| Multilingual | 26% (7) | 37% (10) | 37% (10) | 0% (0) | 0% (0) | 2.11 | (5.08) |
| Local–global perspective | 22% (6) | 33% (9) | 19% (5) | 22% (6) | 4% (1) | 2.52 | (2.88) |
| Understanding of how leadership is conceptualized in other cultures | 52% (14) | 33% (9) | 7% (2) | 7% (2) | 0% (0) | 1.70 | (5.90) |

Five of the items from Round 2 had a mean of 2.5 or above or a standard deviation of 2.0 or below, which indicated items for which there was a lack of consensus. The participants judged the latter items and eliminated them from further consideration. Of the items eliminated, four had a mean above 2.5 and one had a standard deviation below 2.0. A list of the five eliminated items can be found in Table A.13.

### Round 3 of the Delphi Study

Round 3, the final round of this Delphi Study, consisted of a fixed-alternative instrument containing nine questions with 34 items from Round 2 that had

*Table A.13* Five eliminated items from round 2

|  | Mean | Standard Deviation |
|---|---|---|
| Adopting a "global–local" perspective | 2.50 | 3.05 |
| Using general communication and interpersonal relations models | 2.67 | 4.04 |
| Ethics-based perspective | 2.44 | 1.50 |
| Empathy/compassion | 2.78 | 3.85 |
| Bridging/synthesizing | 2.74 | 5.17 |

*Table A.14* Items modified for round 3 of the delphi study

| Round 2 item | Modifications or additions |
|---|---|
| Effective communication | "Ability to understand another's ideas and having the other person understand your own" |
| Local–global perspective | "Ability to attend to both global and local consequences of one's own actions" |

received a mean score above the threshold. Given some of the comments from participants in Round 2, for example, slight modifications emerged, specifically adding definitions. The modifications appear in Table A.14. Participants ranked each item in an effort to achieve full consensus on specific items. Only one open-ended question was included, which appeared at the end of the questionnaire.

We sent an electronic mail invitation to participate in the survey to all of our potential intercultural experts. Then, we sent participants the Round 3 instrument, which included the mean and standard deviation from each item so that they could view the group's position on each item. Twenty-six of the 31 experts returned the completed instruments.

We performed analyses of the questionnaire data two ways. In the first method of analysis, we used relative ranking of the number of items accepted by the group, and the second method involved calculating standard deviation. Both methods assisted in determining the items for which the respondents reached consensus. In Delphi studies, an arbitrary consensus point is determined.

For the purposes of Round 3, a relative ranking process occurred to gain consensus for priority competencies. The average of the importance levels assigned by group participants to each category appeared, and we calculated the standard deviation. If the deviation of the individual preference values for a particular feature was small, effectively the group reached a consensus. If the deviation for a feature was large, effectively there was variability within the group. Relative ranking occurs extensively in the nominal group technique and Delphi processes to reach consensus.

*Table A.15* Relative to how U.S. leaders can become aware of culture as a factor in conducting business, please rank each of the items in order of importance

|  | 1 | 2 | 3 | 4 | Relative Ranking | Standard Deviation |
|---|---|---|---|---|---|---|
| Formal training/ education (Higher education, academic courses, training programs) | 15% (4) | 12% (3) | 27% (7) | 46% (12) | 3.04 | (3.06) |
| Self-education (Reading, observation, research, language tapes, interviewing people) | 0% (0) | 12% (3) | 42% (11) | 46% (12) | 3.35 | (4.89) |
| Cultural immersion (Learning the language, customs, living in the culture) | 65% (17) | 15% (4) | 15% (4) | 4% (1) | 1.58 | (5.69) |
| Coach/consultant/ mentor (Using the services of a person from other culture, or who has worked within another culture for some time) | 19% (5) | 62% (16) | 15% (4) | 4% (1) | 2.04 | (5.16) |

*Table A.16* Relative to how U.S. business leaders can utilize the concept of culture in understanding their own cultural background and bias, please rank each of the items in order of importance

|  | 1 | 2 | 3 | Relative Ranking | Standard Deviation |
|---|---|---|---|---|---|
| Recognition (Awareness of own culture, perspectives, differences between cultures) | 31% (8) | 23% (6) | 46% (12) | 2.15 | (3.63) |
| Engagement (Meaningfully interacting with other cultures) | 42% (11) | 46% (12) | 12% (3) | 1.69 | (4.75) |
| Intentionality (Purposefully seeking to broaden perspective and knowledge) | 27% (7) | 31% (8) | 42% (11) | 2.15 | (3.26) |

*Table A.17* Relative to which schools of thought, paradigms, and tools U.S. business leaders can use to analyze and evaluate intercultural situations, please rank each of the items in order of importance

|  | *1* | *2* | *Relative Ranking* | *Standard Deviation* |
|---|---|---|---|---|
| The use of intercultural assessments and inventories | 50% (13) | 50% (13) | 1.50 | (6.17) |
| The use of intercultural models | 50% (13) | 50% (13) | 1.50 | (6.12) |

*Table A.18* Relative to which schools of thought, paradigms, and tools U.S. business leaders can use to negotiate and make decisions within intercultural situations, please rank each of the items in order of importance

|  | *1* | *2* | *3* | *Relative Ranking* | *Standard Deviation* |
|---|---|---|---|---|---|
| Values-based perspective | 23% (6) | 42% (11) | 35% (9) | 2.12 | (3.23) |
| Context-based perspective | 42% (11) | 42% (11) | 15% (4) | 1.73 | (4.75) |
| Ambiguity tolerance | 35% (9) | 15% (4) | 50% (13) | 2.15 | (4.38) |

*Table A.19* Relative to how U.S. business leaders can motivate and lead in intercultural situations, please rank each of the items in order of importance

|  | *1* | *2* | *3* | *4* | *5* | *Relative Ranking* | *Standard Deviation* |
|---|---|---|---|---|---|---|---|
| Engaging the culture and its people | 35% (9) | 8% (2) | 19% (5) | 23% (6) | 15% (4) | 2.77 | (1.88) |
| "Self–other" awareness and appreciation | 15% (4) | 12% (3) | 31% (8) | 31% (8) | 12% (3) | 3.12 | (2.42) |
| Global perspective | 4% (1) | 19% (5) | 8% (2) | 15% (4) | 54% (14) | 3.96 | (4.41) |
| Build intercultural understanding/ sensitivity/ communication effectiveness | 27% (7) | 38% (10) | 23% (6) | 8% (2) | 4% (1) | 2.23 | (2.97) |
| Culture is integrated and part of business practices (Feedback/ rewards/ goal-setting) | 19% (5) | 23% (6) | 19% (5) | 23% (6) | 15% (4) | 2.92 | (1.09) |

*Table A.20* Relative to how U.S. business leaders can develop intercultural teams, please rank each of the items in order of importance

|  | 1 | 2 | 3 | 4 | Relative Ranking | Standard Deviation |
|---|---|---|---|---|---|---|
| Shared or joint leadership | 15% (4) | 8% (2) | 31% (8) | 46% (12) | 3.08 | (3.44) |
| Cultural preparation prior to assignment | 31% (8) | 15% (4) | 35% (9) | 19% (5) | 2.42 | (2.66) |
| Select people with cultural understanding to staff the team | 31% (8) | 58% (15) | 12% (3) | 0% (0) | 1.81 | (5.91) |
| Use processes, systems, and business models that are appropriate to the culture | 23% (6) | 19% (5) | 23% (6) | 35% (9) | 2.69 | (2.38) |

*Table A.21* Relative to the most important competencies that U.S. business leaders need to possess to work within intercultural situations, please rank each of the items in order of importance (intrapersonal dimension)

|  | 1 | 2 | 3 | 4 | 5 | 6 | 7 | Relative Ranking | Standard Deviation |
|---|---|---|---|---|---|---|---|---|---|
| Self-awareness (including knowing one's biases) | 46% (12) | 23% (6) | 15% (4) | 4% (1) | 8% (2) | 4% (1) | 0% (0) | 2.15 | (4.12) |
| Curiosity, learning | 19% (5) | 12% (3) | 23% (6) | 12% (3) | 12% (3) | 19% (5) | 4% (1) | 3.58 | (1.72) |
| Flexibility and adaptability | 19% (5) | 19% (5) | 23% (6) | 23% (6) | 12% (3) | 0% (0) | 4% (1) | 3.04 | (2.57) |
| Imagination/creativity | 0% (0) | 12% (3) | 4% (1) | 8% (2) | 19% (5) | 12% (3) | 46% (12) | 5.54 | (4.04) |
| Tolerate ambiguity | 12% (3) | 12% (3) | 12% (3) | 19% (5) | 8% (2) | 19% (5) | 19% (5) | 4.35 | (1.27) |
| Patience | 0% (0) | 23% (6) | 15% (4) | 19% (5) | 23% (6) | 15% (4) | 4% (1) | 4.04 | (2.57) |
| Mindfulness | 4% (1) | 0% (0) | 8% (2) | 15% (4) | 19% (5) | 31% (8) | 23% (6) | 5.31 | (2.82) |

*Table A.22* Relative to the most important competencies that U.S. business leaders need to possess to work within intercultural situations, please rank each of the items in order of importance (interpersonal dimension)

|  | *1* | *2* | *Relative Ranking* | *Standard Deviation* |
|---|---|---|---|---|
| Perspective taking | 62% (16) | 38% (10) | 1.38 | (6.43) |
| Nonjudgmental | 38% (10) | 62% (16) | 1.62 | (6.34) |

*Table A.23* Relative to the most important competencies that U.S. business leaders need to possess to work within intercultural situations, please rank each of the items in order of importance (cultural dimension)

|  | *1* | *2* | *3* | *4* | *5* | *Relative Ranking* | *Standard Deviation* |
|---|---|---|---|---|---|---|---|
| Sensitivity/ appreciative of difference | 27% (7) | 31% (8) | 23% (6) | 15% (4) | 4% (1) | 2.38 | (2.68) |
| Effective communication (Ability to understand another's ideas and having them understand yours) | 31% (8) | 27% (7) | 23% (6) | 15% (4) | 4% (1) | 2.35 | (2.49) |
| Multilingual | 12% (3) | 12% (3) | 15% (4) | 12% (3) | 50% (13) | 3.77 | (4.09) |
| Local–global perspective (Ability to pay attention to both global and local consequences of one's actions) | 15% (4) | 12% (3) | 31% (8) | 19% (5) | 23% (6) | 3.23 | (1.48) |
| Understanding of how leadership is conceptualized in other cultures | 15% (4) | 19% (5) | 8% (2) | 38% (10) | 19% (5) | 3.27 | (2.68) |

## Summary of findings

Twenty-six (of 27) panelists participated in Round 3 of the Study by completing the 18-item questionnaire through Internet delivery. All 26 panelists completed the fixed-alternative questionnaire portion, and 15 completed the open-ended feedback question at the end. Eleven women and 15 men completed the final round questionnaire. Sixteen identified themselves as U.S. born, 10 identified themselves as non-U.S. born (two from the United Kingdom, two from France, two from India, one from Germany, one from Senegal, one from the Netherlands, and one from South Africa). All 26 identified their current professional activities as including aspects of intercultural specialization.

### *What intercultural competencies can U.S. business leaders develop to compete globally?*

Certain findings surfaced from the data analysis from Round 3 of this Delphi study. Three sets of leadership competencies were judged important by the study's expert panel. These sets of competencies appeared as intrapersonal, interpersonal, and cultural (social). Within each competency category, participants rank-ordered specific dimensions for importance.

Seven specific dimensions—identified in Round 1 of the study and then rated important in Round 2—in the intrapersonal competency area then appeared in order of importance. The top-ranked competency in the intrapersonal dimension judged by the panel was *self-awareness*, which received a relative ranking of 2.15. The second-highest ranked competency, receiving a score of 3.04, was *flexibility/adaptability*. The third-ranked competency dimension, *curiosity*, received a score of 3.58. The fourth and the fifth dimensions, *patience* and *ambiguity tolerance*, received 4.04 and 4.35, respectively. Rounding out the intrapersonal dimension ranked at sixth and seventh were *mindfulness* at 5.31 and *imagination* at 5.54.

At the culmination of Round 2, two competency areas were rated for importance and in Round 3, they were ranked in order of importance related to the interpersonal dimension. The two competencies, *perspective taking* and *nonjudgmental*, were rated 1.38 and 1.62, respectively.

On the social level, the cultural dimension, five competencies were rated and then ranked for importance. The top-ranked competency according to the panel was *effective communication* at 2.35, followed by *sensitivity/appreciation of difference* at 2.38 and by *local–global perspective* at the third position at 3.23. The fourth and fifth positions were *understanding of how leadership is conceptualized in other cultures* at 3.27 and *multilingual* at 3.77.

### *How can U.S. business leaders recognize the concept of culture?*

Relative to how U.S. business leaders can recognize the concept of culture in conducting business, the expert panel ranked *cultural immersion* as the top means with a score of 1.58. At the second spot, with a score of 2.04, was using the services of *consultants and mentors*. The third-ranked means was judged *formal training or education* with a score of 3.04, and coming in fourth was *self-education* with a score of 3.35.

### How can U.S. business leaders utilize this concept of culture in understanding their own cultural background and bias?

The panel determined that there are three ways that U.S. business leaders can understand their own cultural bias. The first way of understanding was *engagement* with a ranked score of 1.69, narrowly ranked second was *recognition* with a score of 2.15, and at third position was *intentionality* with a ranked score of 2.15.

### How can U.S. business leaders analyze and evaluate intercultural situations?

Relative to analysis and evaluation, the 26 panelists first identified, and then in Round 3 ranked, two tools, or paradigms that U.S. business leaders can use to analyze and evaluate intercultural situations. The two tools, *use of intercultural assessments* and *use of intercultural models*, were ranked equally in terms of importance, with a score of 1.50.

### How can U.S. business leaders negotiate and make decisions within intercultural situations?

The panelists chose three paradigms through the early rounds related to negotiation and decision-making: values-based, context-based, and ambiguity-tolerant perspectives. The context-based perspective garnered the top ranking with a score of 1.73; values-based was second at 2.12 and the ambiguity-tolerant perspective was third with a score of 2.15.

### How can U.S. business leaders motivate and lead in intercultural situations?

The study panelists ranked *building intercultural understanding* as the top priority related to leading and motivating with a score of 2.23. The second priority appeared as *engaging the culture and its people*, which had a score of 2.77. The third priority perceived by the panel was *integrating culture with business processes and practices*, which received a rank of 2.92. The fourth and fifth priorities were having a *self–other appreciation* and having a *global perspective* with scores of 3.12 and 3.96, respectively.

### *How can U.S. business leaders develop intercultural teams?*

The study panelists determined that *selection of team members with intercultural savvy* is the top priority in developing intercultural teams, ranking it with a score of 1.81. In second position was *preparation prior to assignment* with a score of 2.42. Ranked third at 2.69 was *using culturally appropriate business models and processes. Shared or joint leadership* ranked fourth.

# About the authors

**Dr. E.S. Wibbeke** is the most noted intercultural leadership guru in the world. Dr. Wibbeke spent 20 years in business leadership and management roles for Fortune 500 firms including Xerox, Novell, and Siebel Systems, with ten years spent living and working in Silicon Valley.

In addition, Dr. Wibbeke is an international consultant and professor of leadership and management, and teaches global business courses for several leading international universities. Dr. Wibbeke has taught students from over 152 countries.

Dr. Wibbeke holds a Bachelor's Degree in European Studies from Loyola Marymount University, a Master's of Business Administration in International Management from the American Graduate School of International Management (Thunderbird). Dr. Wibbeke also holds a Doctorate in Management (Organizational Leadership).

Dr. Wibbeke was the Founder of the Web of Culture, the leading source of intercultural information on the Internet. Dr. Wibbeke is the former Program Coordinator for the Los Angeles World Affairs Council. Dr. Wibbeke is a dual citizen of the United States and the Republic of Ireland. Dr. Wibbeke can be reached at: docwibbeke@gmail.com and www.geoleadership.com

**Sarah McArthur** is founder of *sdedit, a writing and editing firm based in San Diego, California. With nearly two decades of experience in the publishing field, Sarah has worked with such influential clients as Marshall Goldsmith and Anthony Robbins. She has played significant roles in the best-sellers *What Got You Here Won't Get You There* and *Mojo: How to Get It, How to Keep It, and How to Get It Back If You Lose It*. She is co-editor of the classic *Coaching for Leadership: Writings on Leadership from the World's Greatest Coaches* with Marshall Goldsmith and Laurence S. Lyons and *The AMA Handbook of Leadership* with Marshall Goldsmith and John Baldoni. This book received the Top 10 Business, Management, and Labour Title award of 2010 by Choice.

As managing and developmental editor of numerous highly successful business and leadership titles, Sarah is a highly sought-after freelance editor and writing coach. Sarah has held editorial and management positions at *The San*

*Diego Reader*, Harcourt Brace & Company, and The Anthony Robbins Companies. She is former editor of *Business Coaching Worldwide*, and was graduated from the University of Oregon with degrees in English and Environmental Studies. Contact Sarah at sarahmc@sdedit.com and www.sdedit. com.

# Notes

**Preface**

1  Aristotle. (2012). *Aristotle Quotes*. Available: http://www.brainyquote.com/quotes/quotes/a/aristotle382400.html. Last accessed November 10, 2012.
2  Pedersen, P., and Connerley, M. (2005). *Leadership in a diverse and multicultural environment: Developing awareness, knowledge and skills*. Thousand Oaks, CA: Sage.

**1 Geoleadership Challenges**

1  Epicurus. (2012). *Epicurus Quotes*. Available: http://www.brainyquote.com/quotes/quotes/e/epicurus119456.html. Last accessed November 9, 2012.
2  Adler, N. (2011). Leading beautifully: The creative economy and beyond. *Journal of Management Inquiry*, 20(10), 1–14.
3  Black, J., and Poutsuma, E. (2010). Global management competencies: A theoretical foundation. *Journal of Managerial Psychology*, 25(8), 829–44.
4  Ibid.
5  Moran, R.T., Harris, P.R., and Moran, S.V. (2007). *Managing cultural differences: Global leadership strategies for the 21st Century*. Oxford: Elsevier.
6  Cabrera, Á., and Unruh, G. (2012). *Being global: How to think, act, and lead in a transformed world*. Boston, MA: Harvard Business Review Press, 21.
7  Anonymous.
8  Yule, G. (2010). *The study of language*. Cambridge: Cambridge University Press.
9  Gregersen, H.B., Morrison, A.J., and Black, J.S. (1998). Developing leaders for the global frontier. *Sloan Management Review*, 40, 21–32.
10  Michaels, E., Handfield-Jones, H., and Axelrod, B. (2001). *The war for talent*. Boston, MA: Harvard Business School Press.
11  Sheridan, E.S. (2005). *Intercultural leadership competencies for U.S. business leaders in the new millennium*. Unpublished doctoral dissertation. University of Phoenix, AR.
12  Rothwell, W.J. (2010). *Effective succession planning: Ensuring leadership continuity and building talent from within*, 4th ed. New York: Amacom.
13  Lund, S., Manyika, J., and Ramaswamy, S. (2012). *Preparing for a new era of work*. Available: http://www.mckinseyquarterly.com/Economic_Studies/Productivity_Performance/Preparing_for_a_new_era_of_knowledge_work_3034. Last accessed November 20, 2012.
14  QS Global 200 Business Schools Report (2012). *QS Global 200 Business Schools Report 2012: Intelligence Unit*. http://www.ireg-observatory.org/pdf/QS_Global_200_Business_School_Report_2012_opt.pdf. Last accessed November 21, 2012.
15  Adler (2011).

16 Organization for International Investment (2012). *Organization for International Investment*. Available: http://unctad.org/en/Pages/Statistics.aspx. Last accessed November 20, 2012.

17 Miller, G.A. (2011). *WordNet*. Available: http://wordnet.princeton.edu/. Last accessed 2012.

18 Chen, Z., Veiga, J.F., and Powell, G.N. (2011). A survival analysis of the impact of boundary crossings on managerial career advancement up to mid career. *Journal of Vocational Behavior*, 79(1), 230–40.

19 Offermann, L.R., and Phau, L.U. (2002). Culturally intelligent leadership for a diverse world. In R.E. Riggio, S.E. Murphy, and F.J. Pirozzolo (Eds.), *Multiple intelligences and leadership* (pp. 187–214). Mahwah, NJ: Erlbaum.

20 Earley, P.C., and Ang, S. (2003). *Cultural intelligence: Individual interactions across cultures*. Stanford, CA: Stanford University Press.

21 Pedersen, P., and Connerley, M. (2005). *Leadership in a diverse and multicultural environment: Developing awareness, knowledge, and skills*. Thousand Oaks, CA: Sage.

22 Aschkenazi, J. (2008). *Israeli expatriate managers, knowledge transfer and retention*. Saarbrücken, Germany:VDM Verlag Dr. Müller, 19.

23 Hofstede, G. (2001). *Culture's consequences*. Thousand Oaks, CA: Sage.

24 Hall, E.T. (1976). *Beyond culture*. Garden City, NY: Anchor.

25 Central Intelligence Agency (2012). *The World Factbook*. Available: https://www.cia.gov/library/publications/the-world-factbook/fields/2075.html#. Last accessed 2012.

26 Sheridan (2005).

27 Gill, S. (2012). *Global crises and the crisis of global leadership*. New York: Cambridge University Press.

28 Harrison, A., and McMillan, M. (2011). Offshoring jobs? Multinationals and U.S. manufacturing employment. *Review of Economics and Statistics*. 93 (3), 857–75.

29 Hamzah, N., and Ismail, M.N. (2008). The importance of intellectual capital management in the knowledge-based economy. *Contemporary Management Research*, 4(3), 237–62.

30 Leslie, D., and Rantisi, N. (2012). The rise of a new knowledge/creative economy: Prospects and challenges for economic development, class inequality, and work. In T.J. Barnes, J. Peck, and E. Sheppard (Eds.), *The Wiley-Blackwell Companion to Economic Geography*. Chichester: Blackwell, 458–67.

31 Hamzah and Ismail (2008).

32 Leslie and Rantisi (2012).

33 Lewin, K. (1948) *Resolving social conflicts; selected papers on group dynamics*. Gertrude W. Lewin (Ed.). New York: Harper & Row.

34 Mannix, E., and Lean, M. (2005). Diverse teams in organizations. *Psychological Science in the Public Interest*, 6(2), 31–55, 35.

35 Lin, B., Vassar, J.A., and Clark, L.S. (2011). Information technology services for small businesses. *Journal of Applied Business Research*, 9(2), 25–9.

36 A.T. Kearney. (2012). *2012 Global cities index and emerging cities outlook*. Available: http://www.atkearney.com/documents/10192/dfedfc4c-8a62-4162-90e5-2a3f14f0da3a. Last accessed September 5, 2012.

37 Cabrera and Unruh (2012), 19.

38 Ibid.

39 Williams, F., and Foti, R.J. (2011). Formally developing creative leadership as a driver of organizational innovation. *Advances in Developing Human Resources*, 13(3), 279–96, 283.

40 Ibid.

41 Ibid.

42 Sheridan (2005).

43  Frawley, J., and Fasoli, L. (2012). Working together: Intercultural leadership capabilities for both-ways education. *School Leadership & Management*, 32(4), 309–20.
44  WorldLingo (2012).
45  Ibid.
46  Ibid.
47  Interview with Dr. Magdy Hussein, 2006.
48  Sheridan (2005).
49  Ibid.
50  Ibid.
51  Ibid.
52  Ibid.
53  Ibid.
54  Ibid.
55  Ibid.
56  Harvard Business Review (2012). 50 Most Influential Management Gurus from Harvard Business Review. Available at: http://hbr.org/web/slideshows/the-50-most-influential-management-gurus/42-trompenaars. Accessed August 16, 2012.
57  Hampden-Turner, C., and Trompenaars, T. (1997). *Riding the waves of culture: Understanding diversity in global business*, 2nd ed. New York: McGraw-Hill, 17.
58  Brandenburger, A., Brandenburger, A., and Nalebuff, B. (1997). *Co-opetition*. London: Crown Publishing, 90–3.
59  Ibid.
60  Hampden-Turner, C., and Trompenaars, F. (2000). *Building cross-cultural competence: How to create wealth from conflicting values*. New Haven, CT: Yale University Press, 47–55.
61  Bartlett, C.A., and Ghosahl, S. (2002). *Managing across borders: The transnational solution*, 2nd ed. Boston, MA: Harvard Business Review Press, 29.
62  Bennett, M.J. (2004). Becoming interculturally competent. In J.S. Wurzel (Ed.) *Toward multiculturalism: A reader in multicultural education*. Newton, MA: Intercultural Resource Corporation.
63  ibid.

## 2  Culture and Leadership

1  Democritus. (2012). *Democritus Quotes*. Available: http://www.brainyquote.com/quotes/quotes/d/democritus384620.html. Last accessed October 22, 2012.
2  Youssef, C.M., and Luthans, F. (2012). Positive global leadership. *Journal of World Business*, 47(4), 539–47.
3  Ibid.
4  Carter, S.K., and Bolden, C.L. (2012). Culture work in the research interview. In K.D. McKinney, J.A. Holstein, A.B. Marvasti, and J.F. Gubrium (Eds.), *The SAGE handbook of interview research: The complexity of the craft*, 2nd ed. Thousand Oaks, CA: Sage, 255–6.
5  Hofstede, G. (2001). *Culture's consequences: Comparing values, behaviors, institutions and organizations across nations*, 2nd ed. Thousand Oaks, CA: Sage, 4.
6  N.A. (2012). Available: http://oxforddictionaries.com/definition/english/culture. Last accessed September 20, 2012.
7  Moran, R.T., Harris, P.R., and Moran, S.V. (2011). *Managing cultural differences: Leadership skills and strategies for working in a global world*, 8th ed. Burlington, MA: Butterworth-Heinemann, 10.
8  Hall, E.T., and Hall, M.R. (1990). *Understanding cultural differences: Germans, French, and Americans*. Yarmouth, ME: Intercultural Press.
9  Hall, E.T. (1976). *Beyond culture*. New York: Random House.

10 de Mooij, M. (2011). *Consumer behavior and culture: Consequences for global marketing and advertising*, 2nd ed. Thousand Oaks, CA: Sage.
11 Ibid.
12 Schofer, E., Hironaka, A., Frank, D.J., and Longhofer, W. (2012). Sociological institutionalism and world society. In E. Amenta, K. Nash, and A. Scott (Eds.), *The Wiley-Blackwell Companion to Political Sociology*. Malden, MA: Blackwell, 59.
13 Schein, E.H. (2010). *Organizational culture and leadership*, 4th ed. San Francisco, CA: John Wiley.
14 Ibid.
15 Hall (1976); Hampden-Turner, C., and Trompenaars, F. (2000). *Building cross-cultural competence: How to create wealth from conflicting values*. New Haven, CT: Yale University Press; Hofstede (2001); Kluckhohn, F.R., and Strodtbeck, F.L. (1961). *Variations in value orientations*. Evanston, IL: Row, Peterson.
16 de Mooij, M. (2011). *Consumer behavior and culture: Consequences for global marketing and advertising*, 2nd ed. Thousand Oaks, CA: Sage.
17 Ibid.
18 de Mooij, M. (2004). *Consumer behavior and culture: Consequences for global marketing and advertising*. Thousand Oaks, CA: Sage, 33.
19 de Mooij (2011).
20 Ibid.
21 Ibid.
22 Ibid.
23 Ibid.
24 Ibid.
25 Sheridan, E.S. (2005). *Intercultural leadership competencies for U.S. business leaders in the new millennium*. Unpublished doctoral dissertation. University of Phoenix, AR.
26 de Mooij (2011).
27 Hofstede, G. (2011). Dimensionalizing cultures: The Hofstede Model in context. *Online Readings in Psychology and Culture*, 2(1), 15.
28 Hofstede, G. (2010). *Dimension Data Matrix*. Available: http://www.geerthofstede.com/dimension-data-matrix. Last accessed November 20, 2012.
29 Hofstede (2011).
30 Schein, E.H. (2010). *Organizational culture and leadership*, 4th ed. San Francisco, CA: John Wiley.
31 Ibid.
32 Sheridan (2005).
33 Schein (2010).
34 Ibid.
35 Hofstede (2011).
36 Yukl, G. (2009). Leading organizational learning: Reflections on theory and research. *Leadership Quarterly*, 20(1), 49–53.
37 Caputo, J.S., and Crandall, H.M. (2012). The intercultural communication cultural immersion experience: Preparing leaders for a global future. *Journal of Leadership Studies*, 6(1), 58–63.
38 Sheridan (2005).
39 Ibid.
40 Ibid.
41 Northouse, P. (2013). *Leadership theory and practice*. 6th ed. Thousand Oaks, CA: Sage.
42 Ibid.
43 Goethals, G.R., and Sorenson, G.L.J. (2006). *The quest for a general theory of leadership*. Cheltenham: Edward Elgar.
44 Hemphill, J.K. (1949). The leader and his group. *Journal of Educational Research*, 28, 225–9.
45 Likert, R. (1961). *New patterns of management*. New York: McGraw-Hill.

46  Blake, R.R. and Mouton, J.S. (1964). *The managerial grid*. Houston, TX: Gulf.
47  Fiedler, F.E. (1967). *A theory of leadership effectiveness*. New York: McGraw-Hill.
48  French, J., and Raven, B.H. (1959). The bases of social power. In D. Cartwright (Ed.), *Studies of social power*. Ann Arbor, MI: Institute of Social Research.
49  Burns, J.M. (1978). *Leadership*. New York: Harper & Row.
50  Ibid.
51  Ibid.
52  Bensimon, E., Neumann, A., and Birnbaum, R. (1989). *Making sense of administrative leadership: The "L" word in higher education*. Washington, DC: George Washington University Press.
53  Fuchs, S. (2001). *Against essentialism: A theory of culture*. Cambridge, MA: Harvard University Press; Jones, M.O. (1996). *Studying organizational symbolism*. Newbury Park, CA: Sage.
54  Astin, H., and Leland, C. (1991). *Women of influence, Women of vision*. San Francisco, CA: Jossey-Bass; Ayman, R. (1993). Leadership perception: The role of gender and culture. In M. Chemers and R. Ayman (Eds.), *Leadership theory and research: Perspectives and directions*. San Diego, CA: Academic Press, 137–66; Bensimon, E. (1989). A feminist reinterpretation of presidents' definitions of leadership. *Peabody Journal of Education*, 66(3), 143–56; Rhodes, K. (2001). *The servant leader: Does gender make a difference?* www.eresusltants.com/power of servant leadership.html.
55  Liden, R.C., and Antonakis, J. (2010). Considering context in psychological leadership research. *Human Relations*, 62(11), 1587–605.
56  Bolman, L.G. and Deal, T.E. (1995). *Leading with soul*. San Francisco, CA: Jossey-Bass; Dawson, S. (1992). *Analyzing organizations*, 2nd ed. London: Sage; Kezar, A. (2002). Reconstructing static images of leadership: An application of positionality theory. *Journal of Leadership Studies*, 8, 94–109; Osborn, R.N., Hunt, J.G., and Jauch, L.R. (2002). Toward a contextual theory of leadership, *Leadership Quarterly*, 13, 797–837; Tierney, W. (1988). *The web of leadership*. Greenwich, CT: JAI Press; Calas, M., and Smircich, L. (1991). Voicing seduction to silence leadership. *Organization Studies*, 12, 567–602.
57  Ashcroft, B., Griffiths G., and Tiffin, H. (1995). General introduction. In B. Ashcroft, G. Griffiths, and H. Tiffin (Eds.), *The post-colonial studies reader*. New York: Routledge, 1–4.
58  Calas and Smircich (1991).
59  Grint, K. (1997). *Leadership: Classical, contemporary, and critical approaches*. New York: Oxford University Press; Pearce, C.L., and Conger, J.A. (2003). *Shared leadership: Reframing the hows and whys of leadership*. Thousand Oaks, CA: Sage; Weick, K.E., and Roberts, K.H. (1993). Collective mind in organizations: Heedful interrelating on flight decks. *Administrative Science Quarterly*, 38(3), 357–81; Gronn, P. (2002). Distributed leadership as a unit of analysis. *Leadership Quarterly*, 13, 423–51.
60  Bensimon, Neumann, and Birnbaum (1989).
61  Bolman, L.G., and Deal, T.E. (2008,). *Reframing organizations: Artistry, choice and leadership*. San Francisco, CA: Jossey-Bass.
62  Steers, R., Sanchez-Runde, C., and Nardon, L. (2012). Culture, cognition, and managerial leadership. *Asia Pacific Business Review*, 18, 3.
63  Eagly, A., and Lau Chin, J. (2010). Diversity and leadership in a changing world. *American Psychologist*, 65(3), 216–24; Cantor, D., and Bernay, T. (1992). *Women in power*. New York: Houghton Mifflin; Ferguson, K. (2008). *Gender and globalization in Asia and the Pacific: Method, practice, theory*. Honolulu: University of Hawaii Press; Helgesen, S., and Johnson, J. (2010). *The female vision: Women's real power at work*. San Francisco, CA: Berrett-Koehler Publishing; Kezar, A. (2010). Leadership for a better world: Understanding the social change model of leadership development. *Journal of Higher Education*, 81, 5; Rosener, J. (2009). Ways women lead. *Harvard Business Review*, 68(6), 119–25; Bird, S.R. (2011). Unsettling universities' incongruous, gendered bureaucratic structures: A case-study approach. *Gender, Work & Organization*, 18(2), 202–30.

64  Ayman, R, and Korabik, K. (2010). Leadership: Why gender and culture matter. *American Psychologist*, 65(3), 157–70; Chemers, M. (2007). Comments on the justice model from a leadership perspective. *Applied Psychology: An International Review*, 56(4), 663–6; Schein (2010); Tierney, W. (2008). *The impact of culture on organizational decision-making*. Sterling, VA: Stylus.

65  Ayman and Korabik (2010); Poulson, R., Smith, J., Hood, D., Arthur, C., and Bazemore, K. (2011). The impact of gender on preferences for transactional versus transformational professorial leadership styles: An empirical analysis. *Review of Higher Education & Self-Learning*, 3, 11.

66  Ayman and Korabik (2010); Cantor and Bernay (1992); Ferguson (2008); Helgesen and Johnson (2010); Rosener (2009); Bird (2011).

67  Ayman and Korabik (2010); Cantor and Bernay (1992); Helgesen and Johnson (2010).

68  Ayman and Korabik (2010); Chemers (2007); Tierney (2008).

69  Martin, G., Resick, C., Keating, M., and Dickson, M. (2009). Ethical leadership across cultures: A comparative analysis of German and US perspectives. *Business Ethics: A European Review*, 18(2), 127–44; Punnett, B. (2009). *International perspectives on organizational behavior*, 2nd ed. Amonk: M.E. Sharpe; Varley, P. and Soon Ang and Joo-Seng Tan (2010). *CQ: Developing cultural intelligence at work*. Palo Alto, CA: Stanford Business Books, 1.

70  Resick, Keating, and Dickson (2009).

71  Ayman and Korabik (2010); Boga, I., and Ensari, N. (2009). The role of transformational leadership and organizational change on perceived organizational success. *Psychologist-Manager Journal*, 12, 4.

72  Kirkman, B., Chen, G., Farh, J., Chen, Z., and Lowe, K. (2009). Individual power distance orientation and follower reactions to transformational leaders: A cross-level, cross-cultural examination. *Academy of Management Journal*, 52, 4; Boga and Ensari (2009); Hofstede (1991); Walumbwa, F., Cropanzano, R., and Goldman, B. (2011). How leader–member exchange influences effective work behaviors: Social exchange and internal–external efficacy perspectives. *Personnel Psychology*, 64, 3; Church, A. (2009). Prospects for an integrated trait and cultural psychology. *European Journal of Personality*, 23, 3.

73  Burke, W., Marx, G., and Lowenstein, E. (2012). Leading, leadership, and learning: Exploring new contexts for leadership development in emerging school environments. *Planning & Changing*, 43, 1/2; Pettigrew, A.M. (2011). Scholarship with impact. *British Journal of Management*, 22, 3.

74  Peterson, M.G. (1997). International perspectives on international leadership. *Leadership Quarterly*, 8, 3.

75  Morrison, M., and Lumby, J. (2009). Is leadership observable? Qualitative orientations to leadership for diversity. A case from FE. *Ethnography & Education*, 4, 1; Johnson, A.R. (2007) An anthropological approach to the study of leadership: Lessons learned on improving leadership practice. *Transformation*, 24(3/4), 213–21; Tierney (2008); Pettigrew (2011).

76  Heine, S. (2008). From *Art of War* to Attila the Hun: A critical survey of recent works on philosophy/spirituality and business leadership. *Philosophy East & West*, 58, 1.

77  Tierney (2008).

78  Dawson, S. (1992). *Analyzing organizations*, 2nd ed. London: Sage.

79  Sperandio, J. (2011). Context and the gendered status of teachers: Women's empowerment through leadership of non-formal schooling in rural Bangladesh. *Gender & Education*, 23, 2; Goldstein, J. and Hazy, J., and Lichenstein, B. (2011). *Complexity and the nexus of leadership: Leveraging nonlinear science to create ecologies of innovation*. New York: Palgrave Macmillan; Poulson *et al.* (2011).

80  de Mooij (2011).

81  Ibid.

82  Ibid.

83  Church (2009).

84  Dorfman (2004)

85 Musselwhite, C. (2012). Leader assessment. *Leadership Excellence*, 29(8), 7–8.
86 Heames, J., and Harvey, M. (2006). The evolution of the concept of the "executive" from the 20th century manager to the 21st century global leader. *Journal of Leadership & Organizational Studies* (Baker College), 13, 2.
87 Ibid.
88 Kumar, R., Anjum, B., and Sinha, A. (2011). Cross-cultural interactions and leadership behavior. *Researchers World: Journal of Arts, Science & Commerce*, 2, 3.
89 Rosen, R., and Parker, S. (2009). Pragmatic idealism: Developing the next generation of leaders. *Chief Learning Officer*, 8, 10.
90 Ibid.
91 Rolbin, C., and della Chiesa, B. (2010). "We share the same biology..." Cultivating cross-cultural empathy and global ethics through multilingualism. *Mind, Brain & Education*, 4(4), 196–207; Adler, N. (2010). *Leadership insight*. Oxford: Routledge.
92 Goleman, D. (2011). *Leadership: The power of emotional intelligence*. Florence, MA: More Than Sound; Conger, J., and Hollenbeck, G.P. (2010). What is the character of research on leadership character? *Consulting Psychology Journal: Practice & Research*, 62(4).
93 Kouzes, J., and Posner, B. (2012). *The leadership challenge: How to make extraordinary things happen in organizations*, 5th ed. San Francisco, CA: Jossey-Bass.
94 Horney, N., Pasmore, B., and O'Shea, T. (2010). Leadership agility: A business imperative for a VUCA world. *People and Strategy*, 33, 4.
95 Schwartz, A., Rodríguez, M., Santiago-Rivera, A., Arredondo, P., and Field, L. (2010) Cultural and linguistic competence: Welcome challenges from successful diversification. *Professional Psychology: Research and Practice*, 41, 3.
96 Sue, D.W., Ivey, A., and Pedersen, P.B. (2009). *A theory of multicultural counseling and therapy*. Stamford, CT: Cengage Learning.
97 Ibid.
98 Ibid.
99 Sheridan (2005).
100 Kirmayer, L., Fung, K., Rousseau, C., Hung Tat, L., Menzies, P., Guzder, J. *et al.* (2012). Guidelines for training in cultural psychiatry. *Canadian Journal of Psychiatry*, 57, 3.
101 Hofstede and Hofstede (2004); Sue *et al.* (2009); Sheridan (2005).
102 Lambert, L., Tepper, B., Carr, J., Holt, D., and Barelka, A. (2012). Forgotten but not gone: An examination of fit between leader consideration and initiating structure needed and received. *Journal of Applied Psychology*, 97, 5.
103 Sheridan (2005).

**3 The principle of "Care"**

1 Anaxagoras. (2012). *Anaxagoras Quotes*. Available: http://www.brainyquote.com/quotes/authors/a/anaxagoras.html#GryqBEOH8m29aC3r.99. Last accessed October 22, 2012.
2 Moran, R.T., Harris, P.R., and Moran, S.V. (2011). *Managing cultural differences: Leadership skills and strategies for working in a global world*. 8th ed. Burlington, MA: Elsevier, 43.
3 Freeman, R.E. (2010). *Strategic management: A stakeholder approach*, 2nd ed. Cambridge: Cambridge University Press.
4 Ibid., 52.
5 Ibid.
6 Ditlev-Simonsen, C.D., and Midttun, A. (2010). What motivates managers to pursue corporate responsibility? A survey among key stakeholders. *Corporate Social Responsibility and Environmental Management*, 18(1), 25–38; Roberts, L.M., and Dutton, J.E. (Eds.) (2009). *Exploring positive identities and organizations: Building a theoretical and research foundation*. New York: Taylor & Francis.

7  Ditlev-Simonsen and Midttun (2010).
8  Roberts and Dutton (2009).
9  Ibid.
10 Kluckhohn, F., & and Strodtbeck, F.K. (1961). *Variations in value orientation.* Evanston, IL: Row, Petersen.
11 Hall, E.T. (1976). *Beyond culture.* New York: Random House.
12 Ditlev-Simonsen and Midttun (2010).

## 4  The principle of "Communication"

1  Diogenes. (2012). *Diogenes Quotes.* Available: http://www.brainyquote.com/quotes/authors/d/diogenes.html#t3zmehJThzr6trpU.99. Last accessed October 22, 2012.
2  Mitchell, C. (2009). *A short course in international business culture: Building your international business through cultural awareness*, 3rd ed. Petaluma, CA: World Trade Press.
3  Shafritz, J.M., Ott, J.S., and Jang, Y.S. (2010). *Classics of organization theory*, 7th ed. Stamford, CT: Cengage.
4  Van Vooren, C., and Lindsey, D.B. (2012). Leaders address inequity through a framework of international-mindedness. *Journal of Transformative Leadership and Policy Studies*, 2(1), 25–33.
5  Sheridan, E.S. (2005). *Intercultural leadership competencies for U.S. business leaders in the new millennium.* Unpublished doctoral dissertation. University of Phoenix, AR.
6  Kouzes, J.M., and Posner, B.Z. (2011). *The five practices of exemplary leadership: Financial services.* San Francisco, CA: Pfeiffer.
7  Rockstuhl, T., Seiler, S., Ang, S., Van Dyne, L., and Annen, H. (2011). Beyond general intelligence (IQ) and emotional intelligence (EQ): The role of cultural intelligence (CQ) on cross-border leadership effectiveness in a globalized world. *Journal of Social Issues*, 67(4), 825–40.
8  Van Vooren and Lindsey (2012).
9  Moran, R.T., Harris, P.R., and Moran, S.V. (2011). *Managing cultural differences: Leadership skills and strategies for working in a global world*, 8th ed. Burlington, MA: Butterworth-Heinemann.
10 Ibid.
11 Ibid.
12 Tang, J.C., Zhao, C., Cao, X., and Inkpen, K. (2011). Your time zone or mine? A study of globally time zone-shifted collaboration. *Proceedings of the ACM 2011 Conference on Computer Supported Cooperative Work*, 235–44.
13 Caligiuria, P., and Tariqueb, I. (2012). Dynamic cross-cultural competencies and global leadership effectiveness. *Journal of World Business*, 47(4), 612–22.
14 Goleman, D. (2011). *The brain and emotional intelligence: New insights.* Northampton, MA: More Than Sound.
15 Butler Ellis, J., and Van Dyne, L. (2009). Voice and silence as observers' reactions to defensive voice: Predictions based upon communication competence theory. In J. Greenberg, and M.S. Edwards (Eds.), *Voice and Silence in Organizations.* Bingley, UK: Emerald House, 42.
16 Moran, Harris, and Moran (2011). *Managing cultural differences: Leadership skills and strategies for working in a global world.* 8th edn. Burlington, MA: Butterworth-Heinemann.
17 McCall, M., and Hollenbeck, G. (2002). *The lessons of international experience: Developing global executives*, Boston, MA: Harvard Business School Press.

## 5 The principle of "Consciousness"

1 Aristotle. (2012). *Aristotle Quotes*. Available: http://www.brainyquote.com/quotes/authors/a/aristotle.html#9aOsVxPbjVquUdog.99. Last accessed October 22, 2012.
2 Sheridan, E.S. (2005). *Intercultural leadership competencies for U.S. business leaders in the new millennium*. Unpublished doctoral dissertation. University of Phoenix, AR.
3 Musselwhite, C. (2012). Leader assessment. *Leadership Excellence*, 29(8), 7–8.
4 Trompenaars, F., and C. Hampden-Turner. (2012). *Riding the waves of culture: Understanding diversity in global business*. London: Nicholas Brealey Publishing.
5 Irving, J.A. (2010). Educating global leaders: Exploring intercultural competence in leadership education. *Journal of Business & Cultural Studies*, 3(1).
6 Goleman, D. (2011). Emotional mastery. *Leadership Excellence*, 28(6), 12–13.
7 Ibid.
8 Goleman, D. (2008). The secret to success. *Education Digest*, 74(4), 8–9.
9 Bennis, W. (2009). *On becoming a leader*, 4th ed. Philadelphia, PA: Basic Books.
10 VUCA is an acronym used to describe or reflect on the volatility, uncertainty, complexity, and ambiguity of general conditions and situations.

## 6 The principle of "Contrasts"

1 Socrates. (2012). *Socrates Quotes*. Available: http://www.brainyquote.com/quotes/quotes/s/socrates101211.html. Last accessed October 22, 2012.
2 Barbier, A. (2010). *The political influence on the chiefs of police's leadership in Europe between 2000 and 2010*. Unpublished MBA dissertation. University of Liverpool, UK, 78.
3 Ibid., 23–4.
4 Wibbeke, E.S. (2009). *Global business leadership*. Oxford: Butterworth-Heinemann.
5 Pakes, F. (2007). *Pearls in policing, the discussion continues*. Den Haag: School for Police Leadership, Police Academy of the Netherlands.
6 Ibid., 86.
7 Adlam, R. and Villiers, P. (2003). *Police leadership in the twenty-first century*. Hook, Hampshire: Waterside Press.
8 Wibbeke (2009).
9 Barbier (2010).
10 Hamel, G. (2009) Moon shots for management. *Harvard Business Review*, 87, 2; Kraemer, H.J. (2011). *From values to action: The four principles of value-based leadership*. San Francisco: Jossey-Bass. Pfeffer, J. (2010). *Power: Why some people have it and others don't*. New York: Harper Business.

## 7 The principle of "Context"

1 Epictetus. (2012). *Epictetus Quotes*. Available: http://www.brainyquote.com/quotes/quotes/e/epictetus149126.html. Last accessed October 22, 2012.
2 Urquhart, B. (1987). *A life in peace and war*. New York: Harper & Row.
3 The Aga Khan (2007). Introduction. In *Spirit and life: Masterpieces of Islamic art from the Aga Khan Museum Collection*. London: The Ismaili Centre.
4 *Oxford English Dictionary*, 11th ed. (2008).

## 8 The principle of "Change"

1 Heraclitus. (2012). *Heraclitus Quotes*. Available: http://www.brainyquote.com/quotes/authors/h/heraclitus.html#0ZwRoIe1b4e3SU40.99. Last accessed October 22, 2012.

## 9 The principle of "Capability"

1 Plato. (2012). *Plato Quotes*. Available: http://www.brainyquote.com/quotes/quotes/p/plato162751.html. Last accessed October 23, 2012.
2 Senge, P.M. (1990). *The fifth discipline: The art and practice of the learning organization*. New York: Doubleday/Currency, 1–23.
3 Argyris, C. and Schön, D. (1996). *Organizational learning II: Theory, method and practice*. Reading, MA: Addison-Wesley.
4 Schein, E.H. (2010). *Organizational culture and leadership*, 4th ed. San Francisco, CA: Jossey-Bass.
5 Ibid.
6 Ibid.
7 Ibid.
8 Ibid.
9 Ibid.
10 Ibid.
11 Ibid.
12 Shafritz, J.M., Ott, J.S., and Jang, Y.S. (2010). *Classics of organization theory*, 7th ed. Stamford, CT: Cengage.
13 Ibid.
14 Grouzet, F., Kasser, T., Ahuvia, A., Dols, J., Kim, Y., Lau, S. *et al.* (2005). The structure of goal contents across 15 cultures. *Journal of Personality and Social Psychology*, (89)5, 800–16.
15 Ibid.

## 10 Gender and leadership

1 Protagoras. (2012). *Protagoras Quotes*. Available: http://www.brainyquote.com/quotes/authors/p/protagoras.html#xgmKyXIEPEdJ1DTf.99. Last accessed October 23, 2012.
2 Central Intelligence Agency. (2012). *CIA World Factbook*. Available: https://www.cia.gov/library/publications/the-world-factbook/geos/xx.html. Last accessed October 20, 2012.
3 Ayman, R., and Korabik, K. (2010). Leadership: Why gender and culture matter. *American Psychologist*, 65(3), 157–70.
4 Ibid.
5 Robinson, R. (2012). *Courageous persistence*. Available: http://www.runningtimes.com/Article.aspx?ArticleID=27214. Last accessed October 20, 2012.
6 Ibid.
7 Carli, L.L., and Eagly, A.H. (2012). Leadership and gender. In D.V. Day, and J. Antonakis (Eds.), *The nature of leadership*, 2nd ed. Thousand Oaks, CA: Sage, 437–76.
8 Communications Section of UN Women (2011). *Increasing women's leadership and participation*. Available: http://www.unwomen.org/wp-content/uploads/2011/06/UNwomen_AnnualReport_2010-2011_en.pdf. Last accessed 21 October, 2012.
9 Gannon, M., and Pillai, R. (2010). *Understanding global cultures: Metaphorical journeys through 29 nations, clusters of nations, continents, and diversity*, 4th ed. Thousand Oaks, CA: Sage.
10 de Mooij, M. (2004). *Consumer behavior and culture: Consequences for global marketing and advertising*. Thousand Oaks, CA: Sage, 38.
11 Hofstede, G., Hofstede, G.J., and Minkov, M. (2010). *Cultures and organizations: Software of the mind*, 3rd ed. New York: McGraw-Hill.
12 de Mooij (2004), 34.
13 Paek, H.J., Nelson, M.R., and Vilela, A.M. (2011). Examination of gender-role portrayals in television advertising across seven countries. *Sex Roles: A Journal of Research*, 64(3–4), 192–207.

14 Wren, J.T. (1995). *The leader's companion: Insights on leadership through the ages.* New York: The Free Press.
15 Ibid.
16 Northouse, P.G. (2013). *Leadership: Theory and practice,* 6th ed. Thousand Oaks, CA: Sage.
17 Communications Section of UN Women (2011).
18 Eagly, A.H., Johannesen-Schmidt, M.C., and van Engan, M.L. (2003). Transformational, transactional, and laissez-faire leadership styles: A meta-analysis comparing women and men. *Psychological Bulletin,* 129(4), 569–91.
19 Sen, A.K., and Metzger, J.E. (2010). Women leadership and global power: Evidence from the United States and Latin America. *International Journal of Management and Marketing Research.* 3 (2), 75–84.
20 Bass, B.M. (1998). *Transformational leadership: Industry, military, and educational impact.* Mahwah, NJ: Lawrence Erlbaum.
21 Eagly, A.H., Johannesen-Schmidt, M.C., and van Engan, M.L. (2003). Transformational, transactional, and laissez-faire leadership styles: A meta-analysis comparing women and men. *Psychological Bulletin.* 129 (4), 569–591.
22 Ibid.
23 Carli and Eagly (2012).
24 Avolio, B.J., Bass, B.M., and Jung, D.I. (1999). Re-examining the components of transformational and transactional leadership using the Multifactor Leadership Questionnaire. *Journal of Occupational and Organizational Psychology,* 72, 441–62.
25 Hausmann, R., Tyson, L.D., and Zahidi, S. (2012). *The global gender gap report 2012.* Geneva: World Economic Forum. Available: http://www3.weforum.org/docs/WEF_GenderGap_Report_2012.pdf. Last accessed November 8, 2012.
26 Ibid.
27 Ibid.
28 Gaudiano, N., and Bewley, E. (2012). *Congresswomen find no bathrooms at Saudi Defense Ministry.* Available: http://abcnews.go.com/Politics/congresswomen-find-bathrooms-saudi-defense-ministry/story?id=15443997#.UJxFtbT3DDw. Last accessed November 8, 2012.
29 Kellerman, B., and Rhode, D.L. (Eds.) (2007). *Women and leadership: The state of play and strategies for change.* San Francisco, CA: Jossey-Bass.
30 Heifetz, R.A., and Linsky, M. (2002). *Leadership on the line: Staying alive through the dangers of leading.* Boston, MA: Harvard Business School Press.
31 Ibid.
32 Kark, R., Waismel-Manor, R., and Shamir, B. (2012). Does valuing androgyny and femininity lead to a female advantage? The relationship between gender-role, transformational leadership and identification. *Leadership Quarterly,* 23, 620–40.
33 Ibid.

**11 Technology and leadership**

1 Archimedes. (2012). *Archimedes Quotes.* Available: http://www.brainyquote.com/quotes/authors/a/archimedes.html. Last accessed November 11, 2012.
2 Misa, T.J. (2011). *Leonardo to the Internet: Technology and culture from the Renaissance to the present,* 2nd ed. Baltimore, MD: Johns Hopkins University Press.
3 Merriam-Webster. (2012). *Technology.* Available: http://www.merriam-webster.com/dictionary/technology. Last accessed October 30, 2012.
4 Fidelman, M. (2012). *The latest infographics: Mobile business statistics for 2012.* Available: http://www.forbes.com/sites/markfidelman/2012/05/02/the-latest-infographics-mobile-business-statistics-for-2012/. Last accessed October 20, 2012.
5 Hellström, T. (2012). On the moral responsibility of military robots. *Ethics and Information Technology.* http://www.springerlink.com/content/k745725012225683.
6 Ibid.

7  Murphy, L.L., and Priebe, A.E. (2011). "My co-wife can borrow my mobile phone!" Gendered geographies of cell phone usage and significance for rural Kenyans. *Gender, Technology and Development*, 15(1), 1–23.
8  Mahajan, V. (2010). *Accelerants for growth in Africa: Cell phones and banking.* Upper Saddle River, NJ: FT Press.
9  Murphy and Priebe (2011).
10  Ibid.
11  Ibid.
12  Ibid.
13  Mahajan (2010).
14  LinkedIn. (2012). *About us.* Available: http://press.linkedin.com/About-Us. Last accessed October 30, 2012.
15  LinkedIn Learning Center. (2012). *People you may know: Quickly connect with former classmates and colleagues.* Available: http://learn.linkedin.com/the-homepage/pymk/. Last accessed November 13, 2012.
16  Gerard, J.G. (2012). Linking in with LinkedIn®: Three exercises that enhance professional social networking and career building. *Journal of Management Education*, 36(6), 866–97.
17  Facebook. (2012). Key Facts. Available: http://newsroom.fb.com/Key-Facts. Last accessed November 13, 2012.
18  Chen, A. (2012). *Open courses from America find eager audiences in China.* Available: http://chronicle.com/article/Massive-Excitement-About/134660/. Last accessed November 19, 2012.
19  Lewin, T. (2012). *Instruction for masses knocks down campus walls.* Available: http://www.nytimes.com/2012/03/05/education/moocs-large-courses-open-to-all-topple-campus-walls.html?pagewanted=all. Last accessed November 19, 2012.
20  Chen (2012).
21  Ibid.
22  Monaghan, P. (2012). *What's next in online learning? Stanford names vice provost to lead the way.* Available: http://chronicle.com/article/Massive-Excitement-About/134660/. Last accessed November 19, 2012.
23  Young, J. (2012). *American Council on Education may recommend some Coursera offerings for college credit.* Available: http://chronicle.com/article/American-Council-on-Education/135750/. Last accessed November 19, 2012.
24  Lewin (2012).
25  U.S. Environmental Protection Agency. (2012). *Cleaning up electronic waste.* Available: http://www.epa.gov/international/toxics/ewaste/index.html. Last accessed November 12, 2012.
26  Ibid.
27  Miller, T.R., Gregory, J., Duan, H., and Kirchain, R. (2012). *Characterizing transboundary flows of used electronics: Summary report.* Available: http://msl.mit.edu/publications/CharacterizingTransboundaryFlowsofUsedElectronicsWorkshopSummaryReport%20 1-2012.pdf. Last accessed November 11, 2012.
28  Ibid.
29  Hoque, F. (2011). *The power of convergence: Linking business strategies and technology decisions to create sustainable success.* New York: AMACOM.
30  Ibid.
31  Jeon, S., Kim, S.T., and Lee, D.H. (2011). Web 2.0 business models and value creation. International Journal of Information and Decision Sciences, 3(1), 70–84.
32  Kiva. (2012). Statistics. Available: http://www.kiva.org/about/stats. Last accessed November 12, 2012.
33  Tate, A., Potter, S., Wickler, G. and Hansberger, J.T. (2011). Virtual collaboration spaces and Web 2.0: Bringing presence to distributed collaboration. Reshaping Research and Development Using Web 2.0-Based Technologies.

## 12 Geoleadership and the community

1 Thales. (2012). Thales Quotes. Available: http://www.brainyquote.com/quotes/quotes/t/thales185039.html. Last accessed November 11, 2012.
2 Hofstede, G., and Hofstede, G.J. (2004). *Cultures and organizations: Software of the mind.* New York: McGraw-Hill, 17.
3 Chua, A. (2003). *World on Fire: How Exporting Free Market Democracy Breeds Ethnic Hatred and Global Instability.* New York: Doubleday.

## Appendix A

1 Gundling, E. (2003). *Working GlobeSmart: 12 people skills for doing business across borders.* Palo Alto, CA: Davies-Black, 331.
2 Linstone, H.A., and Turoff, M. (2002). *The Delphi method: Techniques and applications.* Retrieved December 1, 2004, from: http://www.is.njit.edu/pubs/delphibook/
3 Dajani, J.S., Sincoff, M.Z., and Talley, W.K. (1979). Stability and agreement criteria for the termination of Delphi studies. *Technological Forecasting and Social Change,* 13, 83–90.
4 Turoff, M., and Hiltz, S.R. (1996). Computer based Delphi process. Retrieved December 1, 2004, from: http://eies.njit.edu/~turoff/Papers/delphi3.html#Introduction
5 Delbecq, A.L., Van de Ven, A.H., and Gustafson, D.H. (1975). *Group techniques for program planning: A guide to nominal group and Delphi processes.* Glenview, IL: Scott, Foresman.
6 McCoy, R. (2001). Computer competencies for the 21st century information systems educator. *Information Technology, Learning, and Performance Journal,* 19, 21–35.
7 Thach, E.C., and Murphy, K.L. (1995). Competencies for distance education professionals. *Educational Technology Research and Development,* 43, 57–79.
8 Satterlee, B. (1999). The acquisition of key executive skills and attitudes required for international business in the third millennium, ERIC (Document No. ED432175).

# Index

Note: Page numbers in **bold** type refer to **figures**
Page numbers in *italic* type refer to *tables*